Eric Hobsbawm

THE AGE OF CAPITAL
1848–1875

An *Abacus* Book

First published in Great Britain by
Weidenfeld and Nicolson Ltd 1975
First published by Abacus 1997
Reprinted 1980, 1984, 1985, 1988, 1989,
1991, 1992, 1995 (twice), 1997, 1998, 1999, 2003, 2004

Printed in England by Clays Ltd, St Ives plc

ISBN 0 349 10480 8

Abacus
An imprint of
Time Warner Book Group UK
Brettenham House
Lancaster Place
London WC2E 7EN

www.twbg.co.uk

Eric Hobsbawm was born in Alexandria in 1917 and educated in Vienna, Berlin, London and Cambridge. A Fellow of the British Academy and the American Academy of Arts and Sciences, with honorary degrees from universities in several countries, he taught until retirement at Birkbeck College, University of London, and since then at the New York School for Social Research in New York. In addition to *The Age of Revolution 1789–1848*, *The Age of Capital 1848–1875*, *The Age of Empire 1875–1914* and *Age of Extremes: The Short Twentieth Century 1914–1991*, his books include *Revolutionaries*, *On History*, *Bandits*, *Uncommon People* and *The New Century*.

Contents

To Marlene, Andrew and Julia

List of Illustrations

Preface

Though this book is intended to stand on its own, it happens to be the middle volume of a series of three, which will attempt to survey the history of the modern world from the French Revolution to the First World War, of which the first has long been available as *The Age of Revolution, 1789–1848*, and the last is still to be written. Consequently the book is likely to be read by some who know the earlier volume as well as by others who do not. To the former I apologize for including, here and there, material already familiar to them, in order to provide the necessary background for the latter. Similarly I have tried briefly, particularly in the Conclusion, to provide a few pointers to the future. I have naturally tried to keep material which duplicates *The Age of Revolution* to the minimum, and to make it tolerable by distributing it throughout the text. But the book can be read independently, so long as readers bear in mind that it deals not with a self-contained period which can be tidily separated from what went on before and came after. History is not like that.

At all events it ought to be comprehensible to any reader with a modicum of general education, for it is deliberately addressed to the non-expert. If historians are to justify the resources society devotes to their subject, modest though these are, they should not write exclusively for other historians. Still, an elementary acquaintance with European history will be an advantage. I suppose readers could, at a pinch, manage without any previous knowledge of the fall of the Bastille or the Napoleonic Wars, but such knowledge will help.

The period with which this book deals is comparatively short, but its geographical scope is wide. To write about the world from 1789 to 1848 in terms of Europe – indeed almost in terms of Britain and France – is not unrealistic. However, since the major theme of the quarter-century thereafter is the extension of the capitalist economy to the entire world, and hence the impossibility of any longer writing a purely European history, it would be absurd to write about it without paying substantial attention to other continents. Have I nevertheless written it in too Eurocentric a manner? Possibly. Inevitably a European historian not only knows much more about his own continent than about others, but cannot help seeing the global landscape which surrounds him from his particular vantage-point. Inevitably an American historian, say, will see the same landscape

9

somewhat differently. Nevertheless, in the mid-nineteenth century the history of the development of world capitalism was still centred in Europe. For instance, though the USA was already emerging as what was eventually to be the greatest industrial economy in the world, it was as yet somewhat marginal and self-contained. Nor, indeed, was it an unusually large society: in 1870 its population was not much larger than Britain's, about the same size as that of France, and a little less than that of what was about to be the German Empire.

My treatment is divided into three parts. The 1848 revolutions form a prelude to a section on the main developments of the period. These I discuss in both a continental and, where necessary, global perspective, rather than as a series of self-contained 'national' histories, though in the two chapters on the non-European world it would be both impracticable and absurd not to deal specifically with several important areas and countries, notably the USA and Japan, China and India. The chapters are divided by themes, rather than chronologically, though the main sub-periods should be clearly discernible. These are the quiet but expansionist 1850s, the more turbulent 1860s, the boom and slump of the 1870s. The third part consists of a series of cross-sections through the economy, society and culture of the third quarter of the nineteenth century.

My object has not been so much to summarise known facts, or even to show what happened and when, but rather to draw facts together into a general historical synthesis, to 'make sense of' the third quarter of the nineteenth century, and to trace the roots of the present world back to that period, insofar as it is reasonable to do so. But it is also to bring out the extraordinary character of a period which really has no parallel in history, and whose very uniqueness makes it strange and remote. Whether *The Age of Capital* succeeds in 'making sense' and bringing to life this period, must be left to readers to judge. Whether its interpretations are valid, especially when they disagree with more accepted ones, must be left to the discussion of my fellow-historians, who evidently do not all agree with me. I resist the temptation of the writer whose work has been widely and passionately reviewed, in terms ranging from enthusiasm to irritation, to take issue with the reviewers, though I have tried in this edition to eliminate several misprints and some plain mistakes to which some of them have drawn my attention, to straighten out a few syntactical confusions which have apparently led to misunderstanding, and to take account, at least in my formulations, of some criticisms which seem to me to be just. The text remains substantially as before.

Nevertheless, I should like to remove one misunderstanding which appears to exist, especially among reviewers whose natural sympathies are as much with bourgeois society as mine are evidently not. Since it is the duty of the historian to let the reader make allowances for his bias, I wrote (see Introduction p. 17): 'The author of this book cannot conceal a certain distaste, perhaps a certain contempt, for the age with which it deals, though one mitigated by admiration for its titanic material achievements and by the effort to understand even what he does not like.' This has been read by some as a declaration of intent to be unfair to the Victorian bourgeoisie and the age of its triumph. Since some people are evidently unable to read what is on the page, as distinct from what they think must be there, I would like to say clearly that this is not so. In fact, as at least one reviewer has correctly recognised, bourgeois triumph is not merely the organising principle of the present volume, but 'it is the bourgeoisie who receive much the most sympathetic treatment in the book'. For good or ill, it was their age, and I have tried to present it as such, even at the cost of – at least in this brief period – seeing other classes not so much in their own right, as in relation to it.

I cannot claim to be expert on all but a tiny part of the immense subject-matter of this book, and have had to rely almost entirely on second- or even third-hand information. But this is unavoidable. An enormous amount has already been written about the nineteenth century, and every year adds to the height and bulk of the mountain ranges which darken the historical sky. As the range of historical interests widens to include practically every aspect of life in which we of the late twentieth century take an interest, the quantity of information which must be absorbed is far too great for even the most erudite and encyclopedic scholar. Even where he or she is aware of it, it must often, in the context of a wide-ranging synthesis, be reduced to a paragraph or two, a line, a passing mention or a mere nuance of treatment, or omitted with regret. And one must necessarily rely, in an increasingly perfunctory manner, on the work of others.

Unfortunately this makes it impossible to follow the admirable convention by which scholars punctiliously acknowledge their sources, and especially their debts, so that nobody but the originators should claim as their own findings made freely available to all. In the first place, I doubt whether I could trace all the suggestions and ideas I have borrowed so freely back to their origin in some book or article, conversation or discussion. I can only ask those whose work I have looted, consciously or not, to forgive my discourtesy. In the second place, even the attempt to do so, would overload the book with an apparatus of learning quite unsuitable to it. However, there is a general guide to further reading, which includes some of the works I have found most useful and to which I would wish to acknowledge my debt.

11

References have been almost entirely confined to the sources of quotations, of statistics and other figures, and for some statements which are controversial or surprising. Most of the otherwise unacknowledged figures are taken from standard sources or from such invaluable compendia as Mulhall's *Dictionary of Statistics*. References to works of literature – e.g. Russian novels – are to titles only, since they exist in a variety of editions. The one consulted by the author may not be the one available to the reader. References to the works of Marx and Engels, who are major contemporary commentators in this period, are both to the familiar title of work or date of letter and to the volume and page of the existing standard edition (East Berlin 1956–71), cited as *Werke*. Place-names have been given in the English form where there is one (e.g. Munich), otherwise in the form generally used in publications at the time (e.g. Pressburg). This implies no nationalist prejudice one way or another. Where necessary, the current name is added in brackets (e.g. Laibach [– Ljubljana]).

The late Sigurd Zienau and Francis Haskell were kind enough to read my chapters on the sciences and arts and to correct some of my errors. Charles Curwen answered questions on China. Nobody is responsible for mistakes or omissions except myself. W. R. Rodgers, Carmen Claudin and Maria Moisá helped me enormously as research assistants at various times. Andrew Hobsbawm and Julia Hobsbawm helped me to select the illustrations, as did Julia Brown. I am also deeply indebted to my editor, Susan Loden.

E.J.H.

February 1977

Introduction

In the 1860s a new word entered the economic and political vocabulary of the world: 'capitalism'.* It therefore seems apposite to call the present volume *The Age of Capital*, a title which also reminds us that the major work of capitalism's most formidable critic, Karl Marx's *Das Kapital* (1867), was published in these years. For the global triumph of capitalism is the major theme of history in the decades after 1848. It was the triumph of a society which believed that economic growth rested on competitive private enterprise, on success in buying everything in the cheapest market (including labour) and selling in the dearest. An economy so based, and therefore resting naturally on the sound foundations of a bourgeoisie composed of those whom energy, merit and intelligence had raised to their position and kept there, would – it was believed – not only create a world of suitably distributed material plenty, but of ever-growing enlightenment, reason and human opportunity, an advance of the sciences and the arts, in brief a world of continuous and accelerating material and moral progress. The few remaining obstacles in the way of the untrammelled development of private enterprise would be swept away. The institutions of the world, or rather of those parts of the world not still debarred by the tyranny of tradition and superstition or by the unfortunate fact of not having white skins (preferably originating in the central and north-western parts of Europe), would gradually approximate to the international model of a territorially defined 'nation-state' with a constitution guaranteeing property and civil rights, elected representative assemblies and governments responsible to them, and, where suitable, a participation in politics of the common people within such limits as would guarantee the bourgeois social order and avoid the risk of its overthrow.

To trace the earlier development of this society is not the business of

* Its origin may go back to before 1848, as suggested in *The Age of Revolution* (Introduction), but detailed research suggests that it hardly occurs before 1849 or comes into wider currency before the 1860s.[1]

13

the present book. It is enough to remind ourselves that it had already achieved, as it were, its historical breakthrough on both the economic and politico-ideological fronts in the sixty years before 1848. The years from 1789 to 1848 (which I have discussed in an earlier volume [*The Age of Revolution*, see the Preface, p. 9 above] to which readers will be referred back from time to time) were dominated by a dual revolution: the industrial transformation pioneered in, and largely confined to, Britain, and the political transformation associated with, and largely confined to, France. Both implied the triumph of a new society, but whether it was to be the society of triumphant liberal capitalism, of what a French historian has called 'the conquering bourgeois', still seemed more uncertain to contemporaries than it seems to us. Behind the bourgeois political ideologists stood the masses, ready to turn moderate liberal revolutions into social ones. Below and around the capitalist entrepreneurs the discontented and displaced 'labouring poor' stirred and surged. The 1830s and 1840s were an era of crisis, whose exact outcome only optimists cared to predict.

Still the dualism of the revolution of 1789 to 1848 gives the history of that period both unity and symmetry. It is in a sense easy to write and read about, because it appears to possess a clear theme and a clear shape, and its chronological limits are as clearly defined as we have any right to expect in human affairs. With the revolution of 1848, which forms the starting-point of this volume, the earlier symmetry broke down, the shape changed. Political revolution retreated, industrial revolution advanced. Eighteen forty-eight, the famous 'springtime of peoples', was the first and last European revolution in the (almost) literal sense, the momentary realisation of the dreams of the left, the nightmares of the right, the virtually simultaneous overthrow of old regimes over the bulk of continental Europe west of the Russian and Turkish empires, from Copenhagen to Palermo, from Brasov to Barcelona. It had been expected and predicted. It seemed to be the culmination and logical product of the era of dual revolution.

It failed, universally, rapidly and – though this was not realised for several years by the political refugees – definitively. Henceforth there was to be no general social revolution of the kind envisaged before 1848 in the 'advanced' countries of the world. The centre of gravity of such social revolutionary movements, and therefore of twentieth-century socialist and communist regimes, was to be in the marginal and backward regions, though in the period with which this book deals movements of this kind remained episodic, archaic and themselves 'underdeveloped'. The sudden, vast and apparently boundless expansion of the world capitalist economy provided political alternatives in the 'advanced' countries. The (British) industrial revolution had swallowed the (French) political revolution.

The history of our period is therefore lopsided. It is primarily that of the massive advance of the world economy of industrial capitalism, of the social order it represented, of the ideas and beliefs which seemed to legitimatise and ratify it: in reason, science, progress and liberalism. It is the era of the triumphant bourgeois, though the European bourgeoisie still hesitated to commit itself to public political rule. To this – and perhaps only to this – extent the age of revolution was not dead. The middle classes of Europe were frightened and remained frightened of the people: 'democracy' was still believed to be the certain and rapid prelude to 'socialism'. The men who officially presided over the affairs of the victorious bourgeois order in its moment of triumph were a deeply reactionary country nobleman from Prussia, an imitation emperor in France and a succession of aristocratic landowners in Britain. The fear of revolution was real, the basic insecurity it indicated, deep-seated. At the very end of our period the only example of revolution in an advanced country, an almost localised and short-lived insurrection in Paris, produced a greater bloodbath than anything in 1848 and a flurry of nervous diplomatic exchanges. Yet by this time the rulers of the advanced states of Europe, with more or less reluctance, were beginning to recognise not only that 'democracy', i.e. a parliamentary constitution based on a wide suffrage, was inevitable, but also that it would probably be a nuisance but politically harmless. This discovery had long since been made by the rulers of the United States.

The years from 1848 to the middle 1870s were therefore not a period which inspires readers who enjoy the spectacle of drama and heroics in the conventional sense. Its wars – and it saw considerably more warfare than the preceding thirty or the succeeding forty years – were either brief operations decided by technological and organisational superiority, like most European campaigns overseas and the rapid and decisive wars by means of which the German Empire was established between

1864 and 1871; or mismanaged massacres on which even the patriotism of the belligerent countries has refused to dwell with pleasure, such as the Crimean War of 1854–6. The greatest of all the wars of this period, the American Civil War, was won in the last analysis by the weight of economic power and superior resources. The losing South had the better army and the better generals. The occasional examples of romantic and colourful heroism stood out, like Garibaldi in his flowing locks and red shirt, by their very rarity. Nor was there much drama in politics, where the criteria of success were to be defined by Walter Bagehot as the possession of 'common opinions and uncommon abilities'. Napoleon III visibly found the cloak of his great uncle the first Napoleon uncomfortable to wear. Lincoln and Bismarck, whose public images have benefited by the cragginess of their faces and the beauty of their prose, were indeed great men, but their actual achievements were won by their gifts as politicians and diplomats, like those of Cavour in Italy, who entirely lacked what we now regard as their charisma.

The most obvious drama of this period was economic and technological: the iron pouring in millions of tons over the world, snaking in ribbons of railways across the continents, the submarine cables crossing the Atlantic, the construction of the Suez canal, the great cities like Chicago stamped out of the virgin soil of the American Midwest, the huge streams of migrants. It was the drama of European and North American power, with the world at its feet. But those who exploited this conquered world were, if we except the numerically small fringe of adventurers and pioneers, sober men in sober clothes, spreading respectability and a sentiment of racial superiority together with gasworks, railway lines and loans.

It was the drama of *progress*, that key word of the age: massive, enlightened, sure of itself, self-satisfied but above all inevitable. Hardly any among the men of power and influence, at all events in the western world, any longer hoped to hold it up. Only a few thinkers and perhaps a somewhat greater number of intuitive critics predicted that its inevitable advance would produce a world very different from that towards which it appeared to lead: perhaps its very opposite. None of them – not even Marx who had envisaged social revolution in 1848 and for a decade thereafter – expected any immediate reversal. Even his expectations were, by the 1860s, for the long term.

The 'drama of progress' is a metaphor. But for two kinds of people it was a literal reality. For the millions of the poor, transported into a new world, often across frontiers and oceans, it meant a cataclysmic change of life. For the peoples of the world outside capitalism, who were now grasped and shaken by it, it meant the choice between a doomed resistance in terms of their ancient traditions and ways, and a traumatic process of seizing the weapons of the west and turning them against the conquerors: of understanding and manipulating 'progress' themselves. The world of the third quarter of the nineteenth century was one of victors and victims. Its drama was the predicament not of the former, but primarily of the latter.

The historian cannot be objective about the period which is his subject. In this he differs (to his intellectual advantage) from its most typical ideologists, who believed that the progress of technology, 'positive science' and society made it possible to view their present with the unanswerable impartiality of the natural scientist, whose methods they believed themselves (mistakenly) to understand. The author of this book cannot conceal a certain distaste, perhaps a certain contempt, for the age with which it deals, though one mitigated by admiration for its titanic material achievements and by the effort to understand even what he does not like. He does not share the nostalgic longing for the certainty, the self-confidence, of the mid-nineteenth-century bourgeois world which tempts many who look back upon it from the crisis-ridden western world a century later. His sympathies lie with those to whom few listened a century ago. In any case both the certainty and the self-confidence were mistaken. The bourgeois triumph was brief and impermanent. At the very moment when it seemed complete, it proved to be not monolithic but full of fissures. In the early 1870s economic expansion and liberalism seemed irresistible. By the end of the decade they were so no longer.

This turning-point marks the end of the era with which this book deals. Unlike the 1848 revolution, which forms its starting-point, it is marked by no convenient and universal date. If any such date had to be chosen, it would be 1873, the Victorian equivalent of the Wall Street Crash of 1929. For then began what a contemporary observer called 'a most curious and in many respects unprecedented disturbance and depression of trade, commerce and industry' which contemporaries called the 'Great Depression', and which is usually dated 1873–96.

17

'Its most noteworthy peculiarity [wrote the same observer] has been its universality; affecting nations that have been involved in war as well as those which have maintained peace; those which have a stable currency . . . and those which have an unstable currency . . .; those which live under a system of the free exchange of commodities and those whose exchanges are more or less restricted. It has been grievous in old communities like England and Germany, and equally so in Australia, South Africa and California which represent the new; it has been a calamity exceeding heavy to be borne alike by the inhabitants of sterile Newfoundland and Labrador, and of the sunny, fruitful sugar-islands of the East and West Indies; and it has not enriched those at the centres of the world's exchanges, whose gains are ordinarily the greatest when business is most fluctuating and uncertain.'[2]

So wrote an eminent North American in the same year in which, under the inspiration of Karl Marx, the Labour and Socialist International was founded. The Depression initiated a new era, and may therefore properly provide the concluding date for the old.

Part One

Revolutionary Prelude

Chapter One

'The Springtime of Peoples'

*Please read the newspapers very carefully – now they are worth reading
. . . This Revolution will change the shape of the earth – and so it should
and must! – Vive la République!*

The poet Georg Weerth to his mother, 11 March 1848[1]

*Truly, if I were younger and wealthier than I unfortunately am, I'd
emigrate to America today. Not out of cowardice – for the times can
do me personally as little harm as I can do them – but out of over-
powering disgust at the moral rottenness which, to use Shakespeare's
phrase, stinks to high heaven.*

The poet Joseph von Eichendorff to a correspondent, 1 August 1849[2]

I

Early in 1848 the eminent French political thinker Alexis de Tocqueville rose in the Chamber of Deputies to express sentiments which most
Europeans shared: 'We are sleeping on a volcano . . . Do you not see
that the earth trembles anew? A wind of revolution blows, the storm
is on the horizon.' At about the same time two German exiles, the
thirty-year-old Karl Marx and the twenty-eight-year-old Friedrich
Engels, were spelling out the principles of the proletarian revolution
against which de Tocqueville was warning his colleagues, in the programme they had been instructed to draft a few weeks earlier by the
German Communist League, and which was published anonymously
in London around 24 February 1848 under the (German) title
Manifesto of the Communist Party, 'to be published in the English,
French, German, Italian, Flemish and Danish languages'.* Within
weeks, indeed in the case of the *Manifesto* within hours, the hopes and
fears of the prophets seemed to be on the verge of realization. The
French monarchy was overthrown by insurrection, the Republic
proclaimed, and the European revolution had begun.

* It was in fact also translated into Polish and Swedish in the course of that
year, though it is only fair to state that its political reverberations outside small
circles of German revolutionaries were insignificant until it was reissued in the
early 1870s.

There have been plenty of greater revolutions in the history of the modern world, and certainly plenty of more successful ones. Yet there has been none which spread more rapidly and widely, running like a brushfire across frontiers, countries and even oceans. In France, the natural centre and detonator of European revolutions (see *The Age of Revolution*, chapter 6, p. 120), the Republic was proclaimed on 24 February. By 2 March revolution had gained south-west Germany, by 6 March Bavaria, by 11 March Berlin, by 13 March Vienna and almost immediately Hungary, by 18 March Milan and therefore Italy (where an independent revolt was already in possession of Sicily). At this time the most rapid information service available to *anyone* (that of the Rothschild bank) could not carry the news from Paris to Vienna in less than five days. Within a matter of weeks no government was left standing in an area of Europe which is today occupied by all or part of ten states,* not counting lesser repercussions in a number of others. Moreover, 1848 was the first potentially global revolution, whose direct influence may be detected in the 1848 insurrection in Pernambuco (Brazil) and a few years later in remote Colombia. In a sense it was the paradigm of the kind of 'world revolution' of which rebels were henceforth to dream, and which at rare moments, such as in the aftermath of great wars, they thought they could recognise. In fact such simultaneous continent-wide or world-wide explosions are extremely rare. In Europe 1848 is the only one which affected both the 'developed' and the backward parts of the continent. It was both the most widespread and the least successful of such revolutions. Within six months of its outbreak its universal defeat was safely predictable, within eighteen months of its outbreak all but one of the regimes it overthrew had been restored, and the exception (the French Republic) was putting as much distance as it could between itself and the insurrection to which it owed its existence.

The 1848 revolutions thus stand in a curious relationship to the contents of this book. But for their occurrence, and for the fear of their recurrence, the history of Europe in the next twenty-five years would have been very different. Eighteen forty-eight was very far from being 'the turning-point when Europe failed to turn'. What Europe failed to

* France, West Germany, East Germany, Austria, Italy, Czechoslovakia, Hungary, part of Poland, Yugoslavia and Rumania. The political effects of the revolution may also be regarded as serious in Belgium, Switzerland and Denmark.

do was to turn in a revolutionary manner. Because it did not, the year of revolutions stands by itself, an overture but not the main opera, a gateway whose architectural style does not quite lead one to expect the character of what we shall find when we go through it.

II

Revolution triumphed throughout the great central core of the European continent, though not at its periphery. This included countries too remote or too isolated in their history to be directly or immediately affected to any extent (e.g. the Iberian peninsula, Sweden and Greece), too backward to possess the politically explosive social strata of the revolutionary zone (e.g. Russia and the Ottoman Empire), but also the countries already industrialised, whose political game was already played according to rather different rules, Britain and Belgium.* Still the revolutionary zone, consisting essentially of France, the German Confederation, the Austrian Empire stretching far into south-eastern Europe and Italy, was heterogeneous enough, including as it did regions as backward and different as Calabria and Transylvania, as developed as the Rhineland and Saxony, as literate as Prussia and as illiterate as Sicily, as remote from each other as Kiel and Palermo, Perpignan and Bucarest. Most of them were ruled by what can be roughly called absolute monarchs or princes, but France was already a constitutional and indeed bourgeois kingdom, and the only significant republic of the continent, the Swiss Confederation, had actually initiated the year of revolution with a brief civil war at the end of 1847. The states affected by revolution ranged in size from the 35 millions of France to the few thousand inhabitants of the comic opera principalities of central Germany, in status from independent great powers of world standing to foreign-ruled provinces or satellites, in structure from the centralised and uniform to loose conglomerates.

Above all, history – social and economic structure – and politics divided the revolutionary zone into two parts, whose extremes appeared to have little in common. Their social structure differed fundamentally, except for the substantial and pretty universal prevalence of

* There is also the case of Poland, divided since 1796 between Russia, Austria and Prussia, which would certainly have participated in the revolution but for the fact that its Russian and Austrian rulers succeeded in mobilizing the peasantry against the (revolutionary) gentry. See p. 217 below.

countrymen over townsmen, of small towns over big cities; a fact easily overlooked, because the urban population and especially the large cities were disproportionately prominent in politics.* In the west peasants were legally free and large estates relatively unimportant; in much of the east they were still serfs and landownership was highly concentrated in the hands of noble landlords (see chapter 10 below). In the west the 'middle class' meant native bankers, merchants, capitalist entrepreneurs, those practising the 'liberal professions' and senior officials (including professors), though some of these would feel themselves to belong to an upper stratum (*haute bourgeoisie*) ready to compete with the landed nobility, at least in expenditure. In the east the equivalent urban stratum consisted largely of national groups distinct from the native population, such as Germans and Jews, and was in any case much smaller. The real equivalent of the 'middle class' was the educated and/or business-minded sector of the country squires and minor nobles, a stratum which was surprisingly large in certain areas (see *The Age of Revolution*, pp. 16, 183–4). The central zone from Prussia in the north to north-central Italy in the south, which was in a sense the core of the area of revolution, combined the characteristics of the relatively 'developed' and the backward regions in various ways.

Politically the revolutionary zone was equally heterogeneous. Apart from France, what was at issue was not merely the politic and social content of states, but their very form or even existence. Germans strove to construct a 'Germany' – was it to be unitary or federal? – out of an assembly of numerous German principalities of varying size and character. Italians similarly tried to turn what the Austrian Chancellor Metternich, contemptuously, but not inaccurately, described as a 'mere geographical expression' into a united Italy. Both, with the usual biased vision of nationalists, included in their projects peoples who were not and often did not feel themselves to be Germans or Italians, such as the Czechs. Germans, Italians, and indeed all national movements involved in the revolution, aside from the French, found themselves stumbling against the great multi-national empire of the Habsburg dynasty, which stretched into Germany and Italy, as well as

* Of the delegates to the German 'pre-parliament' from the Rhineland, forty-five represented large cities, twenty-four small towns and only ten the countryside, where 73 per cent of the population lived.[3]

24

including the Czechs, Hungarians and a substantial portion of Poles, Rumanians, Yugoslavs and other Slavonic peoples. Some of these, or at least their political spokesmen, saw the Empire as a less unattractive solution than absorption by some expansionist nationalism such as the Germans' or the Magyars'. 'If Austria did not already exist,' Professor Palacky, the Czech spokesman, is supposed to have said, 'it would be necessary to invent it.' Throughout the revolutionary zone politics therefore operated along several dimensions simultaneously.

Radicals admittedly had a simple solution: a unitary centralised democratic republic of Germany, Italy, Hungary or whatever the country happened to be, built according to the tried principles of the French Revolution on the ruins of all kings and princes, and raising its version of the tricolour which, as usual on the French model, was the basic model of the national flag (see *The Age of Revolution*, pp. 128–9). Moderates, on the other hand, were enmeshed in a web of complex calculations, based essentially on the fear of democracy which they believed to equal social revolution. Where the masses had not already swept away the princes, it would be unwise to encourage them to undermine the social order, and where they had, it would be desirable to send or drive them off the streets and to dismantle those barricades which were the essential symbols of 1848. So the question was which of the princes, paralysed but not deposed by the revolution, could be persuaded to support the good cause. How exactly was a federal and liberal Germany or Italy to be brought about, on what constitutional formula and under whose auspices? Could it contain both the King of Prussia and the Emperor of Austria (as the 'greater german' moderates thought – not to be confused with the radical democrats who were by definition 'great-germans' of a different kind) or would it have to be 'little german', i.e. exclude Austria? Similarly moderates in the Habsburg Empire practised the game of devising federal and multi-national constitutions which was to cease only with its demise in 1918. Where revolutionary action or war irrupted, there was not much time for such constitutional speculation. Where they did not, as in most of Germany, it had full scope. Since a large proportion of moderate liberals there consisted of professors and civil servants – 68 per cent of the deputies to the Frankfurt Assembly were officials, 12 per cent belonged to the 'free professions' – the debates of this short-lived parliament have become a by-word for intelligent futility.

The revolutions of 1848 thus require detailed study by state, people and region, for which this is not the place. Nevertheless they had a great deal in common, not least the fact that they occurred almost simultaneously, that their fates were intertwined, and that they all possessed a common mood and style, a curious romantic–utopian atmosphere and a similar rhetoric, for which the French have invented the word *quarante-huitard*. Every historian recognises it immediately: the beards, flowing cravats and broad-brimmed hats of the militants, the tricolours, the ubiquitous barricades, the initial sense of liberation, of immense hope and optimistic confusion. It was 'the springtime of the peoples' – and like spring, it did not last. We must now briefly look at their common characteristics.

In the first place they all succeeded and failed rapidly, and in most cases totally. During the first few months all governments in the revolutionary zone were swept away or reduced to impotence. All collapsed or retreated virtually without resistance. Yet within a relatively short period the revolution had lost the initiative almost everywhere: in France by the end of April, in the rest of revolutionary Europe during the summer, though the movement retained some capacity to counter-attack in Vienna, Hungary and Italy. In France the first landmark of conservative revival was the election of April, in which universal suffrage, though electing only a minority of monarchists, sent to Paris a large majority of conservatives, elected by the votes of a peasantry which was politically inexperienced rather than reactionary, and to which the purely urban-minded left did not yet know how to appeal. (In fact, by 1849 the 'republican' and left-wing regions of the French countryside, familiar to students of later French politics, had already emerged, and here – for instance in Provence – the bitterest resistance to the abolition of the Republic in 1851 was to be encountered.) The second landmark was the isolation and defeat of the revolutionary workers in Paris, defeated in the June insurrection (see below, p. 30).

In central Europe the turning-point came when the Habsburg army, its freedom of manoeuvre increased by the flight of the emperor in May, was allowed to regroup, to defeat a radical insurrection in Prague in June – not without the support of the moderate middle class, Czech and German – thus reconquering the Bohemian lands, the economic core of the Empire, while shortly afterwards it regained control of north Italy. A short-lived and late revolution in the Danubian principalities was put down by Russian and Turkish intervention.

Between the summer and the end of the year the old regimes regained power in Germany and Austria, though it proved necessary to reconquer the increasingly revolutionary city of Vienna by force of arms in October at the cost of over four thousand lives. After this the king of Prussia summoned up the nerve to re-establish his authority over the rebellious Berliners without trouble, and the rest of Germany (except for some opposition in the south-west) fell quickly into line, leaving the German parliament, or rather constitutional assembly, elected in the hopeful spring days, and the more radical Prussian and other assemblies to their discussions, while they waited for dissolution. By the winter only two regions were still in the hands of the revolution – parts of Italy and Hungary. They were reconquered, following a more modest revival of revolutionary action in the spring of 1849, by the middle of that year.

After the capitulation of the Hungarians and Venetians in August 1849 the revolution was dead. With the single exception of France, all the old rulers were restored to power – in some instances, as in the Habsburg Empire, to greater power than ever before – and the revolutionaries scattered into exile. Again with the exception of France, virtually all the institutional changes, all the political and social dreams of the spring of 1848, were soon wiped out, and even in France the Republic had only another two and a half years to live. There had been one and only one major irreversible change: the abolition of serfdom in the Habsburg Empire.* Except for this single, though admittedly important, achievement, 1848 appears as the one revolution in the modern history of Europe which combines the greatest promise, the widest scope, and the most immediate initial success, with the most unqualified and rapid failure. In a sense it resembles that other mass phenomenon of the 1840s, the Chartist movement in Britain. Its specific objects were eventually achieved – but not by revolution or in a revolutionary context. Its wider aspirations were not lost either, but the movements which were to take them

* Broadly speaking, the abolition of serfdom and seignorial rights over peasants in the rest of western and central Europe (including Prussia) had taken place in the French Revolutionary and Napoleonic period (1789–1815), though some remainders of dependency in Germany were abolished in 1848. Serfdom in Russia and Rumania lasted until the 1860s (see chapter 10 below).

up and carry them forward were to be entirely different from those of 1848. It is no accident that the document of that year which has had the most lasting and significant effect on world history is the *Communist Manifesto*.

All the revolutions had something else in common, which largely accounts for their failure. They were, in fact or immediate anticipation, social revolutions of the labouring poor. They therefore frightened the moderate liberals whom they pushed into power and prominence – and even some of the more radical politicians – at least as much as the supporters of the old regimes. Count Cavour of Piedmont, the future architect of united Italy, had put his finger on this weakness some years earlier (1846):

> 'If the social order were to be genuinely menaced, if the great principles on which it rests were to be at serious risk, then many of the most determined oppositionists, the most enthusiastic republicans would be, we are convinced, the first to join the ranks of the conservative party.'[4]

Now those who made the revolution were unquestionably the labouring poor. It was they who died on the urban barricades: in Berlin there were only about fifteen representatives of the educated classes, about thirty master craftsmen, among the three hundred victims of the March fighting; in Milan only twelve students, white-collar workers or landlords among the 350 dead of the insurrection.[5] It was their hunger which powered the demonstrations that turned into revolutions. The countryside of the western regions of revolution was relatively quiet, though south-west Germany saw a great deal more of peasant insurrection than is commonly remembered, but elsewhere the fear of agrarian revolt was sufficiently acute to take the place of its reality, though no one needed to use much imagination in areas like southern Italy, where the peasants everywhere spontaneously marched out with flags and drums to partition the great estates. But fear alone was enough to concentrate the minds of landowners wonderfully. Frightened by false rumours of a huge serf insurrection under the leadership of the poet S. Petöfi(1823–49), the Hungarian Diet–an overwhelmingly landlord assembly – voted the immediate abolition of serfdom as early as 15 March, but only a few days before the imperial government, seeking to isolate the revolutionaries from an agrarian base, decreed the immediate abolition of serfdom in Galicia, the abolition of forced labour and other feudal obligations in the Czech lands. There was no doubt that the 'social order' was in danger.

That danger was not equally acute everywhere. Peasants could be – and were – bought off by conservative governments, especially where it happened that their landlords, or the traders and moneylenders who exploited them, belonged to another, and as likely as not 'revolutionary', nationality, Polish, Hungarian or German. It is improbable that the German middle classes, including the confidently rising businessmen of the Rhineland, were desperately worried by any immediate prospect of proletarian communism, or even proletarian power, which was of little consequence except in Cologne (where Marx made his headquarters) and in Berlin, where a communist printer, Stefan Born, organised a rather important working-class movement. Yet just as the European middle classes of the 1840s thought they recognised the shape of their future social problems in the rain and smoke of Lancashire, so they thought they recognised another shape of the future behind the barricades of Paris, that great anticipator and exporter of revolutions. And the February revolution was not only made by 'the proletariat' but as a conscious social revolution. Its object was not merely any republic, but the 'democratic and social republic'. Its leaders were socialists and communists. Its provisional government actually included a genuine worker, a mechanic known as Albert. For a few days it was uncertain whether its flag was to be the tricolour or the red banner of social revolt.

Except where questions of national autonomy or independence were at issue, the moderate opposition of the 1840s had neither wanted nor seriously worked for revolution, and even on the national question the moderates had preferred negotiation and diplomacy to confrontation. They would no doubt have preferred more, but were quite prepared to settle for concessions which, it might be reasonably argued, all but the most stupid and self-confident of absolutisms such as the tsar's would sooner or later be forced to grant, or for international changes which, sooner or later, were likely to be accepted by the oligarchy of 'great powers' who decided on such matters. Pushed into revolution by the forces of the poor and/or the example of Paris, they naturally tried to turn an unexpectedly favourable situation to the best advantage. Yet they were certainly in the last analysis, and often indeed from the start, much more worried by the danger from their left than by the old regimes. From the moment the barricades went up in Paris, all moderate liberals (and, as Cavour observed, a fair proportion of radicals) were potential conservatives. As moderate opinion more or less rapidly changed sides or dropped out, the workers, the intransigents among the democratic radicals, were left isolated or, what was even more fatal, to face a union of conservative and formerly moderate forces with the old regimes: a 'party of order', as the French called it. Eighteen forty-eight failed because it turned out that the decisive confrontation was not that between the old regimes and the united 'forces of progress', but between 'order' and 'social revolution'. Its crucial confrontation was not that of Paris in February but that of Paris in June, when the workers, manoeuvred into isolated insurrection, were defeated and massacred. They fought and died hard. About 1500 fell in the street-fighting – some two-thirds of them on the government side. It is characteristic of the ferocity of the hatred of the rich for the poor that some three thousand were slaughtered after defeat, while another twelve thousand were arrested, mostly to be deported to Algerian labour camps.[6]*

The revolution therefore maintained its impetus only where the radicals were sufficiently strong and sufficiently linked with the popular movement to drag the moderates forward, or to do without them. This was most likely to occur in countries in which the crucial issue was national liberation, an aim which required the continued mobilisation of the masses. This is why the revolution lasted longest in Italy and above all Hungary.†

In Italy the moderates, rallying behind the anti-Austrian king of Piedmont and joined, after the insurrection of Milan, by the minor principalities with considerable mental reservations, took over the fight against the oppressor, while constantly glancing over their shoulders at the republicans and social revolution. Thanks to the

* The February Revolution in Paris had cost about 370 lives.
† In France national unity and independence was not at issue. German nationalism was preoccupied with the unification of numerous separate states, but what prevented this was not foreign domination but – apart from particularist vested interests – the attitude of two great powers which were considered German themselves, Prussia and Austria. Slav national aspirations conflicted in the first instance with those of 'revolutionary' nations such as the Germans and Magyars, and were therefore muted, if not actually favourable to counter-revolution. Even the Czech left regarded the Habsburg Empire as a protection against absorption into a national Germany. The Poles did not take a large part in this revolution at all.

military weakness of the Italian states, Piedmont's hesitations and, perhaps above all, the refusal to call in the French (who would, it was believed, strengthen the republican cause), they were heavily defeated by the regrouped Austrian army at Custozza in July. (It may be noted in passing that the great republican G. Mazzini [1805–72], with his unfailing instinct for the politically futile, opposed an appeal to the French.) The defeat discredited the moderates and passed the leadership of national liberation to the radicals, who gained power in several Italian states during the autumn, finally actually setting up a Roman republic in early 1849, which gave Mazzini ample opportunity for rhetoric. (Venice, under a sensible lawyer, Daniele Manin [1804–57], had already become an independent republic, which kept out of trouble until it was inevitably reconquered by the Austrians – admittedly later than even the Hungarians – at the end of August 1849.) The radicals were no military match for Austria; when they made Piedmont declare war again in 1849, the Austrians won easily at Novara in March. Moreover, though more determined to expel Austria and unify Italy, they generally shared the moderates' fear of social revolution. Even Mazzini, with all his zeal for the comman man, preferred him to confine his interests to spiritual matters, detested socialism and opposed any interference with private property. After its initial failure, the Italian revolution therefore lived on borrowed time. Ironically, among those who suppressed it were the armies of a by now nonrevolutionary France, which reconquered Rome in early June. The Roman expedition was an attempt to reassert French diplomatic influence in the peninsula against Austria. It also had the incidental advantage of being popular among the Catholics, on whose support the post-revolutionary regime relied.

Unlike Italy, Hungary was already a more or less unified political entity ('the lands of the crown of St Stephen'), with an effective constitution, a not negligible degree of autonomy, and indeed most of the elements of a sovereign state except independence. Its weakness was that the Magyar aristocracy which governed this vast and overwhelmingly agrarian area ruled not only over the Magyar peasantry of the great plain, but over a population of which perhaps 60 per cent consisted of Croats, Serbs, Slovaks, Rumanians and Ukrainians, not to mention a substantial German minority. These peasant peoples were not unsympathetic to a revolution which freed the serfs, but were antagonised by the refusal of even most of the Budapest radicals to make any concessions to their national difference from the Magyars, as their political spokesmen were antagonised by a ferocious policy of Magyarisation and the incorporation of hitherto in some ways autonomous border regions into a centralised and unitary Magyar state. The court at Vienna, following the habitual imperialist maxim 'divide and rule', offered them support. It was to be a Croat army, under Baron Jellacic, a friend of Gaj, the pioneer of a Yugoslav nationalism, which led the assault on revolutionary Vienna and revolutionary Hungary.

Nevertheless, within roughly the present area of Hungary, the revolution retained the mass support of the (Magyar) people for both national and social reasons. The peasants considered that they had been given their freedom not by the emperor but by the revolutionary Hungarian Diet. This was the only part of Europe in which the defeat of the revolution was followed by something like a rural guerilla, which the celebrated bandit Sandor Rósza maintained for several years. When the revolution broke out, the Diet, consisting of an upper house of compromising or moderate magnates and a lower house dominated by radical country squires and lawyers, had merely to exchange protests for action. It did so readily, under the leadership of an able lawyer, journalist and orator, Louis Kossuth (1802–94), who was to become the internationally best-known revolutionary figure of 1848. For practical purposes Hungary, under a moderate-radical coalition government reluctantly authorised by Vienna, was an autonomous reformed state, at least until the Habsburgs were in a position to reconquer it. After the battle of Custozza they thought they were and, by cancelling the Hungarian reform laws of March and invading the country, faced the Hungarians with the choice of capitulation or radicalisation. Consequently, under Kossuth's leadership, Hungary burnt its boats, deposing the Emperor (though not formally proclaiming a republic) in April 1849. Popular support and the generalship of Görgei allowed the Hungarians to do more than hold their own against the Austrian army. They were defeated only when Vienna in despair called in the ultimate weapon of reaction, the Russian forces. This was decisive. On 13 August the remnant of the Hungarian army capitulated – not to the Austrian but to the Russian commander. Alone among the revolutions of 1848, the Hungarian one did not fall or ever look like falling by internal weakness and conflict, but by over-powering military conquest. It is of course true that its chances of avoiding such conquest after the breakdown of all the rest were zero.

Was there any alternative to this general *débacle*? Almost certainly not. Of the main social groups involved in the revolution, the bourgeoisie, as we have seen, discovered that it preferred order to the chance of implementing its full programme, when faced with the threat to property. Confronting 'red' revolution moderate liberals and conservatives drew together. The 'notables' of France, i.e. the respectable, influential and wealthy families who ran the political affairs of that country, stopped their former feuding between supporters of Bourbons, Orléanists, even of a republic, and acquired a national class consciousness through a newly emerging 'party of order'. The key figures in the restored Habsburg monarchy were to be the Minister of the Interior, Alexander Bach (1806–67), a former moderate liberal oppositionist and the shipping and commercial magnate K. von Bruck (1798–1860), key figure in the thriving port of Trieste. The Rhineland bankers and entrepreneurs who spoke for Prussian bourgeois liberalism would have preferred a limited constitutional monarch, but settled down comfortably as pillars of a restored Prussia which at all events avoided a democratic suffrage. In return, the restored conservative regimes were quite prepared to make concessions to the economic, legal, even the cultural liberalism of businessmen, so long as it implied no political retreat. As we shall see the reactionary 1850s were to be, in economic terms, a period of systematic liberalisation. In 1848–9 moderate liberals therefore made two important discoveries in western Europe: that revolution was dangerous and that some of their substantial demands (especially in economic matters) could be met without it. The bourgeoisie ceased to be a revolutionary force.

The large body of the radical lower middle classes, discontented artisans, small shopkeepers, etc., and even agriculturalists, whose spokesmen and leaders were intellectuals, especially young and marginal ones, formed a significant revolutionary force but rarely a political alternative. They stood in general on the democratic left. The German left demanded new elections, because its radicalism made a strong showing in many areas in late 1848 and early 1849, though by then it lacked the focus of the great cities, which had been reconquered by reaction. In France the radical democrats polled 2 million in 1849

33

as against 3 million for the monarchists and 800,000 for the moderates. The intellectuals provided their activists, though perhaps only in Vienna did the 'Academic Legion' of students form actual shock troops of combat. To call 1848 the 'revolution of intellectuals' is misleading. They were no more prominent in it than in most other revolutions which occur, as this one did largely, in relatively backward countries in which the bulk of the middle strata consists of people characterised by schooling and a command of the written word: graduates of all kinds, journalists, teachers, officials. But there is no doubt that intellectuals were prominent: poets like Petöfi in Hungary, Herwegh and Freiligrath in Germany (he was on the editorial board of Marx's *Neue Rheinische Zeitung*), Victor Hugo and the consistently moderate Lamartine in France; academics in large numbers (mainly on the moderate side) in Germany;* medical men like C. G. Jacoby (1804–51) in Prussia, Adolf Fischhof (1816–93) in Austria; scientists like F. V. Raspail (1794–1878) in France; and a vast quantity of journalists and publicists of whom Kossuth was at the time the most celebrated and Marx was to prove the most formidable.

As individuals such men could play a decisive part; as members of a specific social stratum, or as spokesmen for the radical petty-bourgeoisie, they could not. The radicalism of the 'little men', which found expression in the demand for 'a democratic state constitution, whether constitutional or republican, giving a majority to them and their allies, the peasants, as well as democratic local government which would give them control over municipal property and over a series of functions now performed by bureaucrats',[7] was genuine enough, even though secular crisis on one hand, threatening the traditional way of life of master artisans and their like, and temporary economic depression on the other, gave it a special edge of bitterness. The radicalism of the intellectuals was less deeply rooted. It was based largely on the (as it turned out temporary) inability of the new bourgeois society before 1848 to provide enough posts of adequate status for the educated whom it produced in unprecedented numbers, and whose rewards were so much more modest than their ambitions. What happened to all those radical students of 1848 in the prosperous 1850s and 1860s? They established the biographical pattern so familiar, and

* French teachers, though suspect to governments, had been quiet under the July monarchy and appeared to have rallied to 'order' in 1848.

indeed accepted, on the continent of Europe, whereby bourgeois boys sow their political and sexual wild oats in youth, before 'settling down'. And there were plenty of possibilities of settling down, especially as the retreat of the old nobility and the diversion to money-making of the business-bourgeoisie left increasing scope for those whose qualifications were primarily scholastic. In 1842 10 per cent of French lycée professors had still come from the 'notables', but by 1877 none. In 1868 France produced barely more secondary graduates (*bacheliers*) than in the 1830s, but far more of these could then go into banking, commerce, successful journalism and, after 1870, professional politics.[8]

Moreover, when faced with red revolution, even the rather democratic radicals tended to retreat into rhetoric, torn between their genuine sympathy for 'the people' and their sense of property and money. Unlike the liberal bourgeoisie they did not change sides. They merely vacillated, though never very far to the right.

As for the labouring poor, they lacked the organisation, the maturity, the leadership, perhaps most of all the historical conjuncture, to provide a political alternative. Strong enough to make the prospect of social revolution look real and menacing, they were too weak to do more than frighten their enemies. Their forces were disproportionately effective, in so far as they were concentrated in hungry masses in the politically most sensitive spots, the large and especially the capital cities. This concealed some substantial weaknesses: in the first place, their numerical deficiency – they were not always even a majority in the cities, which themselves generally included only a modest minority of the population – and in the second place, their political and ideological immaturity. The most politically conscious and activist stratum among them consisted of the pre-industrial artisans (using the term in the contemporary British sense for journeymen, craftsmen, skilled manual workers in non-mechanised workshops, etc.). Swept into social-revolutionary, even socialist and communist ideologies in Jacobin-Sansculotte France, their aims as a mass were distinctly more modest in Germany, as the communist printer Stefan Born discovered in Berlin. The poor and unskilled in the cities and, outside Britain, the industrial and mining proletariat as a whole, had hardly any developed political ideology as yet. In the industrial zone of northern France even republicanism made hardly any headway before the very end of the Second Republic. Eighteen forty-eight saw Lille and Roubaix exclusively preoccupied with their economic problems, directing their riots not against kings or bourgeois, but against the even more starving immigrant Belgian labourers.

Where the urban plebeians, or more rarely the new proletarians, came within the radius of Jacobin, socialist or democratic-republican ideology or – as in Vienna – of student activists, they became a political force, at least as rioters. (Their participation in elections was as yet low and unpredictable, unlike that of the pauperised rural outworkers who, as in Saxony or Britain, were highly radicalised.) Paradoxically, outside Paris this was rare in Jacobin France, whereas in Germany Marx's Communist League provided the elements of a national network for the extreme left. Outside this radius of influence, the labouring poor were politically insignificant.

Of course we should not underestimate the potential of even so young and immature a social force as the 'proletariat' of 1848, barely as yet conscious of itself as a class. In one sense, indeed, its revolutionary potential was greater than it was to be subsequently. The iron generation of pauperism and crisis before 1848 had encouraged few to believe that capitalism could, still less would, yield them decent conditions of life, or even that it would last. The very youth and weakness of the working class, still emerging from among the mass of labouring poor, independent masters and small shopkeepers, prevented an exclusive concentration on their economic demands among all but the most ignorant and isolated. The *political* demands without which no revolution is made, not even the most purely social one, were built into the situation. The popular objective in 1848, the 'democratic and social republic', was both social and political. Working-class experience injected into it, at least in France, novel institutional elements, based on the practice of trade union and co-operative action, though it created no elements as novel and powerful as the *soviets* of early twentieth-century Russia.

On the other hand, organisation, ideology and leadership were sadly undeveloped. Even the most elementary form, the trade union, was confined to bodies of a few hundred, at best a few thousand, members. Often enough even the societies of the skilled pioneers of unionism only made their first appearance during the revolution – the printers in Germany, the hatters in France. The organised socialists and communists were even more exiguous in number: a few dozen, at

36

most a few hundred. Yet 1848 was the first revolution in which socialists or more likely communists – for pre-1848 socialism was a largely a political movement for building co-operative utopias – appeared at the front of the stage from the beginning. It was the year not only of Kossuth, A. Ledru-Rollin (1807–74) and Mazzini, but of Karl Marx (1818–83), Louis Blanc (1811–82) and L. A. Blanqui (1805–81) (the stern rebel who emerged from a lifetime in jail only when briefly liberated by revolutions), of Bakunin, even of Proudhon. But what did socialism mean to its adherents, other than a name for a self-conscious working class with its own aspirations for a society different from, and based on the overthrow of, capitalism? Even its enemy was not clearly defined. There was plenty of talk about the 'working class' or even the 'proletariat', but during the revolution itself none about 'capitalism'.

Indeed, what were the political perspectives of even a socialist working class? Karl Marx himself did not believe that proletarian revolution was on the agenda. Even in France 'the Paris proletariat was still incapable of going beyond the bourgeois republic other than in *ideas*, in *imagination*'. 'Its immediate, admitted needs did not drive it to want to win the forcible overthrow of the bourgeoisie, nor was it equal to this task.' The most that might be achieved was a bourgeois republic which brought the real nature of the future struggle – that between bourgeoisie and proletariat – into the open, and would in turn unite the remainder of the middle strata with the workers 'as their position became more unbearable and their antagonism to the bourgeoisie became more acute'.[9] It was in the first instance a democratic republic, in the second the transition from an incomplete bourgeois to a proletarian-popular revolution and finally a proletarian dictatorship or, in the phrase which recalls the opinions of Blanqui and which reflected the temporary closeness of the two great revolutionaries in the immediate aftermath of 1848, 'the permanent revolution'. But, unlike Lenin in 1917, Marx did not conceive of the substitution of proletarian for bourgeois revolution until after the defeat of 1848; and, in so far as he then formulated a perspective comparable to Lenin's (including 'backing the revolution with a new edition of the peasant war', as Engels put it), he did not do so for long. There was to be no second edition of 1848 in western and central Europe. The working class, as he soon recognised, would have to follow a different road.

Thus the revolutions of 1848 surged and broke like a great wave leaving little behind except myth and promise. They 'ought to have been' bourgeois revolutions, but the bourgeoisie drew back from them. They might have reinforced one another under the leadership of France, preventing or postponing the restoration of the old rulers, and keeping at bay the Russian tsar. But the French bourgeoisie preferred social stability at home to the rewards and dangers of being once again *la grande nation*, and, for analogous reasons, the moderate leaders of revolution hesitated to call for French intervention. No other social force was strong enough to give them coherence and impetus, except in special cases the struggle for national independence against a politically dominant power, and even this failed, since the national struggles were isolated and in any case too weak to withstand the military force of the old powers. The great and characteristic figures of 1848 played their heroes' parts on the stage of Europe for a few months, to disappear for ever – with the exception of Garibaldi, who was to know an even more glorious moment twelve years later. Kossuth and Mazzini lived out their long lives in exile, contributing little directly to the winning of their countries' autonomy or unification, though rewarded by a secure place in their national pantheons. Ledru-Rollin and Raspail never knew another moment of celebrity like the Second Republic, and the eloquent professors of the Frankfurt parliament retired to their studies and auditoria. Of the passionate exiles of the 1850s, forming great plans and rival governments in exile in the fog of London, nothing survives except the work of the most isolated and untypical, Marx and Engels.

And yet, 1848 was not merely a brief historical episode without consequence. If the changes it achieved were neither those the revolutionaries intended, nor even easily definable in terms of political regimes, laws and institutions, they were none the less profound. It marked the end, at least in western Europe, of the politics of tradition, of the monarchies which believed that their peoples (except for middle-class malcontents) accepted, even welcomed, the rule of divinely appointed dynasties presiding over hierarchically stratified societies, sanctioned by traditional religion, of the belief in the patriarchal rights and duties of social and economic superiors. As the poet Grillparzer, himself by no means a revolutionary, wrote ironically about, presumably, Metternich:

Here lies, all his celebrity forgot
Legitimacy's famous Don Quixote
Who, twisting truth and fact, thought himself wise
And ended by believing his own lies;
An aged fool, who'd been a knave in youth:
He could no longer recognise the truth.[10]

Henceforth the forces of conservatism, privilege and wealth would have to defend themselves in new ways. Even the dark and ignorant peasants of southern Italy in the great spring of 1848 ceased to champion absolutism, as they had done fifty years earlier. When they marched to occupy the land they rarely expressed hostility to 'the constitution'.

The defenders of the social order had to learn the politics of the people. This was the major innovation brought about by the 1848 revolutions. Even the most arch-reactionary Prussian junkers discovered during that year that they required a newspaper capable of influencing 'public opinion' – in itself a concept linked with liberalism and incompatible with traditional hierarchy. The most intelligent of the Prussian arch-reactionaries of 1848, Otto von Bismarck (1815–98), was later to demonstrate his lucid understanding of the nature of the politics of bourgeois society and his mastery of its techniques. However, the most significant political innovations of this kind occurred in France.

There the defeat of the working-class insurrection of June had left a powerful 'party of order', capable of defeating social revolution but not of acquiring much support from the masses, or even from many conservatives who did not wish by their defence of 'order' to commit themselves to the precise brand of moderate republicanism which was now in office. The people were still too mobilised to permit a limitation of elections: not until 1850 was a substantial section of 'the vile multitude' – i.e. about a third in France, about two-thirds in radical Paris – excluded from the vote. But, if in December of 1848 the French did not elect a moderate to the new presidency of the Republic, they did not elect a radical either. (There was no monarchist candidate.) The winner, by an overwhelming majority – 5·5 out of 7·4 million votes cast – was Louis Napoleon, the nephew of the great Emperor. Though he turned out to be a remarkably astute politician, he seemed, when he entered France in late September, to have no assets except a prestigious name and the financial backing of a devoted English mistress. He was evidently not a social revolutionary, but neither was he a conservative; indeed his backers made some play with his youthful interest in Saint-Simonianism (see p. 73 below) and alleged sympathies for the poor. But basically he won because the peasants voted solidly for him under the slogan: 'No more taxes, down with the rich, down with the Republic, long live the Emperor'; in other words, as Marx noted, against the republic of the rich, the workers voted for him, because in their eyes he meant 'the deposition of Cavaignac [who had put down the June rising], the dismissal of bourgeois republicanism, the rescinding of the June victory',[11] the petty-bourgeoisie because he did not appear to stand for the big bourgeoisie.

Louis Napoleon's election signified that even the democracy of universal suffrage, that institution identified with revolution, was compatible with the maintenance of social order. Even a mass of overwhelming discontent was not bound to elect rulers dedicated to the 'overthrow of society'. The wider lessons of this experience were not immediately learned, for Louis Napoleon himself soon abolished the Republic and turned himself into an emperor, though never forgetting the political advantages of a well-managed universal suffrage, which he reintroduced. He was to be the first of the modern chiefs of state who ruled not by simple armed force, but by the sort of demagogy and public relations which are so much more easily operated from the top of the state than from anywhere else. His experience demonstrated not only that 'social order' could masquerade as a force capable of appealing to supporters of 'the left', but that, in a country or an age in which the citizens were mobilised to participate in politics, it had to. The revolutions of 1848 made it clear that the middle classes, liberalism, political democracy, nationalism, even the working classes, were henceforth permanent features of the political landscape. The defeat of the revolutions might temporarily remove them from sight, but when they reappeared they would determine the actions of even those statesmen who had the least sympathy for them.

Part Two

Developments

Chapter Two

The Great Boom

Here the man who is powerful in the weapons of peace, capital and machinery uses them to give comfort and enjoyment to the public, whose servant he is, and thus becomes rich while he enriches others with his goods.

William Whewell, 1852[1]

A people can achieve material well-being without subversive tactics if they are docile, hard-working and constantly apply themselves to their own self-improvement.
From the statutes of the *Société contre l'Ignorance* of Clermont-Ferrand, 1869[2]

The inhabited area of the world is rapidly expanding. New communities, that is, new markets, are daily springing up in the hitherto desert regions of the New World in the West and in the traditionally fertile islands of the Old World in the East.

'Philoponos', 1850[3]

I

Few observers in 1849 would have predicted that 1848 would be the last general revolution in the west. The political demands of liberalism, democratic radicalism and nationalism though not the 'social republic' were to be gradually realised over the next seventy years in most developed countries without major internal upheavals, and the social structure of the developed part of the continent was to prove itself capable of resisting the catastrophic blows of the twentieth century, at least up to the present (1977). The main reason for this lay in the extraordinary economic transformation and expansion of the years between 1848 and the early 1870s which is the subject of this chapter. This was the period when the world became capitalist and a significant minority of 'developed' countries became industrial economies.

This age of unexampled economic advance began with a boom which was all the more spectacular for having been, as it were,

43

temporarily bottled up by the events of 1848. The revolutions had been precipitated by the last, and perhaps greatest, economic crisis of the ancient kind, belonging to a world which depended on the fortunes of harvests and seasons. The new world of the 'trade cycle', which only the socialists as yet recognised as the basic rhythm and mode of operation of the capitalist economy, had its own pattern of economic fluctuations and its own secular difficulties. However, by the middle of the 1840s the gloomy and uncertain era of capitalist development looked like drawing to an end, the great leap forward was beginning. 1847–8 saw a trade-cycle slump and a severe one, probably made worse by coinciding with troubles of the ancient kind. Nevertheless, from a purely capitalist point of view, it was merely a rather sharp dip in what already looked like a very buoyant curve of affairs. James de Rothschild, who regarded the economic situation in early 1848 with notable complacency, was a sensible businessman, though a poor political prophet. The worst of the 'panic' seemed to be over and long-term prospects were rosy. And yet, though industrial production recovered quickly enough, even from the virtual paralysis of the revolutionary months, the general atmosphere remained uncertain. We can hardly date the start of the great global boom before 1850.

What followed was so extraordinary that men were at a loss for a precedent. Never, for instance, did British exports grow more rapidly than in the first seven years of the 1850s. Thus British cotton piece-goods, the vanguard of market penetration for over half a century, actually increased their *rate* of growth over earlier decades. Between 1850 and 1860 they just about doubled. In absolute figures the performance is even more startling: between 1820 and 1850 these exports had grown by about 1,100 million yards, but in the single decade between 1850 and 1860 they grew by considerably more than 1,300 million yards. The number of cotton operatives had grown by about 100,000 between 1819–21 and 1844–6, but at double this rate in the 1850s.[4] And we are here dealing with a large and old-established industry and, moreover, one which actually lost ground in the European markets in this decade because of the speed of local industrial developments. Wherever we look similar evidences of boom may be found. The export of iron from Belgium more than doubled between 1851 and 1857. In Prussia, in the quarter of a century before 1850, sixty-seven joint-stock companies had been founded with a total capital of 45 million Thaler, but in 1851–7 alone 115 such companies were established – *excluding* railway companies – with a total capital of 114·5 millions; almost all of them in the euphoric years between 1853 and 1857.[5] It is hardly necessary to multiply such statistics, though contemporary businessmen, especially company promoters, read and diffused them with avidity.

What made this boom so satisfactory for profit-hungry businessmen was the combination of cheap capital and a rapid rise in prices. Slumps (of the trade-cycle type) always meant low prices, at all events in the nineteenth century. Booms were inflationary. Even so, the rise of about one-third in the British price-level between 1848–50 and 1857 was remarkably large. The profits apparently awaiting producers, merchants and above all promoters were therefore almost irresistible. At one point during this amazing period the rate of profit on paid-up capital of the *Crédit mobilier* of Paris, the finance company which was the symbol of capitalist expansion in this period (see chapter 12 below), touched 50 per cent.[6] And businessmen were not the only ones to benefit. As has already been suggested, employment grew by leaps and bounds, both in Europe and overseas, whither men and women now migrated in enormous numbers (see chapter 11 below). We know next to nothing about actual unemployment, but even in Europe one piece of evidence is decisive. The sharp rise in the cost of cereals (i.e. the main element in the cost of living) between 1853 and 1855 no longer precipitated hunger-riots anywhere except in some very backward regions such as northern Italy (Piedmont) and Spain. High employment and the readiness to concede temporary wage rises where necessary, blunted the edge of popular discontent. But for capitalists the ample labour supplies now moving into the market were relatively cheap.

The political consequence of this boom was far-reaching. It gave the governments shaken by the revolution invaluable breathing-space, and, conversely, wrecked the hopes of the revolutionaries. In a word, politics went into hibernation. In Britain Chartism died away, and the fact that its death was more protracted than historians used to suppose did not make it any the less final. Even Ernest Jones (1819–69), its most persistent leader, gave up the attempt to revive an independent movement of the working classes by the late 1850s and threw in his lot, like most old Chartists, with those who wanted to organise the workers as a pressure group on the radical left of liberalism. Parliamentary reform ceased to preoccupy British politicians for a while, leaving them free to dance their complicated parliamentary ballets. Even the middle-class radicals, Cobden and Bright, having achieved the abolition of the Corn Laws in 1846, were now an isolated fringe minority in politics.

For the restored monarchies of the continent and that unintended child of the French Revolution, Napoleon III's Second Empire, the breathing-space was even more vital. To Napoleon they gave those reasonably genuine and impressive electoral majorities which lent colour to his claim to be a 'democratic' emperor. To the old monarchies and principalities it gave time for political recovery and the legitimation of stability and prosperity, which was now politically more relevant than the legitimacy of their dynasties. It also gave them revenues without the need to consult representative assemblies and other troublesome interests, and left their political exiles to bite their nails and attack each other savagely in impotent exile. For the time being it left them weak in international affairs but strong internally. Even the Habsburg Empire, which had only been restored in 1849 by the intervention of the Russian army, was now able, for the first and only time in its history, to administer all its territories – including the recalcitrant Hungarians – as a single centralised bureaucratic absolutism.

This period of calm came to an end with the depression of 1857. Economically speaking, this was merely an interruption of the golden era of capitalist growth which resumed on an even larger scale in the 1860s and reached its peak in the boom of 1871–3. Politically it transformed the situation. Admittedly it disappointed the hopes of the revolutionaries, who had expected it to produce another 1848, though admitting that 'the masses will have become damned lethargic as a result of this prolonged prosperity'.[7] Yet politics did revive. Within a short space of time all the old questions of liberal politics were once again on the agenda – Italian and German national unification, constitutional reform, civil liberties and the rest. Whereas the economic expansion of 1851–7 had taken place in a political vacuum, prolonging the defeat and exhaustion of 1848–9, after 1859 it coincided with increasingly intense political activity. On the other hand, though interrupted by various external factors such as the American Civil

46

War of 1861–5, the 1860s were economically relatively stable. The next trade-cycle slump (which occurred, according to taste and region, some time in 1866–8) was not as concentrated, as global nor as dramatic as that of 1857–8. In short, politics revived in a period of expansion, but it was no longer the politics of revolution.

II

If Europe had still lived in the era of the baroque princes, it would have been filled with spectacular masques, processions and operas distributing allegorical representations of economic triumph and industrial progress at the feet of its rulers. In fact the triumphant world of capitalism had their equivalent. The era of its global victory was initiated and punctuated by giant new rituals of self-congratulation, the Great International Exhibitions, each encased in a princely monument to wealth and technical progress – the Crystal Palace in London (1851), the Rotunda ('larger than St Peter's in Rome') in Vienna, each displaying the growing number and variety of manufactures, each attracting native and foreign tourists in astronomic quantities. Fourteen thousand firms exhibited in London in 1851 – the fashion was suitably enough inaugurated in the home of capitalism – 24,000 in Paris in 1855, 29,000 in London in 1862, 50,000 in Paris in 1867. True to its claims, the largest of all was the Philadelphia Centennial of 1876 in the United States, opened by the President in the presence of the Emperor and Empress of Brazil – crowned heads now habitually inclined themselves before the products of industry – and 130,000 cheering citizens. They were the first of ten million who paid tribute on this occasion to the 'Progress of the Age'.

What were the reasons for this progress? Why did economic expansion accelerate so spectacularly in our period? The question ought really to be reversed. What strikes us retrospectively about the first half of the nineteenth century is the contrast between the enormous and rapidly growing productive potential of capitalist industrialisation and its inability, as it were, to broaden its base, to break the shackles which fettered it. It could grow dramatically, but appeared unable to expand the market for its products, the profitable outlets for its accumulating capital, let alone the capacity to generate employment at a comparable rate or at adequate wages. It is instructive to remember

47

that even in the late 1840s intelligent and informed observers in Germany – on the eve of the industrial explosion in that country – could still assume, as they do today in underdeveloped countries, that no conceivable industrialisation could provide employment for the vast and growing 'surplus population' of the poor. The 1830s and 1840s had for this reason been a period of crisis. Revolutionaries had hoped that it might be final, but even businessmen had feared that it might strangle their industrial system (see *The Age of Revolution*, chapter 16).

For two reasons these hopes or fears proved groundless. In the first place the early industrial economy discovered – thanks largely to the pressure of its own profit-seeking capital accumulation – what Marx called its 'crowning achievement'; the railway. In the second place – and partly due to the railway, the steamer and the telegraph 'which finally represented the means of communication adequate to modern means of production'[8] – the geographical size of the capitalist economy could suddenly multiply as the intensity of its business transactions increased. The entire globe became part of this economy. This creation of a single expanded world is probably the most significant development of our period (see chapter 3 below). Looking back from almost half a century later H. M. Hyndman, both a Victorian businessman and a Marxist (though untypical in both these roles), quite rightly compared the ten years from 1847 to 1857 with the era of the great geographical discoveries and conquests of Columbus, Vasco da Gama, Cortez and Pizarro. Though no dramatic new discoveries were made and (with relatively minor exceptions) few formal conquests by new military conquistadors, for practical purposes an entirely new economic world was added to the old and integrated into it.

This was particularly crucial for economic development because it provided the basis for that gigantic export boom – in both goods, capital and men – which played so large a part in the expansion, at all events in what was still the major capitalist country, Britain. The mass consumer economy still lay in the future, except perhaps in the United States. The domestic market of the poor, in so far as it was not supplied by peasants and small craftsmen, was not yet considered a major foundation for really spectacular economic advance.* It was, of course,

* While the exports of British cotton goods tripled in quantity between 1850 and 1875, the consumption of cotton for the British domestic market merely increased by two-thirds.[9]

far from negligible at a time when the population of the developed world both grew rapidly and probably improved its average standard of life (see chapter 12 below). Yet the enormous lateral extension of the market for both consumer goods and, perhaps above all, the goods required to construct the new industrial plants, transport undertakings, public utilities and cities was indispensable. Capitalism now had the entire world at its disposal, and the expansion of both international trade and international investment measures the zest with which it proceeded to capture it. The world's trade between 1800 and 1840 had not quite doubled. Between 1850 and 1870 it increased by 260 per cent. Anything saleable was sold, including goods which met with distinct resistance from the receiving countries, such as the opium whose export from British India to China more than doubled in quantity and almost trebled in value.* By 1875 £1,000 millions had been invested abroad by Britain – three-quarters since 1850 – while French foreign investment multiplied more than tenfold between 1850 and 1880.

Contemporary observers, their eyes fixed on less fundamental aspects of the economy, would almost certainly have stressed a third factor: the great gold discoveries in California, Australia and other places after 1848 (see chapter 3 below). These multiplied the means of payment available to the world economy and removed what many businessmen regarded as a crippling stringency, lowered interest rates and encouraged the expansion of credit. Within seven years the world gold supply increased between six and sevenfold, and the amount of gold coinage issued by Britain, France and the United States multiplied from an annual average of £4·9 millions in 1848–9 to one of £28·1 millions in each year between 1850 and 1856. The role of bullion in the world economy continues to be a matter of fairly passionate debate even today, a debate into which we need not enter. Its absence probably did not inconvenience commerce as seriously as was then thought, since other means of payment such as cheques – a fairly new device – bills of exchange, etc., were easily expandable and already increasing at a considerable rate. However, three aspects of the new gold supplies are reasonably uncontroversial.

In the first place they helped, perhaps crucially, to produce that relatively rare situation between about 1810 and the end of the nine-

* The average number of chests of Bengal and Malwa opium exported annually in 1844–9 was 43,000, in 1869–74, 87,000.[10]

teenth century, an era of rising prices or moderate, though fluctuating, inflation. Basically most of this century was deflationary, due largely to the persistent tendency of technology to cheapen manufactured products, and of newly opened sources of food and raw materials to cheapen (though more intermittently) primary products. Long-term deflation – i.e. a pressure on margins of profit – did not do business-men much harm, because they made and sold so much vaster quantities. However, until after the end of our period, it did not do the workers much good, because either their cost of living did not fall to the same extent or their income was too meagre to allow them to benefit significantly. On the other hand, inflation undoubtedly raised profit-margins and in doing so encouraged business. Our period was basic-ally an inflationary interlude in a deflationary century.

Second, the availability of bullion in large quantities helped to establish that stable and reliable monetary standard based on the pound sterling (linked to a fixed gold parity) without which, as the experience of the 1930s and 1970s shows, international trade becomes more difficult, complex and unpredictable. Third, the gold-rushes themselves opened new areas, notably round the Pacific, to intensive economic activity. In doing so they 'created markets out of nothing', as Engels ruefully put it to Marx. And by the middle 1870s neither Cali-fornia nor Australia and the other zones on the new 'mineral frontier' were by any means negligible. Between them they contained well over three million inhabitants with considerably more ready cash than other populations of comparable size.

Contemporaries would certainly also have stressed the contribution of yet another factor: the liberation of private enterprise, the engine which, by common agreement, powered the progress of industry. Never has there been a more overwhelming consensus among econo-mists or indeed among intelligent politicians and administrators about the recipe for economic growth: economic liberalism. The remaining institutional barriers to the free movement of the factors of production, to free enterprise and to anything which could conceivably hamper its profitable operation, fell before a world-wide onslaught. What makes this general raising of barriers so remarkable is that it was not confined to the states in which political liberalism was triumphant or even influential. If anything it was more drastic in the restored absolute monarchies and principalities of Europe than in England,

France and the Low Countries, because so much more remained to be swept away there. The control of gilds and corporations over artisan production, which had remained strong in Germany, gave way to *Gewerbefreiheit* – freedom to enter and practise any trade – in Austria in 1859, in most of Germany in the first half of the 1860s. It was finally established completely in the North German Federation (1869) and the German Empire; to the displeasure of the numerous artisans who were consequently to become increasingly hostile to liberalism, and would in time provide a political basis for right-wing movements from the 1870s on. Sweden, which had abolished gilds in 1846, established complete freedom in 1864; Denmark abolished the old gild legislation in 1849 and 1857; Russia, most of which had never known a gild system, removed the last traces of one in the (German) towns of its Baltic provinces (1866), though for political reasons it continued to restrict the right of Jews to practise trade and business to a specific area, the so-called 'pale of settlement'.

This legal liquidation of the medieval and mercantilist periods was not confined to craft legislation. The laws against usury, long a dead letter, were dropped in Britain, Holland, Belgium and north Germany between 1854 and 1867. The strict control which governments exercised over mining – including the actual operation of mines – was virtually withdrawn, e.g. in Prussia between 1851 and 1865, so that (subject to government permit) any entrepreneur could now claim the right to exploit any minerals he found, and conduct his operations as he thought fit. Similarly the formation of business companies (especially joint-stock companies with limited liability or their equivalent) now became both considerably easier and independent of bureaucratic control. Britain and France led the way, though Germany did not establish automatic company registration until 1870. Commercial law was adapted to the prevailing atmosphere of buoyant business expansion.

But in some ways the most striking tendency was the movement towards total freedom of trade. Admittedly only Britain (after 1846) abandoned protectionism completely, maintaining customs duties – at least in theory – only for fiscal purposes. Nevertheless, apart from the elimination or reduction of restrictions, etc., on international waterways such as the Danube (1857) and the Sound between Denmark and Sweden, and the simplification of the international monetary system by the creation of larger monetary areas (e.g. the Latin Monetary Union of France, Belgium, Switzerland and Italy in 1865), a series of 'free trade treaties' substantially cut down the tariff barriers between the leading industrial nations in the 1860s. Even Russia (1863) and Spain (1868) joined to some extent in the movement. Only the United States, whose industry relied heavily on a protected home market and little on exports, remained a bastion of protectionism, and even here there was a modest improvement in the early 1870s.

We may even go a step further. Hitherto even the most daring and ruthless capitalist economies had hesitated to rely entirely on the free market to which they were theoretically committed, notably in the relation between employers and workers. Yet even in this sensitive field non-economic compulsion retreated. In Britain the 'Master and Servant' law was changed, establishing equality of treatment for breaches of contract between both parties; the 'annual bond' of the north of England miners was abolished, the standard hiring contract being increasingly (for workers) one which could be terminated at minimal notice. What is at first sight more surprising, between 1867 and 1875 all significant legal obstacles to trade unions and the right to strike were abolished with remarkably little fuss (see chapter 6 below). Many other countries as yet hesitated to give such freedom to labour organisations, though Napoleon III relaxed the legal prohibition of unions quite significantly. Nevertheless, the general situation in the developed countries now tended to become as described in the German *Gewerbeordnung* of 1869: 'Relations between those independently practising a trade or business and their journeymen, assistants and apprentices, are determined by free contract.' Only the market was to rule the sale and purchase of labour power, as of everything else.

Undoubtedly this vast process of liberalisation encouraged private enterprise and the liberalisation of trade helped economic expansion, though we should not forget that much formal liberalisation was unnecessary. Certain kinds of free international movement which are today controlled, notably those of capital and labour, i.e. migration, were by 1848 taken so much for granted in the developed world that they were hardly even discussed (see chapter 11 below). On the other hand, the question of what part institutional or legal changes play in fostering or hindering economic development is too complex for the simple mid-nineteenth-century formula: 'liberalisation creates economic progress'. The era of expansion had already begun even before the Corn Laws were repealed in Britain in 1846. No doubt liberalisation brought all sorts of specific positive results. Thus Copenhagen began to develop rather more rapidly as a city after the abolition of the 'Sound Tolls' which discouraged shipping from entering the Baltic (1857). But how far the global movement to liberalise was cause, concomitant or consequence of economic expansion must be left an open question. The only certain thing is that, when other bases for capitalist development were lacking, it did not achieve much by itself. Nobody liberalised more radically than the Republic of New Granada (Colombia) between 1848 and 1854, but who will say that the great hopes of prosperity of its statesmen were realised immediately or at all?

Nevertheless, in Europe these changes indicated a profound and striking confidence in economic liberalism, which seemed to be justified, at all events for a generation. Within each country this was not very surprising, since free capitalist enterprise clearly flourished so impressively. After all, even freedom of contract for the workers, including the toleration of such trade unions as were strong enough to establish themselves by the sheer bargaining-power of their workers, hardly seemed to threaten profits, since the 'reserve army of labour' (as Marx called it), consisting chiefly of masses of countrymen, ex-artisans and others streaming into the cities and industrial regions, looked like keeping wages at a satisfactorily modest level (see chapters 11 and 12 below). The enthusiasm for international free trade is at first sight more surprising, except among the British for whom it meant firstly that they were allowed freely to undersell everybody in all markets of the world, and secondly that they encouraged underdeveloped countries to sell them their own products – chiefly foodstuffs and raw materials – cheaply and in large quantities, thus earning the income with which to buy British manufactures.

But why did Britain's rivals (with the exception of the United States) accept this apparently unfavourable arrangement? (For underdeveloped countries which did not seek to compete industrially at all, it was of course attractive: the Southern states of the United States, for instance, were quite content to have an unlimited market for their cotton in Britain and therefore remained strongly attached to free trade until conquered by the North.) It is too much to say that international free trade progressed because, at this brief moment, the liberal utopia genuinely carried away even governments – if only with the force of what they believed to be its historic inevitability; though there is no doubt that they were deeply influenced by economic arguments which appeared to have almost the force of natural laws. However, intellectual conviction is rarely stronger than self-interest. But the fact is that most industrialising economies could at this period see two advantages in free trade. In the first place, the general expansion of world commerce, which was really quite spectacular compared to the period before the 1840s, benefited all of them, even if it benefited the British disproportionately. Both a large and unimpeded export trade and a large and unimpeded supply of foodstuffs and raw materials, where necessary by imports, were evidently desirable. If specialised interests might be adversely affected, there were others whom liberalisation suited. In the second place, whatever the future rivalry between capitalist economies, at this stage of industrialisation the advantage of being able to draw upon the equipment, the resources and know-how of Britain was distinctly helpful. To take merely one example, illustrated by the following table,

EXPORTS OF BRITISH RAILROAD IRON AND STEEL AND MACHINERY

(quinquennial totals: 000 tons)[11]

	rail iron and steel	machinery	
1845–49	1,291	4·9	(1846–50)
1850–54	2,846	8·6	
1856–60	2,333	17·7	
1861–65	2,067	22·7	
1866–70	3,809	24·9	
1870–75	4,040	44·1	

the railway iron and machinery, whose exports from Britain soared, did not inhibit the industrialisation of other countries, but facilitated it.

The capitalist economy thus received simultaneously (which does not mean accidentally) a number of extremely powerful stimuli. What was the result? Economic expansion is most conveniently measured in statistics and its most characteristic measures in the nineteenth century are steam power (since the steam engine was *the* typical form of power) and the associated products of coal and iron. The mid-nineteenth century was pre-eminently the age of smoke and steam. Coal output had long been measured in millions of tons, but now came to be measured in tens of millions for individual countries, in hundreds of millions for the world. About half of it – rather more at the beginning of our period – came from the incomparably largest producer, Great Britain. Iron production in Britain had reached the order of magnitude of millions in the 1830s (it stood at about 2·5 million tons in 1850), but nowhere else. But by 1870 France, Germany and the United States each produced between one and two million tons, though Britain, still the 'workshop of the world', remained far ahead with almost 6 million or about half the world output. In these twenty years world coal output multiplied about two-and-a-half times, world iron output about four times. Total steam power, however, multiplied by four-and-a-half, rising from an estimated 4 million HP in 1850 to about 18·5 million HP in 1870.

Such crude data indicate little more than that industrialisation was progressing. The significant fact is that its progress was now geographically much more widespread, though also extremely uneven. The spread of railways and, to a lesser extent, steamships, now introduced mechanical power into all continents and into otherwise un-industrialised countries. The arrival of the railway (see chapter 3 below) was in itself a revolutionary symbol and achievement, since the forging of the globe into a single interacting economy was in many ways the most far-reaching and certainly the most spectacular aspect of industrialisation. But the 'fixed engine' itself, in factory, mine or forge, made dramatic progress. In Switzerland there had been no more than thirty-four such engines in 1850, but by 1870 there were almost one thousand; in Austria the number rose from 671 (1852) to 9,160 (1875) with a more than fifteenfold increase in horse power. (For comparison, a really backward European country like Portugal still had a mere seventy engines with a total of 1,200 HP even in 1873.) The total steam power of the Netherlands multiplied thirteenfold.

There were minor industrial regions, and some European industrial economies such as Sweden had hardly begun to industrialise in a big way. Yet the most significant fact was the uneven development of the major centres. At the start of our period Britain and Belgium were the only countries where industry had developed intensively, and both remained the most highly industrialised *per capita*. Their consumption of iron per inhabitant in 1850 was 170 lb. and 90 lb. respectively, compared to 56 lb. in the United States, 37 lb. in France and 27 lb. in Germany. Belgium was a small economy, though relatively important: in 1873 it still produced about half as much iron as its much larger neighbour France. Britain, of course, was the industrial country *par excellence* and, as we have seen, managed to maintain its relative position, though its productive steam power had begun to lag seriously. In 1850 it still contained well over a third of the global engine power (of 'fixed engines'), whereas by 1870 it contained rather less than a quarter: 900,000 HP out of a total of 4·1 millions. In sheer quantity the United States was already slightly larger in 1850 and far outdistanced Britain in 1870 with more than double the engine power of the old country, but American industrial expansion, though extraordinary, seemed less striking than that of Germany. The fixed steam power of that country had been extremely modest in 1850 – perhaps 40,000 HP in all, much less than 10 per cent of the British. By 1870 it was 900,000 HP, or about the same as the British, incidentally far outdistancing France which had been considerably larger in 1850 (67,000 HP), but managed to reach no more than 341,000 in 1870 – less than twice as much as little Belgium.

The industrialisation of Germany was a major historical fact. Quite apart from its economic significance, its political implications were far-reaching. In 1850 the German Federation had about as many inhabitants as France, but incomparably less industrial capacity. By 1871 a united German empire was already somewhat more populous than France, but very much more powerful industrially. And, since political and military power now came to be increasingly based on industrial potential, technological capacity and know-how, the political consequences of industrial development were more serious than ever before. The wars of the 1860s demonstrated this (see chapter

4 below). Henceforth no state could maintain its place in the club of 'great powers' without it.

The characteristic products of the age were iron and coal, and the railway, its most spectacular symbol, combined both. Textiles, the most typical product of the first phase of industrialisation, grew comparatively less. Cotton consumption in the 1850s was about 60 per cent higher than in the 1840s, remained fairly static in the 1860s (because the industry was disrupted by the American Civil War) and increased by about 50 per cent in the 1870s. Woollen production in the 1870s was about double that of the 1840s. But coal and pig-iron output multiplied by five, while for the first time the mass production of steel became feasible. Indeed during this period the technological innovations in the iron and steel industry played a role analogous to that of the textile innovations in the previous era. On the continent (except in Belgium, where it had long prevailed), coal replaced charcoal as the chief fuel for smelting in the 1850s. Everywhere new processes – the Bessemer converter (1856), the Siemens–Martin open hearth furnace (1864) – now made possible the manufacture of cheap steel, which was eventually almost to replace wrought iron. However its significance lay in the future. In 1870 only 15 per cent of the finished iron produced in Germany, less than 10 per cent of that made in Britain, emerged as steel. Our period was not yet an age of steel, not even as yet in armaments, which gave the new material a significant impetus. It was an age of iron.

Still, though it made possible the revolutionary technology of the future, the new 'heavy industry' was not particularly revolutionary except perhaps in scale. Globally speaking, the Industrial Revolution up to the 1870s still ran on the impetus generated by the technical innovations of 1760–1840. Nevertheless the mid-century decades did develop two kinds of industry based on a far more revolutionary technology: the chemical and (in so far as it was concerned with communications) the electrical.

With few exceptions the main technical inventions of the first industrial phase had not required much advanced scientific knowledge. Indeed, and fortunately for Britain, they had been within the grasp of practical men with experience and common sense, such as George Stephenson, the great railway builder. From the mid-century this ceased increasingly to be so. Telegraphy was closely linked with academic science, through men like C. Wheatstone (1802–75) of London and William Thompson (Lord Kelvin) (1824–1907) of Glasgow. The artificial dye-stuffs industry, a triumph of mass chemical synthesis, though its first product (the colour mauve) is not universally acclaimed aesthetically, came from the laboratory into the factory. So did explosives and photography. At least one of the crucial innovations in steel production, the Gilchrist–Thomas 'basic' process, came out of higher education. As witness the novels of Jules Verne (1828–1905), the professor became a much more significant industrial figure than ever before: did not the wine producers of France appeal to the great L. Pasteur (1822–95) to solve a difficult problem for them (see p. 302 below)? Furthermore, the research laboratory now became an integral part of industrial development. In Europe it remained attached to universities or similar institutions – that of Ernst Abbe at Jena actually developed into the famous Zeiss works – but in the United States the purely commercial laboratory had already appeared in the wake of the telegraph companies. It was soon to be made celebrated by Thomas Alva Edison (1847–1931).

One significant consequence of this penetration of industry by science was that henceforth the educational system became increasingly crucial to industrial development. The pioneers of the first industrial phase, Britain and Belgium, had not been among the most literate of peoples, and their systems of technological and higher education (if we except the Scottish one) were far from distinguished. From now on it was to be almost impossible for a country lacking both mass education and adequate higher educational institutions to become a 'modern' economy; and conversely poor and retrograde countries with a good educational system found it easier to break into development, as, for example, Sweden.*

The practical value of a good primary education for science-based technologies, both economic and military, is obvious. Not the least reason for the ease with which the Prussians beat the French in 1870–1

---

* Illiteracy in selected European countries (males)[12]

England	(1875)*	17%	Sweden	(1875)†	1%
France	(1875)†	18%	Denmark	(1859–60)†	3%
Belgium	(1875)†	23%	Italy	(1875)†	52%
Scotland	(1875)*	9%	Austria	(1875)†	42%
Switzerland	(1879)†	6%	Russia	(1875)†	79%
Germany	(1875)†	2%	Spain	(1877)†	63%

* Illiterate bridegrooms.   † Illiterate conscripts.

was the vastly greater literacy of their soldiers. On the other hand, what economic development needed at a higher level was not so much scientific originality and sophistication – these could be borrowed – as the capacity to grasp and manipulate science: 'development' rather than research. The American universities and technical academies, which were undistinguished by the standards of, say, Cambridge and the *Polytechnique*, were economically superior to the British ones because they actually provided a systematic education for engineers such as did not yet exist in the old country.* They were superior to the French, because they mass produced engineers of adequate level instead of producing a few superbly intelligent and well-educated ones. The Germans in this respect relied on their excellent secondary schools rather than on their universities, and in the 1850s pioneered the *Realschule*, a technically oriented non-classical secondary school. When in 1867 the notoriously 'educated' industrialists of the Rhineland were asked to contribute to the fiftieth anniversary celebration of Bonn university, all but one of the fourteen industrial cities approached refused, because 'the eminent local industrialists have neither themselves enjoyed a higher academic [*wissenschaftlich*] education at universities, nor hitherto given it to their sons'.[13]

Still, technology was science-based and it is remarkable how rapidly the innovations of a relatively few scientific pioneers, provided they thought in terms readily translatable into machinery, were widely adopted. New raw materials, often only to be found outside Europe, therefore acquired a significance which was only to become evident in the later period of imperialism.† Thus oil had already attracted the attention of ingenious Yankees as a convenient fuel for lamps, but rapidly acquired new uses with chemical processing. In 1859 a mere two thousand barrels had been produced, but by 1874 almost 11 million barrels (mostly from Pennsylvania and New York) were already enabling John D. Rockefeller (1839–1937) to establish a stranglehold over the new industry by the control of its transport through his Standard Oil Company.

Nevertheless, these innovations look more significant in retrospect

* Until 1898 the only way into the British engineering profession was by apprenticeship.
† European deposits of chemical raw materials also boomed. Thus the German deposits of potash produced 58,000 tons in 1861–5, 455,000 tons in 1871–5 and over one million tons in 1881–5.

than they did at the time. After all, at the end of the 1860s an expert still thought that the only metals which had a serious economic future were those known to the ancients: iron, copper, tin, lead, mercury, gold and silver. Manganese, nickel, cobalt and aluminium, he held, 'do not seem destined to play such an important part as their elders'.[14] The growth of rubber imports into Britain from 7,600 cwt. in 1850 to 159,000 cwt. in 1876 was indeed notable, but the quantities were negligible even by the standards of twenty years later. The main uses of this material – still overwhelmingly collected wild in South America – were still such things as waterproof clothing and elastic. In 1876 there were exactly 200 telephones working in Europe and 380 in the United States, and at the Vienna International Exhibition the operation of a pump by electricity was a striking novelty. Looking back we can see that the breakthrough was quite close: the world was about to enter the era of electric light and power, of steel and high-speed steel alloys, of telephone and phonograph, of turbines and the internal combustion engine. However, in the mid-1870s it had not yet entered it.

The major industrial innovation, other than in the science-based fields already mentioned, was probably the mass production of machinery, which had been constructed virtually by craft methods, as locomotives and ships still continued to be. Most of the advances in mass production engineering came from the United States, pioneer of the Colt revolver, the Winchester rifle, the mass-produced clock, the sewing-machine and (via the slaughter-houses of Cincinnati and Chicago in the 1860s) the modern assembly-line, i.e. the mechanical conveyance of the object of production from one operation to the next. The essence of the machine-produced machine (which implied the development of the modern automatic or semi-automatic machine-tools) was that it was required in far larger standardised quantities than any other machine – i.e. by individuals and not by firms or institutions. The entire world in 1875 contained perhaps 62,000 locomotives, but what was this demand against the 400,000 brass clocks mass-produced in the United States in a single year (1855) and the rifles required by the 3 million Federal and Confederate soldiers mobilised between 1861 and 1865 by the American Civil War? Hence the products most likely to be mass produced were those which could be used by very large numbers of small producers such as farmers and needle-women (the sewing-machine), in offices (the typewriter), consumer goods such as watches, but above all the small arms and ammunition of war. Such products were still somewhat specialised and untypical. They worried intelligent Europeans, who already noted in the 1860s the technological superiority of the United States in mass production, but not yet the 'practical men' who merely thought that the Americans would not have to bother to invent machines to produce inferior articles, if they had as ready a supply of skilled and versatile craftsmen as the Europeans. After all, did not a French official as late as the early 1900s claim that, while France might not be able to keep up with other countries in mass-production industry, it could more than hold its own in the industry where ingenuity and craft skill were decisive: the manufacture of automobiles?

IV

The businessman, looking round at the world at the start of the 1870s, could therefore exude confidence, not to say complacency. But was it justified? Though the gigantic expansion of the world economy, now firmly based on industrialisation in several countries and on a dense and genuinely global flow of goods, capital and men, continued and even accelerated, the effect of the specific injections of energy it had received in the 1840s did not last. The new world opened to capitalist enterprise would continue to grow – but it would no longer be absolutely *new*. (Indeed, as soon as their products, such as the grain and wheat of American prairies and pampas and Russian steppes, began to pour into the old world, as they did in the 1870s and 1880s, they would disrupt and unsettle the agriculture of both old and new countries.) For a generation the building of the world's railways went on. But what would happen when the building had to be less universal, because most railway lines had already been completed? The technological potential of the first Industrial Revolution, the British one of cotton, coal, iron and steam engines, seemed vast enough. Before 1848 it had, after all, hardly been exploited at all outside Britain and only incompletely within Britain. A generation which began to exploit this potential more adequately could be pardoned for thinking it inexhaustible. But it was not, and in the 1870s the limits of this kind of technology were already visible. What would happen if it were to be exhausted?

61

As the world entered the 1870s such gloomy reflections seemed absurd. True, the process of expansion was, as everyone now discovered, curiously catastrophic. Sharp, sometimes dramatic and increasingly global slumps succeeded stratospheric booms, until prices had fallen sufficiently to dissipate the glutted markets and cleared the ground of bankrupt enterprises, until businessmen began to invest and expand to renew the cycle. It was in 1860, after the first of these genuine world slumps (see p. 85 below) that academic economics, in the form of a brilliant French doctor Clement Juglar (1819–1905), recognised and measured the periodicity of this 'trade cycle', hitherto considered chiefly by socialists and other heterodox elements. Still, dramatic though these interruptions to expansion were, they were temporary. Never was economic euphoria among businessmen higher than in the early 1870s, the famous *Gründerjahre* (the years of company promotion) in Germany, the era when the most absurd and obviously fraudulent company prospectus found unlimited sucker-money for its promises. Those were the days when, as a Viennese journalist put it, 'companies were founded to transport the aurora borealis in pipelines to St Stephen's Square and to win mass sales for our boot polish among the natives of the South Sea islands'.[15]

Then came the crash. Even for the taste of a period which liked its economic booms high-stepping and highly coloured, it was dramatic enough: 21,000 miles of American railroads collapsed into bankruptcy, German share values fell by some 60 per cent between the peak of the boom and 1877 and – more to the point – almost half the blast-furnaces in the main iron-producing countries of the world stopped. The flood of migrants to the New World was reduced to a modest river. Between 1865 and 1873 every year well over 200,000 arrived in the port of New York, but in 1877 a mere 63,000. But unlike earlier slumps of the great secular boom, this one did not seem to end. As late as 1889 a German study describing itself as 'an introduction to economic studies for officials and businessmen' observed that 'since the stock-market collapse of 1873 . . . the word "crisis" has constantly, with only brief interruptions, been in everyone's mind'.[16] And this in Germany, the country whose economic growth during this period continued to be quite spectacular. Historians have doubted the existence of what has been called the 'Great Depression' of 1873 to 1896, and of course it was nothing like as dramatic as that of 1929 to 1934, when the world capitalist economy almost ground to a halt. However, contemporaries were in no doubt that the great boom had been succeeded by a great depression.

A new era of history, political as well as economic, opens with the depression of the 1870s. It lies beyond the boundaries of this volume, though we may note, in passing, that it undermined or destroyed the foundations of mid-nineteenth-century liberalism which appeared to have been so firmly established. The period from the late 1840s to the mid-1870s proved to be not so much, as the conventional wisdom of the time held, the model of economic growth, political development, intellectual progress and cultural achievement, which would persist, no doubt with suitable improvements, into the indefinite future, but rather a special kind of interlude. But its achievements were nevertheless extremely impressive. In this era industrial capitalism became a genuine world economy and the globe was therefore transformed from a geographical expression into a constant operational reality. History from now on became world history.

Chapter Three

The World Unified

*The bourgeoisie, by the rapid improvement of all instruments of pro-
duction, by the immensely facilitated means of communication, draws
all, even the most barbarian nations into civilisation . . . In one word,
it creates a world after its own image.*

K. Marx and F. Engels, 1848[1]

*As commerce, education, and the rapid transition of thought and
matter, by telegraph and steam have changed everything, I rather
believe that the great Maker is preparing the world to become one
nation, speaking one language, a consummation which will render
armies and navies no longer necessary.*

President Ulysses S. Grant, 1873[2]

*'You should have heard all he said – I was to live on a mountain some-
where, go to Egypt or to America.'*
  *'Well, what of it ?' Stolz remarked coolly. 'You can be in Egypt in
a fortnight and in America in three weeks.'*
  *'Whoever goes to America or Egypt ? The English do, but then
that's the way the Lord God made them and besides, they have no
room to live at home. But which of us would dream of going ? Some
desperate fellow, perhaps, whose life is worth nothing to him.'*

I. Goncharov, 1859[3]

I

When we write the 'world history' of earlier periods, we are in fact
making an addition of the histories of the various parts of the globe, but
which, in so far as they had knowledge of one another, had only
marginal and superficial contacts, unless the inhabitants of some
region had conquered or colonised another, as the west Europeans
did the Americas. It is perfectly possible to write the earlier history of
Africa with only a casual reference to that of the Far East, with (except
along the west coast and the Cape) little reference to Europe, though

not without fairly persistent reference to the Islamic world. What happened in China was, until the eighteenth century, irrelevant to the political rulers of Europe, other than the Russians, though not to some of their specialised groups of traders; what happened in Japan was beyond the direct knowledge of all except the handful of Dutch merchants who were allowed to maintain a foothold there between the sixteenth and the mid-nineteenth centuries. Conversely, Europe was for the Celestial Empire merely a region of outer barbarians fortunately remote enough to pose no problem of assessing the precise degree of their undoubted subservience to the Emperor, though raising some minor problems of administration for the officials in charge of some ports. For that matter, even within the regions in which there was significant interaction, much could be ignored without inconvenience. For whom in western Europe – merchants or statesmen – was it of any consequence what went on in the mountains and valleys of Macedonia? If Libya had been entirely swallowed by some natural cataclysm, what real difference would it have made to anybody, even in the Ottoman Empire of which it was technically a part, and among the Levant traders of various nations?

The lack of interdependence of the various parts of the globe was not simply a matter of ignorance, though of course, outside the region concerned and often within it, ignorance of 'the interior' was still considerable. Even in 1848 large areas of the various continents were marked in white on even the best European maps – notably in Africa, central Asia, the interior of South and parts of North America and Australia, not to mention the almost totally unexplored Arctic and Antarctic. The maps which might have been drawn up by any other cartographers would certainly have shown even vaster spaces of the unknown; for if the officials of China or the illiterate scouts, traders and *coureurs de bois* of each continental hinterland knew a great deal more about some areas, large or small, than Europeans did, the sum total of their geographical knowledge was much more exiguous. In any case, the mere arithmetical addition of everything that any expert knew about the world would be a purely academic exercise. It was not generally available: in fact, there was not, even in terms of geographical knowledge, *one* world.

Ignorance was a symptom rather than a cause of the lack of the world's unity. It reflected both absence of diplomatic, political and administrative relations, which were indeed slender enough,* and the weakness of economic links. It is true that the 'world market', that crucial pre-condition and characteristic of capitalist society, had long been developing. International trade† had more than doubled in value between 1720 and 1780. In the period of the Dual Revolution (1780–1840) it had increased more than threefold – yet even this substantial growth was modest by the standards of our period. By 1870 the value of foreign trade for every citizen of the United Kingdom, France, Germany, Austria and Scandinavia was between four and five times what it had been in 1830, for every Dutchman and Belgian about three times as great, and even for every citizen of the United States – a country for which foreign commerce was only of marginal importance – well over double. During the 1870s an annual quantity of about 88 million tons weight of seaborne merchandise were exchanged between the major nations, as compared with 20 million in 1840. Thirty-one million tons of coal crossed the seas, compared to 1·4 million; 11·2 million tons of grain, compared to less than 2 million; 6 million tons of iron, compared to 1 million; even – anticipating the twentieth century – 1·4 million tons of petroleum, which had been unknown to overseas trade in 1840.

Let us measure the tightening of the net of economic interchanges between parts of the world remote from each other more precisely. British exports to Turkey and the Middle East rose from 3·5 million pounds in 1848 to a peak of almost 16 million in 1870; to Asia from 7 millions to 41 millions (1875); to Central and South America from 6 millions to 25 millions (1872); to India from around 5 millions to 24 millions (1875); to Australasia from 1·5 millions to almost 20 millions (1875). In other words in, say, thirty-five years, the value of the exchanges between the most industrialised economy and the most remote or backward regions of the world had increased about sixfold. Even this is of course not very impressive by present standards, but in sheer volume it far surpassed anything that had previously been con-

* That bible of European diplomatic, genealogical and political reference, the *Almanach de Gotha*, though careful to record what little was known about the ex-colonies which were now American republics, did not include Persia before 1859, China before 1861, Japan before 1863, Liberia before 1868 and Morocco before 1871. Siam only entered in 1880.

† i.e., the sum total of all the exports and imports for all the countries within the purview of European economic statistics at this period.

ceived. The net which linked the various regions of the world was visibly tightening.

Precisely how the continuing process of exploration, which gradually filled the empty spaces on the maps, was linked with the growth of the world market, is a complex question. Some of it was a by-product of foreign policy, some of missionary enthusiasm, some of scientific curiosity and, towards the end of our period, some of journalistic and publishing enterprise. Yet neither J. Richardson (1787–1865), H. Barth (1821–65) and A. Overweg (1822–52), who were sent by the British Foreign Office to explore central Africa in 1849, nor the great David Livingstone (1813–73), who criss-crossed the heart of what was still known as 'the dark continent' from 1840 to 1873 in the interests of Calvinist Christianity, nor Henry Morton Stanley (1841–1904), the journalist from the *New York Herald* who went to discover his whereabouts (especially not he!), nor S. W. Baker (1821–92) and J. H. Speke (1827–64), whose interests were more purely geographical or adventurous, were or could be unaware of the economic dimension of their travels. As a French Monsignor with missionary interests put it:

'The Good Lord has need of no man, and the propagation of the Gospel proceeds without human help; nevertheless, it would redound to the glory of European commerce, were it to lend assistance in the task of breaking down the barriers which stand in the way of evangelisation . . .[4]

To explore meant not only to know, but to develop, to bring the unknown and therefore by definition backward and barbarous into the light of civilisation and progress; to clothe the immorality of savage nakedness with shirts and trousers, which a beneficent providence manufactured in Bolton and Roubaix, to bring the goods of Birmingham which inevitably dragged civilisation in their wake.

Indeed, what we call the 'explorers' of the mid-nineteenth century were merely one well-publicised, but numerically not very important, sub-group of a very large body of men who opened the globe to knowledge. They were those who travelled in areas in which economic development and profit were not yet sufficiently active to replace the 'explorer' by the (European) trader, the mineral prospector, the surveyor, the builder of railway and telegraph, in the end, if the climate were to prove suitable, the white settler. 'Explorers' dominated the cartography of inner Africa, because that continent had no very obvious economic assets for the west between the abolition of the Atlantic slave-trade and the discovery, on the one hand of precious stones and metals (in the south), on the other of the economic value of certain primary products which could only be grown or collected in tropical climates, and were still far from synthetic production. Neither was yet of great significance or even promise until the 1870s, though it seemed inconceivable that so large and under-utilised a continent should not, sooner rather than later, prove to be a source of wealth and profit. (After all, British exports to sub-Saharan Africa had risen from about 1·5 million pounds in the late 1840s to about 5 millions in 1871 – they doubled in the 1870s to reach about 10 millions in the early 1880s – which was by no means unpromising.) 'Explorers' also dominated the opening of Australia, because the interior desert was vast, empty and, until the mid-twentieth century, devoid of obvious resources for economic exploitation. On the other hand, the oceans of the world ceased, except for the Arctic – the Antarctic attracted little interest during our period – to preoccupy the 'explorers'.* Yet the vast extension of shipping, and above all the laying of the great submarine cables, implied a great deal of what can properly be called exploration.

The world in 1875 was thus a great deal better known than ever before. Even at the national level, detailed maps (mostly initiated for military purposes) were not available in many of the developed countries: the publication of the pioneer enterprise of this kind, the Ordnance Survey maps of England – but not yet of Scotland and Ireland – was completed in 1862. However, more important than mere knowledge, the most remote parts of the world were now beginning to be linked together by means of communication which had no precedent for regularity, for the capacity to transport vast quantities of goods and numbers of people, and above all, for speed: the railway, the steamship, the telegraph.

By 1872 they had achieved the triumph chronicled by Jules Verne: the possibility of travelling round the world in eighty days, even allowing for the numerous mishaps which dogged the indomitable Phileas Fogg. Readers may recall the imperturbable traveller's route.

* The incentive here was largely economic – the search for a practicable north-west and north-east passage for shipping from Atlantic to Pacific, which would – like the transpolar flights of our days – have saved a great deal of time, and therefore money. The search for the actual North Pole was not, during this period, pursued with any great persistence.

He went by rail and channel steamer across Europe from London to Brindisi and thence by boat through the newly opened Suez Canal (an estimated seven days). The journey from Suez to Bombay by boat was to take him thirteen days. The rail journey from Bombay to Calcutta should, but for the failure to complete a stretch of the line, have taken him three days. Thence by sea to Hong Kong, Yokohama and across the Pacific to San Francisco was still a long stretch of forty-one days. However, since the railroad across the American continent had been completed by 1869, only the still not wholly controlled perils of the West – herds of bison, Indians etc. – stood between the traveller and a normal journey of seven days to New York. The remainder of the trip – Atlantic crossing to Liverpool and railway to London – would have posed no problems but for the requirements of fictional suspense. In fact, an enterprising American travel agent offered a similar round-the-world trip not long after.

How long would such a journey have taken Fogg in 1848? It would have had to be almost entirely by sea, since no railway lines as yet crossed the continent, while virtually none existed anywhere else in the world except in the United States, where they hardly yet went further inland than two hundred miles. The speediest of sailing ships, the famous tea clippers, would most usually take an average of 110 days for the journey to Canton around 1870, when they were at the peak of their technical achievement; they could not do it in less than ninety days but had been known to take 150. We can hardly suppose a circumnavigation in 1848 to have taken, with anything but the best of fortunes, much less than eleven months, or say four times as long as Phileas Fogg, not counting time spent in port.

This improvement in the time of long-distance travel was relatively modest, entirely because of the lag in the improvement of maritime speeds. The average time for a transatlantic steamer trip from Liverpool to New York in 1851 had been eleven to twelve and a half days; it remained substantially the same in 1873, though the White Star line prided itself on pushing it down to ten days.[5] Except where the sea-route was itself shortened, as by the Suez Canal, Fogg could not hope to do much better than a traveller in 1848. The real transformation took place on land – through the railway, and even this not so much by raising the speeds of which steam locomotives were technically capable, as by the extraordinary extension of railway building. The railway of 1848 was indeed generally rather slower than that of the 1870s, though it already reached Holyhead from London in eight and a half hours, or three and a half hours more than in 1974. (By 1865, however, Sir William Wilde – Oscar's father and a notable fisherman – could suggest to his London readers a weekend trip to and from Connemara for a little fishing, such as would be impossible in as short a time by rail and ship today, and far from easy without recourse to air travel.) However, the locomotive as developed in the 1830s was a remarkably efficient engine. But what did not exist in 1848, outside England, was anything like a railway network.

II

The period with which this book deals saw the construction of such a long-distance network almost everywhere in Europe, in the United States, and even in a few other parts of the world. The following tables, the first giving an overall picture, and the second slightly more detail, speak for themselves. In 1845, outside Europe, the only 'under-developed' country which possessed even a mile of railway line was Cuba. By 1855 there were lines in all five continents, though those of South America (Brazil, Chile, Peru) and Australia were hardly visible. By 1865 New Zealand, Algeria, Mexico and South Africa had their

RAILWAY MILEAGE OPEN (000 miles)[6]

	1840	1850	1860	1870	1880
Europe	1,7	14,5	31,9	63,3	101,7
North America	2,8	9,1	32,7	56,0	100,6
India	—	—	0.8	4,8	9,3
Rest of Asia	—	—	—	—	*
Australasia	—	—	*	1,2	5,4
Latin America	—	—	*	2,2	6,3
Africa (inc. Egypt)	—	—	*	0,6	2,9
Total world	4,5	23,6	66,3	128,2	228,4

* Less than 500 miles.

70

	1845	1855	1865	1875
Number of countries in Europe				
with railways	9	14	16	18
with over 1,000 km. railway line	3	6	10	15
with over 10,000 km. railway line	—	3	3	5
Number of countries in the Americas				
with railways	3	6	11	15
with over 1,000 km. railway line	1	2	2	6
with over 10,000 km. railway line	—	1	1	2
Number of countries in Asia				
with railways	—	1	2	5
with over 1,000 km. railway line	—	—	1	1
with over 10,000 km. railway line	—	—	—	1
Number of countries in Africa				
with railways	—	1	3	4
with over 1,000 km. railway line	—	—	—	1
with over 10,000 km. railway line	—	—	—	—

first railways, and by 1875, while Brazil, Argentina, Peru and Egypt had around a thousand miles or more of track, Ceylon, Java, Japan and even remote Tahiti had acquired their first lines. Meanwhile by 1875 the world possessed 62,000 locomotives, 112,000 carriages and almost half a million goods wagons, carrying between them, so it was estimated, 1,371 million passengers and 715 million tons of goods, or about nine times as much as was carried by sea each year (on average) during this decade. The third quarter of the nineteenth century was, in quantitative terms, the first real railway age.

The construction of the great trunk lines naturally gained the most publicity. It was indeed, taken as a whole, the largest body of public works and almost the most dazzling achievement of engineering known to human history up to that date. As the railways left the unexacting topography of England, their technical achievements became ever more remarkable. The Southern Railway from Vienna to Trieste already crossed the Semmering Pass at a height of almost 3,000 feet in 1854; by 1871 tracks across the Alps reached elevations of up to 4,500 feet; by 1869 the Union Pacific touched 8,600 feet as it crossed the

71

Rockies; and by 1874 that triumph of the mid-nineteenth-century economic conquistador, Henry Meiggs' (1811–77) Peruvian Central Railway, steamed slowly along at a height of up to 15,840 feet. As they rose between the peaks they tunnelled under the rock, dwarfing the modest passages of the early English railways. The first of the great Alpine tunnels, the Mont Cenis, was begun in 1857 and completed in 1870, and its seven and a half miles traversed by the first mail train, thus cutting twenty-four hours off the journey to Brindisi (a fact utilised by Phileas Fogg, as we recall).

It is impossible not to share the mood of excitement, of self-confidence, of pride, which seized those who lived through this heroic age of the engineers, as the railway first linked Channel and Mediterranean, as it became possible to travel by rail to Seville, to Moscow, to Brindisi, as the iron tracks pushed westwards across the North American prairies and mountains and across the Indian sub-continent in the 1860s, up the Nile valley, and into the hinterlands of Latin America in the 1870s.

How can we withhold admiration from the shock-troops of industrialisation who built them, the armies of peasants, often organised in co-operative teams, who shifted earth and rocks in unimaginable quantities with pick and shovel, the professional English and Irish navvies and foremen who constructed lines far from their native country, the engine-drivers or mechanics from Newcastle or Bolton who settled down to run the new railways in Argentina or New South Wales?* How can we fail to pity the armies of coolies who left their bones along each mile of track? Even today Satyadjit Ray's beautiful film *Pather Panchali* (based on a nineteenth-century Bengali novel) enables us to recapture the wonder of the first steam train ever experienced, a massive iron dragon, the irresistible and inspiring force of the industrial world itself, pushing its way where previously nothing but bullock-carts or pack-mules had passed.

Neither can we fail to be moved by the hard men in top hats who organised and presided over these vast transformations of the human landscape – material and spiritual. Thomas Brassey (1805–70), who at

* We find their traces among the successful businessmen, such as the locomotive mechanic William Pattison of Newcastle, who went abroad as a repair foreman for a French railway, and in 1852 helped to form what soon became the second-largest mechanical engineering firm in Italy.[8]

times employed eighty thousand men on five continents, was merely the most celebrated of these entrepreneurs, the list of his overseas enterprises an equivalent of the battle honours and campaign medals of generals in less enlightened days: the Prato and Pistoia, the Lyons and Avignon, the Norwegian Railway, the Jutland, the Grand Trunk of Canada, the Bilbao and Miranda, the Eastern Bengal, the Mauritius, the Queensland, the Central Argentine, the Lemberg and Czernowitz, the Delhi Railway, the Boca and Barracas, the Warsaw and Terespol, the Callao Docks.

The 'romance of industry', a phrase which generations of public orators and commercial self-congratulators were to drain of its original, and indeed of any, meaning surrounds even the bankers, the financiers, the stock-jobbers, who merely found the money for railway construction. Rockets of self-intoxicated rather than crooked finance, men like George Hudson (1800–71) or Bethel Strousberg (1823–84) exploded into bankruptcy as they had into wealth and social prominence. Their collapses have become landmarks in economic history. (No such allowance can be made for the genuine 'robber barons' among American railroad men – Jim Fisk [1834–72], Jay Gould [1836–92], Commodore Vanderbilt [1794–1877], etc. – who merely bought up and looted existing railroads as well as everything else they could lay their hands on.) It is hard to deny a grudging admiration even to the most obvious crooks among the great railway builders. Henry Meiggs was by any standards a dishonest adventurer, leaving behind him a trail of unpaid bills, bribes and memories of luxurious spending along the entire western edge of the American continents, at home in the wide open centres of villainy and exploitation like San Francisco and Panama rather than among respectable businessmen. But can anyone who has ever seen the Peruvian Central Railway deny the grandeur of the concept and achievement of his romantic if rascally imagination?

This combination of romanticism, enterprise and finance was perhaps most dramatically displayed by the curious French sect of the Saint-Simonians. These apostles of industrialisation graduated, especially after the failure of the 1848 revolution, from a set of beliefs which has got them into the history books as 'utopian socialists' to a dynamic, adventurous entrepreneurship as 'captains of industry', but above all as constructors of communications. They were not the only ones to dream of a world linked by commerce and technology. So improbable a centre of global enterprise as the virtually landlocked Habsburg Empire produced the *Austrian Lloyd* of Trieste, whose ships, anticipating the as yet unbuilt Suez Canal, were named *Bombay* and *Calcutta*. Yet it was a Saint-Simonian, F. M. de Lesseps (1805–94), who actually built the Suez Canal and planned the Panama Canal, to his later misfortune.

The brothers Isaac and Emile Pereire were to become known chiefly as adventurous financiers who came into their own in Napoleon III's Empire. Yet Emile himself had supervised the building of the first French railway in 1837, living in an apartment over the workshops, gambling on demonstrating the superiority of the new form of transport. During the Second Empire the Pereires were to construct railway lines all over the continent in a titanic duel with the more conservative Rothschilds, which eventually ruined them (1869). Another Saint-Simonian, P. F. Talabot (1789–1885), constructed among other things the railways of south-eastern France, the Marseilles docks and the Hungarian railways, and bought up the barges made redundant by the ruin of shipping on the river Rhône, hoping to use them for a commercial fleet along the Danube to the Black Sea – a project vetoed by the Habsburg Empire. Such men thought in continents and oceans. For them the world was a single unit, bound together with rails of iron and steam engines, because the horizons of business were like their dreams world-wide. For such men human destiny, history and profit were one and the same thing.

From the global point of view, the network of trunk railways remained supplementary to that of international shipping. In so far as it existed in Asia, Australia, Africa and Latin America, the railway, considered economically, was primarily a device for linking some area producing bulky primary goods to a port, whence they could be shipped to the industrial and urban zones of the world. Shipping, as we have seen, did not become notably faster in our period. Its comparative technical sluggishness is indicated by the fact, by now well known, that the sailing ship continued to hold its own against the new steamship surprisingly well, thanks to technologically less dramatic but still substantial improvements in its own efficiency. Steam had indeed increased notably, from about 14 per cent of the world's carrying capacity in 1840 to 49 per cent in 1870, but sail was still slightly in the

74

lead. It was not until the 1870s and especially the 1880s that it dropped out of the race. (By the end of the latter decade it was reduced to about 25 per cent of global carrying capacity.) The triumph of the steamship was essentially that of the British mercantile marine, or rather of the British economy which stood behind it. In 1840 and 1850 British vessels made up about a quarter – more or less – of world nominal steamer tonnage, in 1870 rather over one-third, in 1880 over half. To put it another way, between 1850 and 1880 British steam tonnage increased by 1,600 per cent, that of the rest of the world by about 440 per cent. This was natural enough. If cargo was to be loaded in Callao, Shanghai or Alexandria, the odds were that it would be destined for Britain. And plenty of ships were loaded. One and a quarter million tons (900,000 of them British) passed through the Suez Canal in 1874 – in the first year of operation there had been less than half a million. The regular traffic across the North Atlantic was even larger: 5·8 million tons entered the three main east coast ports of the United States in 1875.

Rail and shipping, between them, transported goods and men. However in a sense the most startling technological transformation of our period was in the communication of messages through the electric telegraph. This revolutionary device seems to have been ready for discovery in the middle 1830s, in the mysterious way in which such problems suddenly break through towards their solution. In 1836–7 it was invented almost simultaneously by a number of different re-searchers, of whom Cooks and Wheatstone were the most immediately successful. Within a few years it was applied on the railways, and, what was more important, plans for submarine lines were considered from 1840, though they did not become practicable until after 1847, when the great Faraday suggested insulating the cables with gutta-percha. In 1853 an Austrian, Gintl, and two years later another, Stark, demon-strated that two messages could be sent along the same wire in both directions; by the late 1850s a system for sending two thousand words an hour was adopted by the American Telegraph Company; by 1860 Wheatstone patented an automatic printing telegraph, ancestor of the ticker-tapes and telexes.

Britain and the United States were already in the 1840s applying this new device, one of the first examples of a technology developed by scientists, and which could hardly have been developed except on the basis of sophisticated scientific theory. The developed parts of Europe adopted it rapidly in the years after 1848: Austria and Prussia in 1849 Belgium in 1850, France in 1851, Holland and Switzerland in 1852, Sweden in 1853, Denmark in 1854. Norway, Spain, Portugal, Russia and Greece introduced it in the second half of the 1850s, Italy, Rumania and Turkey in the 1860s. The familiar telegraph lines and poles multiplied: 2,000 miles in 1849 on the European continent, 15,000 in 1854, 42,000 in 1859, 80,000 in 1864, 111,000 in 1869. So did the messages. In 1852 less than a quarter of a million were sent in all the six continental countries which had by then introduced telegraphy. In 1869 France and Germany sent over 6 million each, Austria over 4 million, Belgium, Italy and Russia over 2 million, even Turkey and Rumania between 600,000 and 700,000 each.[9]

However, the most significant development was the actual construction of submarine cables, first pioneered across the Channel in the early 1850s (Dover–Calais 1851, Ramsgate–Ostend 1853), but increasingly over long distances. A north-Atlantic cable was proposed in the mid-1840s, and actually laid in 1857–8, but broke down due to inadequate insulation. The second attempt, with the celebrated *Great Eastern* – the largest ship in the world – as cable-layer, succeeded in 1865. There followed a burst of international cable-laying which, within five or six years, virtually girdled the globe. In 1870 alone cables were being laid from Singapore to Batavia, Madras–Penang, Penang–Singapore, Suez–Aden, Aden–Bombay, Penzance–Lisbon, Lisbon–Gibraltar, Gibraltar–Malta, Malta–Alexandria, Marseille–Bône, Emden–Teheran (by landline), Bône–Malta, Salcombe–Brest, Beachy Head–Havre, Santiago de Cuba–Jamaica, Möen-Bornholm–Libau and another couple of lines across the North Sea. By 1872 it was possible to telegraph from London to Tokyo and to Adelaide. In 1871 the result of the Derby was flashed from London to Calcutta in no more than five minutes, though the news was considerably less exciting than the achievement. What were Phileas Fogg's eighty days compared with this? Such speed of communication was not merely without precedent, or indeed without possible comparison. For most people in 1848 it would have been beyond imagination.

The construction of this world-wide telegraph system combined both political and commercial elements: with the major exception of the United States, inland telegraphy was or became almost entirely

76

state-owned and operated, even Britain nationalising it under the Post Office in 1869. On the other hand, the submarine cables remained almost entirely the reserve of the private enterprise which had built them, though it is evident from the map that they had a substantial strategic interest, at all events for the British Empire. They were indeed of very direct importance to government, not only for military and police purposes, but for administration – as witness the unusually large numbers of telegrams sent in countries such as Russia, Austria and Turkey, whose commercial and private traffic would hardly have accounted for them. (The Austrian traffic consistently exceeded that of north Germany until the early 1860s.) The larger the territory, the more useful was it for the authorities to have a rapid means of communicating with its remoter outposts.

Obviously businessmen used the telegraph extensively, but private citizens soon discovered its use – mainly of course for urgent, and usually dramatic, communications with relatives. By 1869 about 60 per cent of all Belgian telegrams were private. But the most significant new use of the device cannot be measured by the mere number of messages. Telegraphy transformed *news*, as Julius Reuter (1816–99) foresaw when he founded his telegraph agency at Aix-la-Chapelle (Aachen) in 1851. (He broke into the British market, with which Reuters was henceforth associated, in 1858.) From the journalistic point of view the middle ages ended in the 1860s when international news could be cabled freely from a sufficiently large number of places on the globe to reach the next morning's breakfast-table. Scoops were no longer measured in days, or if from remoter territories in weeks or months, but in hours or even minutes.

Yet this extraordinary acceleration of the speed of communication had one paradoxical result. In widening the gap between the places accessible to the new technology and the rest, it intensified the relative backwardness of those parts of the world where horse, ox, mule, human bearer or boat still set the speed of transport. At a time when New York could telegraph Tokyo in a matter of minutes or hours, it became all the more striking that the full resources of the *New York Herald* could not get a letter from David Livingstone in central Africa to that newspaper in less than eight or nine months (1871–2); all the more striking when *The Times* in London could reprint that same letter on the day after its New York publication. The 'wildness' of the

'Wild West', the 'darkness' of the 'dark continent', were due partly to such contrasts.

So was the remarkable passion of the public for the explorer and the man who came increasingly to be called the 'traveller' *tout court* – i.e. the person who voyaged at or beyond the frontiers of technology, outside the area within which the state-room of the steamer, the sleeping compartment of the *wagon-lit* (both inventions of our period), the hotel and the *pension* took care of the tourist. Phileas Fogg travelled on this frontier. The interest of his enterprise lay both in the demonstration that rail, steamer and telegraph now almost encompassed the globe, and in the margin of uncertainty and the remaining gaps which still prevented world travel from becoming a routine.

However, the 'travellers' whose accounts were most avidly read were those who faced the hazards of the unknown with no more aid from modern technology than could be carried on the backs of stout and numerous native porters. They were the explorers and missionaries, especially those who penetrated the interior of Africa, the adventurers, especially those who ventured into the uncertain territories of Islam, the naturalists hunting butterflies and birds in South American jungles or on the islands of the Pacific. The third quarter of the nineteenth century was, as publishers were quick to discover, the start of a golden age for a new breed of armchair travellers, following Burton and Speke, Stanley and Livingstone through bush and primeval forest.

III

Nevertheless the tightening net of the international economy drew even the geographically very remote areas into direct and not merely literary relations with the rest of the world. What counted was not simply speed – though growing intensity of traffic also brought a powerful demand for rapidity – but the range of repercussion. This can be vividly illustrated from the example of an economic event which both opens our period and, it has been argued, very largely determined its shape: the discovery of gold in California (and, shortly afterwards, in Australia).

In January 1848 a man called James Marshall discovered gold in what appeared to be vast quantities at Sutter's Mill near Sacramento in

California, a northern extension of Mexico which had only just been annexed to the United States, and was of no significant economic interest except to a few large Mexican–American estate-owners and ranchers, to fishermen and to the whalers who used the convenient harbour of San Francisco Bay, which supported a village of 812 white inhabitants. Since this territory faced the Pacific and was separated from the rest of the United States by large tracts of mountain, desert and prairie, its evident natural wealth and attractions were not of immediate relevance to capitalist enterprise, though they were of course recognised. The gold-rush promptly changed this. Fragmentary news of it filtered to the rest of the United States by August and September of the year, but raised little interest until confirmed by President Polk in his presidential message of December. Hence the gold-rush is identified with the 'Forty-niners'. By the end of 1849 the population of California had swelled from 14,000 to not quite 100,000, by the latter part of 1852 to a quarter of a million; San Francisco was already a city of almost 35,000. In the last three-quarters of 1849 about 540 ships docked there, about half from American, half from European, ports, in 1850 1,150 ships docked there of almost half a million tons in all.

The economic effects of this sudden development here, and from 1851 in Australia, have been much debated, but contemporaries had no doubt of its importance. Engels remarked bitterly to Marx in 1852: 'California and Australia are two cases not provided for in the [*Communist*] *Manifesto*: the creation of large new markets out of nothing. We shall have to allow for this.'[10] How far they were responsible for the general boom in the United States, for the world-wide economic upsurge (see chapter 2 above), or for the sudden burst of mass emigration (see chapter 11 below), we need not decide here. What is clear, at all events, is that localised developments several thousand miles distant from Europe had, in the opinion of competent observers, an almost immediate and far-reaching effect on that continent. The interdependence of the world economy could hardly be better demonstrated.

That the gold-rushes should affect the metropoles of Europe and the eastern United States, and the globally-minded merchants, financiers and shippers there, is not of course surprising. Their immediate repercussions in other, and geographically remote, parts of the globe is more unexpected, though it was greatly assisted by the fact that for practical purposes California was accessible only by sea, where distance is not a serious obstacle to communication. The gold-fever spread rapidly across the oceans. The sailors of Pacific vessels deserted to try their luck in the gold-fields, as the bulk of San Franciscans had done as soon as the news reached them. In August 1849 two hundred vessels, abandoned by their crews, clogged the waterside, their timbers eventually being used for building. In the Sandwich Islands (Hawaii), China and Chile sailors heard the news, wise captains – like the English trading on the west coast of South America – refused the profitable temptation to sail north, freights and sailors' wages shot up with the prices of anything exportable to California; and nothing was not exportable. By the end of 1849 the Chilean Congress, observing that the bulk of national shipping had been drawn to California, where it was immobilised by desertion, authorised foreign vessels to practise the coastal (cabotage) trade temporarily. California for the first time created a genuine network of trade linking the Pacific coasts, by means of which Chilean cereals, Mexican coffee and cocoa, Australian potatoes and other foodstuffs, sugar and rice from China, and even – after 1854 – some imports from Japan were transported to the United States. (Not for nothing had the Boston *Bankers Magazine* predicted in 1850 that 'it can hardly be unreasonable to anticipate a partial extension of the influence [of enterprise and trade] even to Japan'.)[11]

More significant, from our point of view, even than trade were people. The immigration of Chileans, Peruvians and 'Cacknackers who belong to the different islands' (Pacific islanders),[12] though it attracted attention in the early stages, was not of major numerical importance. (In 1860 California contained only about 2,400 Latin Americans other than Mexicans and less than 350 Pacific Islanders.) On the other hand, 'one of the most extraordinary results of the wonderful discovery is the impulse it has given to the enterprise of the Celestial Empire. Chinamen, hitherto the most impassive and domestic creatures of the universe, have started into new life at the tidings of the mines and have poured into California by the thousands.'[13] In 1849 there were seventy-six of them, by the end of 1850 4,000, in 1852 no less than 20,000 landed, until by 1876 there were about 111,000 or 25 per cent of all non-California-born inhabitants of the state. They brought with them their skill, intelligence and enterprise, and incidentally introduced western civilisation to that most powerful cultural export of the east, the Chinese restaurant, which was already flourishing in 1850. Oppressed, hated, ridiculed and from time to time lynched – eighty-eight were murdered during the slump of 1862 – they showed the usual capacity of this great people to survive and prosper, until the Chinese Restriction Act of 1882, climax of a long racialist agitation, brought to an end what was perhaps the first example in history of a voluntary, economically induced, mass migration from an oriental to an occidental society.

Otherwise the stimulus of the gold-rush moved only the traditional sources of migrants to the west coast, among whom the British, Irish and Germans were in a large majority, and the Mexicans.

They came overwhelmingly by sea, except for some of the North Americans (notably those from Texas, Arkansas and Missouri, and from Wisconsin and Iowa – states with a disproportionately heavy migration to California) who presumably came overland, a cumbersome journey which would take three to four months coast to coast. The major route along which the Californian gold-rush passed along its effects led eastwards over the sixteen to seventeen thousand miles of sea which linked Europe on the one hand, the east coast of the United States on the other, with San Francisco via Cape Horn. London, Liverpool, Hamburg, Bremen, Le Havre and Bordeaux already had direct sailings in the 1850s. The incentive to shorten this journey of four to five months, as well as to make it more secure, was overwhelming. The clippers constructed by Boston and New York ship-builders for the Canton-London tea-trade could now carry an outward cargo. Only two had rounded the Horn before the gold-rush, but in the second half of 1851 twenty-four (or 34,000 tons) reached San Francisco, cutting the trip from Boston to the west coast down to less than a hundred – or even in one case eighty days' – sailing. Inevitably an even shorter potential route asked to be developed. The Isthmus of Panama once again became what it had been in Spanish colonial times, the major point of trans-shipment, at least until the building of an isthmian canal, which was immediately envisaged by the Anglo-American Bulwer–Clayton Treaty of 1850, and actually begun – against American opposition – by the maverick French Saint-Simonian de Lesseps, fresh from his triumph at Suez, in the 1870s. The United States government fostered a mail service across the isthmus of

Panama, thus making possible the establishment of a regular monthly steamer service from New York to the Caribbean side and from Panama to San Francisco and Oregon. The scheme, essentially started in 1848 for political and imperial purposes, became commercially more than viable with the gold-rush. Panama became what it has remained, a Yankee-owned boom town, where future robber barons like Commodore Vanderbilt and W. Ralston (1828–89), founder of the Bank of California, cut their teeth. The saving of time was so enormous that the isthmus soon became the crossroads of international shipping: through it Southampton could be linked with Sydney in fifty-eight days, and the gold discovered in the early 1850s in that other great mining centre, Australia, not to mention the older precious metals of Mexico and Peru, passed through it on their way to Europe and the eastern United States. Together with the Californian gold, perhaps 60 million dollars per annum may have been transported through Panama. No wonder that as early as January 1855 the first railway train traversed the isthmus. It had been planned by a French company but, characteristically, built by an American one.

Such were the visible and almost immediate results of events which occurred in one of the remotest corners of the world. No wonder that observers saw the economic world not merely as a single interlocking complex, but as one where each part was sensitive to what happened elsewhere, and through which money, goods and men moved smoothly and with increasing rapidity, according to the irresistible stimuli of supply and demand, gain and loss and with the help of modern technology. If even the most sluggish (because the least 'economic') of these men responded to such stimuli *en masse* – British emigration to Australia rose from twenty thousand to almost ninety thousand in a year after gold was discovered there – then nothing and no one could resist them. Obviously there were still many parts of the globe, even of Europe, more or less isolated from this movement. Could it be doubted that they would all sooner or later be drawn into it?

IV

We are today more familiar than the men of the mid-nineteenth century with this drawing together of all parts of the globe into a single world. Yet there is a substantial difference between the process as we experience it today and that in the period of this book. What is most striking about it in the later twentieth century is an international standardisation which goes far beyond the purely economic and technological. In this respect our world is more massively standardised than Phileas Fogg's, but only because there are more machines, productive installations and businesses. The railroads, telegraphs and ships of 1870 were not less recognisable as international 'models' wherever they occurred than the automobiles and airports of 1970. What hardly occurred then was the international, and interlinguistic standardisation of culture which today distributes, with at best a slight time-lag, the same films, popular music-styles, television programmes and indeed styles of popular living across the world. Such standardisation did affect the numerically modest middle classes and some of the rich, up to a point, or at least in so far as it was not brought up against the barriers of language. The 'models' of the developed world were copied by the more backward in the handful of dominant versions – the English throughout the Empire, in the United States and, to a much smaller extent, on the European continent, the French in Latin America, the Levant, and parts of eastern Europe, the German–Austrian throughout central and eastern Europe, in Scandinavia and also to some extent in the United States. A certain common visual style, the overstuffed and overloaded bourgeois interior, the public baroque of theatres and operas, could be discerned, though for practical purposes only where European or colonists descended from Europeans had established themselves (see chapter 13 below). Nevertheless, except in the United States (and Australia) where high wages democratised the market, and therefore the life styles, of the economically more modest classes, this remained confined to a comparative few.

There is no doubt that the bourgeois prophets of the mid-nineteenth century looked forward to a single, more or less standardised, world where all governments would acknowledge the truths of political economy and liberalism carried throughout the globe by impersonal missionaries more powerful than those Christianity or Islam had ever had; a world reshaped in the image of the bourgeoisie, perhaps even one from which, eventually, national differences would disappear. Already the development of communications required novel kinds of international co-ordinating and standardising organisms – the International Telegraph Union of 1865, the Universal Postal Union of 1875, the International Meterological Organisation of 1878, all of which still survive. Already it had posed – and for limited purposes solved by means of the International Signals Code of 1871 – the problem of an internationally standardised 'language'. Within a few years attempts to devise artificial cosmopolitan languages were to become fashionable, headed by the oddly named *Volapük* (—'world-speak') excogitated by a German in 1880. (None of these succeeded, not even the most promising contender, *Esperanto*, another product of the 1880s.) Already the labour movement was in the process of establishing a global organisation which was to draw political conclusions from the growing unification of the world – the International (see chapter 6 below).*

Nevertheless international standardisation and unification in this sense remained feeble and partial. Indeed, to some extent the rise of new nations and new cultures with a democratic base, i.e. using separate languages rather than the international idioms of educated minorities, made it more difficult, or rather, more circuitous. Writers of European or global reputation had to become so through translation. And while it is significant that by 1875 readers of German, French, Swedish, Dutch, Spanish, Danish, Italian, Portuguese, Czech and Hungarian were able to enjoy some or all of Dickens's works (as Bulgarian, Russian, Finnish, Serbo-Croat, Armenian and Yiddish ones were to before the end of the century), it is equally significant that this process implied an increasing linguistic division. Whatever the long-term prospects, it was accepted by contemporary liberal observers that, in the short and medium term, development proceeded by the formation of different and rival nations (see chapter 5 below). The most that could be hoped was that these would embody the same type of institutions, economy and beliefs. The unity of the world implied division. The world system of capitalism was a structure of rival 'national economies'. The world triumph of liberalism rested on its conversion of all peoples, at least among those regarded as 'civilised'. No doubt the champions of progress in the third quarter

* Whether the International Red Cross (1860), also the child of our period, belongs to this group is more doubtful, since it was based on the most extreme form of lack of internationalism, namely wars between states.

of the nineteenth century were confident enough that this would happen sooner or later. But their confidence rested on insecure foundations.

They were indeed on safe ground in pointing to the ever-tightening network of global communications, whose most tangible result was a vast increase in the flow of international exchanges of goods and men – trade and migration, which will be considered separately (see chapter 11 below). Yet even in the most plainly international field of business, global unification was not an unqualified advantage. For if it created a world economy, it was one in which all parts were so dependent on each other that a pull on one thread would inevitably set all others into movement. The classical illustration of this was the international slump.

As has been suggested, two major kinds of economic fluctuation affected the fortunes of the world in the 1840s, the ancient agrarian cycle, based on the fortunes of crops and livestock, and the novel 'trade cycle', an essential part of the mechanism of the capitalist economy. In the 1840s the first of these had still been dominant in the world, though its effects tended to be regional rather than global, since even the most widespread natural uniformities – the weather, epidemics of plants, animals and humans – hardly occurred simultaneously in all parts of the world. Industrialised economies were already dominated by the business cycle, at least from the end of the Napoleonic Wars, but this affected, in practice, only Britain, perhaps Belgium and the small sectors of other economies geared to the international system. Crises not linked with simultaneous agrarian disturbances, e.g. that of 1826, 1837 or 1839–42, shook England and the business circles of the eastern American seaboard or Hamburg, but left most of even Europe reasonably untroubled.

Two developments occurred after 1848 to change this. In the first place, the business-cycle became genuinely world wide. That of 1857, which began with a bank collapse in New York, was probably the first world slump of the modern type. (This may not have been accidental: Karl Marx observed that communications had brought those two major sources of business disturbance, India and America, much closer to Europe.) From the United States the crisis passed to Britain, thence to north Germany, thence to Scandinavia and back to Hamburg, leaving a trail of bankruptcies and unemployment, mean-

85

while leaping the oceans to South America. The slump of 1873, which began in Vienna, spread in the opposite direction and more widely. Its long-term effects were, as we shall see, much more profound – as might be expected. In the second place, at least in the industrialising countries, the old agrarian fluctuations lost a good deal of their effect, both because the mass transportation of foodstuffs diminished local shortages and tended to equalise prices, and because the social effect of such shortages was now offset by good employment generated in the industrial sector of the economy. A series of bad harvests would still affect agriculture, but not necessarily the rest of the country. Moreover, as the world economy strengthened its grip, even the fortunes of agriculture were to depend much less on the fluctuations of nature than on those of world market prices – as the great agrarian depressions of the 1870s and 1880s were to demonstrate.

All these developments affected only that sector of the world which was already drawn into the international economy. Since vast areas and populations – virtually all of Asia and Africa, most of Latin America, and quite substantial parts even of Europe – still existed outside any economies but those of purely local exchange and remote from port, railway and telegraph, we ought not to exaggerate the unification of the world achieved between 1848 and 1875. After all, as an eminent chronicler of the time pointed out, 'The *world economy* is only at its beginning'; but, as he also added, correctly, 'even these beginnings allow us to guess at its future importance, inasmuch as the present stage already represents a truly amazing transformation in the productivity of humanity'.[14] If we were to consider only, say, a region so near to Europe as the southern shore of the Mediterranean and northern Africa, in 1870 little of what has been said above would apply anywhere except in Egypt and in the modest patches of Algeria colonised by French settlers. Morocco only granted foreigners the freedom to trade throughout its territory in 1862; Tunisia did not hit on the idea, almost as disastrous here as in Egypt, to speed its slow progress by means of loans until after 1865. It was about this time that, a product of the growth of global trade, tea is first recorded south of the Atlas in Ouargla, Timbuctoo and Tafilelt, though still as an article of considerable luxury: a pound cost the equivalent of a Moroccan soldier's monthly wage. Until the second half of the century there was no sign of the characteristic population increase of the modern world in the Islamic countries, and, conversely, throughout the Saharan countries, as well as in Spain, the traditional combination of the famine and epidemic of 1867–9 (which ravaged so much of India at the same time) is of far greater economic, social and political importance than any developments associated with the rise of world capitalism, though perhaps – as in Algeria – intensified by it.

Chapter Four

Conflicts and War

And English history speaks loudly to kings as follows:
If you march at the head of the ideas of your century, these ideas
will follow and sustain you.
If you march behind them, they will drag you with them.
If you march against them, they will overthrow you!

Napoleon III[1]

The speed with which the military instinct developed among this nation
of shipowners, merchants and tradesmen ... is well known. [The
Baltimore Gun Club] had only one interest: the destruction of mankind
for philanthropic purposes, and the improvement of armaments, which
they looked upon as instruments of civilisation.

Jules Verne, 1865[2]

I

For the historian the great boom of the 1850s marks the foundation
of a global industrial economy and a single world history. For the
rulers of mid-nineteenth-century Europe, as we have seen, it provided
a breathing-space during which the problems which neither the
revolutions of 1848 nor their suppression had solved might be forgotten or at least mitigated by prosperity and sound administration.
And indeed the social problems now seemed a good deal more
manageable by virtue of the great expansion, the adoption of institutions and policies suitable for unrestrained capitalist development,
and the opening of safety-valves – good employment and migration –
sufficiently large to lower the pressures of mass discontent. But the
political problems remained and by the end of the 1850s it was clear
that they could no longer be avoided. They were, for each government, essentially problems of domestic politics, but because of the
peculiar nature of the European state-system east of the line from
Holland to Switzerland, domestic and international affairs were in-
extricably intertwined. Liberalism and radical democracy, or at least
the demand for rights and representation, could not be separated, in

88

Germany and Italy, in the Habsburg Empire, and even in the Ottoman Empire and on the fringes of the Russian Empire, from the
demands for national autonomy, independence or unification.
And this in turn might, and in the case of Germany, Italy and the
Habsburg Empire was bound to, produce international conflict.

For, quite apart from the interests of other powers in any substantial change in the frontiers of the continent, the unification of Italy
implied the expulsion of the Habsburg Empire, to which most of
northern Italy belonged. The unification of Germany raised three
questions: what exactly the Germany that was to be unified consisted
of,* how – if at all – the two major powers which were members of
the Germanic Confederation, Prussia and Austria, were to be fitted
into it, and what was to happen to the numerous other principalities
within it, ranging from middle-sized kingdoms to comic-opera
midgets. And both, as we have seen, directly involved the nature and
frontiers of the Habsburg Empire. In practice both unifications
implied wars.

Fortunately for the rulers of Europe, such a mixed charge of
domestic and international problems had now ceased to be explosive;
or rather the defeat of the revolution followed by the economic
boom had defused it. Broadly speaking, from the end of the 1850s
governments found themselves again faced with domestic political
agitation by a moderate liberal middle class and more radical
democrats, sometimes even by the newly emerging forces of a working-class movement. Some of them – especially when, like Russia in
the Crimean War (1854–6) and the Habsburg Empire in the Italian
War of 1859–60, they had been defeated – now found themselves
more vulnerable than before to internal discontent. Nevertheless,
these new agitations were not revolutionary, except in one or two
places where they could be isolated or contained. The characteristic
episode of these years was the confrontation between a strongly
liberal Prussian parliament, elected in 1861, and the Prussian king

* The *Germanic Confederation* included the smaller part of the Habsburg
Empire, the greater part of Prussia, as well as Holstein–Lauenburg, which also
belonged to Denmark, and Luxemburg, which also had non-German ties. It did
not include the then Danish Schleswig. On the other hand, the *German Customs
Union* (*Zollverein*), originally formed in 1834, by the mid-1850s included all of
Prussia, but no part of Austria. It also left out Hamburg, Bremen, and a large
area of north Germany (Mecklenburg and Holstein–Lauenburg as well as
Schleswig). The complications of such a situation may be imagined.

and aristocracy, who had not the slightest intention of abdicating to its demands. The Prussian government, knowing perfectly well that the liberal threat was mere rhetoric, provoked a confrontation and simply called in the most ruthless conservative available – Otto von Bismarck – as prime minister, to rule without and in defiance of the parliamentary refusal to vote taxes. He did so without difficulty.

And yet the significant thing about the 1860s is not that the governments almost always maintained the initiative and hardly ever lost more than momentary control of a situation they could always manipulate, but that some of the demands of their popular oppositions were *always* conceded, at all events west of Russia. This was a decade of reform, of political liberalisation, even of some concession to what was called 'the forces of democracy'. In Britain, Scandinavia and the Low Countries, where there were already parliamentary constitutions, the electorate was widened within them, not to mention a crop of associated reforms. The British Reform Act of 1867 was actually believed to put electoral power in the hands of working-class voters. In France, where Napoleon III's government had visibly lost the city vote by 1863 – it could elect only one out of fifteen deputies for Paris – increasingly extensive attempts were made to 'liberalise' the imperial system. But this change in mood is even more strikingly demonstrated in the non-parliamentary monarchies.

The Habsburg monarchy after 1860 simply gave up trying to rule as though its subjects had no political opinions. Henceforth it concentrated on discovering some coalition of forces among its numerous and obstreperous nationalities which would be strong enough to keep the rest politically ineffective, though all of them had now to be given certain educational and linguistic concessions (see pp. 119–20 below). Until 1879 it was usually to find its most convenient base among the middle-class liberals of its German-speaking component. It was unable to retain any effective control over the Magyars who won something not far short of independence by the 'Compromise' of 1867, which turned the empire into the Dual Monarchy of Austro–Hungary. But even more striking was what happened in Germany. In 1862 Bismarck became Prussian premier on a programme of maintaining the traditional Prussian monarchy and aristocracy against liberalism, democracy and German nationalism. In 1871 the same statesman appeared as the Chancellor of a German Empire united by his own efforts, with a parliament (admittedly of little significance) elected by universal male vote, and relying on the enthusiastic support of the (moderate) German liberals. Bismarck was in no sense a liberal, and far from a German nationalist in the political sense (see chapter 5 below). He was merely intelligent enough to be able to realise that the world of Prussian *junkers* could henceforth be preserved not by head-on conflict with liberalism and nationalism, but only by twisting the framework of both to its advantage. This implied doing what the British Conservative leader Benjamin Disraeli (1804–81), when introducing the Reform Act of 1867, described as 'catching the Whigs bathing and walking off with their clothes'.

The politics of rulers in the 1860s were therefore shaped by three considerations. First, they found themselves in a situation of economic and political change which they could not control, but to which they had to adapt. The only choice – and statesmen recognised this clearly – was whether to sail before the wind or use their skill as sailors to steer their ships into another direction. The wind itself was a fact of nature. Second, they had to determine what concessions to the new forces could be made without threatening the social system, or in special cases the political structures, to whose defence they were committed, and the point beyond which they could not safely go. But thirdly, they were fortunate to be able to make both kinds of decisions under circumstances which permitted them a considerable initiative, scope for manipulation and in some cases actually left them virtually free to control the course of events.

The statesmen who figure most prominently in the traditional histories of Europe during this period were therefore those who most systematically combined political management with diplomacy and control of the machines of government, like Bismarck in Prussia, Count Camillo Cavour (1810–61) in Piedmont, and Napoleon III, or those best able to manage the difficult process of a controlled broadening of an upperclass system of rule, e.g. the Liberal W. E. Gladstone (1809–98) and the Conservative Disraeli in Britain. And the most successful were those who understood how to turn both old and new unofficial political forces to their own advantage, whether or not they approved of them. Napoleon III fell in 1870, because eventually he failed to do so. But two men proved unusually good as this difficult operation, the moderate liberal Cavour and the conservative Bismarck.

Both were remarkably lucid politicians, a fact reflected in the unambitious clarity of Cavour's style and the remarkable mastery of German prose by Bismarck, an altogether more complex and greater figure. Both were profoundly anti-revolutionary and entirely out of sympathy with the political forces, whose programme they took over and carried out in Italy and Germany, minus its democratic and revolutionary implications. Both took care to separate national unity from popular influence: Cavour by insisting on turning the new Italian kingdom into a prolongation of Piedmont, even to the point of refusing to renumber the title of its king Victor Emmanuel ii (of Savoy) into Victor Emmanuel i (of Italy), Bismarck by building Prussian supremacy into the new German Empire. Both were flexible enough to integrate the opposition into their system, though making it impossible for it to win control.

Both faced enormously complex problems of international tactics and (in Cavour's case) national politics. Bismarck, who needed no outside help and did not have to worry about internal opposition, could consider a united Germany only if it was neither democratic nor too large to be dominated by Prussia. This implied the exclusion of Austria, which he achieved by means of two brilliantly conducted short wars in 1864 and 1866, the paralysis of Austria as a force in German politics, which he achieved by supplying and ensuring the autonomy of Hungary within the Habsburg monarchy (1867), and at the same time the preservation of Austria, to which he hence forth devoted his remarkable diplomatic gifts.* It also implied making Prussian supremacy more palatable than Austrian to the rather anti-Prussian lesser German states, which Bismarck achieved by an equally brilliantly provoked and managed war against France in 1870–71. Cavour, on the other hand, had both to mobilise an ally (France) to expel Austria from Italy for him, and thereafter to immobilise him, when the process of unification went far beyond what Napoleon iii

---

* For, if the Habsburg monarchy collapsed into its component nationalities, it would be impossible to prevent the Austrian Germans joining Germany, thus upsetting the carefully constructed Prussian supremacy. This is in fact what happened after 1918, and, as it happens, the most lasting result of the 'greater Germany' of Hitler (1938–45) was the total disappearance of Prussia. Today not even its name remains, except in history books.

had envisaged. More seriously, he found himself with an Italy half-unified by controlled management from above and half-unified by revolutionary war from below, led by the forces of the democratic-republican opposition under the military leadership of that frustrated Fidel Castro of the mid-nineteenth century, the red-shirted guerilla chief Giuseppe Garibaldi (1807–82). Quick thinking, fast talking and some brilliant manoeuvring were required before Garibaldi was persuaded to hand over power to the king in 1860.

The operations of these statesmen still command admiration for their sheer technical brilliance. Yet what made them so dazzling was not only personal talent, but the unusual scope which the absence of serious revolutionary danger and of uncontrollable international rivalry gave to them. The actions of peoples or unofficial movements, too weak at this period to achieve much on their own, either failed or became the ancillaries of change organised from above. The German liberals, democratic radicals and social revolutionaries contributed little except cheering or dissent to the actual process of German unification. The Italian left, as we have seen, played a greater role. Garibaldi's Sicilian expedition, which rapidly conquered southern Italy, forced the hands of Cavour, but, though this was a significant achievement, it would have been impossible but for the situation created by Cavour and Napoleon. In any case the left failed to achieve the Italian democratic republic which it regarded as the essential complement of unity. The moderate Hungarian gentry achieved autonomy for their country under the wing of Bismarck, but the radicals were disappointed. Kossuth continued to live in exile and died there. The rebellions of the Balkan peoples in the 1870s were to result in a sort of independence for Bulgaria (1878), but only in so far as this suited the interests of the great powers: the Bosnians, who began these insurrections in 1875–6, merely exchanged Turkish rule for the probably superior administration of the Habsburgs. Conversely, as we shall see, independent revolutions ended badly (see chapter 9 below). Even the Spanish one of 1868, which actually produced a short-lived radical republic in 1873, ended with the rapid return of the monarchy.

We do not diminish the merits of the great political operators of the 1860s by pointing out that their task was made considerably easier because they could introduce major constitutional changes without drastic political consequences, and, even more to the point, because they could start and stop wars almost at will. In this period both the domestic and the international order could therefore be considerably modified with comparatively little political risk.

II

This is why the thirty years after 1848 were a period of even more spectacular changes in the pattern of international relations than in that of domestic politics. In the age of revolution, or at any rate after the defeat of Napoleon (see *The Age of Revolution*, chapter 5), governments of great powers had been extremely careful to avoid major conflicts among themselves, since experience had seemed to show that major wars and revolutions went together. Now that the revolutions of 1848 had come and gone, this motive for diplomatic restraint was much weaker. The generation after 1848 was an age not of revolutions but of wars. Some of these were indeed the product of internal tensions, and revolutionary or quasi-revolutionary phenomena. These – the great civil wars of China (1851–64) and the United States (1861–5) – do not strictly speaking belong in the present discussion, except in so far as this must also deal with the technical as well as the diplomatic aspects of war in this period. We shall consider them separately (see chapters 7 and 8 below). Here we are concerned primarily with the tensions and shifts within the system of international relations, bearing in mind the curious intertwining of international and domestic politics.

If we had asked a surviving practitioner of the pre-1848 international system about the problems of foreign policy – say, Viscount Palmerston, who had been British Foreign Secretary long before the revolutions and continued to manage foreign affairs with some interruptions until his death in 1865 – he would have explained them something as follows. The only world affairs that counted were the relations between the five European 'great powers' whose conflicts might result in a major war: Britain, Russia, France, Austria and Prussia (see *The Age of Revolution*, chapter 5). The only other state with sufficient ambition and power to count, the United States, was negligible, since it confined its interests to other continents, and no European power had active ambitions in the Americas other than

94

economic ones – and these were the concern of private businessmen and not governments. In fact, as late as 1867 Russia sold Alaska to the United States for some 7 million dollars, plus enough bribes to persuade the American Congress to accept what was universally regarded merely as a collection of rocks, glaciers and arctic tundra. The European powers themselves, or those which seriously counted – Britain, because of her wealth and navy, Russia, because of her size and army, and France, because of her size, army and rather formidable military record – had ambitions and reasons for mutual distrust, but not such as to be beyond the scope of diplomatic compromise. For over thirty years after the defeat of Napoleon in 1815 no great powers had used their arms against each other, confining their military operations to the suppression of domestic or international subversion, to various local trouble-spots, and to expanding into the backward world.

There was indeed one fairly constant source of friction, arising mainly out of the combination of a slowly disintegrating Ottoman Empire, from which various non-Turkish elements were liable to break away, and the conflicting ambitions of Russia and Britain in the eastern Mediterranean, the present Middle East and the area lying between Russia's eastern borders and the western ones of Britain's Indian empire. In so far as foreign ministers were not worried about the danger of a general breakdown in the international system through revolution, they were fairly constantly preoccupied by what was called the 'Eastern Question'. Still, matters had not got out of hand. The 1848 revolutions proved this, for even though three out of the five great powers had been simultaneously shaken by them, the international system of the powers emerged virtually unchanged from them. Indeed, with the one partial exception of France, so did the domestic political systems of all of them.

The subsequent decades were to be strikingly different. In the first place, the power considered (at least by the British) as potentially the most disruptive, France, emerged from the revolution as a populist empire under another Napoleon, and, what is more, the fear of a return to the Jacobinism of 1793 no longer restrained it. Napoleon, in spite of occasional announcements that 'the Empire means Peace', specialised in world-wide interventions: military expeditions to Syria (1860), jointly with Britain in China (1860), the conquest of

95

the southern part of Indochina (1858–65), and even – while the United States was otherwise occupied – an adventure in Mexico (1861–7), where the French satellite Emperor Maximilian (1864–7) did not long survive the end of the American Civil War. There was nothing particularly French in these exercises in brigandage, except perhaps Napoleon's appreciation of the electoral value of imperial glory. France was merely strong enough to take part in the general victimisation of the non-European world; as Spain, for instance, was not, in spite of her grandiose ambitions to recover some of its lost imperial influence in Latin America during the American Civil War. In so far as such French ambitions were pursued overseas, they did not particularly affect the European power system; but in so far as they were pursued in regions where the European powers were in rivalry, they disturbed what was always a rather delicately balanced arrangement.

The first major result of this disturbance was the Crimean War (1854–6), the nearest thing to a general European war between 1815 and 1914. There was nothing new or unexpected about the situation which turned into a major, notoriously incompetent, international butchery between Russia on one side, Britain, France and Turkey on the other, and in which it is estimated that over 600,000 men perished, almost half a million of them of disease: 22 per cent of the British, 30 per cent of the French and about half the Russian forces. Neither before nor after did the Russian policy of either partitioning Turkey or turning it into a satellite (in this instance the former) envisage, require or indeed lead to a war between the powers. But both before and during the next phase of Turkish disintegration, in the 1870s, the power-conflict was conducted essentially as a two-power game between two old contestants, Russia and Britain, the others being unwilling or unable to intervene other than symbolically. But in the 1850s there was a third player, France, whose style and strategy were, moreover, unpredictable. There is little doubt that nobody wanted such a war, and it was called off, without making any visibly lasting difference to the 'Eastern Question', as soon as the powers could extricate themselves. The fact was that the mechanism of 'Eastern-Question' diplomacy, designed for simpler confrontations, temporarily broke down – at the cost of a few hundred thousand lives.

The direct diplomatic results of the war were temporary or insignificant, though Rumania (formed by the union of two Danubian principalities still nominally under Turkish suzerainty until 1878) became *de facto* independent. The wider political results were more serious. In Russia the rigid crust of the tsarist autocracy of Nicholas I (1825–55), already under growing strain, cracked. An era of crisis, reform and change began, culminating in the emancipation of the serfs (1861) and the emergence of a Russian revolutionary movement in the late 1860s. The political map of the rest of Europe was also shortly to be transformed, a process facilitated, if not made possible, by the shifts in the international power-system precipitated by the Crimean episode. As we have noted, a united kingdom of Italy emerged in 1858–70, a united Germany in 1862–71, incidentally leading to the collapse of Napoleon's Second Empire in France and the Paris Commune (1870–71). Austria was excluded from Germany and profoundly restructured. In brief, with the exception of Britain, all the European 'powers' were substantially – in most cases even territorially – changed between 1856 and 1871, and a new large state, soon to be considered among them, was founded: Italy.

Most of these changes arose directly or indirectly out of the political unifications of Germany and Italy. Whatever the original impetus of these movements for unification, the process was undertaken by governments, i.e. under the circumstances by military force. In Bismarck's famous phrase it was solved 'by blood and iron'. In twelve years Europe passed through four major wars: France, Savoy and the Italians against Austria (1858–9), Prussia and Austria against Denmark (1864), Prussia and Italy against Austria (1866), Prussia and the German states against France (1870–71). They were relatively brief and, by the standards of the great butcheries in the Crimea and the United States, not exceptionally costly, though some 160,000 perished, mostly on the French side, in the Franco-Prussian war. But they helped to make the period of European history with which this volume deals a rather warlike interlude in what was otherwise an unusually peaceable century between 1815 and 1914. Nevertheless, though war was common enough in the world between 1848 and 1871, the fear of a *general* war, in which the twentieth century has lived virtually without interruption since the early 1900s, did not as yet haunt the citizens of the bourgeois world. It only began to do so slowly after 1871. Wars between the states could still be started and finished deliberately by governments, a situation brilliantly exploited by Bismarck. Only civil wars, and the relatively few conflicts which turned into genuine people's wars, like the war between Paraguay and her neighbours (1864–70), turned into those episodes of uncontrollable slaughter and destruction with which our own century is so familiar. Nobody knows the extent of the losses in the Taiping Wars, but it has been claimed that some Chinese provinces have not to this day recovered their former population. The American Civil War killed over 630,000 soldiers, and casualties totalled between 33 and 40 per cent of the Union and Confederate forces. The Paraguayan War killed 330,000 (in so far as Latin-American statistics have any meaning), reducing the population of its chief victim to some 200,000, of whom perhaps 30,000 were men. By any standards, the 1860s were a decade of blood.

What made this period of history relatively so bloody? In the first place, it was the very process of global capitalist expansion which multiplied tensions within the overseas world, the ambitions of the industrial world, and direct and indirect conflicts arising out of it. Thus the American Civil War, whatever its political origins, was the triumph of the industrialised North over the agrarian South, almost, one might even say, the transfer of the South from the informal empire of Britain (to whose cotton industry it was the economic pendant) into the new major industrial economy of the United States. It might be regarded as an early if giant step on the road which was in the twentieth century to turn all the Americas from a British to an American economic dependency. The Paraguayan War may be best regarded as part of the integration of the River Plate basin into the British world economy: Argentina, Uruguay and Brazil, their faces and economies turned to the Atlantic, forced Paraguay out of the self-sufficiency in which the only area in Latin America in which the Indians resisted the settlement of the whites effectively had so long maintained itself, thanks perhaps to the original dominion of the Jesuits (see chapter 7 below).* The Taiping rebellion and its suppression are inseparable from the rapid penetration of western

* The remainder of the Indians who resisted white conquest were pressed back by the frontier of settlement. Only in the upper La Plata basin did Indian settlement remain solid, and Guaraní rather than Spanish or Portuguese the *de facto* idiom of communication among both natives and settlers.

guns and capital in the Celestial Empire since the first Opium War (1839–42) (see pp. 157–8 below).

In the second place, as we have seen – especially in Europe – it was due to the reversion to war as a normal instrument of policy by governments who now ceased to believe that it must be avoided for fear of consequent revolution, and who were also rightly convinced that the power-mechanism was capable of keeping them within limits. Economic rivalry hardly led to more than local friction in an era of expansion when there seemed plainly to be room for everyone. Moreover, in this classic era of economic liberalism, business competition was more nearly independent of government support than ever before or after. Nobody – not even Marx, contrary to a common assumption – thought of European wars as primarily economic in origin in this period.

Thirdly, however, these wars could now be waged with the new technology of capitalism. (Since this technology, through the camera and the telegraph, also transformed the reporting of war in the press, it now brought its reality more vividly before the literate public, but except for the foundation of the International Red Cross in 1860 and the Geneva Convention recognising it in 1864, this had little effect. Still our century has produced no more effective controls over its more horrible bloodbaths.) The Asian and Latin-American Wars remained substantially pre-technological, except for the small incursions of European forces. The Crimean War, with characteristic incompetence, failed to use adequately the technology already available. But the wars of the 1860s already employed the railway to good effect for mobilisation and transport, had the telegraph available for rapid communication, developed the armoured warship and its pendant, heavy armour-piercing artillery, could use mass-produced fire-arms including the Gatling machine gun (1861) and modern explosives – dynamite was invented in 1866 – with significant consequences for the development of industrial economies. Hence they were on the whole closer to modern mass warfare than anything that had preceded them. The American Civil War mobilised 2·5 million men out of a total population of, say, 33 million. The rest of the wars of the industrial world remained smaller, for even the 1·7 million mobilised in 1870–71 in the Franco–German war represented less than 2·5 per cent of the 77 or so million inhabitants of the two countries or, say, 8 per cent of the 22 million capable of bearing arms. Still it is worth noting that from the mid-1860s giant battles involving over 300,000 men ceased to be unusual (Sadowa [1866], Gravelotte, Sedan [1870]). There had been only one such battle in the entire course of the Napoleonic Wars (Leipzig [1813]). Even the Battle of Solferino in the Italian War of 1859 was larger than all but one Napoleonic battle.

We have already observed the domestic by-products of these government initiatives and wars. Yet in the long run their international consequences were to prove even more dramatic. For during the third quarter of the nineteenth century the international system was fundamentally altered – much more profoundly than most contemporary observers recognised. Only one aspect of it remained unchanged: the extraordinary superiority of the developed world over the underdeveloped, which was actually underlined (see chapter 8 below) by the career of the only non-white country which in this period succeeded in imitating the west, namely Japan. Modern technology put any government which did not possess it at the mercy of any government which did.

On the other hand, the relations between the powers were transformed. For half a century after the defeat of Napoleon I there had been only one power which was essentially industrial and capitalist, and only one which had a genuinely global policy, i.e. a global navy: Britain. In Europe there were two powers with potentially decisive armies, though their strength was essentially non-capitalist: that of Russia rested on its vast and physically tough population, that of France on the possibility and tradition of revolutionary mass mobilisation. Austria and Prussia were not of comparable politico-military importance. In the Americas there was a single power without rivals, the United States, which, as we have seen, did not venture into the area of effective power-rivalry. (This area did not, before the 1850s, include the Far East.) But between 1848 and 1871, or more precisely during the 1860s, three things happened. First, the expansion of industrialisation produced other essentially industrial-capitalist powers besides Britain: the United States, Prussia (Germany) and, to a much greater extent than before, France, later to be joined by Japan. Second, the progress of industrialisation increasingly made wealth and industrial capacity the decisive factor in international power; hence devaluing the relative standing of Russia and France, and greatly increasing that of Prussia (Germany). Third, the emergence as independent powers of two extra-European states, the United States (united under the North in the Civil War) and Japan (systematically embarking on 'modernisation' with the Meiji Restoration of 1868), created for the first time the possibility of global power-conflict. The increasing tendency of European businessmen and governments to expand their activities overseas, and to find themselves involved with other powers in such areas as the Far East and the Middle East (Egypt), reinforced this possibility.

Overseas these changes in the power-structure were as yet of no great consequence. Within Europe they immediately made themselves felt. Russia, as the Crimean War showed, had ceased to be the potentially decisive force on the European continent. So, as the Franco-Prussian War demonstrated, had France. Conversely Germany, a new power which combined both a remarkable industrial and technological strength with a substantially larger population than any other European state except Russia, became the new decisive force in this part of the world, and was to remain so until 1945. Austria, in the restyled version of an Austro–Hungarian Dual Monarchy (1867), remained what she had long been, a 'great power', merely by size and international convenience, though stronger than the newly united Italy, whose large population and diplomatic ambitions also allowed her to be treated as a participant in the power game.

Increasingly, therefore, the formal international structure came to diverge from the real one. International politics became global politics, in which at least two non-European powers were to intervene effectively, though this was not evident until the twentieth century. Furthermore, it became a sort of oligopoly of capitalist-industrial powers, jointly exercising a monopoly over the world, but competing among themselves; though this did not become evident until the era of 'imperialism' after the end of our period. Around 1875 all this was as yet hardly visible. But the foundations of the new power-structure were laid in the 1860s, including the fear of a general European war, which began to haunt observers of the international scene from the 1870s. In fact, there was to be no such war for another forty years, a longer period than the twentieth century has ever managed. Yet our own generation, which can look back at the time of writing on

101

more than thirty years without war between any of the great or even the medium-sized powers,* knows better than any other that the absence of war can be combined with the permanent fear of it. In spite of conflicts, the era of liberal triumph had been stable. It was no longer so after 1875.

* With the exception of the conflict between the United States and China in Korea in 1950–53, at a time when China was not yet considered a major power.

Chapter Five

Building Nations

But what . . . is a nation? Why is Holland a nation, while Hanover and the Grand Duchy of Parma are not?

Ernest Renan, 1882[1]

What's national? When nobody understands a word of the language you speak.

Johann Nestroy, 1862[2]

If a great people does not believe that the truth is to be found in itself alone . . . if it does not believe that it alone is fit and destined to raise up and save all the rest by its truth, it would at once sink into being ethnographic material, and not a great people . . . A nation which loses this belief ceases to be a nation.

F. Dostoievsky, 1871–2[3]

NATIONS. Réunir ici tous les peuples (?)

Gustave Flaubert, c. 1852[4]

I

If international and domestic politics were closely bound up with one another during this period, the bond which linked them most obviously was what we call 'nationalism' but the mid-nineteenth century still knew as 'the principle of nationality'. What were the international politics of the years from 1848 to the 1870s about? Traditional western historiography had very little doubt: it was about the creation of a Europe of nation-states. There might be considerable uncertainty about the relation between this facet of the age and others which were evidently connected with it, such as economic progress, liberalism, perhaps even democracy, but none about the central role of nationality.

And indeed, how could there be? Whatever else it was, 1848, the 'springtime of peoples', was clearly also, and in international terms primarily, an assertion of nationality, or rather of rival nationalities. Germans, Italians, Hungarians, Poles, Rumanians and the rest

103

asserted their right to be independent and unified states embracing all members of their nations against oppressive governments, as did Czechs, Croats, Danes and others, though with growing misgivings about the revolutionary aspirations of bigger nations which seemed excessively ready to sacrifice their own. France was already an independent national state, but none the less nationalist for that.

The revolutions failed, but the European politics of the next twenty-five years were dominated by the same aspirations. As we have seen, they were actually achieved, in one form or another, though by non-revolutionary or only marginally revolutionary means. France returned to a caricature of the 'great nation' under a caricature of the great Napoleon, Italy and Germany were united under the kingdoms of Savoy and Prussia, Hungary achieved virtual home rule by the Compromise of 1867, Rumania became a state by the merger of the two 'Danubian principalities'. Only Poland, which had failed to take an adequate part in the 1848 revolution, also failed to win independence or autonomy by the insurrection of 1863.

In the extreme west, as in the extreme south-east, of Europe the 'national problem' obtruded itself. The Fenians in Ireland raised it in the form of radical insurrection, backed by the millions of their countrymen driven by famine and hatred of Britain to the United States. The endemic crisis of the multi-national Ottoman Empire took the form of revolts by the various Christian peoples it had so long ruled in the Balkans. Greece and Serbia were already independent, though still much smaller than they thought they ought to be. Rumania won independence of a sort at the end of the 1850s. Popular insurrections in the early 1870s precipitated yet another internal and international Turkish crisis, which was to make Bulgaria independent at the end of the decade and accelerate the 'Balkanisation' of the Balkans. The so-called 'Eastern Question', that permanent pre-occupation of foreign ministers, now appeared primarily as the question of how to redraw the map of European Turkey among an uncertain number of new states of uncertain size which claimed and were believed to represent 'nations'. And a little further to the north the internal problems of the Habsburg Empire were even more patently those of its constituent nationalities, several of which – and potentially all of which – put forward demands ranging from a mild cultural autonomy to secession.

Even outside Europe the construction of nations was dramatically visible. What was the American Civil War, if not the attempt to maintain the unity of the American nation against disruption? What was the Meiji Restoration, if not the appearance of a new and proud 'nation' in Japan? It seemed hardly deniable that 'nation-making', as Walter Bagehot (1826–77) called it, was taking place all over the world and was a dominant characteristic of the age.

So obvious, that the nature of the phenomenon was hardly investigated. 'The nation' was taken for granted. As Bagehot put it: 'We cannot imagine those to whom it is a difficulty: "we know what it is when you do not ask us", but we cannot very quickly explain or define it',[5] and few thought they needed to. Surely the Englishman knew what being English was, the Frenchman, German, Italian or Russian had no doubt about their collective identity? Perhaps not, but in the age of nation-building this was believed to imply the logical necessary, as well as desirable transformation of 'nations' into sovereign nation-states, with a coherent territory defined by the area settled by the members of a 'nation', which was in turn defined by its past history, its common culture, its ethnic composition and, increasingly, its *language*. But there is nothing logical about this implication. If the existence of differing groups of men, distinguishing themselves from other groups by a variety of criteria is both undeniable and as old as history, the fact that they imply what the nineteenth century regarded as 'nationhood' is not. Still less so is the fact that they are organised in territorial states of the nineteenth-century kind, let alone states coinciding with 'nations'. These were relatively recent historic phenomena, though some older territorial states – England, France, Spain, Portugal and perhaps even Russia – could have been defined as 'nation-states' without obvious absurdity. Even as a general programme, the aspiration to form nation-states out of non-nation-states was a product of the French Revolution. We must therefore distinguish rather clearly between the formation of nations and 'nationalism', in so far as this took place during our period, and the creation of nation-states.

The problem was not merely analytical but practical. For Europe, let alone the rest of the world, was evidently divided into 'nations' about whose states or aspirations to found states there was, rightly or wrongly, little doubt, and those about which there was a considerable amount of uncertainty. The safest guide to the first was political fact, institutional history or the cultural history of the literate. France, England, Spain, Russia were undeniably 'nations' because they had states identified with the French, English, etc. Hungary and Poland were nations because a Hungarian kingdom existed as a separate entity even within the Habsburg Empire and a Polish state had long existed until destroyed at the end of the eighteenth century. Germany was a nation both because its numerous principalities, though never united into a single territorial state, had long formed the so-called 'Holy Roman Empire of the German Nation' and still formed the Germanic Federation, and also because all educated Germans shared the same written language and literature. Italy, though never a political entity as such, had perhaps the oldest common literary culture of its elite.* And so on.

The 'historic' criterion of nationhood thus implied the decisive importance of the institutions and culture of the ruling classes or educated elites, supposing them to be identified, or not too obviously incompatible with, those of the common people. But the *ideological* argument for nationalism was very different and much more radical, democratic and revolutionary. It rested on the fact that, whatever history or culture said, the Irish were Irish and not English, the Czechs Czech and not German, the Finns were not Russian, and no people ought to be exploited and ruled by another. Historic arguments might be found or invented to back this claim – they can always be discovered – but essentially the Czech movement did not rest on the claim to restore the Crown of St Wenceslas, nor the Irish on the Repeal of the Union of 1801. The basis of this sense of separateness was not necessarily 'ethnic', in the sense of readily identifiable differences of physical appearance, or even linguistic. During our period the movements of the Irish (most of whom already spoke English), the Norwegians (whose literate language was not very distinct from Danish) or the Finns (whose nationalists were both Swedish- and Finnish-speaking), did not make a fundamentally linguistic case for themselves. If it was cultural, it rested not on 'high culture', of which several of the peoples concerned as yet had little,

* No modern Englishman, German or Frenchman can read the works of fourteenth-century literature written in their countries without learning what amounts to a different language, but all educated Italians today can read Dante with less difficulty than modern English-speakers can read Shakespeare.

but rather on the oral culture – songs, ballads, epics, etc., the customs and ways of life of 'the folk' – the common people, i.e. for practical purposes the peasantry. The first stage of 'national revival' was invariably one of collecting, recovering and acquiring pride in this folk heritage (see *The Age of Revolution*, chapter 14). But in itself this was not political. Those who pioneered it were, as often as not, cultured members of the foreign ruling class or elite, such as the German Lutheran pastors or intellectually minded gentlemen in the Baltic who collected the folklore and antiquities of the Latvian or Estonian peasantry. The Irish were not nationalists because they believed in leprechauns.

Why they were nationalists and how far they were nationalists, we shall discuss below. The significant point here is that the typical 'un-historical' or 'semi-historical' nation was also a *small* nation, and this faced nineteenth-century nationalism with a dilemma which has rarely been recognised. For the champions of the 'nation-state' assumed not only that it must be national, but also that it must be 'progressive', i.e. capable of developing a viable economy, technology, state organisation and military force, i.e. that it must be at least moderately large. It was to be, in fact, the 'natural' unit of the development of the modern, liberal, progressive and *de facto* bourgeois society. 'Unification' as much as 'independence' was its principle, and where no historic arguments for unification existed – as they did for example in Italy and Germany – it was, where feasible, formulated as a programme. There is no evidence whatever that the Balkan Slavs had ever considered themselves parts of the same nation, but the nationalist ideologues who emerged in the first half of the century thought in terms of an 'Illyria' hardly more real than Shakespeare's, a 'Yugoslav' state which was to unite Serbs, Croats, Slovenes, Bosnians, Macedonians and others who to this day demonstrate that their Yugoslav nationalism is, to put it mildly, in conflict with their sentiments as Croats, Slovenes, etc.

The most eloquent and typical champion of the 'Europe of nationalities', Giuseppe Mazzini (1805–72), proposed a map of his ideal Europe in 1857:[6] it consisted of a mere eleven unions of this kind. Clearly his idea of 'nation-states' was very different from that of the Woodrow Wilson who presided over the only systematic redrawing of the European map according to national principles at Versailles in

1919–20. His Europe consisted of twenty-six or (including Ireland) twenty-seven sovereign states, and by Wilsonian criteria a case could have been made out for a few more. What was to happen to the small nations? They must plainly be integrated, federally or otherwise, with or without some as yet undetermined autonomy, into the viable nation-states, though it appeared to escape the notice of Mazzini that a man who proposed uniting Switzerland with Savoy, German Tyrol, Carinthia and Slovenia was hardly in a position to criticise, say, the Habsburg Empire for trampling on the national principle.

The simplest argument for those who identified nation-states with progress was to deny the character of 'real' nations to the small and backward peoples, or to argue that progress must reduce them to mere provincial idiosyncrasy within the larger 'real' nations, or even lead to their actual disappearance by assimilation to some *Kulturvolk*. This did not seem unrealistic. After all, membership of Germany did not stop the Mecklenburgers from talking a dialect which was closer to Dutch than to High German and which no Bavarian could under-stand, or for that matter the Lusatian Slavs from accepting (as they still do) a basically German state. The existence of the Bretons, and a part of the Basques, Catalans and Flemings, not to mention the speakers of *Provençal* and the *Langue d'oc*, appeared perfectly com-patible with the French nation of which they formed a part, and the Alsatians created a problem only because another large nation-state – Germany – disputed their allegiance. Moreover, there were examples of such small linguistic groups whose educated elite looked forward without gloom to the disappearance of their language. Plenty of Welshmen in the mid-nineteenth century were resigned to it, and some welcomed it as a means of facilitating the penetration of progress into a backward region.

There was a strong element of inegalitarianism and perhaps a stronger one of special pleading in such arguments. Some nations – the large, the 'advanced', the established, including certainly the ideologist's own – were destined by history to prevail or (if the ideolo-gist preferred Darwinian phraseology) to be victors in the struggle for existence; others were not. Yet this must not be interpreted simply as a conspiracy of some nations to oppress others, though spokesmen of the unrecognised nations could hardly be blamed for thinking so. For the argument was directed as much against the

regional languages and cultures of the nation itself as against out-
siders, and did not necessarily envisage their disappearance, but only
their down-grading from the status of 'language' to that of 'dialect'.
Cavour did not deny the right of Savoyards to talk their language
(closer to French than Italian) in a united Italy: he spoke it himself
for most domestic purposes. He, and other Italian nationalists,
merely insisted that there should be only one official language and
medium of instruction, namely Italian, and the others should sink or
swim as best they could. As it so happened at this stage, neither the
Sicilians nor the Sardinians insisted on their separate nationhood, so
their problem could be redefined as, at best, 'regionalism'. It only
became politically significant once a small people claimed nationhood, as the Czechs did in 1848 when their spokesmen refused the
invitation of the German liberals to take part in the Frankfurt
parliament. The Germans did not deny that there were Czechs. They
merely assumed, quite correctly, that all educated Czechs read and
wrote German, shared German high culture and (incorrectly) that
they therefore were German. The fact that the Czech elite also spoke
Czech and shared the culture of the local common people seemed to
be politically irrelevant, like the attitudes of the common people in
general and the peasantry in particular.

Faced with the national aspirations of small peoples, the ideologists
of a 'national Europe' therefore had three choices: they could deny
their legitimacy or their existence altogether, they could reduce them
to movements for regional autonomy, and they could accept them as
undeniable but unmanageable facts. Germans tended to do the first
with such peoples as the Slovenes, Hungarians with the Slovaks.*
Cavour and Mazzini took the second view about the Irish movement.
Nothing is more paradoxical than their failure to fit into the nationalist pattern the one national movement about whose mass basis there
could be no conceivable doubt. Politicians of all kinds were con-

* This attitude must be distinguished from that of social revolutionaries who
did not – at least in our period – assign any major significance to nationalism at
all, and therefore took a purely operational view of it. For Marx, Hungarian and
Polish nationalism in 1848 was good, because mobilised on the side of the revolution, Czech and Croat nationalism bad, because objectively on the side of the
counter-revolution. But we cannot deny that there was an element of great-nation
nationalism in such views, very obviously among the highly chauvinist French
revolutionaries (notably the Blanquists), and not easily to be denied even in
Frederick Engels.

strained to take the third view of the Czechs, whose national move-ment, though not then envisaging total independence, could no longer be argued away after 1848. Where possible, of course, they paid no attention to such movements at all. Hardly any foreigner bothered to note that several of the most old-established 'national' states were in fact multinational (e.g. Britain, France, Spain), for the Welsh, the Scots, the Bretons, the Catalans, etc., posed no inter-national problem, and (with the possible exception of the Catalans) no significant problem in the domestic politics of their own countries.

II

There was thus a fundamental difference between the movement to found nation-states and 'nationalism'. The one was a programme to construct a political artifact claiming to be based on the other. There is no doubt that many who thought of themselves as 'Germans' for some purposes, did not believe that this implied a single German state, a German state of a specific type, let alone one which included all Germans living within the area bounded, as the national song had it, by the rivers Meuse in the west and Niemen in the east, the sea-straits of Denmark (the Belt) in the north and the river Adige in the south. Bismarck, for one, would have denied that his rejection of this 'greater German' programme meant that he was not a German as well as a Prussian *junker* and servant of the state. He was a German, but not a German nationalist, probably not even a 'little German' nationalist by conviction, though he actually unified the country (excluding the areas of the Austrian Empire which had belonged to the Holy Roman Empire, but including the areas taken by Prussia from Poland, which had never been part of it). An extreme case of a divergence between nationalism and the nation-state was Italy, most of which was unified under the King of Savoy in 1859–60, 1866 and 1870. There was no historic precedent later than ancient Rome for a single administration of the entire area from the Alps to Sicily, which Metternich had, quite correctly, described as 'a mere geo-graphical expression'. At the moment of unification, in 1860, it has been estimated that not more than $2\frac{1}{2}$ per cent of its inhabitants actually spoke the Italian language for the ordinary purposes of life, the rest talking idioms so different that the schoolmasters sent by the

Italian state into Sicily in the 1860s were mistaken for Englishmen.[7] Probably a much larger percentage, but still a modest minority, at that date would have thought of themselves primarily as Italians. No wonder Massimo d'Azeglio (1792–1866) exclaimed in 1860: 'We have made Italy; now we must make the Italians.'

Nevertheless, whatever their nature and programme movements representing 'the national idea' grew and multiplied. They did not often – or even normally – represent what by the early twentieth century had become the standard (and extreme) version of the national programme, i.e. the necessity of a totally independent, territorially and linguistically homogeneous, secular – and probably republican/parliamentary – state for each 'people'.* However, they all implied some more or less ambitious political changes, and this is what made them 'nationalist'. These we must now try to look at, avoiding both the anachronism of hindsight and the temptation to confuse the ideas of the most vociferous nationalist leaders with those actually held by their followers.

Nor should we overlook the substantial difference between old and new nationalisms, the former including not only the 'historic' nations not yet possessing their own states, but those who had long done so. How British did the British feel? Not very, in spite of the virtual absence at this stage of any movements for Welsh and Scottish autonomy. There was English nationalism, but it was not shared by the smaller nations in the island. English emigrants to the United States were proud of their nationality, and therefore reluctant to become American citizens, but Welsh and Scottish immigrants had no such loyalty. They could remain as proudly Welsh and Scottish under American as under British citizenship, and naturalised themselves freely. How French did the members even of *la grande nation* feel? We do not know, but statistics of draft-evasion earlier in the century suggest that certain regions in the west and south (not to mention the special case of the Corsicans) regarded compulsory military service as a disagreeable imposition rather than as a national duty of the French citizen. The Germans, as we know, had different views about the size, nature and structure of the future united Ger-

* Zionism, by the very extremism of its claims, illustrates this clearly, for it implied taking a territory, inventing a language and secularising the political structures of a people whose historic unity had consisted exclusively in the practice of a common religion.

111

man state, but how many of them cared about German unification at all? Not, by general agreement, the German peasants, even in the 1848 revolution, when the national question dominated politics. These were countries in which mass nationalism and patriotism can hardly be denied, and they demonstrate how unwise it is to take its universality and homogeneity for granted.

In most other nations, especially the emergent ones, only myth and propaganda would have taken it for granted in the mid-nineteenth century. There the 'national' movement tended to become political, after its sentimental and folkloristic phase, with the emergence of more or less large groups of cadres dedicated to 'the national idea', publishing national journals and other literature, organising national societies, attempting to establish educational and cultural institutions, and engaging in various more frankly political activities. But in general at this stage the movement still lacked any serious support among the mass of the population. It consisted primarily of the strata intermediate between the masses and what local bourgeoisie or aristocracy existed (if any), and especially of the literate: teachers, the lower levels of the clergy, some urban shopkeepers and artisans, and the sort of men who had risen about as far as it was possible for the sons of a subordinate peasant people in a hierarchical society. Eventually the students – from some nationally minded faculties, seminaries and high schools – provided them with a ready-made body of active militants. Of course in 'historic' nations, which required little except the removal of foreign rule to re-emerge as states, the local elite – gentry in Hungary and Poland, middle-class bureaucrats in Norway – provided a more immediately political cadre and sometimes a larger base for nationalism (see *The Age of Revolution*, chapter 7). On the whole this phase of nationalism ends between 1848 and the 1860s in northern, western and central Europe, though many of the smaller Baltic and Slav people were only beginning to enter it.

For obvious reasons the most traditional, backward or poor sections of a people were the last to be involved in such movements: workers, servants and peasants, who followed the path traced by the 'educated' elite. The phase of a mass nationalism, which therefore normally came under the influence of organisations of the nationalist liberal-democratic middle strata – except when offset by independent labour and socialist parties – was to some extent correlated with economic and political development. In the Czech lands it began in the revolution of 1848, relapsed in the absolutist 1850s, but grew enormously during the rapid economic progress of the 1860s, when political conditions were also more favourable. A native Czech bourgeoisie had by now acquired sufficient wealth to found an effective Czech bank, and eventually such expensive institutions as a National Theatre in Prague (provisionally opened in 1862). More to our point, mass cultural organisations like the *Sokol* gymnastic clubs (1862) now covered the countryside and the political campaigns after the Austro–Hungarian Compromise were conducted through a series of vast open-air mass rallies – some 140 with an estimated participation of $1\frac{1}{2}$ million in 1868–71[8] – which, incidentally, illustrate both the novelty and the cultural 'internationalism' of the mass national movements. For, lacking a proper name for such activities, the Czech initially borrowed the term 'meeting' for them from the Irish movement which they attempted to copy.* Soon a suitably traditional name was devised by harking back to the Hussites of the fifteenth century, a natural example for Czech national militancy, the 'tabor'; and this in turn was to be adopted by the Croat nationalists for their rallies, though the Hussites had no historical relevance to them.

This kind of mass nationalism was new, and quite distinct from the elite or middle-class nationalism of the Italian and German movements. And yet another form of mass nationalism had long existed: both more traditional, more revolutionary and more independent of local middle classes, if only because these were of no great economic and political consequence. But can we call the rebellions of peasants and mountaineers against foreign rule 'nationalist', when united only by the consciousness of oppression, by xenophobia and by an attachment to ancient tradition, the true faith and a vague sense of ethnic identity? Only when they happened to be attached for one reason or another to modern national movements. Whether they can be so attached in south-eastern Europe, where such risings destroyed much of the Turkish Empire, particularly in the 1870s (Bosnia, Bulgaria),

* The word 'meeting' was also to be borrowed for mass rallies of the working class by the French and the Spaniards, but probably in this instance from English experience.

may be debated, though it is undeniable that they produced independent states (Rumania, Bulgaria) which claimed to be national. At
best we may speak of a proto-nationalism, as among the Rumanians,
conscious of the difference of their language from the surrounding
and intermingled Slavs, Hungarians and Germans, or the Slavs, conscious of a certain 'slavness', which intellectuals and politicians tried
to develop into an ideology of Panslavism in our period;* and even
among them it is probable that the feeling of solidarity of Orthodox
Christians with the great Orthodox empire of Russia was the force
which gave it reality in this period.

One such movement, however, was unquestionably national: the
Irish. The Irish Republican Brotherhood ('Fenians'), with its still
surviving Irish Republican Army, was the lineal descendant of the
secret revolutionary fraternities of the pre-1848 period, and the
longest-lived organisation of its kind. Mass rural support for nationalist politicians was not in itself new, for the Irish combination of
foreign conquest, poverty, oppression and a largely Anglo-Protestant
landlord class imposed on an Irish-Catholic peasantry mobilised the
least political. In the first half of the century the leaders of these
mass movements had belonged to the (small) Irish middle class and
their aim – supported by the only effective national organisation, the
church – had been a moderate accommodation with the English.
The novelty of the Fenians, who first appeared as such in the late
1850s, was that they were entirely independent of the middle-
class moderates, that their support came entirely from among the
popular masses – even, in spite of the open hostility of the Church,
parts of the peasantry – and that they were the first to put forward a
programme of total independence from England, to be achieved by
armed insurrection. In spite of their name, derived from the heroic
mythology of ancient Ireland, their ideology was quite non-
traditional, though its secular, even anti-clerical nationalism cannot
conceal that for the mass of the Fenian Irish the criterion of nation-

* Panslavism appealed both to the conservative and imperial politicians of
Russia, whom it offered an extension of Russian influence, and to those of the
lesser Slavic peoples of the Habsburg Empire, whom it offered a powerful ally
and perhaps also, more remotely, the hope of forming a 'proper' large nation
instead of a collection of small and apparently unviable ones. (The revolutionary
and democratic Panslavism of the anarchist Bakunin may be neglected as utopian.)
It was therefore strongly opposed by the left, which regarded Russia as the main
stronghold of international reaction.

ality was (and still is) the Catholic faith. Their wholehearted concentration on an Irish Republic won by armed struggle replaced a social and economic, even a domestic political programme, and their heroic legend of rebel gunmen and martyrs has up to the present been too strong for those who wanted to formulate one. This is the 'Republican tradition' which survives into the 1970s and has re-emerged in the Ulster civil war, in the 'Provisional' IRA. The readiness of the Fenians to ally themselves with socialist revolutionaries, and of these to recognise the revolutionary character of Fenianism, should not encourage illusions about this.*

But neither should we underestimate the novelty, and the historic significance, of a movement whose financial support came from the masses of Irish labourers driven by famine and hatred of England to the United States, whose recruits came from Irish emigrant proletarians in America and England – there were hardly any industrial workers in what is now the Irish Republic – and from young peasants and farm-workers in the ancient strongholds of Irish 'agrarian terrorism'; whose cadres were men such as these and the lowest strata of revolutionary urban white-collar workers, and whose leaders dedicated their lives to insurrection. It anticipates the revolutionary national movements of under-developed countries in the twentieth century. It lacked the core of socialist labour organisation, or perhaps merely the inspiration of a socialist ideology, which was to turn the combination of national liberation and social transformation into such a formidable force in this century. There was no socialism anywhere, let alone socialist organisation in Ireland, and the Fenians who were also social revolutionaries, notably Michael Davitt (1846–1906), succeeded merely in making explicit in the *Land League* the always implicit relation between mass nationalism and mass agrarian discontent; and even this not until after the end of our period, during the great Agrarian Depression of the late 1870s and 1880s. Fenianism was mass nationalism in the epoch of triumphant liberalism. It could do little except reject England and demand total independence through revolution for an oppressed people, hoping that somehow this would solve all problems of poverty and exploitation. It did not do even this very effectively, for in spite of the

* Marx supported them strongly and was in correspondence with Fenian leaders.

self-abnegation and heroism of the Fenians, their scattered insurrections (1867) and invasions (e.g. of Canada from the United States) were conducted with notable inefficiency, and their dramatic *coups* achieved, as is usual in such operations, little more than temporary publicity; occasionally bad publicity. They generated the force which was to win independence for most of Catholic Ireland but, since they generated nothing else, they left the future of that Ireland to the middle-class moderates, the rich farmers and small-town tradesmen of a small agrarian country who were to take over their heritage.

Though the Irish case was still unique, there is no denying that in our period nationalism increasingly became a mass force, at least in the countries populated by whites. Even though the *Communist Manifesto* was less unrealistic than is often supposed in stating that 'the workers have no country', it probably advanced among the working class *pari passu* with political consciousness, if only because the tradition of revolution itself was national (as in France) and because the leaders and ideologists of the new labour movements were themselves deeply involved in the national question (as almost everywhere in 1848). The alternative to a 'national' political consciousness was not, in practice, 'working-class internationalism' but a sub-political consciousness which still operated on a scale much smaller than, or irrelevant to, that of the nation-state. The men and women on the political left who chose clearly between national and supra-national loyalties, such as the cause of the international proletariat, were few. The 'internationalism' of the left in practice meant solidarity and support for those who fought the same cause in other nations and, in the case of political refugees, the readiness to participate in the struggle wherever they found themselves. But, as the examples of Garibaldi, Cluseret of the Paris Commune (who helped the Fenians in America) and numerous Polish fighters prove, this was not incompatible with passionately nationalist beliefs.

It might also mean a refusal to accept the definitions of the 'national interest' put forward by governments and others. Yet the German and French socialists who in 1870 joined in protesting against the 'fratricidal' Franco–Prussian war were not insensible to nationalism as *they* saw it. The Paris Commune derived its support from the Jacobin patriotism of Paris as much as from the slogans of social emancipation, and the Marxist German Social Democrats of

116

Liebknecht and Bebel derived much of theirs from their appeal to the radical-democratic nationalism of 1848 against the Prussian version of the national programme. What German workers resented was reaction rather than German patriotism; and one of the most unacceptable aspects of reaction was that it called Social Democrats *vaterlandslose Gesellen* (fellows without a fatherland), thus denying them the right to be not only workers but good Germans. And, of course, it was almost impossible for political consciousness not to be in some way or another nationally defined. The proletariat, like the bourgeoisie, existed only conceptually as an international fact. In reality it existed as an aggregate of groups defined by their national state of ethnic/linguistic difference: British, French or, in multinational states, German, Hungarian or Slav. And, in so far as 'state' and 'nation' were supposed to coincide in the ideology of those who established institutions and dominated civil society, politics in terms of the state implied politics in terms of the nation.

III

And yet, however powerful national feelings and (as nations turned into states or the other way round) allegiances, the 'nation' was not a spontaneous growth but an artefact. It was not merely historically novel, though embodying the things members of some very ancient human groups had in common or thought they had in common as against 'foreigners'. It had actually to be constructed. Hence the crucial importance of the institutions which could *impose* national uniformity, which meant primarily the state, especially state education, state employment and (in countries adopting conscription) military service.* The educational systems of developed countries expanded substantially during this period, at all levels. The number of university students remained unusually modest by modern standards. Omitting theology students, Germany led the field at the end of the 1870s with almost seventeen thousand, followed a long way after by Italy and France with nine to ten thousand each and Austria with some eight thousand.[9] It did not grow much except under nationalist pressure and in the United States, where institutions

---

* Conscription operated in France, Germany, Italy, Belgium and Austro–Hungary.

dedicated to higher education were in the process of multiplying.* Secondary education grew with the middle classes, though (like the superior bourgeoisie for whom they were destined) they remained very much elite institutions, except once again in the United States, where the public 'high school' began its career of democratic triumph. (In 1850 there had only been a hundred of them in the entire nation.) In France the proportion of those undergoing a secondary education rose from one in thirty-five (1842) to one in twenty (1864): but secondary graduates – they averaged about five and a half thousand per annum in the first half of the 1860s – formed only one in fifty-five or sixty of the conscript class, though this was better than in the 1840s when they had formed only one in 93.[10] Most countries were situated somewhere between the totally pre-educational or the totally restrictive countries such as Britain with its 25,000 boys in 225 purely private establishments miscalled 'public schools' and the education-hungry Germans whose *gymnasia* contained perhaps a quarter of a million pupils in the 1880s.

But the major advance occurred in the primary schools, whose purpose was by general consent not only to teach the rudiments of literacy and arithmetic but, perhaps even more, to impose the values of society (morals, patriotism, etc.), on their inmates. This was the sector of education which had previously been neglected by the secular state, and its growth was closely linked with the advance of the masses into politics; as witness the setting-up of the state primary education system in Britain three years after the Reform Act of 1867 and the vast expansion of the system in the first decade of the Third Republic in France. Progress was indeed striking: between 1840 and the 1880s the population of Europe rose by 33 per cent, but the number of its children attending school by 145 per cent. Even in well-schooled Prussia the number of primary schools increased by over 50 per cent between 1843 and 1871. But it was not due merely to the educational backwardness of Italy that the fastest increase in the school population in our period occurred there: 460 per cent. In the fifteen years following unification the number of primary-school children doubled.

* Of the eighteen new universities founded between 1849 and 1875, nine were overseas (five in the United States, two in Australia, one each in Algiers and Tokyo), five were in eastern Europe (Jassy, Bucarest, Odessa, Zagreb and Czernowitz). Two very modest foundations were in Britain.

In fact, for new nation-states these institutions were of crucial importance, for through them alone the 'national language' (generally constructed earlier by private efforts) could actually become the written and spoken language of the people, at least for some purposes.* Hence also the crucial importance for struggling national movements of the fight to win 'cultural autonomy', i.e. to control the relevant part of state institutions, e.g. to achieve school instruction in and administrative use for their language. The issue was not one which affected the illiterate, who learned their dialect from their mothers anyway, nor the minority peoples who assimilated *en bloc* to the prevailing language of the ruling class. The European Jews were content to retain their native languages – the Yiddish derived from medieval German and the Ladino derived from medieval Spanish – as a *Mame-Loschen* (mother-tongue) for domestic use, communicating with their gentile neighbours in whatever idiom was required and, if they became bourgeois, abandoning their old language for that of their surrounding aristocracy and middle class, English, French, Polish, Russian, Hungarian, but especially German.† But the Jews at this stage were not nationalist, and their failure to attach importance to a 'national' language, as well as their failure to possess a national territory, led many to doubt that they could be a 'nation'. On the other hand, the issue was vital for the middle class and educated elites emerging from backward or subaltern peoples. It was they who specially resented the privileged access to important and prestigious posts which native speakers of the 'official' language had; even when (as was the case with the Czechs), their own compulsory bilingualism actually gave them a career advantage of the monoglot Germans in Bohemia. Why should a Croat have to learn Italian, the language of a small minority to become an officer in the Austrian navy?

And yet, as nation-states were formed, as the public posts and professions of progressive civilisation multiplied, as school education became more general, above all as migration urbanised rural peoples,

* The 'mass media' – i.e. at this stage the press – could only turn into such when such a mass literate public in the standard language had been created.
† A movement to develop both Yiddish and Ladino into standard literary languages developed, in the first case, from the mid-century, and was later to be taken up by the Jewish revolutionary (Marxist) movements, *not* by Jewish nationalism (Zionism).

these resentments found an increasingly general resonance. For schools and institutions, in imposing one language of instruction, also imposed a culture, a nationality. In areas of homogeneous settlement this did not matter: the Austrian constitution of 1867 recognised elementary education in the 'language of the country'. But why should Slovenes or Czechs, migrating into hitherto German cities, be compelled to become Germans as a price of becoming literate? They demanded the right to their own schools even when they were minorities. And why should the Czechs and Slovenes of Prague or Ljubljana (Laibach), having reduced the Germans from a majority to a smallish minority, have to confront street-names and municipal regulations in a foreign tongue? The politics of the Austrian half of the Habsburg Empire were complex enough for the government to have to think multi-nationally. But what if other governments used schooling, that most powerful weapon for forming the nations upon which they purported to rest, to magyarise, germanise or italianise systematically? The paradox of nationalism was that in forming its own nation it automatically created the counter-nationalism of those whom it now forced into the choice between assimilation and inferiority.

The age of liberalism did not grasp this paradox. Indeed, it did not understand that 'principle of nationality' which it approved, considered itself to embody, and in suitable cases actively supported. Contemporary observers were no doubt right in supposing, or acting as if, nations and nationalism were as yet largely unformed and malleable. The American nation, for instance, was based on the assumption that in migrating across the ocean many millions of Europeans would lightly and quickly abandon any political loyalties to their homeland and any claims to official status for their native languages and cultures. The United States (or Brazil, or Argentina) would not be multi-national, but absorb the immigrants into its own nation. And in our period this is what happened, even though the immigrant communities did not lose their identity in the 'melting-pot' of the new world, but remained or even became consciously and proudly Irish, German, Swedish, Italian, etc. The communities of immigrants might be important national forces in their countries of origin, as the American Irish were in the politics of Ireland; but in the United States itself they were of major significance chiefly to candidates for municipal elections. Germans in Prague by their very existence raised the most far-reaching political problems for the Habsburg Empire; not so Germans in Cincinnati or Milwaukee for the United States.

Nationalism therefore still seemed readily manageable within the framework of a bourgeois liberalism, and compatible with it. A world of nations would, it was believed, be a liberal world, and a liberal world would consist of nations. The future was to show that the relationship between the two was not as simple as this.

Chapter Six

The Forces of Democracy

The bourgeoisie should know that, alongside it, the forces of democracy have grown during the Second Empire. It will find these forces . . . so solidly entrenched that it would be crazy to renew war against it.

Henri Allain Targé, 1868[1]

But as the progress of democracy is the result of general social development, an advanced society, while commanding a greater share of political power, will, at the same time, protect the State from democratic excesses. If the latter should anywhere prevail, for a time, they will be promptly repressed.

Sir T. Erskine May, 1877[2]

I

If nationalism was one historic force recognised by governments, 'democracy', or the growing role of the common man in the affairs of state, was the other. The two were the same, in so far as nationalist movements in this period became mass movements, and certainly at this point pretty well all radical nationalist leaders supposed them to be identical. However, as we have seen, in practice large bodies of common people, such as peasants, still remained unaffected by nationalism even in the countries in which their participation in politics were seriously considered, while others, notably the new working classes, were being urged to follow movements which, at least in theory, put a common international class interest above national affiliations. At all events, from the point of view of ruling classes the important thing was not what 'the masses' believed, but that their beliefs now counted in politics. They were, by definition, numerous, ignorant and dangerous; most dangerous precisely by virtue of their ignorant tendency to believe their eyes, which told them that their rulers paid too little attention to their miseries, and the simple logic which suggested to them that, since they formed the bulk of the people, government should primarily serve their interests.

Yet it became increasingly clear in the developed and industrialised countries of the west that sooner or later the political systems would have to make room for them. Moreover, it also became clear that the liberalism which formed the basic ideology of the bourgeois world had no theoretical defences against this contingency. Its characteristic form of political organisation was representative government through elected assemblies, representing not (as in feudal states) social interests or collectivities, but aggregates of individuals, of legally equal status. Self-interest, caution, or even a certain common sense might well suggest to those on top that all men were not equally capable of deciding the great questions of government, the illiterate less than the university graduates, the superstitious less than the enlightened, the feckless poor less than those who had proved their capacity of rational behaviour by the accumulation of property. However, quite apart from the lack of conviction such arguments carried to those at the bottom, other than the most conservative, they had two major weaknesses. Legal equality could not make such distinctions in theory. What was considerably more important, they became increasingly hard to make in practice, as social mobility and educational progress, both essential to bourgeois society, blurred the division between the middle strata and their social inferiors. Where, in the great and increasing mass of the 'respectable' workers and lower middle classes who adopted so much of the values and, in so far as their means allowed, the behaviour, of the bourgeoisie, was the line to be drawn? Wherever it was drawn, if it included any large number of them, it was likely to include a substantial body of citizens who did not support several of the ideas which bourgeois liberalism regarded as essential to the prospering of society, and who might well oppose them passionately. Furthermore, and most decisively, the 1848 revolutions had shown how the masses could irrupt into the closed circle of their rulers, and the progress of industrial society itself made their pressure constantly greater even in non-revolutionary periods.

The 1850s gave most rulers a breathing-space. For a decade and more they did not seriously have to worry about such problems in Europe. However, there was one country in which the political and constitutional clocks could not simply be turned back. In France, with three revolutions behind it already, the exclusion of the masses from politics seemed a utopian undertaking: they would henceforth

123

have to be 'managed'. The so-called Second Empire of Louis Napoleon (Napoleon III) hence became a sort of laboratory of a more modern kind of politics, though the peculiarities of its character have sometimes obscured its anticipations of later forms of political management. Such experimentation suited the taste, though perhaps less the talents, of the enigmatic personage who stood at its head.

Napoleon III has been notably unfortunate in his public relations. He was unlucky enough to unite against himself all the most powerful polemical talents of his time, and the combined invective of Karl Marx and Victor Hugo are alone sufficient to bury his memory, without counting lesser though at the time equally effective journalistic talents. Furthermore, he was notoriously unsuccessful in his international, and even his domestic political enterprises. A Hitler can survive the unanimous reprobation of world opinion, since it is undeniable that this evil, psychopathological and terrifying man achieved extraordinary things on the way to a probably inevitable catastrophe; not least to maintain the solid support of his people to the end. Napoleon III was plainly not so extraordinary or even mad. The man who was outmanoeuvred by Cavour and Bismarck, whose political support had shrunk dangerously even before his empire disintegrated after a few weeks of war, who turned 'Bonapartism' from a major political force in France into a historical anecdote, will inevitably go down in history as 'Napoleon the Little'. He did not even play his chosen role well. That secretive, saturnine but often charming figure with the long waxed moustaches, increasingly racked by ill-health, horrified by the very battles which were to establish his and French greatness, seemed imperial only *ex officio*.

He was essentially a politician, a backstairs politician and, as it turned out, an unsuccessful one. Yet fate and his personal background had cast him for an entirely novel role. As an imperial pretender before 1848 – though his genealogical claim to being a Bonaparte was doubted – he had to think in untraditional terms. He grew up in the world of the nationalist agitators (joining the Carbonari himself) and the Saint-Simonians. From this experience he derived a strong, perhaps excessive, belief in the inevitability of such historic forces as nationalism and democracy, and a certain heterodoxy about social problems and political methods which stood him in good stead later. The revolution gave him his chance by electing the

124

name Bonaparte to the presidency with an overwhelming majority, but for a variety of motives. He did not need votes to stay in power and, after the *coup d'état* of 1851, to declare himself Emperor, but if he had not been elected first, not all his capacity for intrigue would have persuaded the generals or anyone else of power and ambition to back him. He was thus the first ruler of a large state outside the United States to come to power by means of universal (masculine) suffrage, and never forgot it. He continued to operate with it, initially as a plebiscitary Caesar, rather like General de Gaulle (the elected representative assembly being quite insignificant), after 1860 in-increasingly also with the usual paraphernalia of parliamentarism. Being a believer in the accepted historical verities of the time, he probably did not believe that he could resist this 'force of history' either.

Napoleon III's attitude towards electoralist politics was ambiguous, and this is what makes it interesting. As a 'parliamentarian' he played what was then the standard game of politics, namely collecting to-gether a sufficient majority from among the assembly of elected individuals, grouped in loose and shifting alliances with vaguely ideological labels which must not be confused with modern political parties. Hence both surviving politicians from the July Monarchy (1830–48), like Adolphe Thiers (1797–1877), and future luminaries of the Third Republic, like Jules Favre (1809–80), Jules Ferry (1832–93) and Gambetta (1838–82), restored or made their names in the 1860s. He was not particularly successful at this game, especially when he decided to slacken the firm bureaucratic control over elections and press. On the other hand, as an electoral campaigner himself, he kept in reserve (again like General de Gaulle, only perhaps with greater success) the weapon of the plebiscite. It had ratified his triumph in 1852 by an overwhelming and, in spite of considerable 'management', probably authentic victory of 7·8 million, with 2 million abstentions, and even in 1870, on the eve of collapse, it could still reverse a deteriorating parliamentary situation with a majority of 7·4 million against 1·6 million.

This popular support was politically unorganised (except, of course, through bureaucratic pressures). Unlike modern popular leaders, Napoleon III had no 'movement', but of course as head of the state he hardly needed one. Nor was it at all homogeneous. He would himself have liked the support of the 'progressives' – the Jacobin–Republican vote, which always kept aloof, at all events in the cities – and the working classes, whose social and political significance he appreciated more than orthodox Liberals. However, though he sometimes received the support of important spokesmen of this group, such as the anarchist Pierre-Joseph Proudhon (1809–65), and made serious efforts to conciliate and tame the rising labour movement in the 1860s – he legalised strikes in 1864 – he failed to break both their traditional and their logical affinity with the left. In practice he therefore relied on the conservative element and especially on the peasantry, mainly of the western two-thirds of the country. For these he was a Napoleon, a stable and anti-revolutionary government firm against threats to property; and (if they were Catholics), the defender of the Pope in Rome, a situation from which Napoleon would have wanted to escape for diplomatic reasons, but could not for domestic political ones.

But his rule was even more significant. Karl Marx observed with his habitual insight the nature of his relationship with the French peasantry,

> 'incapable of enforcing their class interest in their own name, whether through a parliament or a convention. They cannot represent themselves, they must be represented. Their representative must at the same time appear as their master, as an authority over them, as an unlimited governmental power that protects them against other classes and sends them the rain and sunshine from above. The political influence of the small peasants, therefore, finds its final expression in the executive power subordinating society to itself.'[3]

Napoleon was that executive power. Many politicians of the twentieth century – nationalist, populist, and in the most dangerous form, fascist – were to rediscover the sort of relationship which he pioneered with masses unable to 'enforce their class interest in their own name'. They were also to discover that there were other strata of the population similar in this respect to the post-revolutionary French peasantry.

With the exception of Switzerland, whose revolutionary constitution remained in being, no other European state operated on the basis of universal (masculine) suffrage in the 1850s.* (It should perhaps be

* The Swiss *Nationalrat* was chosen by all males aged twenty or more without property qualifications, but the second chamber was chosen by the Cantons.

noted that even in the nominally democratic United States electoral participation was strikingly lower than in France: in 1860 Lincoln was elected by less than half of 4·7 million voters out of a population of roughly comparable size.) Representative assemblies, generally lacking serious power or influence outside Britain, Scandinavia, Holland, Belgium, Spain and Savoy, were familiar enough, but invariably either elected very indirectly, or something like the old 'estates', or with more or less rigorous age- and property-qualifications for both voters and candidates. Almost invariably elected assemblies of this kind were flanked and braked by more conservative first chambers, mostly appointed or composed of hereditary or *ex officio* members. The United Kingdom, with something like 1 million electors out of 27·5 million inhabitants, was doubtless less restrictive than, say, Belgium, with something like 60,000 out of 4·7 million, but neither was, nor intended to be, democratic.

The revival of popular pressure in the 1860s made it impossible to keep politics isolated from it. By the end of our period only tsarist Russia and imperial Turkey maintained themselves as simple autocracies in Europe, while conversely universal suffrage was no longer the prerogative of regimes sprung from revolution. The new German Empire used it to elect its *Reichstag*, though largely for decorative purposes. Very few states in this decade escaped some more or less significant widening of their franchise, and hence the problems which had hitherto preoccupied only the minority of countries in which voting had real significance – the choice between voting by lists or by candidates, 'electoral geometry' or the gerrymandering of social and geographical constituencies, the checks which first chambers could exercise upon second chambers, the rights reserved to the Executive, etc. – now troubled most governments. They were still hardly acute. The Second Reform Act in Britain, while more or less doubling the number of voters, still left them as no more than 8 per cent of the population, while in the recently united Kingdom of Italy they amounted to a bare 1 per cent. (At this period manhood suffrage would in practice enfranchise 20–25 per cent of the population, to judge by French, German and American elections of the mid-1870s.) Still, there had been changes, and further ones could only be delayed.

These advances towards representative government raised two

quite distinct problems in politics: those of 'the classes' and 'the masses' to use contemporary British jargon, i.e., of the upper- and middle-class elites, and of the poor who remained largely outside the official processes of politics. Between them stood the intermediate strata – small shopkeepers, craftsmen and other 'petty-bourgeois', peasant proprietors, etc. – who as property-owners were already, at least in part, involved in such representative politics as existed. Neither the old landed and hereditary aristocracies nor the new bourgeoisie had the strength of numbers, but unlike the aristocracy, the bourgeoisie needed it. For while both had (at least in their upper reaches) wealth, and the sort of personal power and influence in their communities which made them automatically into at least potential 'notables', i.e. persons of political consequence, only the aristocracies were firmly entrenched in institutions safeguarding them against voting: in Houses of Lords or similar upper chambers, or by means of more or less flagrant over-representation as in the 'class-suffrage' of the Prussian and Austrian Diets or in the surviving – but rapidly disappearing – ancient estates. Moreover, in the monarchies which were still the prevailing form of European government, they normally found systematic political support as a class.

The bourgeoisies, on the other hand, relied on their wealth, their indispensability and the historic destiny which made them and their ideas the foundations of 'modern' states in this period. However, what actually turned them into forces within the political systems was the ability to mobilise the support of the non-bourgeois who possessed numbers and hence votes. Deprive them of this, as happened in Sweden in the late 1860s, and was to happen elsewhere later with the rise of genuine mass politics, and they were reduced to an electorally impotent minority, at least in national politics. (In municipal politics they were to maintain themselves better.) Hence the crucial importance for them of retaining the support of, or at least the hegemony over, the petty-bourgeoisie, the working classes and, more rarely, the peasants. Broadly speaking, in this period of history they were successful. In representative political systems the Liberals (normally the classical party of the urban and industrial business classes) were generally in power and/or office with only occasional interruptions. In Britain this was so from 1846 to 1874, in the Netherlands for at least twenty years after 1848, in Belgium from 1857 to 1870, in

Denmark more or less until the shock of defeat in 1864. In Austria and Germany they were the major formal support of governments from the mid-1860s until the end of the 1870s.

However, as pressure grew from below, a more democratic radical (progressive, republican) wing tended to split off from them, where it was not already more or less independent. In Scandinavia peasant parties seceded as 'the Left' (*Venstre*) in 1848 (Denmark) and during the 1860s (Norway), or as an agrarian anti-city pressure group (Sweden 1867). In Prussia (Germany) the rump of the democratic radicals, with their base in the non-industrial south-west, refused to follow the bourgeois National Liberals into their alliance with Bismarck after 1866, though some of them tended to join the anti-Prussian Marxist Social Democrats. In Italy the Republicans remained in opposition, while the moderates became the mainstay of the newly united kingdom. In France the bourgeoisie had long ceased to be able to sail under its own, or even the Liberal flag, and its candidates sought popular support under increasingly inflammatory labels. 'Reform' and 'Progressive' were to give way to 'Republican', and this in turn to 'Radical' and, even in the Third Republic, 'Radical-Socialist', each concealing a new generation of substantially the same bearded, frock-coated, golden-tongued and frequently gold-lined Solons, rapidly shifting towards moderation after their electoral triumphs on the left. Only in Britain did the radicals remain a permanent wing of the Liberal Party; probably because there the peasants and petty bourgeoisie which allowed them to establish their political independence elsewhere hardly existed as a class.

Nevertheless, for practical purposes liberalism remained in power, because it represented the only economic policy which was believed to make sense for development ('Manchesterism' as the Germans called it), and the forces almost universally believed to represent science, reason, history and progress by those who had any ideas on these matters. In this sense almost every statesman and civil servant of the 1850s and 1860s was a Liberal, irrespective of his ideological affiliation, just as today nobody is any longer. The Radicals themselves had no viable alternative to it. At all events, to join with the genuine opposition against Liberalism was, if not impossible, then at least politically almost unthinkable for them. They both formed part of 'the Left'.

The genuine opposition ('the Right') came from those who resisted the 'forces of history', irrespective of argument. In Europe few really hoped for a return to the past, as in the days of romantic reactionaries after 1815. All they aimed for was to hold up, or even merely to slow down, the menacing progress of the present, an objective rationalised by such intellectuals as they had into the need for both parties of 'movement' and 'stability', of 'order' and 'progress'. Hence conservatism was liable to attract from time to time such members and groups of the Liberal bourgeoisie as felt that further progress would once again bring revolution dangerously close. Naturally such Conservative parties attracted the support of particular groups whose immediate interests happened to clash with prevailing Liberal policy (e.g. agrarians and protectionists), or groups opposed to the Liberals for reasons irrelevant to their Liberalism, e.g. the Belgian Flemings, resenting an essentially Walloon bourgeoisie and its cultural predominance. No doubt also, especially in rural society, family or local rivalries were naturally assimilated into an ideological dichtomy which had little to do with them. Colonel Aureliano Buendía, in Garcia Marquez's novel *A Hundred Years of Solitude*, organised the first of his thirty-two Liberal uprisings in the Colombian hinterland not because he was a Liberal or even knew what the word meant, but because he was outraged by a local official who happened to represent a Conservative government. There may be a logical or historical reason why mid-Victorian English butchers should have been predominantly Conservative (a link with agriculture?) and grocers overwhelmingly Liberal (a link with overseas trade?), but none has been established, and perhaps what needs explaining is not this, but why these two omnipresent types of shopkeepers refused to share the same opinions, whatever they were.

But essentially Conservatism rested on those who stood for tradition, the old and ordered society, custom and no change, on opposition to what was new. Hence the crucial importance in it of the official churches, organisations both threatened by all that Liberalism stood for, and still capable of mobilising immensely powerful forces against it, not to mention inserting a fifth column into the very centre of the bourgeois power by virtue of the notably greater piety and traditionalism of wives and daughters, by clerical control over

130

the ceremonies of birth, marriage and death, and over a large sector of education. Control of these was bitterly contested, and provided the major content of Conservative–Liberal political struggles in a number of countries.

All official churches were *ipso facto* Conservative, though only the greatest of them, the Roman Catholic, formulated its position as flat hostility to the rising Liberal tide. In 1864 Pope Pius IX defined its views in the *Syllabus of Errors*. This condemned, with equal implacability, eighty errors including 'naturalism' (which denied the action of God upon men and the world), 'rationalism' (the use of reason without reference to God), 'moderate rationalism' (the refusal of ecclesiastical supervision by science and philosophy), 'indifferentism' (the free choice of any religion or none), secular education, the separation of church and state and in general (error no. 80) the view that 'the Roman Pontiff can and ought to reconcile himself and come to terms with progress, liberalism and modern civilisation'. Inevitably the line between right and left became largely that between clerical and anticlerical; the latter being mainly frank unbelievers in Catholic countries, but also – notably in Britain – believers in minority or independent religions outside the state church* (see chapter 14 below).

What was new about the politics of 'the classes' in this period was chiefly the emergence of the Liberal bourgeoisie as a force in more or less constitutionalist politics, with the decline of absolutism, notably in Germany, Austro–Hungary and Italy, i.e. in an area covering about a third of the population of Europe. (Something less than a third of the population of the continent still lived under governments in which it played no such part.) The progress of the periodical press – outside Britain and the United States still addressed almost wholly to bourgeois readers – illustrates the change vividly: between 1862 and 1873 the number of periodicals in Austria (without Hungary) increased from 345 to 866. Otherwise they introduced little that had not been familiar to the nominally or genuinely electoral assemblies of the period before 1848.

---

* The position of state churches where they happened to be minority religions was anomalous. The Dutch Catholics might find themselves on the Liberal side against the predominant Calvinists, and the German ones, unable to join either the Protestant Right or the Liberal Left of the Bismarckian empire, formed a special 'Centre Party' in the 1870s.

The franchise remained so restricted in most cases that there could be no question of modern or any other mass politics. Indeed often the stage armies of the middle class could almost take the place of the real 'people' they claimed to represent. Few cases were as extreme as Naples and Palermo in the early 1870s, 37·5 and 44 per cent of whose respective electors were on the voting list by virtue of being graduates of some kind. But even in Prussia the Liberal triumph of 1863 looks less impressive if we recall that the 67 per cent of the city vote which went to them represented in fact only about 25 per cent of the urban electors, since almost two-thirds even of the restricted electorate did not bother to go to the polls in the towns.[4] Did the splendid electoral triumphs of Liberalism in the 1860s represent anything more in such countries of restricted franchise and popular apathy than the opinions of a minority of respectable town burghers?

In Prussia Bismarck at least thought they did not, and consequently solved the constitutional conflict between a Liberal Diet and the monarch (which arose in 1862 over plans of army reform) by simply governing without reference to parliament. So long as nobody stood behind the Liberals except the bourgeoisie, and the bourgeoisie were unable or unwilling to mobilise any genuine force, armed or political, all talk about the Long Parliament of 1640 or the Estates General of 1789 was so much vapour.* He realised that, in the most literal sense of the word, a 'bourgeois revolution' was an impossibility, since it would only be a real revolution if others except the bourgeoisie were mobilised, and in any case businessmen and professors were rarely inclined to mount the barricades themselves. This did not prevent him from applying the economic, legal and ideological programme of the Liberal bourgeoisie, in so far as it could be combined with the predominance of the landed aristocracy in a Protestant Prussian monarchy. He did not wish to drive the Liberals into an alliance of despair with the masses, and in any case theirs was the obvious programme for a modern European state, or at least seemed inevitable. As we know, he succeeded brilliantly. The bulk of the Liberal bourgeoisie accepted the offer of programme minus political

* Conversely, what gave the Liberals real power in some backward countries, in spite of their minority position, was the existence of Liberal landowners whose hold over their regions was virtually beyond government influence, or of officers ready to make pronunciamentos in the Liberal interest. This was the case in several Iberian countries.

132

power – it had little option – and transferred itself in 1866 to the National Liberal party which was the foundation of Bismarck's domestic political manoeuvres for the remainder of our period.

Bismarck and other conservatives knew that, whatever the masses were, they were not Liberals in the sense in which the urban businessmen were. Consequently they sometimes felt that they could hold over the Liberals the threat of expanding the franchise. They might even carry it out, as Benjamin Disraeli did in 1867 and the Belgian Catholics more modestly in 1870. Their error was to suppose that the masses were conservatives in their own sense. No doubt the bulk of the peasantry in most parts of Europe were still traditionalists, ready to support church, king or emperor and their hierarchic superiors automatically, especially against the evil designs of the townsmen. Even in France large regions of the west and south continued in the Third Republic to vote for supporters of the Bourbon dynasty. No doubt also, as Walter Bagehot, the theorist of harmless democracy, pointed out after the Reform Act of 1867, there were plenty of people including even workers whose political behaviour was governed by deference to 'their betters'. But once the masses entered the political scene they inevitably did so sooner or later as actors rather than as mere extras in a well-designed crowd tableau. And while backward peasants could still be relied on in many places, the growing industrial and urban sectors could not. What their inhabitants wanted was not classical Liberalism, but it was not necessarily welcome to conservative rulers either, especially to those devoted, as most increasingly were, to an essentially Liberal economic and social policy. This was to become evident during the era of economic depression and uncertainty which followed the collapse of Liberal expansion in 1873.

II

The first and most dangerous group to establish its separate identity and role in politics was the new proletariat, its numbers swollen by twenty years of industrialisation.

The labour movement had not so much been destroyed as decapitated by the failure of the 1848 revolutions and the subsequent decade of economic expansion. The various theorists of a new social future who had turned the unrest of the 1840s into the 'spectre of com-

133

munism', and given the proletariat an alternative political perspective to both the conservative and the liberal or radical, were in jail like Auguste Blanqui, in exile like Karl Marx and Louis Blanc, forgotten like Constantin Pecueur (1801–87), or all three like Etienne Cabet (1788–1857). Some had even made their peace with the new regime, as P. J. Proudhon did with Napoleon III. The age was hardly propitious for believers in the imminent doom of capitalism. Marx and Engels, who maintained some hope of a revived revolution for a year or two after 1849, and then put their faith in the next major economic crisis (that of 1857), resigned themselves to a long haul thereafter. While it is perhaps an exaggeration to say that socialism died out completely, even in Britain, where the native socialists during the 1860s and 1870s might all have been comfortably got into one smallish hall, probably hardly anyone in 1860 was a socialist who had not already been one in 1848. We may be grateful to this interval of enforced isolation from politics, which enabled Karl Marx to mature his theories and lay the foundations of *Das Kapital*, but he himself was not. Meanwhile the surviving political organisations of, or dedicated to, the working class collapsed, like the Communist League in 1852, or subsided gradually into insignificance, like British Chartism.

However, on the more modest level of economic struggle and self-defence, working-class organisation persisted, and could not but grow. This in spite of the fact that, with the notable if partial exception of Britain, trade unions and strikes were legally prohibited almost everywhere in Europe though Friendly Societies (Mutual Aid Societies) and co-operatives – on the continent generally for production, in Britain generally shops – were considered acceptable. It cannot be said that they flourished notably: in Italy (1862) the average membership of such Mutual Aid Societies in Piedmont, where they were strongest, was a little under fifty.[5] Only in Britain, Australia and – curiously enough – the United States were trade unions of workmen of real significance, in both the latter cases largely arriving in the baggage of class-conscious and organised British immigrants.

In Britain not only the skilled craftsmen of the machine-building industries as well as the artisans of more ancient occupations, but even – thanks to the nucleus of highly skilled adult male spinners – the cotton workers maintained strong local unions, more or less effectively linked nationally, and in one or two instances (the Amalgamated Society of Engineers [1852], the Amalgamated Society of Carpenters and Joiners [1860]) financially, if not strategically, co-ordinated national societies. They formed a minority, but not a negligible one and among the skilled in some instances a majority. Moreover, they provided a base from which unionism could be readily extended. In the United States the unions were perhaps even more powerful, though they were to prove unable to withstand the impact of really rapid industrialisation towards the end of the century. However they were less powerful than in that paradise of organised labour, the Australian colonies, where the building workers actually gained the Eight Hour Day as early as 1856, soon to be followed by other trades. Admittedly nowhere was the bargaining position of the worker stronger than in this under-populated and dynamic economy in which the gold-rushes of the 1850s tempted away thousands, raising the wages of the unadventurous ones who remained.

Sensible observers did not expect this relative insignificance of the labour movement to last. Indeed from about 1860 it became clear that the proletariat was returning to the scene, with the other *dramatis personae* of the 1840s, though in a less turbulent mood. It emerged with unexpected rapidity, soon to be followed by the ideology henceforth identified with its movements: socialism. This process of emergence was a curious amalgam of political and industrial action, of various kinds of radicalism from the democratic to the anarchist, of class struggles, class alliances and government or capitalist concessions. But above all it was *international*, not merely because, like the revival of liberalism, it occurred simultaneously in various countries, but because it was inseparable from the international solidarity of the working classes, or the international solidarity of the radical left (a heritage of the period before 1848). It was actually organised as and by the International Workingmen's Association, Karl Marx's First International (1864–72). Whether it was true that 'the workingmen have no country', as the *Communist Manifesto* had put it, may be debated: certainly the organised and radical workers of both France and England were patriots in their manner – the French revolutionary tradition being notoriously nationalist (see chapter 5 above). But in an economy where the

135

factors of production moved freely even the unideological British trade unions could appreciate the need to stop employers from importing strike-breakers from abroad. For all radicals the triumphs and defeats of the left anywhere still seemed to have an immediate and direct bearing on their own. In Britain the International emerged from a combination of a revived agitation for electoral reform with a series of campaigns for international solidarity – with Garibaldi and the Italian left in 1864, with Abraham Lincoln and the North in the American Civil War (1861–5), with the hapless Poles in 1863, all of which were believed, quite correctly, to reinforce the labour movement in its least political, most 'trade unionist' form. And the mere organised contact between workers in one country and those in another could not but have repercussions on their respective movements, as Napoleon III found when he permitted the French workers to send a large delegation to London on the occasion of an international exhibition in 1862.

The International, founded in London and rapidly taken into the capable hands of Karl Marx, began as a curious combination of insular and liberal–radical British trade-union leaders, ideologically mixed but rather more left-wing French union militants, and a shadowy general staff of old continental revolutionaries of increasingly assorted and incompatible views. Their ideological battles were eventually to ruin it. Since they have tended to pre-empt the interest of many other historians, they need not detain us long here. Broadly speaking, the first major struggle, between the 'pure' (i.e. in effect liberal or liberal–radical) trade unionists and those with more ambitious perspectives of social transformation, was won by the socialists (though Marx was careful to keep the British, his main backers, out of continental battles). Subsequently Marx and his supporters confronted (and defeated) the French supporters of Proudhon's 'mutualism', militantly class-conscious and anti-intellectual artisans, and thereafter the challenge of Michael Bakunin's (1814–76) anarchist alliance, all the more formidable for operating through the highly un-anarchic methods of disciplined secret organisations, fractions, etc. (see chapter 9 below). Unable to maintain control of the International any longer, Marx quietly wrote it off in 1872 by transferring its headquarters to New York. However, by this time the back of the great working-class mobilisation, of which the International was part and to some extent co-ordinator, was broken anyway. Still, as it turned out, Marx's ideas had triumphed.

In the 1860s this was not readily predictable. There was only one Marxist, or indeed socialist, mass labour movement, that which developed in Germany after 1863. (Indeed, if we except the abortive National Labour Reform Party of the United States [1872] – a political extension of the ambitious National Labour Union [1866–72] which affiliated to the IWMA – there was only one political labour movement operating on a national scale independent of the 'bourgeois' or 'petty-bourgeois' parties.) This was the achievement of Ferdinand Lassalle (1825–65), a brilliant agitator who fell victim to a rather highly coloured private life (he died of wounds received in a duel over a woman), and who regarded himself as a follower of Marx, in so far as he followed anyone, which was not very far. Lassalle's General German Workers Association (*Allgemeiner Deutscher Arbeiterverein* [1863]) was officially radical–democratic rather than socialist, its immediate slogan being universal suffrage, but it was both passionately class-conscious and anti-bourgeois, and – in spite of its initially modest membership – organised like a modern mass party. It was not particularly welcome to Marx, who backed a rival organisation under the leadership of two more wholehearted (or at least more acceptable) disciples, the journalist Wilhelm Liebknecht and the gifted young wood-turner August Bebel. This body, based on central Germany, though officially more socialist, paradoxically followed a rather less intransigent policy of alliance with the (anti-Prussian) democratic left of the old '48ers. The Lassalleans, an almost entirely Prussian movement, though essentially in terms of a Prussian solution of the German problem. Since this was the solution which clearly prevailed after 1866, these differences, passionately felt in the decade of German unification, ceased to be significant. The Marxists (together with a Lassallean breakaway which insisted on the purely proletarian character of the movement) formed a Social Democratic Party in 1869 and eventually (in 1875) fused with – and as it turned out effectively took over – the Lassalleans in 1875, forming the powerful Social Democratic Party of Germany (SPD).

The important fact is that both movements were in one way or another linked with Marx, whom they regarded (especially after Lassalle's death) as their theoretical inspirer and *guru*. Both emancipated themselves from radical–liberal democracy and functioned as independent working-class movements. And both (under the universal suffrage given by Bismarck to north Germany in 1866 and to Germany in 1871) gained immediate mass support. The leaders of both were elected to parliament. In Barmen, the birthplace of Frederick Engels, 34 per cent voted socialist as early as 1867, 51 per cent by 1871.

But if the International did not yet inspire working-class parties of any significance (the two German ones were officially not even affiliated to it), it was associated with the emergence of labour in a number of countries in the form of a massive industrial and trade-union movement, which it systematically set out to foster, at least from 1866. How far it actually did so is not so clear. (The IWMA happened to coincide with the first international upsurge of labour struggles, some of which, like those of the Piedmontese woollen workers in 1866–7, certainly had nothing to do with it.) However, particularly from 1868 on, such struggles converged with it, since the leaders of these movements tended increasingly to be attracted to the International, or even to be militants of it already. This wave of labour unrest and strikes swept through the continent, reaching as far as Spain and even Russia: in 1870 strikes took place in St Petersburg. It gripped Germany and France in 1868, Belgium in 1869 (retaining its force for some years), Austro–Hungary shortly after, finally reaching Italy in 1871 (where it was at its peak in 1872–4) and Spain in the same year. Meanwhile the strike wave was also at its height in Britain in 1871–3.

New trade unions sprang up. They gave the International its masses: to take only the Austrian figures, its reported supporters grew from 10,000 in Vienna to 35,000 between 1869 and 1872, from 5,000 in the Czech lands to almost 17,000, from 2,000 in Styria and Carinthia to almost 10,000 in Styria alone.[6] This does not look much by later standards, but it represented a far greater power of mobilisation – unions in Germany learned to take strike decisions only in mass meetings, representing also the unorganised – and it certainly frightened governments, especially in 1871 when the peak of the International's popular appeal coincided with the Paris Commune (see chapter 9 below).

Governments and at least sections of the bourgeoisie had become aware of the rise of labour fairly early in the 1860s. Liberalism was too wedded to an orthodoxy of economic *laissez-faire* to consider policies of social reform seriously, though some of the democratic radicals, keenly aware of the danger of losing the support of the proletariat, were prepared for even this sacrifice and, in countries where 'Manchesterism' was never totally victorious, officials and intellectuals increasingly considered the need for them. Thus in Germany, under the impact of the rising socialist movement, a rather misnamed group of 'Socialist Professors' (*Kathedersozialisten*) in 1872 formed the influential Society for Social Policy (*Verein für Sozialpolitik*), which advocated social reform as an alternative to, or rather a prophylactic against, the Marxist class struggle.*

However, even those who regarded any public interference in the free market mechanism as a certain recipe for ruin were now convinced that labour organisation and activities had to be recognised if they were to be tamed. As we have seen, some of the more demagogic politicians, not least Napoleon III and Benjamin Disraeli, were keenly aware of the electoral potential of the working class. Throughout Europe in the 1860s the law was modified to permit at least some limited labour organisation and strikes; or, to be more exact, to make room in the theory of the free market for the free collective bargaining of workers. However, the legal position of unions remained highly uncertain. Only in Britain was the political weight of the working class and its movements sufficiently great – by general consent they formed the majority of the population – to produce, after some years of transition (1867–75), a virtually complete system of legal recognition, so favourable to trade unionism that periodic attempts have been made ever since to whittle away the freedom they were then granted.

The object of these reforms was plainly to prevent the emergence of labour as an independent political, and still more as a revolutionary force. This was successful in countries with already established non-political or liberal–radical labour movements. Where the power of organised labour was already strong, as in Britain and Australia, independent parties of labour were not to emerge until very much

* The term 'socialist', unlike the more inflammatory 'communist' could still be used vaguely for anyone who recommended state economic action and social reform, and was widely so used until the general rise of socialist labour movements in the 1880s.

later, and even then they remained essentially non-socialist. But, as we have seen, over most of Europe the trade-union movement emerged in the period of the International, largely under the leadership of the socialists, and the labour movement was to be politically identified with them, and more especially with Marxism. Thus in Denmark, where the International Workers' Association was formed in 1871 with the object of organising strikes and producers' co-operatives, the sections of this body, after the government had dissolved the International in 1873, formed independent unions most of which later reunited as a 'social democratic league'. This was the most significant achievement of the International. It had made labour both independent and socialist.

On the other hand, it did not make it insurrectionary. In spite of the terror it inspired among governments, the International did not plan immediate revolution. Marx himself, though no less revolutionary than before, did not consider this a serious prospect. Indeed, his attitude to the only attempt to make a proletarian revolution, the Paris Commune, was notably cautious. He did not believe it had the slightest chance of success. The best it might have achieved was to make a bargain with the Versailles government. After its inevitable end, he wrote its obituary in the most moving terms, but the object of this magnificent pamphlet (*The Civil War in France*) was to instruct the revolutionaries of the future, and in this he succeeded. However, the International, i.e. Marx, remained silent while the Commune was actually in being. During the 1860s he worked for long-term perspectives and remained modest about short term ones. He would have been content with the establishment, at least in the major industrial countries, of independent political labour movements organised (where this was legally possible) as mass movements and for the conquest of political power, and emancipated from the intellectual influence of liberal–radicalism (including simple 'republicanism' and nationalism) as well as from the kind of left-wing ideology (anarchism, mutualism, etc.) which he regarded with some justification as a hangover from an earlier era. He did not even ask for such movements to be 'Marxist'; indeed, under the circumstances, this would have been utopian, since Marx had virtually no followers except in Germany and among a few old emigrés. He did not expect capitalism either to collapse or to be in immediate danger of over-

140

throw. He merely hoped to achieve the first steps in the organisation of the armies which would wage the long campaign against the well-entrenched enemy.

By the early 1870s it looked as though the movement had failed to achieve even these modest objectives. British labour remained firmly in the tow of the liberals, its leaders too feeble and corrupt even to extort significant parliamentary representation from their now decisive electoral strength. The French movement lay in ruins as a result of the defeat of the Paris Commune, and among these ruins no signs of anything better than the obsolete Blanquism, sansculottism and mutualism could be discerned. The great wave of labour unrest broke in 1873–5, leaving behind trade unions hardly stronger, and in some instances actually weaker, than those of 1866–8. The International itself broke, having been unable to eliminate the influence of the obsolete left, whose own failure was only too evident. The Commune was dead, and the only other European revolution, that of Spain, was rapidly drawing to a close: by 1874 the Bourbons were back in Spain, postponing the next Spanish Republic for almost sixty years. Only in Germany had there been a distinct advance. Admittedly a new, as yet shadowy, perspective of revolution might be discerned in the underdeveloped countries, and from 1870 on Marx began to pin some hopes on Russia. However, the most immediately interesting of these movements, because the one most likely to shake Britain, the main bastion of world capitalism, had also collapsed. The Fenian movement in Ireland also apparently lay in ruins (see chapter 5 above).

A mood of withdrawal and disappointment pervades the final years of Marx. He wrote comparatively little,* and was politically more or less inactive. Yet we can now see that two achievements of the 1860s were permanent. There were henceforth to be organised, independent, political, socialist mass labour movements. The influence of the pre-Marxian socialist left had been largely broken. And consequently the structure of politics was to be permanently changed.

Most of these changes did not become evident until the end of the 1880s, when the International itself revived, now as a common

* The bulk of the material posthumously ordered by Engels as *Capital*, vols. II and III, and the 'Theories on Surplus Value', had actually been written before the publication of vol. I in 1867. Of Marx's major writings, apart from some letters, only the *Critique of the Gotha Programme* (1875) follows the fall of the Commune.

front of, mainly Marxist, mass parties. But even in the 1870s at least one state had to face the new problem: Germany. There the socialist vote (102,000 in 1871) began to rise again with an apparently inexorable force after a short setback: to 340,000 in 1874, to half a million in 1877. Nobody knew what to do about it. Masses who neither remained passive nor were prepared to follow the lead of their traditional 'superiors' or of the bourgeoisie, and whose leaders could not be assimilated, did not fit into the scheme of politics. Bismarck, who could play the game of Liberal parliamentarism for his own purposes as well as, indeed better than, anyone else, could think of nothing else to do except to prohibit socialist activity by law.

Chapter Seven

Losers

An imitation of European customs, including the perilous art of borrowing, has been lately affected: but, in the hands of Eastern rulers, the civilisation of the West is unfruitful; and, instead of restoring a tottering state, appears to threaten it with speedier ruin.

Sir T. Erskine May, 1877[1]

The Word of God gives no authority to the modern tenderness for human life ... It is necessary in all Eastern lands to establish a fear and awe of the Government. Then, and only then, are its benefits appreciated.

J. W. Kaye, 1870[2]

I

In that 'struggle for existence' which provided the basic metaphor of the economic, political, social and biological thought of the bourgeois world, only the 'fittest' would survive, their fitness certified not only by their survival but by their domination. The greater part of the world's population therefore became the victims of those whose superiority, economic, technological and therefore military, was unquestioned and seemed unchallengeable: the economies and states of north-western and central Europe and the countries settled by its emigrants abroad, notably the United States. With the three major exceptions of India, Indonesia and parts of North Africa few of them became or were formal colonies in the third quarter of the nineteenth century. (We may leave aside the areas of Anglo-Saxon settlement like Australia, New Zealand and Canada which, though not yet formally independent, were clearly not treated like the areas inhabited by 'natives', a term in itself neutral, but which acquired a strong connotation of inferiority.) Admittedly these exceptions were not negligible: India alone accounted for 14 per cent of the world's population in 1871. Still, the political independence of the rest counted for little. Economically they were at the mercy of capitalism,

143

in so far as they came within its reach. From a military point of view their inferiority was blatant. The gunboat and the expeditionary force appeared to be all-powerful.

In fact, they were not quite as decisive as they looked, when Europeans blackmailed feeble or traditional governments. There were plenty of what British administrators liked to call, not without admiration, 'martial races', which were quite capable of defeating European forces in pitched battles on land, though never at sea. The Turks enjoyed a well-merited reputation as soldiers, and indeed their ability not only to defeat and massacre the rebel subjects of the Sultan but to stand up to their most dangerous adversary, the Russian army, preserved the Ottoman Empire as effectively as the rivalries between the European powers, or at least slowed down its disintegration. British soldiers treated the Sikhs and Pathans in India and the Zulus in Africa, French ones the North African Berbers, with considerable respect. Again experience showed that expeditionary forces were severely troubled by consistent irregular or guerilla warfare, especially in rather remote mountainous areas where the foreigners lacked local support. The Russians struggled for decades against such resistance in the Caucasus, and the British gave up the attempt to control Afghanistan directly, and contented themselves with little more than supervising the north-western frontier of India. Lastly, the permanent occupation of vast countries by small minorities of foreign conquerors was extremely difficult and expensive, and, given the ability of the developed countries to impose their will and interests on them without it, the attempt hardly seemed worth making. Still, hardly anybody doubted that it could be done if necessary.

The greater part of the world was therefore in no position to determine its own fate. It could at best react to the outside forces which pressed upon it with increasing weight. By and large this world of the victims consisted of four major sectors. First, there were the surviving non-European empires or independent large kingdoms, of the Islamic world and Asia: the Ottoman Empire, Persia, China, Japan and a few lesser ones such as Morocco, Burma, Siam and Vietnam. The greater ones of these survived, though – with the exception of Japan which will be considered separately (see chapter 8 below) – increasingly undermined by the new forces of nineteenth-century capitalism;

PENNY POLITICAL PICTURE FOR THE PEOPLE,
WITH A FEW WORDS UPON PARLIAMENTARY REFORM.
BY THEIR OLD FRIEND, GEORGE CRUIKSHANK

1 The social order of 'the richest country in the world' symbolised in 1867

2 The aristocracy of labour: group of foremen at the International Exhibition of 186.

3 The labourer: 'Mr Ashton's ingenious steam winch' (1862) with operative

4 A musical comment on city reconstruction and building booms: Johann Strauss' 'Demolition Polka'

5 Shovel, barrow, cart and crane: building the underground railway, London 1869

The private face of the city
6   *Over London by Rail* as seen by Gustave Doré, 1872

7   Manchester, from the river Irwell, 1859

The new public face of the city: Paris, Boulevard Sébastopol

Life on the public street:
Boulevard des Italiens, Paris
1864

10 The middle-class family setting, c.1860

11 Working-class family setting, 1861

12 The social life of elegance: a Paris salon, 1867

13 School: Mr Williams' Academy – the last private school in Deptford before the Education Act of 1870

14   Working-class life idealised: *The Dinner Hour at Wigan* by Eyre Crowe (1874)

15   Working-class life in reality: view of Fore Street, Lambeth, *c.* 1860

the smaller ones were eventually occupied after the end of our period, with the exception of Siam which survived as a buffer state between British and French zones of influence. Second, there were the former colonies of Spain and Portugal in the Americas, now nominally independent states. Third, there was sub-Saharan Africa, about which little need be said since it attracted no major attention in this period. Finally, there were the already formally colonised or occupied victims, mainly Asian.

All of them faced the fundamental problem of what their attitude should be to the formal or informal conquest by the west. That the whites were too strong to be merely rejected was, alas, evident. The Maya Indians of the Yucatan jungles might attempt in 1847 to expel them, returning to their ancient ways, and actually succeeded to some extent in doing so as a result of the 'Race War' which began in 1847, until eventually – in the twentieth century – sisal and chewing-gum brought them back into the orbit of western civilisation. But theirs was an exceptional case, for Yucatan was isolated, the nearest white power (Mexico) was weak, and the British (one of whose colonies adjoined them) did not discourage their efforts. Fighting nomad raiders and mountain tribesmen might continue to keep them at bay, and imagine that the rarity with which they appeared was due to their strength rather than to their remoteness and lack of economic profitability. But for most politically organised peoples of the non-capitalist world the issue was not whether the world of white civilisation could be avoided, but how its impact was to be met: by copying it, by resisting its influence, or by a combination of both.

Of the dependent sectors of the world two had already compulsorily undergone 'westernisation' by European rule or were in the process of doing so: the former colonies in the Americas and the actual ones in various parts of the world.

Latin America had emerged from Spanish and Portuguese colonial status as an aggregate of technically sovereign states in which liberal middle-class institutions and laws of the familiar nineteenth-century pattern (both British and French) were superimposed on the institutional heritage of the Spanish and Portuguese past, notably a passionate and deep-rooted if locally coloured Roman Catholicism of the indigenous population – which was Indian, mixed and, in the

145

Caribbean zone and the coastal belt of Brazil, largely African.* The imperialism of the capitalist world was to make no such systematic attempt to evangelise its victims. These were all agrarian countries, and virtually inaccessible to a remote world market so far as they lay beyond the reach of river, seaports and mule-trains. Leaving aside the slave plantation area and the tribes of the inaccessible interiors or remote frontiers of the extreme north and south, they were inhabited primarily by peasants and cattlemen of various colours, in autonomous communities, directly enserfed by the owners of large estates or, more rarely, independent. They were ruled by the wealth of the large estate-owners, whose position was notably strengthened by the abolition of Spanish colonialism, which had attempted to maintain a certain control over them, including some protection of peasant (mainly Indian) communities. They were also ruled by the armed men whom lords of the land or anyone else could mobilise. These formed the basis of the *caudillos* who, at the head of their armies, became such a familiar part of the Latin-American political scenery. Basically the countries of the continent were almost all oligarchies. In practice this meant that national power and the national states were feeble, unless a republic was unusually small or a dictator sufficiently ferocious to instil at least temporary terror into his more remote subjects. In so far as these countries were in contact with the world economy, it was through the foreigners who dominated the import and export of their staples and their shipping (with the exception of Chile, which had a flourishing fleet of its own). In our period these were mostly the English, though some French and Americans might also be noted. The fortunes of their governments depended on their rake-off from foreign trade and their success in raising loans, once again mostly from the British.

The first decades after independence saw economic and in many areas demographic regression, with notable exceptions such as Brazil, which separated peacefully from Portugal under a local emperor and avoided disruption and civil war, and Chile, isolated in its temperate strip by the Pacific. The liberal reforms instituted by the new regimes – the largest accumulation of republics in the world –

* Cults of African origin survived in the slave areas, more or less syncretising with Catholicism, but, except in Haiti, appear not to have competed with the dominant religion.

had as yet little practical consequence. In some of the largest and subsequently most important states, such as Argentina under the dictator Rosas (1835–52), home-grown, inward-looking oligarchs, hostile to innovation, dominated. The astonishing world-wide expansion of capitalism in the third quarter of the century was to change this.

In the first place, north of the isthmus of Panama, it led to a great deal more direct interference by the 'developed' powers than Latin America had been used to since the disappearance of Spain and Portugal. Mexico, the chief victim, lost vast territories to the United States as a result of American aggression in 1846. In the second place, Europe (and to a lesser extent the United States) discovered commodities worth importing from this great undeveloped region – *guano* from Peru, tobacco from Cuba and various other areas, cotton from Brazil and elsewhere (especially during the American Civil War), coffee, after 1840 above all in Brazil, nitrates from Peru, etc. Several of these were temporary boom products, liable to decline as rapidly as they had risen: the *guano* era in Peru had hardly begun before 1848 and did not survive the 1870s. Not until after the 1870s did Latin America develop that relatively permanent pattern of products for export which was to last until the middle decades of our century, or our own day. Capital investment from abroad began to develop the infrastructure of the continent – railways, port installations, public utilities; even European immigration increased substantially, at all events into Cuba, Brazil and above all the temperate areas of the River Plate estuary.*

These developments strengthened the hands of the minority of Latin Americans devoted to the modernisation of their continent, as poor in the present as it was rich in potentiality and resources; 'a beggar sitting on a heap of gold', as an Italian traveller described Peru. The foreigners, even where actually threatening as in Mexico, seemed less of a danger than the formidable combination of native inertia represented by a traditionalist peasantry, old-fashioned backwoods lords and, above all, the church. Or rather, if these were not first overcome, the chances of standing up to the foreigners would be negligible. And they could only be overcome by ruthless modernisation and 'Europeanisation'.

* Roughly a quarter of a million Europeans settled in Brazil between 1855 and 1874, while over 800,000 went to Argentina and Uruguay in a comparable period.

The ideologies of 'progress' which gripped educated Latin Americans were not simply those of 'enlightened' Freemasonry and Benthamite liberalism, which had been so popular in the independence movement. In the 1840s various forms of utopian socialism had captured intellectuals, promising not only social perfection but economic development, and from the 1870s Auguste Comte's positivism penetrated deeply into Brazil (whose national motto is still the Comtian 'Order and Progress') and, to a lesser extent, Mexico. Still, classical 'liberalism' remained prevalent. The combination of 1848 revolution and world capitalist expansion gave the liberals their chance. They brought about the real destruction of the old colonial legal order. The two most significant – and linked – reforms were the systematic liquidation of any land tenures other than those by private property, purchase and sale (as by the Brazilian Land Law and the Colombian removal of limits on the breaking up of Indian lands, both 1850), and above all a ferocious anti-clericalism, which incidentally also sought to abolish the landholdings of the church. The extremes of anti-clericalism were reached in Mexico under President Benito Juarez (1806–72) in the Constitution of 1857, where church and state were separated, tithes abolished, priests forced to take an oath of loyalty, officials forbidden to attend religious services and ecclesiastical lands sold. However, other countries were hardly less militant.

The attempt to transform society by institutional modernisation imposed through political power failed, essentially because it could not be backed by economic independence. The liberals were an educated and urban elite in a rural continent and, in so far as they had genuine power it rested on unreliable generals and on local clans of land-owning families which, for reasons which often had only the remotest connection with John Stuart Mill or Darwin, chose to mobilise their clients on their side. Socially and economically speaking, very little had changed in the backlands of Latin America by the 1870s, except that the power of landlords had been strengthened, that of peasants weakened. And, in so far as it had changed under the impact of the intruding world market, the result was to subordinate the old economy to the demands of the import-export trade, operated through a few great ports or capitals and controlled by the foreigners or foreign settlers. The only major exception was in the lands of the

148

River Plate, where eventually massive European immigration was to produce an entirely new population with an entirely untraditional social structure. Latin America in the third quarter of the nineteenth century took to the road of 'westernisation' in its bourgeois-liberal form with greater zeal, and occasionally greater ruthlessness, than any other part of the world outside Japan, but the results were disappointing.

Leaving aside the areas inhabited by – normally fairly recent – settlers from Europe, and lacking a large native population (Australia, Canada), the colonial empires of the European powers consisted of a few regions where a majority or minority of white settlers coexisted with a fairly important indigenous population (South Africa, Algeria, New Zealand) and a larger number of regions without a significant or permanent European population at all.* 'White settler' colonies were notoriously to create the most intractable problem of colonialism, though in our period it was not of great international significance. In any case, the major problem of the indigenous populations was now to resist the advance of the white settlers and, though the Zulus, the Maori and the Berbers were formidable enough in arms, they could do no more than score local successes. The colonies of solid indigenous population raised more problems, because the scarcity of whites made it essential to use natives on a large scale to administer and overawe them on behalf of their rulers, and these had in any case to administer through the already existing local institutions, at least at the local level. In other words, they faced the dual problem of creating a body of assimilated natives to take the place of white men and of bending the traditional institutions of the countries, often far from suitable to their purposes. Conversely, the indigenous peoples confronted the challenge of westernisation as something much more complex than mere resistance.

* Miscegenation did not develop on a large scale in these areas, unlike the old pre-industrial empires – parts of which still survived (e.g. Cuba, Puerto-Rico, the Philippines), and appears, in India at least, to have been increasingly discouraged from the middle of the nineteenth century. Such groups of *mestizos* as were not simply assimilated to the 'coloured' race (as in the United States) or could 'pass' as white, were sometimes used as a caste of subaltern administrators or technicians, as in Indonesia, or India, where they monopolised the running of the railways; but in principle the line between 'white' and 'coloured' was sharp.

149

India – by far the largest colony – illustrates the complexities and paradoxes of this situation. The mere existence of foreign rule in itself posed no major problem here, for vast regions of the sub-continent had in the course of its history been conquered and re-conquered by various kinds of foreigners (mostly from central Asia) whose legitimacy had been sufficiently established by effective power. That the present rulers had marginally whiter skins than the Afghans, and an administrative language a little more incomprehensible than classical Persian raised no special difficulties; that they did not seek conversions to their peculiar religion with any great zeal (to the sorrow of missionaries), was a political asset. Yet the changes they imposed, deliberately or in consequence of their curious ideology and unprecedented economic activities, were more profound and dis-turbing than anything hitherto brought across the Khyber Pass.

Yet they were at the same time both revolutionary and limited. The British strove to westernise – even in some respects to assimilate – not only because local practices like the burning of widows (*suttee*) genuinely outraged many of them, but chiefly because of the require-ments of administration and the economy. Both also disrupted the existing economic and social structure even when this was not their intention. Thus, after long debates, T. B. Macaulay's (1800–59) famous Minute (1835) had established a purely English system of education for the few Indians in whose education and training the British Raj took any official interest, namely the subaltern adminis-trators. A small anglicised elite emerged, sometimes so remote from the Indian masses as actually to lack fluency in their own vernacular language, or anglicising their names, though even the most assimilated Indian would not be treated as an Englishman by the English.* On the other hand, the British refused or failed to westernise, both be-cause the Indians were, after all, subject peoples whose function was *not* to compete with British capitalism, because the political risks of excessive interference with popular practices were serious, and also because the differences between the ways of the British and the 190 or

* The British left, to its honour, was more egalitarian and eventually one or two Indian immigrants were actually elected to the British parliament, the first of them as a Radical member for a London constituency in 1893.

so million Indians (1871) appeared to be so great as to be virtually insurmountable, at least by tiny handfuls of British administrators. The extremely able literature produced by the men who ruled or had experience of India in the nineteenth century, and which contributed significantly to the development of the disciplines of sociology, social anthropology and comparative history (see chapter 14 below), is a series of variations on the theme of this incompatibility and impotence.

'Westernisation' was eventually to produce the leadership and the ideologies and programmes of the Indian liberation struggle, whose cultural and political leaders were to emerge from the ranks of those who collaborated with the British, benefited from their rule as a compradore bourgeoisie or in other ways, or set out to 'modernise' themselves by imitating the west. It produced the beginnings of a class of indigenous industrialists whose interests were to bring them into conflict with the metropolitan economic policy. Yet it has to be pointed out that in this period the 'westernised' elite, whatever its discontents, saw the British both as providing a model and as opening new possibilities. The anonymous nationalist in *Mukherjee's Magazine* (Calcutta 1873) was as yet an isolated figure when he wrote: 'Dazzled by the superficial lustre around them . . . the natives hitherto accepted the views of their superiors [and] rested their belief in them as it were in a commercial veda. But day by day the light of intelligence is clearing up the fog in their minds.'[3] In so far as there was resistance to the British as British, it came from the traditionalists, and even this was – with one major exception – muted in an age when, as the nationalist B. G. Tilak was later to recall, people 'were dazzled at first by the discipline of the British. Railways, Telegraph, Roads, Schools bewildered the people. Riots ceased and people could enjoy peace and quiet . . . People began to say that even a blind person can travel safely from Benares to Rameshwar with gold tied to a stick.'[4]

The major exception was the great rising of 1857–8 on the north Indian plains, known to British historical tradition as the 'Indian Mutiny', a turning-point in the history of the British administration which has been retrospectively claimed as a forerunner of the Indian national movement. It was the last kick of traditional (north) India against the imposition of direct British rule, and finally brought down the old East India Company. This curious survival of private enterprise colonialism, increasingly absorbed into the British state apparatus, was finally replaced by it. The policy of systematic annexation of hitherto merely dependent Indian territories, associated with the rule of the Viceroy Lord Dalhousie (1847–56),* and especially the annexation in 1856 of the Kingdom of Oudh, last relic of the old Mughal Empire, provoked it. The speed and tactlessness of the changes imposed, or believed to be intended, by the British, precipitated it. The actual occasion was the introduction of greased cartridges, which the soldiers of the Bengal army regarded as a deliberate provocation of their religious sensibilities. (The establishments of Christians and missionaries were among the first targets of popular fury.) Though the rising began as a mutiny of the Bengal army (those of Bombay and Madras remained quiet), it turned into a major popular insurrection in the northern plains, under the leadership of traditional nobles and princes, and an attempt to restore the Mughal Empire. That economic tensions such as those arising out of the British changes in the land tax, the main source of public revenue, played their part, is obvious, but whether these alone would have produced so enormous and widespread a revolt is doubtful. Men rose against what they believed to be the increasingly rapid and ruthless destruction of their way of life by a foreign society.

The 'Mutiny' was suppressed in a welter of blood, but it taught the British caution. For practical purposes annexation ceased, except on the eastern and western borders of the sub-continent. The large areas of India not yet taken under direct administration were left to the rule of puppet indigenous princes, controlled by the British yet officially flattered and respected, and these in turn became the pillars of the regime which guaranteed them wealth, local power and status. A marked tendency to rely on the more conservative elements in the country – landowners, and especially the powerful Moslem minority – developed, following the ancient imperial precept 'Divide and Rule'. As time went on, this shift in policy became more than a recognition of the powers of resistance by traditional India to its foreign rulers. It became a counter-weight to the slowly developing resistance of the new Indian middle-class elite – the products of

* Between 1848 and 1856 Britain annexed the Punjab, large parts of central India, parts of the west coast and Oudh, thus adding about a third to the territory directly administered by the British.

colonial society, sometimes its actual servants.* For whatever the policies of Indian empire, its economic and administrative realities continued to weaken and disrupt the forces of tradition, to strengthen the forces of innovation and to intensify the conflicts between these and the British. After the end of Company rule the growth of a new community of expatriate British, accompanied by their wives, which increasingly emphasised its separatism and racial superiority, increased social friction with the new indigenous middle strata. The economic tensions of the last third of the century (see chapter 16 below) multiplied anti-imperialist arguments. By the end of the 1880s the Indian National Congress – the main vehicle of Indian nationalism and ruling party of independent India – was already in existence. In the twentieth century the Indian masses themselves were to follow the ideological lead of the new nationalism.

III

The Indian Rising of 1857–8 was not the only mass colonial rebellion of past against present. Within the French Empire the great Algerian rising of 1871, precipitated both by the withdrawal of French troops during the Franco–Prussian War and the mass resettlement of Alsatians and Lorrainers in Algeria after it, is an analogous phenomenon. Yet, by and large, the scope for such rebellions was limited, if only because the bulk of the victims of western capitalist society were not conquered colonies but increasingly enfeebled and disrupted though nominally independent societies and states. The fortunes of two of these may be singled out in our period: Egypt and China.

Egypt, a virtually independent principality though formally still within the Ottoman Empire, was predestined for victimisation by its agricultural wealth and its strategic situation. The first of these turned it into an agricultural export economy supplying the capitalist world with wheat but especially with cotton, the sales of which expanded dramatically. From the early 1860s on it provided 70 per cent of the country's export earnings and, during the great boom of the 1860s

* The first major economic critique of British imperialism in India, R. C. Dutt's *Economic History of India* and *India in the Victorian Age*, was to be written by the Indian whose career in the British administration was the most brilliant of his or previous times. Similarly the Indian national anthem was written by an Indian functionary of the British, the novelist Bankim Chandra Chatterjee.

(when American cotton supplies were disrupted by the Civil War), even the peasants temporarily benefited from it, though half of them in Lower Egypt also acquired parasitic diseases due to the extension of perennial irrigation. This vast expansion brought Egyptian trade firmly into the international (British) system, and attracted those floods of foreign businessmen and adventurers who were only too ready to extend credit to the Khedive Ismail. The financial sense of this as of earlier viceroys of Egypt was defective, but while in the 1850s Egyptian state expenditure had only exceeded revenue by perhaps 10 per cent, between 1861 and 1871, when revenues almost trebled, expenditure averaged distinctly more than double government income, the gap being filled by some 70 million pounds in loans which left a variety of financiers, ranging from the businesslike to the shady, with distinctly satisfactory profits. By these means the Khedive hoped to turn Egypt into a modern and imperial power and to reconstruct Cairo along the lines of Napoleon III's Paris, which then provided the standard model of paradise for well heeled rulers of his kind. The second fact, the strategic situation, attracted the interests of the western powers and their capitalists, especially the British, to whose world position the country became crucial with the construction of the Suez Canal. World culture may be modestly grateful to the Khedive for commissioning Verdi's *Aïda* (1871), first performed in the Khedive's new Opera House to celebrate the opening of the Canal (1869), but the cost to his countrymen was excessive.

Egypt was thus integrated as an agrarian supplier in the European economy. The bankers, through the pashas, battened on the Egyptian people, and when Khedive and pashas could no longer pay the interest on the loans they had accepted with frivolous enthusiasm – in 1876 they totalled almost half of the actual revenue receipts for that year – the foreigners imposed control.[5] The Europeans would probably have remained content to exploit an independent Egypt, but the collapse both of the economic boom and of the administrative and political structure of the Khedive's government, undermined by economic forces and temptations its rulers could neither understand nor manage, made this difficult. The British, whose position was more powerful and whose interests were much more crucially involved, emerged as the new rulers of the country in the 1880s.

But meanwhile the unusual exposure of Egypt to the west had

created a new elite of landlords, intellectuals, civil functionaries and army officers, which led the national movement of 1879–82, directed against both the Khedive and the foreigners. In the course of the nineteenth century the old Turkish or Turko-Circassian ruling group had been Egyptianised, while Egyptians had risen to positions of wealth and influence. Arabic replaced Turkish as the official language, reinforcing the already powerful position of Egypt as a centre of Islamic intellectual life. The notable pioneer of modern Islamic ideology, the Persian Jamal ad-din Al Afghani, found an enthusiastic public among the Egyptian intellectuals during his influential stay in that country (1871–9).* The point about Al Afghani, as about his Egyptian disciples and equivalents, was that he did *not* advocate a merely negative Islamic reaction against the west. His own religious orthodoxy has been effectively questioned (he became a freemason in 1875), though he was realistic enough to know that the religious convictions of the Islamic world must not be shocked and were indeed a powerful political force. His call was for a revitalisation of Islam which would permit the Moslem world to absorb modern science and thus emulate the west; to demonstrate that Islam actually enjoined modern science, parliaments and national armies.[6] The anti-imperialist movement in Egypt looked forward and not back.

While the pashas of Egypt were imitating the tempting example of Napoleon III's Paris, the greatest of nineteenth-century revolutions was taking place in the greatest of the non-European empires, the so-called Taiping rebellion in China (1850–66). It has been ignored by euro-centric historians, though Marx at least was sufficiently aware of it to write, as early as 1853: 'Perhaps the next uprising of the people of Europe may depend more on what is now taking place in the Celestial Empire than on any other existing political cause.' It was the greatest not merely because China, more than half whose territory the Taipings controlled at one point, was even then, with perhaps 400 million inhabitants, by far the most populated state of the world, but also because of the extraordinary scale and ferocity of the civil wars to which it gave rise. Probably something like 20 million Chinese

* Al Afghani continued the cosmopolitan tradition of Islamic intellectuals in the course of a migrant life which took him from his native Iran to India, Afghanistan, Turkey, Egypt, France, Russia and elsewhere.

perished during this period. These convulsions were in important respects the direct product of the western impact on China.

Perhaps alone among the great traditional empires of the world, China possessed a popular revolutionary tradition, both ideological and practical. Ideologically its scholars and its people took the permanence and centrality of their Empire for granted: it would always exist, under an emperor (except for occasional interludes of division), administered by the scholar-bureaucrats who had passed the great national civil service examinations introduced almost two thousand years before – and only abandoned when the Empire itself was about to die in 1910. Yet its history was that of a succession of dynasties each passing, it was believed, through a cycle of rise, crisis and supersession: gaining and eventually losing that 'mandate of Heaven' which legitimised their absolute authority. In the process of changing from one dynasty to the next, popular insurrection, growing from social banditry, peasant risings and the activities of popular secret societies to major rebellion, was known and expected to play a significant part. Indeed its success was itself an indication that the 'mandate of Heaven' was running out. The permanence of China, the centre of world civilisation, was achieved through the ever-repeated cycle of dynastic change, which included this revolutionary element.

The Manchu dynasty, imposed by northern conquerors in the mid-seventeenth century, had thus replaced the Ming dynasty, which had in turn (through popular revolution) overthrown the Mongol dynasty in the fourteenth century. Though in the first half of the nineteenth century the Manchu regime still seemed to function intelligently and effectively – though it was said with an unusual amount of corruption – there had been signs of crisis and rebellion since the 1790s. Whatever else they may have been due to, it seems clear that the extraordinary increase of the country's population during the past century (whose reasons are still not fully elucidated) had begun to create acute economic pressures. The number of Chinese is claimed to have risen from round 140 million in 1741 to about 400 million in 1834. The dramatic new element in the situation of China was the western conquest, which had utterly defeated the Empire in the first Opium War (1839–42). The shock of this capitulation to a modest naval force of the British was enormous, for it

156

revealed the fragility of the imperial system, and even parts of popular opinion outside the few areas immediately affected may have become conscious of it. At all events there was a marked and immediate increase in the activities of various forces of opposition, notably the powerful and deeply rooted secret societies such as the *Triad* of south China, dedicated to the overthrow of the foreign Manchurian dynasty and the restoration of the Ming. The imperial administration had set up militia forces against the British, and thus helped to distribute arms among the civilian population. It only required a spark to produce an explosion.

That spark was provided in the shape of an obsessed, perhaps psychopathic prophet and messianic leader, Hung Hsiu Chuan (1813–64), one of those failed candidates for the imperial Civil Service examination who were so readily given to political discontent. After his failure at the examination he evidently had a nervous breakdown, which turned into a religious conversion. Around 1847–8 he founded a 'Society of those who venerate God', in Kwangsi province, and was rapidly joined by peasants and miners, by men from the large Chinese population of pauperised vagrants, by members of various national minorities and by supporters of the older secret societies. Yet there was one significant novelty in his preaching. Hung had been influenced by Christian writings, had even spent some time with an American missionary in Canton, and thus embodied significant western elements in an otherwise familiar mixture of anti-Manchu, heretico-religious and social-revolutionary ideas. The rebellion broke out in 1850 in Kwangsi and spread so rapidly that a 'Celestial Realm of Universal Peace' could be proclaimed within a year with Hung as the supreme 'Celestial King'. It was unquestionably a regime of social revolution, whose major support lay among the popular masses, and dominated by Taoist, Buddhist and Christian ideas of equality. Theocratically organised on the basis of a pyramid of family units, it abolished private property (land being distributed only for use, not ownership), established the equality of the sexes, prohibited tobacco, opium and alcohol, introduced a new calendar (including a seven-day week) and various other cultural reforms, and did not forget to lower taxes. By the end of 1853, the Taipings with at least a million active militants controlled most of south and east China and had captured Nanking, though failing –

largely for want of cavalry – to push effectively into the north. China was divided, and even those parts not under Taiping rule were convulsed by major insurrections such as those of the *Nien* peasant rebels in the north, not suppressed until 1868, the Miao national minority in Kweichow, and other minorities in the south-west and north-west.

The Taiping revolution did not maintain itself, and was in fact unlikely to. Its radical innovations alienated moderates, traditionalists and those with property to lose – by no means only the rich – the failure of its leaders to abide by their own puritanical standards weakened its popular appeal, and deep divisions within the leadership soon developed. After 1856 it was on the defensive, and in 1864 the Taiping capital of Nanking was recaptured. The imperial government recovered, but the price it paid for recovery was heavy and eventually proved fatal. It also illustrated the complexities of the western impact.

Paradoxically the rulers of China had been rather less ready to adopt western innovations than the plebeian rebels, long used to living in an ideological world in which unofficial ideas drawn from foreign sources (such as Buddhism) were acceptable. To the Confucian scholar-bureaucrats who governed the empire what was not Chinese was barbarian. There was even resistance to the technology which so obviously made the barbarians invincible. As late as 1867 Grand Secretary Wo Jen memorialised the throne warning that the establishment of a college for teaching astronomy and mathematics would 'make the people proselytes of foreignism' and result 'in the collapse of uprightness and the spread of wickedness',[7] and resistance to the construction of railways and the like remained considerable. For obvious reasons a 'modernising' party developed, but one may guess that they would have preferred to keep the old China unchanged, merely adding to it the capacity to produce western armaments. (Their attempts to develop such production in the 1860s were not very successful for this reason.) The powerless imperial administration in any case saw itself with little but the choice between different degrees of concession to the west. Faced with a major social revolution, it was even reluctant to mobilise the enormous force of Chinese popular xenophobia against the invaders. Indeed, the overthrow of the Taiping seemed politically by far its most urgent problem, and for this purpose the help of the foreigners was, if not essential, then at any rate desirable; their good-will indispensable. Thus imperial China found itself tumbling rapidly into complete dependence on the foreigners. An Anglo-Franco-American triumvirate had controlled the Shanghai customs since 1854, but after the second Opium War (1856–8) and the sack of Peking (1860) which ended with total capitulation,* an Englishman actually had to be appointed 'to assist' in the administration of the entire Chinese customs revenue. In practice Robert Hart, who was Inspector General of Chinese Customs from 1863 until 1909, was the master of the Chinese economy and, though he came to be trusted by the Chinese governments and to identify himself with the country, in effect the arrangement implied the entire subordination of the imperial government to the interests of the westerners.

In fact, when it came to the point, the westerners preferred propping up the Manchus to their overthrow, which would have produced either a militant nationalist revolutionary regime or, more likely, anarchy and a political void which the west was reluctant to fill. (The initial sympathy of some foreigners for the apparently Christian elements in the Taiping soon evaporated.) Conversely, the Chinese empire recovered from the Taiping crisis by a combination of concession to the west, a return to conservatism and a fatal erosion of its central power. The real victors in China were the old scholar-bureaucrats. Faced with mortal danger the Manchu dynasty and aristocracy drew closer to the Chinese elite, forfeiting much of their former power. The ablest of the scholar-administrators – men like Li Hung-Chang (1823–1901) – had saved the empire, when Peking had been powerless, by raising provincial armies based on provincial resources. In doing so they anticipated the later collapse of China into a collection of regions under independent 'warlords'. The great and ancient Empire of China was henceforth to live on borrowed time.

In one way or another, therefore, the societies and states which

* This time not only Britain but also France, Russia and the United States received concessions. A number of further ports were opened, foreign merchants were granted freedom of movement and immunity from Chinese law, there was to be freedom of action for foreign missionaries, free trade, including free navigation by foreigners of inland waters, heavy war indemnities, etc.

became victims of the capitalist world, with the exception of Japan (to be considered separately, see chapter 8 below), failed to come to terms with it. Their rulers and elites soon became convinced that a mere refusal to accept the ways of the white westerners or northerners was impracticable and, if practicable, would merely have perpetuated their weakness. Those in colonies conquered, dominated or administered by the west had not much choice: their fate was determined by their conquerors. The others were divided between policies of resistance and collaboration or concession, between a wholehearted 'westernisation' and some sort of reform which would allow them to acquire the science and technology of the west without losing their own culture and institutions. On the whole the former colonies of European states in the Americas opted for an unconditional imitation of the west, the chain of independent and sometimes ancient monarchies stretching from Morocco on the Atlantic to China on the Pacific, for some version of reform, when they could no longer cut themselves off completely from western expansion.

The cases of China and Egypt are, in their different ways, typical of this second choice. Both were independent states based on ancient civilisations and a non-European culture, undermined by the penetration of western trade and finance (accepted willingly or under duress), and powerless to resist the military and naval forces of the west, modest though those mobilised against them were. The capitalist powers at this stage were not particularly interested in occupying and administering either, so long as their citizens were given total freedom to do what they wanted, including extra-territorial privileges. They merely found themselves drawn into growing involvement in the affairs of such countries by the crumbling of indigenous regimes under the western impact, as well as by the rivalries between western powers. The rulers of both China and Egypt rejected a policy of national resistance, preferring – in so far as they had the option – a dependency on the west, which maintained their own political power. At this stage relatively few among those who in such countries wanted resistance through national regeneration, favoured straightforward 'westernisation'. Instead they opted for some sort of ideological reform which would allow them to embody whatever made the west so formidable in their own cultural system.

160

These policies failed. Egypt was soon under the direct control of its conquerors, China became an ever more helpless hulk on the way to disintegration. Since the existing regimes and their rulers had opted for western dependence, it is improbable that the national reformers could have succeeded, for revolution was the pre-condition for their success.* But its time had not yet come.

Thus what is today called the 'Third World' or the 'underdeveloped countries' lay at the mercy of the west, its helpless victim. But did these countries derive no compensating advantages from their subordination? As we have seen, there were those in the backward countries who believed that they did. Westernisation was the only solution, and if this meant not only learning from and imitating the foreigners but accepting their alliance against the local forces of traditionalism, i.e. their domination, then the price had to be paid. It is a mistake to see such passionate 'modernisers' in the light of later nationalist movements simply as traitors and agents of foreign imperialism. They might merely take the view that the foreigners, quite apart from their invincibility would help them to break the stranglehold of tradition, and thus allow them eventually to create a society capable of standing up to the west. The Mexican elite of the 1860s was pro-foreign because it despaired of its country.[8] Such arguments were also used by western revolutionaries. Marx himself welcomed the American victory over Mexico in the war of 1846–8, because it brought historical progress and created the conditions for capitalist development, that is to say for the eventual overthrow of capitalism. His views of the British 'mission' in India, expressed in 1853, are familiar. It was a double mission: 'the annihilation of the old Asiatic society, and the laying of the material foundations of Western society in India'. True, he believed that:

'the Indians will not reap the fruits of the new elements of society scattered among them by the British bourgeoisie, till in Great Britain itself the now ruling classes shall have been supplanted by the industrial proletariat, or till the Hindus themselves shall have grown strong enough to throw off the English yoke altogether.'

* In fact, the greatest of the old independent non-western empires were overthrown or transformed by revolution in the early twentieth century – Turkey, Iran and China.

Nevertheless, in spite of the 'blood and dirt . . . misery and degrada-tion' through which the bourgeoisie dragged the peoples of the world, he saw its conquest as positive and progressive.

Yet, whatever the ultimate prospects (and modern historians are less optimistic than the Marx of the 1850s), in the immediate present the most obvious result of western conquest was 'the loss of [the] . . . old world with no gain of a new one', which imparted 'a peculiar kind of melancholy to the present misery of the Hindu',[9] as of other peoples who were the victims of the west. The gains were hard to discern in the third quarter of the nineteenth century, the losses only too evident. On the positive side there were steamships, railways and telegraphs, small knots of western-educated intellectuals, even smaller ones of local landlords and businessmen who amassed enormous fortunes out of their control of the sources of exports and the dis-posal of foreign loans, like the *hacendados* of Latin America, or their position as middlemen for foreign business, like the *Parsi* million-aires of Bombay. There was communication – material and cultural. There was a growth of exportable production in some suitable areas, though hardly as yet on a huge scale. There was, arguably, a sub-stitution of order for public disorder, security for insecurity in some areas which came under direct colonial rule. But only the congenital optimist would argue that these outweighed the negative side of the balance-sheet at this period.

The most obvious contrast between developed and underdeveloped worlds was and still remains that between poverty and wealth. In the first, people still starved to death, but by now in what the nineteenth century regarded as small numbers: say an average of five hundred a year in the United Kingdom. In India they died in their millions – one in ten of the population of Orissa in the famine of 1865–6, anything between a quarter and a third of the population of Rajputana in 1868–70, $3\frac{1}{2}$ million (or 15 per cent of the population) in Madras, one million (or 20 per cent of the population) in Mysore during the great hunger of 1876–8, the worst up to that date in the gloomy history of nineteenth-century India.[10] In China it is not easy to separate famine from the numerous other catastrophes of the period, but that of 1849 is said to have cost nearly 14 million lives, while another 20 million are believed to have perished between 1854 and 1864.[11] Parts of Java were ravaged by a terrible famine in 1848–50. The late

1860s and early 1870s saw an epidemic of hunger in the entire belt of countries stretching from India in the east to Spain in the west.[12] The Moslem population of Algeria dropped by over 20 per cent between 1861 and 1872.[13] Persia, whose total people were estimated to number between 6 and 7 million in the mid-1870s, was believed to have lost between $1\frac{1}{2}$ and 2 million in the great famine of 1871-3.[14] It is difficult to say whether the situation was worse than in the first half of the century (though this was probably so in India and China), or merely unchanged. In any case the contrast with the developed countries during the same period was dramatic, even if we grant (as seems likely for the Islamic world) that the age of traditional and catastrophic demographic movements was already giving way to a new population pattern in the second half of the century.

In short, the bulk of the peoples in the Third World did not as yet appear to benefit significantly from the extraordinary, the unprecedented, progress of the west. If they were aware of it at all as something other than the mere disruption of their ancient ways of life, it was as a possible example rather than as a reality; as something done by and for red- and sallow-faced men in curious hard hats with cylindrical trousers who came from far countries or lived in big cities. It did not belong to their world, and most of them very much doubted whether they wanted it to. But those who resisted it in the name of their ancient ways were defeated. The day of those who resisted it with the weapons of progress itself had not yet arrived.

Chapter Eight

Winners

*What classes and strata of society will now become the real repre-
sentatives of culture, will give us our scholars, artists and poets, our
creative personalities?
Or is everything to turn into big business, as in America?*

Jakob Burkhardt, 1868–71[1]

*The administration of Japan has become enlightened and progressive:
European experience is accepted as its guide: foreigners are employed
in its service: and Eastern customs and ideas are giving way before
Western civilisation.*

Sir T. Erskine May, 1877[2]

I

Never, therefore, did Europeans dominate the world more completely
and unquestionably than in the third quarter of the nineteenth
century. To be more exact, never did white men of European descent
dominate it with less challenge, for the world of capitalist economy
and power included at least one non-European state, or rather
federation, the United States of America. The United States did not
as yet play a major part in world affairs, and thus the statesmen of
Europe paid it only intermittent attention, unless they had interests
in the two regions of the world in which it took a direct interest,
namely the American continents and the Pacific Ocean; but, with the
exception of Britain, whose perspectives were consistently global, no
other state was constantly involved in both these areas. The liberation
of Latin America had removed all European colonies from the main-
land of Central and South America, except in the Guyanas, which
provided the British with some sugar, the French with a jail for
dangerous criminals and the Dutch with a reminder of their past links
with Brazil. The Caribbean islands, omitting the island of Hispaniola
(which consisted of the Negro republic of Haiti and the Dominican
Republic, finally emancipating itself from both Spanish domination

and Haitian preponderance), remained colonial possessions of Spain (Cuba and Puerto Rico), Britain, France, the Netherlands and Denmark. Except for Spain, which hankered after a partial restoration of its American empire, none of the European states bothered about their possessions in the West Indies more than they could help. Only on the North American continent did a large European presence remain by 1875, the vast but underdeveloped and largely empty British dependency of Canada, separated from the United States by a long and open frontier running in a straight line from the borders of Ontario to the Pacific Ocean, the areas in dispute on either side of this line being peacefully – though not without hard diplomatic bargaining – adjusted, mainly in favour of the United States, in the course of the century. But for the construction of the trans-Canadian railway, British Columbia might well have been unable to resist the attraction of the Pacific states of the United States. As for the Asian shores of this ocean, only the Russian Far East of Siberia, the British colony of Hong Kong and the British foothold in Malaya marked the direct presence of the European great powers, though the French were beginning the occupation of Indochina. The relics of Spanish and Portuguese colonialism, and the Dutch in what is now Indonesia, raised no international problems.

The territorial expansion of the United States thus caused no great political stir in the chanceries of Europe. A large part of the southwest – California, Arizona, Utah and parts of Colorado and New Mexico – were ceded by Mexico in 1848–53 after a disastrous war. Russia sold Alaska in 1867: these and older western territories were transformed into states of the Union as and when they became economically sufficiently interesting or accessible: California in 1850, Oregon in 1859, Nevada in 1864, while in the Middle West Minnesota, Kansas, Wisconsin and Nebraska acquired statehood between 1858 and 1867. Beyond this American territorial ambitions did not go at this point, though the slave states of the South hankered after an extension of slave society to the large islands of the Caribbean and expressed even wider Latin-American ambitions. The basic pattern of American domination was that of indirect control, since no foreign power appeared as an effective direct challenger: weak but nominally independent governments which knew that they had to keep on the right side of the northern giant. Only at the end of the century, during the international fashion for formal imperialism, was the United States to break for a while with this established tradition. 'Poor Mexico,' President Porfirio Diaz (1828–1915) was to sigh, 'so far from God, so near to the USA', and even the Latin-American states which felt themselves to be on closer terms with the Almighty were increasingly aware that in this world Washington was what they had chiefly to keep their eye on. The occasional North American adventurer attempted to establish direct power in and around the narrow land-bridges between the Atlantic and Pacific Oceans, but nothing came of it until the Panama Canal was actually constructed, occupied by American forces in a small independent republic detached for this purpose from the larger South American state of Colombia. But this was later.

Most of the world, and especially Europe, was keenly aware of the United States, if only because during this period (1848–75) several million Europeans emigrated to it, and because its vast size and extraordinary progress rapidly made it into the technical miracle of the globe. It was, as the Americans were the first to point out, the land of superlatives. Where else could one find a city like Chicago, with a modest 30,000 inhabitants in 1850, which had become the sixth largest urban centre in the world, with more than a million inhabitants, a mere forty years later? No railroads spanned greater distances than its transcontinental lines, or were exceeded in total mileage (49,168 in 1870) by any other country. No millionaires were or seemed more dramatically self-made than those of the United States, and if they were not yet the richest of their kind – though they soon would be – they were certainly the most numerous. No newspapers were more adventurously journalistic, no politicians more flamboyantly corrupt, no country more unlimited in its possibilities.

'America' was still the New World, the open society in an open country, where the penniless immigrant could, it was widely believed, remake himself (the 'self-made man') and in so doing make a free egalitarian, democratic republic, the only one of any size and significance in the world until 1870. The image of the United States as a revolutionary political alternative to the Old World of monarchy, aristocracy and subjection was perhaps no longer as vivid as it had once been, at least outside its borders. The image of America as a place of escape from poverty, of personal hope through personal enrichment, replaced it. The New World increasingly confronted Europe not as the new society, but as the society of the newly rich.

And yet within the United States, the revolutionary dream was far from dead. The image of the republic remained that of a land of equality, democracy, perhaps above all of untrammelled, anarchic freedom, of unlimited opportunity which had as its obverse what later came to be called 'manifest destiny'.* Nobody can make sense of the United States in the nineteenth or, for that matter, the twentieth century, without an appreciation of this utopian component, though it was increasingly obscured by and transformed into a complacent economic and technological dynamism, except at moments of crisis. It was, by origin, an agrarian utopia of free and independent farmers on free land. It never came to terms with the world of great cities and great industry, and was not yet reconciled to the domination of either in our period. Even in so typical a centre of American industry as the textile town of Paterson, New Jersey, the ethos of business was not yet dominant. During the ribbon weavers' strike of 1877 the mill-owners complained bitterly, and with justification, that Republican mayor, Democratic aldermen, press, courts and public opinion failed to support them.[4]

Still, the bulk of Americans were still rural: in 1860 only 16 per cent lived in cities of eight thousand or more inhabitants. The rural utopia in its most literal form – the free yeoman on free soil – could mobilise more political power than ever, notably among the growing population of the Middle West. It contributed to the formation of the Republican Party, and not least to its anti-slavery orientation (for though the programme of a classless republic of freeholding farmers had nothing to do with slavery and little interest in the Negro, it excluded slavery). It achieved its greatest triumph in the Homestead Act of 1862, which offered any American family man over twenty-one 160 acres *gratis* of surveyed public domain after five years' continous residence, or purchase for $1·25 an acre after six months. It is hardly necessary to add that this utopia failed. Between 1862 and 1890 less than 400,000 families benefited under the Homestead Act, while the population of the United States increased by 32 million, that of the

---

* 'The Atlantic States ... are steadily renovating the Governments and the social constitutions of Europe and Africa. The Pacific States must necessarily perform the same sublime and beneficent functions in Asia' (William H. Seward, 1850).[3]

167

western states by more than 10 million. The railways alone (which received enormous grants of public land so that they might recoup the losses of construction and operation by the profits of property speculation and development) sold more land at $5 than was conveyed under the Act. The real beneficiaries of free land were speculators, financiers and capitalist entrepreneurs. In the last decades of the century little more was heard of the bucolic dream of a free yeomanry.

Whether we choose to regard this transformation of the United States as the end of a revolutionary dream or a coming of age, it happened in the third quarter of the nineteenth century. Mythology itself bears witness to the importance of this era, for the two most profound and lasting themes of American history, as enshrined in popular culture, belong to it: the Civil War and the West. Both are intimately connected, in as much as it was the opening of the West (or more exactly its southern and central parts) which precipitated the conflict between the states of the republic, the ones representing the free settlers and the rising capitalism of the North, the others the slave society of the South. It was the Kansas–Nebraska conflict of 1854, about the introduction of slavery into the Middle West, which precipitated the formation of the Republican Party. This was to elect Abraham Lincoln (1809–65) as president in 1860, an event that led to the eventual secession of the Confederate States of the South from the Union in 1861.*

The westward expansion of settlement was not new. It was merely accelerated dramatically in our period by the railroads – the first of them reached and bridged the Mississippi in 1854–6 – and by the development of California (see chapter 3 above). After 1849 'the West' ceased to be a sort of frontier of infinity and became instead a large empty space of prairie, desert and mountain, suspended between two rapidly developing areas to the east and along the Pacific. The first transcontinental lines were built simultaneously eastwards from the Pacific and westwards from the Miss ssippi and met somewhere in Utah, whither the Mormons sect had transferred their Zion from Iowa in 1847, under the mistaken impression that it lay beyond

* Virginia, North and South Carolina, Georgia, Alabama, Florida, Mississippi, Louisiana, Tennessee, Arkansas, Texas. Some border states hesitated, but did not leave the Union: Maryland, West Virginia, Kentucky, Missouri, Kansas.

the reach of the gentiles. In fact, the region between the Mississippi and California (the 'Wild West') remained pretty empty in our period; which was unlike the 'tame' or Middle West, increasingly heavily settled, cultivated and even industrialised. It has been estimated that the total labour for building farms in the whole vast area of the prairie, south-west and mountain states for the period from 1850 to 1880 was barely larger than that expended during the same period in the south-east or in the long-settled mid-Atlantic states.[5]

The prairie lands west of the Mississippi were slowly being colonised by farmers, which implied the removal (by forced transfer) of the Indians, including those already transferred there by earlier legislation, and (by massacre) of the buffalo on whom the Plains Indians lived. Their extermination began in 1867, the same year in which Congress established the major Indian reservations. By 1883 about 13 million of them had been killed. The mountains never became much of an area of agricultural settlement. They were and remained a prospectors' and miners' frontier, populated by a series of stampedes after the precious metals – mostly silver – of which the Comstock Lode in Nevada (1859) proved to be the largest. It produced $300 million in twenty years, made spectacular fortunes for half a dozen men, a score or so of lesser millionaires and a fairly large number of smaller but by contemporary standards still impressive accumulations of wealth, before it ran out, leaving behind an empty Virginia City peopled by the ghosts of Cornish and Irish miners haunting the Union Hall and Opera House of its wild prime. Similar rushes occurred into Colorado, Idaho and Montana.[6] Demographically they did not amount to much. In 1870 Colorado (admitted to statehood in 1876) had less than 40,000 inhabitants.

The south-west remained essentially cattle, i.e. cowboy, country. Thence the vast herds of longhorns – some 4 million between 1865 and 1879 – were driven to the trans-shipment points and the railheads edging westward, on their way to the giant slaughter-houses of Chicago. The traffic gave to otherwise negligible settlements in Missouri, Kansas and Nebraska, like Abilene and Dodge City, the reputation which lives in a thousand Westerns, and which has not been overlaid by the stern biblical rectitude and populist fervour of the prairie farmers.[7]

The 'Wild West' is so powerful a myth that it is difficult to analyse

169

it with any realism. Very nearly the only historically accurate fact about it that has entered general knowledge is that it lasted only a short time, its heyday falling between the Civil War and the collapse of mining and cattle booms in the 1880s. Its 'wildness' was not due to the Indians, who were ready enough to live at peace with the whites, except perhaps in the extreme south-west, where tribes like the Apache (1871–86) and the (Mexican) Yaqui (1875–1926) fought the last of several centuries' wars to maintain their independence from the white men. It was due to the institutions, or rather the absence of effective institutions, of government and law in the United States. There was no 'Wild West' in Canada, where even gold-rushes were not anarchic, and the Sioux, who fought and beat Custer in the United States before being massacred, lived quietly there. The anarchy (or, to use a more neutral term, the passion for armed self-help) was perhaps exaggerated by the dream of freedom as well as of gold which lured men to the west. Beyond the frontier of farm-settlement and city there were no families: in 1870 Virginia City had more than two men for every woman, and only 10 per cent children. It is true that the Western myth has degraded even this dream. Its heroes are more often than not desperadoes and barroom gunmen like Wild Bill Hickok who never had much to be said in their favour, rather than the unionised immigrant miners. Yet, even allowing for this, it should not be idealised. The dream of freedom did not apply to the Indians or the Chinese (who formed almost a third of the population of Idaho in 1870). In the racist south-west – Texas belonged to the Confederacy – it certainly did not apply to the Negroes. And though so much of what we regard as 'Western', from the cowboy's costume to the Spanish-based 'Californian custom' which became the effective mining law in the American mountains,[8] derived from the Mexicans, who probably also supplied more cowboys than any other single group, it did not apply to the Mexicans. It was a dream of poor whites, who hoped to replace the private enterprise of the bourgeois world by gambling, gold and guns.

If there is nothing very obscure about the 'opening of the West', the nature and origins of the American Civil War (1861–5), have led to endless dispute among historians. This centres on the nature of the slave society of the Southern states and its possible compatibility with the dynamically expanding capitalism of the North. Was it a slave society at all, given that Negroes were always in a minority even in the Deep South (apart from a few patches), and considering that the majority of slaves worked not on the classical large plantation but in small numbers on white farms or as domestics? It can hardly be denied that slavery was the central institution of Southern society, or that it was the major cause of friction and rupture between the Northern and Southern states. The real question is why it should have led to secession and civil war, rather than to some sort of formula of coexistence. After all, though no doubt most people in the North detested slavery, militant abolitionism alone was never strong enough to determine the Union's policy. And Northern capitalism, whatever the private views of businessmen, might well have found it as possible and convenient to come to terms with and exploit a slave South as international business has with the 'apartheid' of South Africa.

Of course slave societies, including that of the South, were doomed. None of them survived the period from 1848 to 1890 – not even Cuba and Brazil (see chapter 10 below). They were already isolated both physically, by the abolition of the African slave-trade, which was pretty effective by the 1850s, and, as it were, morally, by the overwhelming consensus of bourgeois liberalism which regarded them as contrary to history's march, morally undesirable and economically inefficient. It is difficult to envisage the survival of the South as a slave society into the twentieth century, any more than the survival of serfdom in eastern Europe, even if (like some schools of historians) we consider both economically viable as systems of production. But what brought the South to the point of crisis in the 1850s was a more specific problem: the difficulty of coexisting with a dynamic northern capitalism and a flood of migration into the West.

In purely economic terms, the North was not much worried about the South, an agrarian region hardly involved in industrialisation. Time, population, resources and production were on its side. The main stumbling-blocks were political. The South, a virtual semi-colony of the British to whom it supplied the bulk of their raw cotton, found free trade advantageous, whereas the Northern industry had long been firmly and militantly committed to protective tariffs, which it was unable to impose sufficiently for its desires because of

171

the political leverage of the Southern states (who represented, it must be recalled, almost half the total number of states in 1850). Northern industry was certainly more worried about a nation half-free trading and half-protectionist than about one half-slave and half-free. What was equally to the point, the South did its best to offset the advantages of the North by cutting it off from its hinterland, attempting to establish a trading and communications area facing south and based on the Mississippi river system rather than facing east to the Atlantic, and so far as possible pre-empting the expansion to the West. This was natural enough since its poor whites had long explored and opened the West.

But the very economic superiority of the North meant that the South had to insist with increasing stubbornness on its political force – to stake its claims in the most formal terms (e.g. by insisting on the official acceptance of slavery in new western territories), to stress the autonomy of states ('states' rights') against the national government, to exercise its veto over national policies, to discourage northern economic developments, etc. In effect it had to be an obstacle to the North while pursuing an expansionist policy in the West. Its only assets were political. For (given that it could not or would not beat the North at its own game of capitalist development) the currents of history ran dead against it. Every improvement in transport strengthened the links of the West with the Atlantic. Basically the railroad system ran from east to west with hardly any long lines from north to south. Moreover, the men who peopled the West, whether they came from North or South, were not slave-owners but poor, white and free, attracted by free soil or gold or adventure. The formal extension of slavery to new territories and states was therefore crucial to the South, and the increasingly embittered conflicts of the two sides during the 1850s turned mainly on this question. At the same time slavery was irrelevant to the West, and indeed western expansion might actually weaken the slave system. It provided no such reinforcement as that which Southern leaders hoped for when envisaging the annexation of Cuba and the creation of a Southern-Caribbean plantation empire. In brief, the North was in a position to unify the continent and the South was not. Aggressive in posture, its real recourse was to abandon the struggle and secede from the Union, and this is what it did when the election of Abraham

Lincoln from Illinois in 1860 demonstrated that it had lost the 'Middle West'.

For four years civil war raged. In terms of casualties and destruction it was by far the greatest war in which any 'developed' country was involved in our period, though relatively it pales beside the more or less contemporary Paraguayan War in South America, and absolutely beside the Taiping Wars in China. The Northern states, though notably inferior in military performance, eventually won because of their vast preponderance of manpower, productive capacity and technology. After all, they contained over 70 per cent of the total population of the United States, over 80 per cent of the men of military age, and over 90 per cent of its industrial production. Their triumph was also that of American capitalism and of the modern United States. But, though slavery was abolished, it was not the triumph of the Negro, slave or free. After a few years of 'Reconstruction' (i.e. forced democratisation) the South reverted to the control of conservative white Southerners, i.e. racists. Northern occupying troops were finally withdrawn in 1877. In one sense it achieved its object: the Northern Republicans (who retained the presidency for most of the time from 1860 to 1932) could not break into the solidly Democratic South, which therefore retained substantial autonomy. The South, in turn, through its block vote, could exercise some national influence, since its support was essential for the success of the other great party, the Democrats. In fact, it remained agrarian, poor, backward and resentful; the whites resenting the never-forgotten defeat, the blacks the disfranchisement and ruthless subordination reimposed by the whites.

American capitalism developed with dramatic speed and impressiveness after the Civil War, which had probably slowed its growth temporarily, though it also provided considerable opportunities for the great buccaneering business entrepreneurs aptly nicknamed 'robber barons'. This extraordinary advance forms the third great strand in the history of the United States during our period. Unlike the Civil War and the Wild West the age of the robber barons has not become part of American popular myth, except as part of the demonology of democrats and populists, but it still remains part of American reality. Robber barons are still a recognisable part of the business scene. Attempts have been made to defend or rehabilitate

173

the men who changed the vocabulary of the English language: when the Civil War broke out the word 'millionaire' was still italicised, but when the greatest robber of the first generation, Cornelius Vanderbilt, died in 1877 his wealth of 100 million dollars required the coining of a new term, 'multi-millionaire'. It has been argued that many of the great American capitalists were in fact creative innovators without whom the triumphs of American industrialisation, which are indeed impressive, would not have been achieved so rapidly. Their wealth was therefore due not to economic banditry but, as it were, to the generosity with which society rewarded its benefactors. Such arguments cannot be applied to all the robber barons, for even the mind of the apologist boggles when faced with barefaced crooks such as the financiers Jim Fisk or Jay Gould, but it would be senseless to deny that a number of the tycoons of this period made positive, and sometimes important, contributions to the development of the modern industrial economy or (what is not quite the same thing) to the operations of a system of capitalist enterprise.

However, such arguments are beside the point. They simply amount to another way of saying the obvious, namely that the nineteenth-century United States was a capitalist economy, in which money – a very great deal of money – was to be made, among other ways, by the development and rationalisation of the productive resources of a vast and rapidly growing country in a rapidly growing world economy. Three things distinguish the era of the American robber barons from the other flourishing capitalist economies of the same period, which also bred their generations of sometimes rapacious millionaires.

The first was the total absence of any kind of control over business dealings, however ruthless and crooked, and the really spectacular possibilities of corruption both national and local – especially in the post-Civil War years. There was indeed little that could be called government by European standards in the United States, and the scope for the powerful and unscrupulous rich was virtually unlimited. In fact, the phrase 'robber barons' should carry its accent on the second rather than the first word, for, as in a weak medieval kingdom, men could not look to the law but only to their own strength – and who were stronger in a capitalist society than the rich? The United States, alone among the states of the bourgeois world, was a country of private justice and private armed forces, and never more so than in our period. Between 1850 and 1889 self-appointed Vigilante squads killed 530 alleged or real lawbreakers, or six out of seven of all the victims in the entire history of this characteristic American phenomenon which stretches from the 1760s to 1909.[9]* In 1865 and 1866 *every* railroad, colliery, iron-furnace and rolling mill in Pennsylvania was granted statutory authority to employ as many armed policemen as it wished to act as they thought fit, though in other states sheriffs and other local officials had formally to appoint the members of such private police forces. And it was during this period that the most notorious of the private forces of detectives and gunmen, 'the Pinkertons', gained their shady reputation, first in the fight against criminals but increasingly against labour.

The second distinguishing characteristic of this pioneer era of American big business, big money and big power was that most of its successful practitioners, unlike so many of the great entrepreneurs of the Old World, who often seemed obsessed with technological construction as such, seemed uncommitted to any special way of making money. All they wanted was to maximise profits, though it happens that most of them met in and through the great money-maker of the age, railroads. Cornelius Vanderbilt had a mere 10–20 million dollars before he got into railroads, which brought him an extra 80–90-odd millions in sixteen years. Small wonder, when men like the California crowd – Collis P. Huntington (1821–1900), Leland Stanford (1824–93), Charles Crocker (1822–88) and Mark Hopkins (1813–78) – could unblushingly charge three times the actual cost of building the Central Pacific Railroad, and racketeers like Fisk and Gould could scoop up millions by rigged dealing and looting without actually organising the laying of a single sleeper or the departure of a single locomotive.

Few of the first-generation millionaires made their career in a single branch of activity. Huntington began by selling hardware to gold-rush miners in Sacramento. Perhaps his customers included the meat magnate Philip Armour (1832–1901) who tried his luck in the goldfields before turning to the grocery business in Milwaukee, which in turn enabled him to make a killing in pork during the Civil War. Jim Fisk was in turn circus hand, hotel waiter, pedlar and dry-goods

* Of the 326 recorded Vigilante movements, 230 occurred during this period.

salesman, before discovering the possibilities of war contracts and thereafter the stock exchange. Jay Gould was in turn cartographer and leather merchant, before discovering what could be done with railway stock. Andrew Carnegie (1835–1919) did not concentrate his energies on steel until he was almost forty. He began as a telegraphist, continued as a railway executive – his income already made from investments whose value was rapidly increasing – dabbled in oil (which was the chosen field of John D. Rockefeller, who began life as a clerk and book-keeper in Ohio), while gradually moving into the industry he was to dominate. All these men were speculators and ready to move towards the big money wherever it was. None had noticeable scruples or could afford to have in an economy and an age where fraud, bribery, slander and if necessary guns were normal aspects of competition. All were hard men, and most would have regarded the question whether they were honest as considerably less relevant to their affairs than the question whether they were smart. Not for nothing did 'Social Darwinism', the dogma that those who climbed to the top of the heap were the best, because the fittest to survive in the human jungle, become something like a national theology in the late-nineteenth-century United States.

The third characteristic of the robber barons will already be obvious, but has been overemphasised by the mythology of American capitalism: a considerable proportion of them were 'self-made men', and they had no competitors in wealth and social standing. Of course, in spite of the prominence of several 'self-made' multi-millionaires, only 42 per cent of the businessmen of our period who have entered the *Dictionary of American Biography* came from lower- or lower-middle-class backgrounds.* Most came from business or professional families. Only 8 per cent of the 'industrial elite of the 1870s' were sons of working-class fathers.[10] Still, for comparison it may be worth recalling that of the 189 British millionaires who died between 1858 and 1879 something like a minimum of 70 per cent must have been the descendants of at least one and probably several generations of wealth, over 50 per cent of them being landowners.[11] Of course America contained its Astors and Vanderbilts, inheritors of old money, and the greatest of its financiers, J. P. Morgan (1837–1913),

* Those born between 1820 and 1849 are counted. The calculation comes from C. Wright Mills.

176

was a second-generation banker whose family grew rich as one of the main intermediaries for channelling British capital to the United States. But what attracted attention were, understandably enough, the careers of young men who simply saw opportunity, seized it and fought off all challengers: men who were above all penetrated by the capitalist imperative of accumulation. The opportunities were indeed colossal for men prepared to follow the logic of profit-making rather than living, and with sufficient competence, energy, ruthlessness and greed. The distractions were minimal. There was no old nobility to tempt men into titles and the gracious life of the landed aristocrat, and politics was something to buy rather than to practise, except of course as another way of making money.

In a sense, therefore, the robber barons felt themselves to represent America as nobody else did. And they were not quite wrong. The names of the greatest multi-millionaires – Morgan, Rockefeller – entered the realm of myth, which is why, with the very different myth-names of the gunmen and marshals of the West, they are probably the only names of individual Americans of this period (other perhaps than Abraham Lincoln) which are widely known abroad, except among those who claim a special interest in the history of the United States. And the great capitalists imposed their stamp on their country. Once, said the *National Labor Tribune* in 1874, men in America could be their own rulers. 'No one could or should become their masters.' But now 'these dreams have not been realised . . . The working people of this country . . . suddenly find capital as rigid as an absolute monarchy.'[12]

II

Of all the non-European countries only one actually succeeded in meeting and beating the west at its own game. This was Japan, somewhat to the surprise of contemporaries. For them it was perhaps the least known of all developed countries, since it had been virtually closed to direct contact with the west early in the seventeenth century, maintaining only a single point of mutual observation, where the Dutch were allowed to trade on a restricted scale. By the mid-nineteenth century it seemed to the west no different from any other oriental country, or at least equally predestined by economic back-

177

wardness and military inferiority to become the victim of capitalism. Commodore Perry of the United States, whose ambitions in the Pacific extended far beyond the interests of its very active whalers (who had recently – 1851 – been the subject of the greatest work of artistic creation of nineteenth-century America, Herman Melville's *Moby Dick*), forced them to open certain ports in 1853–4 by the usual methods of naval threats. The British, and later the united western forces in 1862, bombarded them with the usual frivolity and impunity: the city of Kagoshima was attacked simply as a reprisal for the murder of a single Englishman. It hardly looked as though within half a century Japan would be a major power capable of defeating a European power in a major war singlehanded, and within three-quarters of a century it would come close to rivalling Britain's navy; still less that in the 1970s some observers would expect it to surpass the economy of the United States within a matter of years.

Historians, with the wisdom of hindsight, have perhaps been less surprised at the Japanese achievement than they might have been. They have pointed out that in many respects Japan, though entirely alien in its cultural tradition, was surprisingly analogous to the west in social structure. At all events it possessed something very like the feudal order of medieval Europe, a hereditary landed nobility, semi-servile peasants and a body of merchant-entrepreneurs and financiers surrounded by an unusually active body of crafts, based on growing urbanisation. Unlike Europe, cities were not independent nor merchants free, but the growing concentration of the nobility (the *samurai*) in cities made them increasingly dependent on the non-agricultural sector of the population, and the systematic development of a closed national economy cut off from foreign trade created a body of entrepreneurs both essential for the formation of a national market and intimately linked with the government. The Mitsui, for instance – still one of the major forces in Japanese capitalism – began as provincial brewers of *sake* (rice-wine) in the early seventeenth century, turned to money-lending and in 1673 established themselves in Edo (Tokyo) as shopkeepers, founding branches in Kyoto and Osaka. By 1680 they were what Europe would have called active on the stock exchange, shortly after they became financial agents of the imperial family and the Shogunate (the *de facto* rulers of the country) as well as of several major feudal clans. The Sumitomo, also still prominent, began in the drug and hardware trade in Kyoto and soon became great merchants and refiners in the copper business. In the late eighteenth century they acted as regional administrators of the copper monopoly and exploited mines.

It is not impossible that Japan, left to itself, might have independently evolved in the direction of a capitalist economy, though the question can never be settled. What is beyond doubt is that Japan was more willing to imitate the west than many other non-European countries and more capable of doing so. China was plainly capable of beating the westerners at their own game, at least in as much as it amply possessed the technical skills, intellectual sophistication, education, administrative experience and business capacities required for the purpose. But China was too enormous, too self-sufficient, too accustomed to considering itself the centre of civilisation for the incursion of yet another brand of dangerous and long-nosed barbarians, however technically advanced, to suggest immediately the wholesale abandonment of the ancient ways. China did not want to imitate the west. Educated men in Mexico did want to imitate liberal capitalism as exemplified by the United States, if only as a means of becoming strong enough to resist their northern neighbour. But the weight of a tradition they were too weak to break or destroy made it impossible for them to do so effectively. Church and peasantry, Indian or hispanicised in a medieval pattern, were too much for them, and they were too few. The will was greater than the capacity. But Japan possessed both. The Japanese elite knew their country to be one among many confronted by the dangers of conquest or subjection which they had faced in the course of a long history. It was (to use contemporary European phraseology) a potential 'nation' rather than an ecumenical empire. At the same time it possessed the technical and other capacities and cadres required for a nineteenth-century economy. And what is perhaps more important, the Japanese elite possessed a state apparatus and a social structure capable of controlling the movement of an entire society. To transform a country from above without risking either passive resistance, disintegration or revolution is extremely difficult. The Japanese rulers were in the historically exceptional position of being able to mobilise the traditional mechanism of social obedience for the purposes of a sudden, radical but controlled 'westernisation' with no greater

179

resistance than a scattering of *samurai* dissidence and peasant rebellion.

The problem of confronting the west had preoccupied the Japanese for some decades – certainly since the 1830s – and the British victory over China in the first Opium War (1839–42) demonstrated the achievement and possibilities of the western ways. If China itself could not resist them, were they not bound to prevail everywhere? The discovery of gold in California, that crucial event in world history in our period, brought the United States squarely into the Pacific area and Japan squarely into the centre of western attempts to 'open' its markets as the Opium War had 'opened' those of China. Direct resistance was hopeless, as the feeble attempts to organise it proved. Mere concessions and diplomatic evasions could be no more than temporary expedients. The need to reform, both by adopting the relevant techniques of the west and by restoring (or creating) the will to national self-assertion, was hotly debated among educated officials and intellectuals, but what turned it into the 'Meiji Restoration' of 1868, i.e. a drastic 'revolution from above', was the evident failure of the feudal-bureaucratic military system of the Shoguns to cope with the crisis. In 1853–4 the rulers were divided and uncertain what to do. For the first time the government formally asked for the opinions and advice of the *daimyo*, or feudal lords, most of whom favoured resistance or temporisation. In doing so it demonstrated its own inability to act effectively, and its military counter-measures were both ineffective and costly enough to strain the finances and administrative system of the country. While the bureaucracy revealed its clumsy ineffectiveness and the factions of nobles within the Shogunate competed, the second defeat of China in another Opium War (1857–8) underlined the weakness of Japan against the west. But the new concessions to the foreigners and the growing disintegration of the domestic political structure produced a counter-reaction among the younger *samurai* intellectuals, who in 1860–63 launched one of those waves of terror and assassination (against both foreigners and unpopular leaders) which punctuate Japanese history. Since the 1840s embattled patriotic activists had come together in military and ideological study both in the provinces and in certain schools of swordsmanship in Edo (Tokyo), where they came under the influence of suitable philosophers, returning to their feudal territories with the two slogans 'Expel the barbarians' and 'venerate the Emperor'. Both slogans were logical: Japan must not be allowed to fall victim to the foreigners and, given the failure of the Shogunate, it was natural that conservative attention should turn to the surviving traditional political alternative, the theoretically all-powerful but practically impotent and unimportant Imperial Throne. Conservative reform (or revolution from above) was almost bound to take the form of a restoration of imperial power against the Shogunate. The foreign reaction to the terrorism of the extremists, e.g. the British bombardment of Kagoshima, merely intensified the domestic crisis and undermined the already tottering regime. In January 1868 (following the death of the old emperor and the appointment of a new Shogun) the imperial restoration was finally proclaimed, with the forces of certain powerful and dissident provinces, and established after a brief civil war. The 'Meiji Restoration' was accomplished.

Had it consisted merely of a conservative-xenophobic reaction, it would have been comparatively insignificant. The great feudalities of west Japan, especially Satsuma and Chōshū, whose forces overthrew the old system, had traditionally disliked the House of Tokugawa which monopolised the Shogunate. Neither their power nor the militant traditionalism of the young extremists provided a programme in itself, and the men who now took over the fortunes of Japan, predominantly young *samurai* (on average just over thirty years of age in 1868) did not represent the forces of social revolution, though clearly they came to power in an epoch when economic and social tensions were increasingly acute and reflected both in a growing number of localised and not markedly political peasant risings and the emergence of middle-class and peasant activists. But between 1853 and 1868 the bulk of the surviving young *samurai* activists (several of the most xenophobic perished in the course of their terrorism) had recognised that their object, to save the country, required systematic westernisation. Several had by 1868 had contact with foreigners; some had actually travelled abroad. All recognised that preservation implied transformation.

The parallelism between Japan and Prussia has often been made. In both countries capitalism was formally installed not by bourgeois revolution but from above, by an old bureaucratic-aristocratic order

181

which recognised that its survival could not otherwise be assured. In both countries the consequent economic-political regimes retained important characteristics of the old order: an ethic of obedient discipline and respect which pervaded both the middle classes and even the new proletariat, and incidentally helped capitalism to solve the problems of labour discipline, a strong dependence of the economy of private enterprise on the help and supervision of the bureaucratic state, and not least a persistent militarism which was to make both into formidable powers in war, and an undercurrent of passionate and at times pathological extremism of the political right. Yet there are differences. In Germany the liberal bourgeoisie was strong, conscious of itself as a class and an independent political force. As the 1848 revolutions demonstrated, 'bourgeois revolution' was a genuine possibility. The Prussian way to capitalism was through the combination of a bourgeoisie reluctant to make a bourgeois revolution and a Junker state prepared to give them most of what they wanted without a revolution, for the price of preserving the political control of the landed aristocracy and the bureaucratic monarchy. The Junkers did not initiate this change. They merely (thanks to Bismarck) made sure that they would not be overwhelmed by it. In Japan, on the other hand, the initiative, the direction and the cadres of the 'revolution from above' came from sections of the feudalists themselves. The Japanese bourgeoisie (or its equivalent) played a part only in so far as the existence of a stratum of business-men and entrepreneurs made it practicable to install a capitalist economy on lines derived from the west. The Meiji Restoration cannot therefore be regarded in any real sense as a 'bourgeois revolution', however aborted, though it can be regarded as the functional equivalent of part of one.

This makes the radicalism of the changes introduced by it all the more impressive. It abolished the old feudal provinces and replaced them by a centralised state administration, which acquired a new decimal currency, a financial foundation through inflation, by means of public loans based on a banking system inspired by the American, and (in 1873) a comprehensive land tax. (It must be remembered that in 1868 the central government possessed no independent income, relying temporarily on the help of the feudal provinces, soon to be abolished, on forced loans, and on the private estates of the Tokugawa ex-Shoguns.) This financial reform implied a radical social reform, the Regulation of Landed Property (1873) which established individual and not communal liability for tax and consequently individual assignment of property rights, with the consequent right of sale. The former feudal rights, already in decline as regards cultivated land, consequently fell by the wayside. The high nobles and a few eminent *samurai* retained some mountain and forest land, the government took over former communal property, the peasants increasingly became tenants of wealthy landowners – and the nobles and *samurai* lost their economic basis. In return they received compensation and government help, but even before these proved inadequate for many of them the change in their situation was nevertheless profound. It was made even more drastic by the military reform, and especially the Military Service Law of 1873 which, on the Prussian model, introduced conscription. Its most far-reaching consequence was egalitarian, for it abolished the last vestiges of separate and higher status for the *samurai* as a class. However the resistance of both peasants and *samurai* against the new measures – there was an average of perhaps thirty peasant risings per year between 1869 and 1874 and a substantial *samurai* rebellion in 1877 – was put down without major difficulty.

It was not the object of the new regime to abolish aristocracy and class distinctions, though these were simplified and modernised. A new aristocracy was even founded. At the same time westernisation implied the abolition of old ranks, a society in which wealth, education and political influence more than birth determined status, and therefore some genuinely egalitarian tendencies: unfavourable for the poorer *samurai*, many of whom declined into common workers, favourable for the common people who were (from 1870) permitted to take family names and choose their occupation and place of residence freely. For the rulers of Japan these were, unlike western bourgeois society, not a programme in themselves, but instruments for achieving the programme of national revival. They were necessary, hence they had to be made. And they were justifiable to the cadres of the old society partly because of the enormous power of the traditional ideology of service to the state, or more concretely the need to 'strengthen the state', and made less unpalatable by the substantial openings in military, administrative, political and business careers

183

which the new Japan provided for many of them. They were resisted by the traditionalist peasants and *samurai*, especially those for whom the new Japan in effect provided no very glowing future. Nevertheless, the radicalism of the changes introduced within a matter of a few years by men formed in the old society and belonging to the proud class of its military gentry, remains an extraordinary and unique phenomenon.

The driving force was westernisation. The west clearly had the secret of success, and hence, at all costs, it must be imitated. The prospect of taking over wholesale the values and institutions of another society was perhaps less unthinkable for the Japanese, than for many other civilisations because they had already once done so – from China – but nevertheless it was an astonishing endeavour, both traumatic and problematic. For it could not be done merely by superficial, selective and controlled borrowing, especially not in a society so profoundly different in its culture from the west as the Japanese. Hence the exaggerated passion with which many champions of westernisation threw themselves into their task. To some it seemed to imply the abandonment of all that was Japanese in so far as the entire past was backward and barbaric: the simplification, perhaps even the abandonment of the Japanese language, the renovation of inferior Japanese genetic stock by miscegenation with superior western stock – a suggestion, based on the eagerly swallowed western theories of social-Darwinist racism, which actually had temporary support in the highest quarters.[13] Western costume and hair-styles, western diet (the Japanese had not hitherto eaten meat) were adopted with hardly less zeal than western technology, architectural styles and ideas.[14] Did not westernisation involve the adoption of the ideologies which were fundamental to western progress, including even Christianity? Did it not eventually imply the abandonment of all ancient institutions including the emperor?

Yet here westernisation, unlike the earlier sinification, posed a major dilemma. For 'the west' was not a single coherent system, but a complex of rival institutions and rival ideas. Which of them were the Japanese to choose? In practical terms, the choice was not difficult. The British model naturally served as a guide for railways, telegraphs, public works, the textile industry and much of business methods. The French model inspired legal reform, and initially army reform, until the Prussian model prevailed. (The navy naturally followed the British.) Universities owed much to German as well as American examples, primary education, agricultural innovation and postal services to the United States. By 1875–6, five to six hundred foreign experts, by 1890 three thousand or so, were employed – under Japanese supervision. But politically and ideologically the choice was more difficult. How was Japan to choose between the rival systems of bourgeois-liberal states – the British and French – or the more authoritarian Prusso–German monarchy? Above all, how was it to choose between the intellectual west represented by the missionaries (who had a surprising appeal to declassed and disoriented *samurai* ready to transfer their traditional loyalty from a secular lord to the Lord in heaven) and the west represented by agnostic science – by Herbert Spencer and Charles Darwin? Or between the rival secular and religious schools?

Within a couple of decades a reaction against the extremes of westernisation and liberalism had set in, partly with the help of western traditions critical of total liberalism, such as the German, which helped to inspire the constitution of 1889, mainly by a neo-traditionalist reaction which was virtually to invent a new state-religion centred on emperor-worship, the Shinto cult. It was this combination of neo-traditionalism and selective modernisation (as exemplified in the Imperial Educational Edict of 1890) which prevailed. But the tension between those for whom westernisation implied fundamental revolution and those for whom it merely meant a strong Japan, remained. The revolution was not to occur, but the transformation of Japan into a formidable modern power did. Economically the achievement of Japan still remained modest in the 1870s, and based as yet almost entirely on what amounted to an extreme economy of state-mercantilism, which contrasted oddly with the official ideology of economic liberalism. The military activities of the new army were still directed entirely against the recalcitrant fighters of the old Japan, though as early as 1873 a war against Korea was planned, and only avoided because the more sensible members of the Meiji elite believed that internal transformation must precede foreign adventure. Hence the west continued to underestimate the significance of the transformation of Japan.

Western observers could not quite understand this strange country

185

Some could see little in it except an exotic and appealing aestheticism and those elegant and subservient women who so readily confirmed both male and (so it was supposed) western superiority: the land of Pinkerton and Madame Butterfly. Others were too convinced of non-western inferiority to see anything. 'The Japanese are a happy race, and being content with little, are not likely to achieve much,' wrote the *Japan Herald* in 1881.[15] Until after the Second World War the belief that technologically the Japanese could only produce cheaper imitations of western goods formed part of white mythology. Yet there were already hard-headed observers – mainly Americans – who noted the remarkable efficiency of Japanese agriculture,* the skills of Japanese artisans, the potentialities of Japanese soldiers. As early as 1878 an American general predicted that thanks to them the country 'was destined to play an important part in the history of the world'.[17] And as soon as the Japanese proved that they could indeed win wars, the views of westerners about them became considerably less self-satisfied. But at the end of our period they were still seen chiefly as a living proof that the bourgeois civilisation of the west was triumphant and superior to all others; and at this stage the educated Japanese themselves would not have disagreed.

* By 'thrift, economy and skill in agriculture, without livestock to convert the luxuriant vegetation of the unoccupied land into manure for their tilled fields, or any system of *rotation* of *crops* . . . and unaided by mechanical appliances of any sort, the Japanese farmer produces annually from one acre of land the crops which require four seasons under their system in the United States'.[16]

Chapter Nine

Changing Society

According to [the communists]: 'From everyone according to his abilities: to everyone according to his needs.' In other words, no man is to profit by his own strength, abilities or industry; but is to minister to the wants of the weak, the stupid and the idle.

Sir T. Erskine May, 1877[1]

Government is passing from the hands of those who own something to the hands of those who own nothing, from the hands of those with a material interest in the preservation of society to those who have no concern whatever for order, stability and conservation . . . Perhaps, in the great law of terrestrial change, for our modern societies the workers are what the barbarians were for the societies of antiquity, the convulsive agents of dissolution and destruction?

The Goncourts during the Paris Commune[2]

As capitalism and bourgeois society triumphed, the prospects of alternatives to it receded, in spite of the emergence of popular politics and labour movements. These prospects could hardly have seemed less promising in, say 1872–3. And yet within a very few years the future of the society that had triumphed so spectacularly once again seemed uncertain and obscure, and movements to replace it or to overthrow it had once again to be taken seriously. We must therefore consider these movements for radical social and political change as they existed in the third quarter of the nineteenth century. This is not simply to write history with the wisdom of hindsight, though there is no good reason why the historian should deprive himself of his most powerful asset, for which any betting man and investor would give his eye-teeth, namely the knowledge of what actually happened later. It is also to write history as contemporaries saw it. The rich and powerful are rarely so self-confident that they do not fear an end to their rule. What is more, the memory of revolution was young and strong. Any person aged forty in 1868 had lived through the greatest European revolution in his late teens. Anyone aged fifty had lived through the revolutions of 1830 as a child, through those of 1848 as an adult. Italians, Spaniards, Poles and others had lived through insurrections, revolutions or events with a strong insurrectionary component, like Garibaldi's liberation of southern Italy, within the last fifteen years. We can hardly be surprised that the hope or fear of revolution was powerful and vivid.

We now know that it was not of major consequence in the years after 1848. Indeed, to write about social revolution in these decades is rather like writing about snakes in Britain: they exist, but not as a very significant part of the fauna. The European revolution, so near – perhaps so real – in the great year of hope and disappointment, disappeared from sight. Marx and Engels had, as we know, hoped for its revival in the years immediately following. They seriously looked forward to another general outbreak in the aftermath of, and as a consequence of, the global economic depression of 1857. When this did not happen, they no longer expected it within the concretely foreseeable future, and certainly not in the form of another 1848. It is, of course, quite mistaken to suppose that Marx turned into some sort of gradualist social democrat (in the modern sense of the word), or even that he expected the transition to socialism, when it occurred, to happen peacefully. Even in the countries where the workers might be able to seize power peacefully through winning elections (he mentioned the United States, Britain and perhaps the Netherlands), their seizure of power and the destruction of the old politics and institutions, which he regarded as essential, would probably, he thought, lead to violent resistance by the old rulers. And in this he was undoubtedly realistic. Governments and ruling classes might be ready to accept a labour movement which did not threaten their rule, but there was no reason whatever to suppose, especially after the sanguinary suppression of the Paris Commune, that they were ready to accept one which did.

Nevertheless, the prospects of revolution, let alone socialist revolution, in the developed countries of Europe, were no longer a matter of practical politics and, as we have seen, Marx discounted them, even in France. The immediate future in the European capitalist countries lay in the organisation of independent mass parties of the working class, whose short-term political demands were not revolutionary. When Marx himself dictated the programme of the German Social Democrats (*Gotha* [1875]) to an American interviewer, he left out the only clause which envisaged a socialist future ('the establishment of socialist production co-operatives ... under the democratic control of the working people') as a mere tactical concession to the Lassalleans. Socialism, he observed, 'will be the result of the movement. But this will be a question of time, of education, and of the development of new forms of society'.[3]

This unpredictably remote future might be brought significantly closer by developments in the margins rather than at the centre of bourgeois society. From the late 1860s on Marx began seriously to envisage this strategy of an indirect approach to the overthrow of bourgeois society, along three lines, two of which were to prove prophetic and one of which was mistaken: colonial revolution, Russia and the United States. The first of these became part of his calculations through the rise of the Irish revolutionary movement (see chapter 5 above). Britain was then decisive for the future of proletarian revolution because it was the metropolis of capital, the ruler of the world market, and at the same time 'the *only* country where the material conditions of this revolution have developed to a certain degree of maturity'.[4] Hence the chief object of the International must be to accelerate the English revolution, and the only means of doing so was to win Irish independence. Irish revolution (or more generally, the revolution of subject peoples) was envisaged not for its own sake, but as a possible accelerator of revolution in the central bourgeois countries, as the Achilles heel of metropolitan capitalism.

The role of Russia was to be perhaps more ambitious. From the 1860s, as we shall see, a Russian revolution became not merely a possibility, but a probability, perhaps even a certainty. But whereas in 1848 such a contingency would have been welcomed merely because it removed the major block in the way of the victory of a western revolution, it now became significant in its own right. A Russian revolution might actually 'give the signal to a proletarian revolution in the West, so that both complement each other' (as Marx and Engels put it in the preface to a new Russian edition of the *Communist Manifesto*).[5] Even more: it might conceivably – though Marx never fully committed himself to this hypothesis – lead to a direct transition in Russia from the communalism of the village to a communist development, by-passing the development of a mature capitalism. As Marx foresaw quite correctly, a revolutionary Russia changed the prospects of revolution everywhere.

The role of the United States was to be less central. Its chief effect was negative: to break, by virtue of its massive development, the industrial monopoly of western Europe and in particular of Britain, and to shatter, by virtue of its agrarian exports, the bases of large and small landed property in Europe. This was of course a correct assessment. But would it contribute positively to the triumph of revolution? In the 1870s Marx and Engels certainly and not unrealistically expected a crisis in the political system of the United States, as the agrarian crisis would weaken the farmers, 'the basis of the entire Constitution', and the increasing capture of politics by speculators and big business would produce a revulsion among the citizens. They also stressed the tendencies towards the formation of a mass proletarian movement. Perhaps they did not expect too much from these tendencies, though Marx expressed some optimism: in the United States 'the people is more resolute than in Europe ... Everything matures more rapidly.'[6] Still, they were mistaken to bracket Russia and the United States as the two great countries which had been omitted from the original *Communist Manifesto*: their future development was to be very different.

Marx's views carry the weight of his posthumous triumphs. At the time they represented no serious political force, though by 1875 two symptoms of his subsequent influence were already visible: a strong German Social Democratic Party and a dramatic penetration of his ideas – unexpected by him, but not in retrospect surprising – into the Russian *intelligentsia* (see p. 196 below). In the late 1860s and early 1870s the 'red doctor' was sometimes made responsible for the activities of the International (see chapter 6 above) of which he was undoubtedly by far the most formidable figure and the grey eminence. However, as we have seen, the International was not in any sense a Marxist movement, or even a movement which contained more than a handful of Marx's followers, most of them German *émigrés* of his own generation. It consisted of a jumble of left-wing groups united primarily, perhaps exclusively, by the fact that they all sought to organise 'the workers', and with substantial, though not always permanent, success. Their ideas represented both the remnants of 1848 (or even of 1789 as transformed between 1830 and 1848), some anticipations of reformist labour movements and a peculiar sub-variety of the revolutionary dream, anarchism.

In a sense all the theories of revolution at the time were, and had to be, attempts to come to terms with the experience of 1848. This applies to Marx as well as to Bakunin, to the Paris Communards as well as to the Russian populists whom we shall discuss below. One might have said that they all came out of the ferment of the years 1830–48, had not one of the pre-48 colours disappeared for good from the spectrum of the left: utopian socialism. The major utopian currents had ceased to exist as such. Saint-Simonianism had cut its links with the left. It has transformed itself into Auguste Comte's (1798–1857) 'Positivism' and into a youthful experience held in common by a group of (mainly French) capitalist adventurers. Robert Owen's (1771–1858) followers had turned their intellectual energies to spiritualism and secularism, their practical energies to the modest field of co-operative stores. Fourier, Cabet and the other inspirers of communist communities, mainly in the land of freedom and unlimited opportunities, were forgotten. Horace Greeley's (1811–72) slogan 'Go West Young Man' proved more successful than his earlier Fourierist ones. Utopian socialism did not survive 1848.

On the other hand the intellectual offspring of the Great French Revolution did. They ranged from radical democratic republicans (sometimes emphasising national liberation, sometimes their interest in social problems) to Jacobin communists of the stamp of L. A. Blanqui. This traditional left had learned and forgotten nothing. Some of its extremists in the Paris Commune could think of nothing better than to reproduce as exactly as they could the events of the Great Revolution. Blanquism, determined and conspiratorially organised, survived in France and played a crucial part in the Commune, but this was its swan song. It was never to play a significant independent role again thereafter, and was to be lost among the conflicting tendencies of the new French socialist movement.

Democratic radicalism was more resistant, because its programme provided both a genuine expression of the aspirations of 'little men' everywhere (shopkeepers, teachers, peasants), an essential component of the aspirations of the workers, and a convenient appeal for liberal politicians asking for their votes. Liberty, equality and fraternity may not be precise slogans, but poor and modest people confronted with rich and powerful ones know what they mean. Even

191

when the official programme of democratic radicalism was realised, in a republic based on universal equal unconditional suffrage, as in the United States,* the need for 'the people' to exercise real power against the rich and the corrupt, kept democratic passion alive. But, of course, democratic radicalism was a reality hardly anywhere else, even in the modest field of local government.

And yet by this period radical democracy itself was no longer a revolutionary slogan in itself, but rather a means, though not an automatic means, to an end. The revolutionary republic was the 'social republic', the revolutionary democracy 'social democracy' – the title increasingly adopted by the Marxist parties. This was not quite so obvious among the primarily nationalist revolutionaries, such as the Mazzinians in Italy, since the winning of independence and unification (on a basis of democratic republicanism) would, they believed, somehow solve all the other problems. The real nationalism was automatically both democratic and social, and if it was not, it was not real. But even the Mazzinians did not disclaim social liberation, and Garibaldi actually declared himself a socialist, whatever he meant by that. After the disappointments of unification or republicanism, the cadres of the new socialist movement were to emerge from among the former radical republicans.

Anarchism, though it can be traced back to the revolutionary ferment of the 1840s, is much more clearly a product of the period after 1848, or more precisely of the 1860s. Its two political founders were P.-J. Proudhon, a self-educated French printer and voluminous writer, who took practically no part in political agitation, and Michael Bakunin, a peripatetic Russian aristocrat, who plunged into it at every opportunity.† Both, from an early stage, attracted the unfavourable attention of Marx, and, though admiring him, returned his hostility. Proudhon's unsystematic, prejudiced and profoundly non-liberal theory – he was both anti-feminist and anti-semitic, and has been claimed by the extreme right – is not of great interest in itself, but it contributed two themes to anarchist thought: a belief in small mutually supporting groups of producers instead of dehuman-

* Male suffrage: no country as yet seriously considered citizen rights for women, though militants in the United States, where Victoria Woodhull actually stood for President in 1872, had begun seriously to campaign for it.

† An intellectual pedigree for anarchism can be drawn up, but it has little bearing on the development of the actual anarchist movement.

ised factories, and a hatred of government as such, *any* government. These appealed strongly to independent small craftsmen, skilled but relatively autonomous workers resisting proletarianisation, to men who had not forgotten a peasant or small-town provincial childhood in the growing cities, to regions on the margins of developed industrialism. It was to such men and in such regions that anarchism made its strongest appeal: it was among the Swiss village watchmakers of the 'Jura Federation' that the most devoted anarchists of the First International were to be found.

Bakunin added little to Proudhon as a thinker, except an unquenchable passion for actual revolution – 'the passion for destruction', he said, 'is at the same time a creative passion' – an ill-advised enthusiasm for the revolutionary potential of criminals and the socially marginal, a real sense of the peasantry and some powerful intuitions. He was not much of a thinker at all, but a prophet, an agitator and – in spite of the disbelief of anarchists in disciplined organisation, that foreshadowing of the tyranny of the state – a formidable conspiratorial organiser. As such he spread the anarchist movement in Italy, Switzerland and (through disciples) Spain, and organised what turned out to be the disruption of the International in 1870–72. And as such he virtually created an anarchist movement, for the (French) Proudhonists as a body were little more than a rather undeveloped form of trade unionism, mutual aid and co-operation, and politically not in themselves very revolutionary. Not that anarchism was a major force by the end of our period. But it had established some foundations in France and French Switzerland, some nuclei of influence in Italy, and above all it has made startling progress in Spain, where both the artisans and workers of Catalonia and the rural labourers of Andalusia welcomed the new gospel. There it merged with the home-grown belief that villages and workshops could manage perfectly well if the superstructure of the state and the rich was simply removed, and that the ideal of a country constituted of autonomous townships was easily realisable. Indeed the 'cantonalist' movement during the Spanish Republic of 1873–4 actually tried to realise it, and its leading ideologist, F. Pi y Margall (1824–1901), was to be adopted into the anarchist pantheon together with Bakunin, Proudhon – and Herbert Spencer.

For anarchism was both a revolt of the pre-industrial past against the present, and a child of that present. It rejected tradition, though the intuitive and spontaneous nature of both thought and movement caused it to retain – perhaps even to emphasise – a number of traditional elements such as anti-semitism or more generally xenophobia. Both occur in Proudhon and Bakunin. At the same time it passionately hated religion and churches, and hailed the cause of progress, including science and technology, or reason, and, perhaps above all, of 'enlightenment' and education. And since it rejected any authority, it found itself curiously converging with the ultra-individualism of the *laissez-faire* bourgeois, who also did so. Ideologically Spencer (who was to write *Man against the State*) was as much an anarchist as Bakunin. The only thing anarchism did not represent was the future, about which it had nothing to say except that it couldn't happen until after the revolution.

Anarchism is of no great political significance (outside Spain), and concerns us chiefly as a distorting mirror of the age. The most interesting revolutionary movement of the age was a very different one: Russian populism. It was not then and never became a mass movement, and its most dramatic acts of terrorism, culminating in the assassination of Tsar Alexander II (1881) occurred after the end of our period. But it is the ancestor both of an important family of movements in the backward countries of the twentieth century and of Russian bolshevism. It provides a direct link between the revolutionism of the 1830s and 1840s and that of 1917 – a more direct link, one might argue, than the Paris Commune. Moreover, because it was a movement composed almost wholly of intellectuals in a country in which all serious intellectual life was political, it was immediately projected on the screen of global literature through the Russian writers of genius who were its contemporaries: Turgenev (1789–1871) and Dostoievsky (1821–81). Even western contemporaries soon heard about 'the Nihilists', and confused them with Bakuninite anarchism. This was comprehensible, since Bakunin dabbled in Russian as in all other revolutionary movements and got himself temporarily mixed up with a genuinely Dostoievskyan figure (life and literature being very close in Russia), the young advocate of an almost pathological belief in terror and violence, Sergei Gennadevich Nechaev. But Russian populism was by no means anarchist.

That Russia 'ought to' have a revolution was not seriously questioned by anyone in Europe from the most moderate liberals to the left. Its political regime, a straightforward autocracy under Nicholas I (1825–55) was patently an anachronism and could not, in the long run, be expected to last. It was maintained in power by the absence of anything like a strong middle class and above all by the traditional loyalty or passivity of the backward and largely servile peasantry, who accepted the rule of the 'gentry' because it was God's will, because the tsar represented Holy Russia, and also because they were largely left in peace to conduct their own modest affairs by means of the powerful village communities, to whose existence and significance both Russian and foreign observers drew attention from the 1840s. They were not contented. Quite apart from their poverty and coercion by the lords, they never accepted the gentry's right to landed estates: the peasant belonged to the lord, but the land belonged to the peasants for they alone tilled it. They were merely inactive or impotent. If they were to shake off their passivity and rise, it would go hard with the tsar and the ruling classes of Russia. And if their unrest were to be mobilised by the ideological and political left, the result would not be a mere repetition of the great risings of the seventeenth and eighteenth century – that 'Pugachevshchina' which haunted Russian rulers – but a social revolution.

After the Crimean War a Russian revolution no longer seemed merely desirable, but became increasingly probable. This was the major innovation of the 1860s. The regime which, however reactionary and inefficient, had hitherto appeared internally stable and externally powerful, both immune to continental revolution in 1848 and in a position to march its armies against it in 1849, was now revealed as internally unstable and externally rather weaker than had been supposed. Its key weaknesses were both political and economic, and the reforms of Alexander II (1855–81) could be seen as symptoms rather than as remedies of these weaknesses. In fact, as we shall see (in chapter 10 below), the emancipation of the serfs (1861) created the conditions for a revolutionary peasantry, while the administrative, judicial and other reforms of the tsar (1864–70) failed to remove the weakness of the tsarist autocracy, or indeed to compensate for the traditional acceptance it was now in the process of losing. Revolution in Russia was no longer a utopian prospect.

Given the feebleness of the bourgeoisie and (at this stage) of the new industrial proletariat, only one exiguous but articulate social stratum existed which could 'carry' political agitation, and in the 1860s it acquired both self-consciousness, an association with political radicalism and a name: the *intelligentsia*. Its very exiguity probably helped this group of persons with a higher education to feel itself a coherent force: even in 1897 the 'educated' consisted of no more than a hundred thousand men and somewhat over six thousand women in all Russia.[7] The numbers were tiny, though increasing rapidly. Moscow in 1840 had possessed little more than 1,200 educators, doctors, lawyers and persons active in the arts in all, but by 1882 it sheltered 5,000 teachers, 2,000 doctors, 500 lawyers and 1,500 in 'the arts'. But what is significant about them is that they joined neither the ranks of the business classes, which in the nineteenth century hardly required academic qualifications anywhere outside Germany, except perhaps as a certificate of social advancement, nor the only major employer of intellectuals, the bureaucracy. Of the 333 St Petersburg graduates in 1848–50 only ninety-six entered the civil service.

Two things distinguished the Russian *intelligentsia* from the other strata of intellectuals: recognition as a special social group, and a political radicalism which was socially rather than nationally orien- ted. The first distinguished it from the western intellectuals, who were readily absorbed into the prevailing middle classes and into the pre- vailing liberal or democratic ideology. Apart from the literary and artistic *bohème* (see chapter 15 below), a licensed or at least tolerated sub-culture, there was no significant group of dissidents, and bohe- mian dissidence was only marginally political. Even the universities, so revolutionary up to and in 1848, became politically conformist. Why indeed should intellectuals be otherwise in the age of bourgeois triumph? The second distinguished it from the intellectuals of the emergent European peoples, whose political energies were taken up almost exclusively with nationalism, i.e. with the struggle to construct a liberal bourgeois society of their own into which they could be integrated. The Russian *intelligentsia* could not follow the first path, since Russia was patently not a bourgeois society, and the tsarist system made even moderate liberalism a slogan of political revolu- tion. Tsar Alexander II's reforms in the 1860s – the liberation of the serfs, **the** judicial and educational changes and the establishment of some local government for the gentry (the *zemstvos* of 1864) and the towns (1870) – were too hesitant and limited to mobilise the potential enthusiasm of reformers permanently, and in any case this reforming phase was short-lived. Nor did they follow the second path, not so much because Russia was already an independent nation or because they lacked national pride, but because the slogans of Russian nationalism – Holy Russia, pan-Slavism, etc. – were already pre-empted by tsar, church, and all that was reactionary. Tolstoi's (1828–1910) Pierre Bezuhov, in some ways the most Russian of the characters in *War and Peace*, was obliged to seek cosmopolitan ideas, even to defend Napoleon the invader, because he was not content with Russia as it was; and his spiritual nephews and grandsons, the *intelligentsia* of the 1850s and 1860s, were forced to do the same.

They were – as natives of what was *par excellence* the backward country of Europe they had to be – modernisers, i.e. 'westernisers'. Yet they could not be *only* 'westernisers', because western liberalism and capitalism at the time provided no viable model for Russia to follow, and because the only potentially revolutionary mass force in Russia was the peasantry. The result was 'populism', which briefly held this contradiction in a tense balance. In doing so 'populism' illuminates much about the revolutionary movements of the Third World in the mid-twentieth century. The rapid progress of capitalism in Russia after our period, which implied the rapid growth of an organisable industrial proletariat, appeared to overcome the uncertainties of the populist era, and the collapse of the heroic phase of populism – roughly from 1868 to 1881 – encouraged theoretical reappraisals. The Marxists, who emerged out of the ruins of populism, were, at least in theory, pure westernisers. Russia, they argued, would go the same way as the west, generating the same forces of social and political change – a bourgeoisie which would establish a democratic republic, a proletariat which would dig its grave. But even some Marxists soon became aware – during the 1905 revolution – that this prospect was unreal. The Russian bourgeoisie would be too weak to play its historic role, and the proletariat, backed by the irresistible force of the peasantry, would overthrow both tsarism and an immature and doomed Russian capitalism, led by 'the professional revolutionaries'.

The populists were modernisers. The Russia of their dreams was new – a Russia of progress, science, education and revolutionised production – but socialist and not capitalist. Yet it was to be based on the most ancient and traditional of popular Russian institutions, the *obshchina* or village commune, which would thus become the direct parent of and model for socialist society. Time and again the populist intellectuals of the 1870s asked Marx, whose theories they made their own, whether he thought this was possible, and Marx wrestled with this attractive but by his theories implausible proposition, concluding hesitantly that perhaps it might be. On the other hand, Russia must reject the traditions of western Europe – including the patterns of its liberalism and democratic doctrines – because Russia lacked such traditions. For even the one aspect of populism which had the most direct apparent links with the western revolutionism of the period 1789–1848 was in a sense different and new.

The men and women who now banded together in secret conspiracies to overthrow tsarism by insurrection and terror were more than the heirs of the Jacobins or the professional revolutionaries who descended from them. They were to break all links with existing society to devote their lives totally to 'the people' and its revolution, to penetrate among the people and express its will. There was an unromantic intensity, a totality, of self-sacrifice about their dedication which had hardly any parallel in the west. They were closer to Lenin than to Buonarroti. And they found their first cadres, like so many later revolutionary movements, among the students, especially the new and poor students who now entered the universities, no longer confined to the children of the nobility.

The activists of the new revolutionary movement were indeed 'new' people rather than children of the nobility. Of 924 persons imprisoned or exiled between 1873 and 1877, only 279 came from noble families, 117 from non-noble officials, 33 from merchants; 68 were Jews, 92 came from what may best be described as the urban petty-bourgeoisie or modest city folk (*meshchane*), 138 were nominal peasants – presumably from similar urban milieus – and no less than 197 were children of priests. The number of girls among them was particularly striking. No less than 15 per cent of the 1,600 or so propagandists arrested in the same years were women.[8] The movement initially oscillated between an anarchising small-group terrorism (under the influence of Bakunin and Nechaev) and the advocates of mass political education among 'the people'. But what eventually prevailed was the rigidly disciplined and centralised secret conspiratorial organisation of Jacobin-Blanqui affinity, elitists in practice whatever its theory, which anticipated the bolsheviks.

Populism is significant not for what it achieved, which was hardly anything, nor for the numbers it mobilised, which hardly exceeded a few thousand. Its significance lies in the fact that it marks the start of a continuous history of Russian revolutionary agitation which, within fifty years, was to overthrow tsarism and install the first regime in world history dedicated to the construction of socialism. They were symptoms of the crisis which, between 1848 and 1870, rapidly – and for most western observers unexpectedly – transformed tsarist Russia from an unshakable pillar of world reaction into a clay-footed giant, certain to be overthrown by revolution. But they were more than this. They formed, as it were, the chemical laboratory in which all the major revolutionary ideas of the nineteenth century were tested, combined and developed into those of the twentieth century. No doubt this is due to some extent to the good fortune – the reasons for which are quite mysterious – that populism coincided with one of the most brilliant and astonishing outbursts of intellect and cultural creation in the world's history. Backward countries seeking to break through to modernity are normally derivative and unoriginal in their ideas, though necessarily not so in their practice. Often enough they have little discrimination in their borrowing: Brazilian and Mexican intellectuals took uncritically to August Comte,[9] Spanish ones at this very period to an obscure and second-rate German philosopher of the early nineteenth century, one Karl Krause, whom they made into a battering-ram of anti-clerical enlightenment. The Russian left was not merely in touch with the best and most advanced thought of the time, and made it its own – students in Kazan were reading Marx even before *Capital* had been translated into Russian – but almost immediately transformed the social thinking of the advanced countries themselves, and were recognised as capable of doing so. Some of its great names retain a primarily national reputation – N. Chernishevsky (1828–89), V. Belinsky (1811–48), N. Dobrolyubov (1836–61), even, in a way, the splendid Alexander Herzen (1812–70). Others merely transformed – though perhaps a decade or two later – the sociology, anthropology and historiography of western countries, for example P. Vinogradov (1854–1925) in Britain, V. Lutchisky (1877–1949) and N. Kareiev (1850–1936) in France. Marx himself immediately appreciated the intellectual achievement of his Russian readers, and not only because they were his earliest intellectual public.

We have so far considered the social revolutionaries. What of the revolutions? The greatest one of our period was virtually unknown to most observers, and certainly unconnected with the revolutionary ideologies of the west: the Taiping (see chapter 7 above). The most frequent, those of Latin America, appeared to consist mainly of pronunciamentos (military coups) or regional secessions which did not noticeably change the complexion of their countries, so much so that the social component in some of them was generally overlooked. The European ones were either failures, like the Polish insurrection of 1863, absorbed by moderate liberalism, like Garibaldi's revolutionary conquest of Sicily and south Italy in 1860, or of purely national significance, like the Spanish revolutions of 1854 and 1868–74. The first of these Spanish revolutions was, like the Colombian revolution of the early 1850s, an afterglow of the outbreaks of 1848. The Iberian world was habitually out of phase with the rest of Europe. The second seemed to nervous contemporaries, in the midst of political unrest and the International, to presage a new round of European revolutions. But there was to be no new 1848. There was only the Paris Commune of 1871.

The Paris Commune was, like so much of the revolutionary history of our period, important not so much for what it achieved as for what it forecast; it was more formidable as a symbol than as a fact. Its actual history is overlaid by the enormously powerful myth it generated, both in France itself and (through Karl Marx) in the international socialist movement; a myth which reverberates to this day, notably in the Chinese People's Republic.[10] It was extraordinary, heroic, dramatic and tragic, but in terms of hard fact it was a brief, and in the opinion of most serious observers doomed, insurrectionary government of the workers in a single city, whose major achievement was that it actually was a *government*, even though it lasted less than two months. Lenin, after October 1917, was to count the days until the date when he could triumphantly say: we have lasted longer than the Commune. Yet historians should resist the temptation to diminish it retrospectively. If it did not threaten the bourgeois order seriously, it frightened the wits out of it by its mere existence. Its life and death were surrounded by panic and hysteria, especially in the international press, which accused it of instituting communism, expropriating the rich and sharing their wives, terror, wholesale massacre, chaos, anarchy and whatever else haunted the nightmares of the respectable classes – all, needless to say, deliberately plotted by the International. More to the point, governments themselves felt the need to take action against the international threat to order and civilisation. Apart from the international collaboration of policemen and a tendency (regarded as more scandalous then than it would be today) to deny fugitive Communards the protected status of political refugees, the Austrian Chancellor – backed by Bismarck, not a man given to panic reactions – suggested the formation of a capitalists' counter-International. Fear of revolution was a major factor in the construction of the Three Emperors' League of 1873 (Germany, Austria, Russia), which was seen as a new Holy Alliance 'against European radicalism that has been threatening all thrones and institutions',[11] though the rapid decline of the International had made this object less urgent by the time it was actually signed. The significant fact about this nervousness was that what governments now feared was not social revolution in general, but *proletarian* revolution. Marxists, who have seen the International and the Commune essentially as a proletarian movement, were thus at one with the governments and 'respectable' public opinion of the time.

And indeed the Commune was a *workers'* insurrection – and if the word described men and women 'halfway between "people" and "proletariat"' rather than factory workers, it would also fit the activists of labour movements elsewhere at this period.[12] The 36,000 arrested Communards were virtually a cross-section of popular labouring Paris: 8 per cent white-collar workers, 7 per cent servants, 10 per cent small shopkeepers and the like, but the rest overwhelmingly workers – from the building trades, the metal trades, general labouring, followed by the more traditional skilled crafts (furniture, luxury articles, printing, clothing), which also provided a disproportionate number of the cadres;* and of course the ever-radical shoemakers.

* Thirty-two per cent of the arrested printers in the National Guard were officers or non-commissioned officers, 19 per cent of the woodworkers, but only 7 per cent of the building workers.

But was the Commune a *socialist* revolution? Almost certainly yes, though its socialism was still essentially the pre-1848 dream of self-governing co-operative or corporative units of producers, now also appealing for radical and systematic government intervention. Its practical achievements were far more modest, but that was hardly its fault.

For the Commune was a beleaguered regime, the child of war and the siege of Paris, the response to capitulation. The advance of the Prussians in 1870 broke the neck of Napoleon iii's empire. The moderate republicans who overthrew him continued the war half-heartedly and then gave up, realising that the only resistance that remained possible implied a revolutionary mobilisation of the masses, a new Jacobin and social republic. In Paris, besieged and abandoned by its government and bourgeoisie, effective power had in any case fallen into the hands of the mayors of the *arrondissements* (districts) and the National Guard, i.e. in practice the popular and working-class quarters. The attempt to disarm the National Guard after the capitulation which provoked the revolution took the form of the independent municipal organisation of Paris (the 'Commune'). But the Commune was almost immediately itself besieged by the national government (now situated at Versailles) – the surrounding and victorious German army refraining from intervention. The two months of the Commune were a period of almost unbroken war against the overwhelming forces of Versailles: hardly a fortnight after its proclamation on 18 March it had lost the initiative. By 21 May the enemy had entered Paris and the final week merely demonstrated that the working people of Paris could die as hard as they had lived. The Versaillais lost perhaps 1,100 in killed and missing, and the Commune had also executed perhaps a hundred hostages.

Who knows how many Communards were killed during the fighting? Thousands were massacred after it: the Versaillais admitted to 17,000, but the number cannot be more than half of the truth. Over 43,000 were taken prisoner, 10,000 were sentenced, of whom almost half were sent to penal exile in New Caledonia, the rest to prison. This was the revenge of the 'respectable people'. Henceforth a river of blood ran between the workers of Paris and their 'betters'. And henceforth also the social revolutionaries knew what awaited them if they did not manage to maintain power.

202

Part Three

Results

Chapter Ten

The Land

As soon as the Indian earns three reales *a day, he will never work more than half the week, so that he will still have the same nine* reales *he gets at present. When you have changed everything, you will have to return to where you started: to freedom, to that true freedom which wants neither taxes nor regulations nor measures to develop agriculture: to that marvellous* laissez-faire *which is the last word of political economy.*

A Mexican landowner, 1865[1]

The prejudice which used to operate against all the popular classes still exists against the peasants. They do not receive the education of the middle class: hence their differences, the lack of esteem for the countryman, his vigorous desire to escape from the oppression of this contempt. Hence the decadence of old customs, the corruption and deterioration of our race.

A Mantua newspaper, 1856[2]

I

In 1848 the population of the world, even of Europe, still consisted overwhelmingly of countrymen. Even in Britain, the first industrialised economy, city-dwellers did not outnumber country-dwellers until 1851, and then only just (51 per cent). Nowhere else except in France, Belgium, Saxony, Prussia and the United States did more than one in ten of the population live in cities of 10,000 and over. By the middle and late 1870s this situation had been substantially modified, but with few exceptions the rural population still largely prevailed over the urban. So, for by far the greater part of humanity, the fortunes of life still depended on what happened to and on the land.

What happened on the land depended partly on economic, technical and demographic factors which, allowing for all local peculiarities and lags, operated on the scale of the globe, or at least of large geographical-climatic zones, and on institutional factors (social, political, legal, etc.) which differed much more profoundly, even when the general trends of world development operated through them. Geographically the North American prairies, the South American pampas, the steppes of south Russia or of Hungary were quite comparable: great plains in the more or less temperate zone, suited to the large-scale cultivation of cereals. All of them indeed developed what was, from the point of view of the world economy, the same kind of agriculture, becoming massive exporters of grain. Socially, politically and legally there was a very large difference between the American plains, largely unoccupied except by hunting Indian tribes, and the European ones, long if thinly settled by an agricultural population; between the free farmer–settlers of the New World and the serf peasants of the Old, between the forms of peasant liberation after 1848 in Hungary and those after 1861 in Russia, between the large ranchers or estate owners of Argentina and the noble landlords and gentry of eastern Europe, between the legal systems, the administration, the land policies of the various states involved. For the historian it is equally illegitimate to overlook what they had in common as it is to neglect the differences.

What a growing part of agriculture all over the world had in common was subjection to the industrial world economy. Its demands multiplied the commercial market for agricultural products – mostly foodstuffs and the raw materials of the textile industry, as well as some industrial crops of lesser importance – both domestically, through the rapid growth of cities, and internationally. Its technology made it possible to bring hitherto unexploitable regions effectively within the range of the world market by means of the railway and the steamer. The social convulsions which followed the transfer of agriculture to a capitalist, or at least a large-scale commercialised pattern, loosened the traditional ties of men to the land of their forefathers, especially when they found they owned none of it, or too little to maintain their family. At the same time the insatiable demand of new industries and urban occupations for labour, the growing gap between the backward and 'dark' country and the advancing city and industrial settlement, attracted them away. During our period we see the simultaneous and enormous growth of trade in agricultural produce, a remarkable extension of the area in agricultural use, and – at least in the countries directly affected

206

by world capitalist development – a major 'flight from the land'.

For two reasons this process became particularly massive during the third quarter of the nineteenth century. Both are aspects of that extraordinary widening and deepening of the world economy which forms the basic theme of world history at this period. Technology made possible the opening of geographically remote or inaccessible areas to export production, most notably the plains of the central United States and of south-eastern Russia. In 1844–53 Russia exported about 11·5 million hectolitres of grains per year, but in the second half of the 1870s between 47 and 89 million. The United States, which had exported negligible quantities in the 1840s – perhaps 5 million hectolitres – now sold abroad more than 100 million.[3] At the same time we find the first attempts to develop certain overseas areas as specialist producers of such exports to the 'developed' world – indigo and jute in Bengal, tobacco in Colombia, coffee in Brazil and Venezuela, not to mention cotton in Egypt, etc. These replaced or supplemented the now traditional export crops of the same kind – the declining sugar from the Caribbean and Brazil, cotton from the southern states of America, whose trade was at least temporarily wrecked by the Civil War of 1861–5. On the whole, with certain exceptions – such as Egyptian cotton and Indian jute – these economic specialisations did not prove to be permanent, or else, where permanent, they did not develop on any scale comparable to that of the twentieth century. The lasting pattern of this world-market agriculture did not establish itself until the period of the imperialist world economy of 1870–1930. Boom products rose and fell; areas which provided the main body of such exports in our period were later to stagnate or abandon them. Thus, if Brazil was already the major producer of coffee, the state of São Paulo, which is predominantly identified with this crop in our century, as yet harvested only about a quarter of the production of Rio and at most a fifth of the entire country; about half the production of Indonesia and only about twice as much as Ceylon, where the development of tea-culture was still so negligible that exports were not separately registered until the second half of the 1870s, and then in tiny quantities.

Still, a major international trade in agricultural produce was now in being, normally – for obvious reasons – leading to extreme specialisation or even monoculture in the exporting regions. Technology made it possible, for after all the major means of transporting bulk produce over long land distances, the railroad, was hardly available before the 1840s. At the same time technology visibly followed demand, or sought to anticipate it. This was most evident on the wide plains of the south-western United States and several parts of South America, where cattle multiplied virtually without human effort, herded by *gauchos, llaneros, vaqueros* and cowboys, and called loudly to all profit-minded citizens for means of converting it into money. Texas drove some beasts to New Orleans and after 1849 to California, but it was the promise of the great north-eastern market which urged ranchers to explore those long routes which have become part of the heroic romance of the 'Wild West', linking the remote south-west with the slowly approaching railheads and through them with the giant transport centre of Chicago, whose stockyards were opened in 1865. They came each year in tens of thousands before the Civil War, in hundreds of thousands for the twenty years after it, until the completion of the railway network and the advance of the plough on the prairies brought the classical period of the 'Wild West' (which was essentially a cattle economy) to an end in the 1880s. Meanwhile another method of utilising livestock was explored: the preservation of slaughtered meat, by the traditional methods of salting and drying, by some sort of concentration (Liebig's meat extract began to be produced in the River Plate states in 1863), by canning and finally by the decisive device of refrigeration. However, though Boston received some refrigerated meat in the late 1860s, and London a little from Australia from 1865, the trade did not really develop until after the end of our period. It is no accident that its two great American pioneers, the packing tycoons Swift and Armour, did not establish themselves in Chicago until 1875.

The dynamic element in agricultural development was thus demand: the ever-growing demand for food of the urban and industrial parts of the world, the ever-growing demand of the same sectors for labour and, linking the two, the boom economy which raised the standards of consumption of the masses and thus their *per capita* demand. For with the construction of a genuinely global capitalist economy new markets sprang from nowhere (as Marx and Engels noted), while old ones grew dramatically. For the first time since the

Industrial Revolution, the capacity of the new capitalist economy to give employment caught up with its capacity to multiply production (see chapter 12 below). In consequence, to take one example, the British *per capita* consumption of tea trebled between 1844 and 1876, and the *per capita* consumption of sugar rose from *c.* 17 to *c.* 60 lbs in the same period.[4]

World agriculture thus increasingly divided into two parts, one dominated by the capitalist market, national or international, the other largely independent of it. This does not mean that nothing was bought and sold in the independent sector, still less that the agricultural producers in it were self-sufficient, though it is probable that a rather high proportion of peasant agriculture was consumed on the peasant holding, or within the narrow limits of a local system of exchange, if only because the food demands of the small cities in so many areas could be supplied from within a radius of little more than one or two dozen miles. Still, there is a substantial difference between the sort of agricultural economy in which sales to the wider world are marginal or optional, and the sort whose fortunes depend on them; between – to put it another way – those haunted by the spectre of a bad harvest and consequent famine, and those haunted by its opposite, overproduction or sudden competition and a collapse of prices. By the 1870s sufficient of world agriculture was in the second position to make agrarian depression both world-wide and politically explosive.

Economically the traditional sector of agriculture was a negative force: it was immune to the fluctuations of the great markets or, if not, it resisted their impact as best it could. Where it was strong, it kept men and women on the land, in so far as the land could give them a living, or sent its excess population along the well-beaten traditional tracks of seasonal migration, like those which took the smallholders of central France to and from the building sites of Paris. In extreme cases it might actually be beyond the range of townsmen's knowledge. The murderous droughts of the *sertão* of north-eastern Brazil brought a periodic exodus of starveling backwoodsmen, as scrawny as their scrub cattle; the news that the drought was over took them back again, to the dry, cactus-riddled landscape where no 'civilised' Brazilian went, unless on a military expedition against some wild-eyed back-country messiah. There were areas in the Carpathians, in the Balkans, in the western marches of Russia, in Scandinavia and Spain – to confine ourselves only to the most developed continent – where the world economy, and hence the rest of the modern world, material or mental, meant little enough. As late as 1931 the inhabitants of Polesia, when asked by the Polish census officials about their nationality, quite failed to understand the question. They answered 'We are from hereabouts' or 'We are locals'.[5]

The market-sector was more complex, since its fortunes depended both on the nature of the market, or in some cases of its mechanism of distribution, on the degree of specialisation of the producers, and on the social structure of agriculture. At one extreme, there might be the virtual monoculture of the new agricultural areas, imposed by their orientation towards a remote world market, and intensified, if not created, by the characteristic mechanism of foreign merchant firms in the great port cities which controlled this export trade – the traditional Greeks who ran the Russian corn trade through Odessa, the Bunges and Borns from Hamburg who were about to fulfil the same function for the River Plate countries from Buenos Aires and Montevideo. Where such exports were produced by large estates, as was usual in tropical plantations (sugar, cotton, etc.), almost invariable with overseas cattle and sheep-ranching, though rather less common with tillage crops, the pattern of specialisation was complete. Incidentally, in such cases identity of interest produced a close symbiosis between the large producers – where they happened to be natives and not themselves foreigners – the great trading houses and compradore interests of the export/import ports, and the policies of the states representing the European markets and suppliers. The slave-owning aristocracy of the Southern United States, the *estancieros* of Argentina, the great wool-ranchers of Australia, were as enthusiastically devoted to free trade and foreign enterprise as the British, on whom they depended, since their incomes depended exclusively on the free sale of the produce of their estates, in return for which they were more than ready to accept any non-agricultural products which their customers exported. Where crops were sold both by large estates and small farmers or peasants, the situation was more complex, though in peasant economies, for obvious reasons, the proportion of the crop which came on the world market – i.e. which

210

was not consumed by the producers – from large estates was normally much larger than that which came from the peasant holdings.

At the other extreme, the growth of urban areas multiplied the demand for a variety of different foodstuffs, in whose production the sheer size of the farming unit gave no special advantages, at any rate compared with those to be drawn from intensive cultivation and from the natural protection of high transport costs and defective technology. Those who produced staple grains might have to worry about the competition of national or world markets which hardly troubled those who sold dairy products, eggs, vegetables, fruit or even fresh meat – or any other perishable commodity which could not be transported over large distances. The great agrarian depression of the 1870s and 1880s was thus essentially a depression of the staple national and international food-crops. Mixed farming, peasant agriculture, especially that of commercially-minded rich peasants, could flourish in such situations.

This was one reason why the predictions of ruin which were made for the peasantry failed at this stage even to look like coming true in some of the most industrialised and developed countries. It was easy to establish that a peasant unit was unviable below a certain minimum size of holding and resources, which varied with soil, climate and type of production. It was much harder to show that the economy of large estates was superior to that of medium or even small units, especially when most of the labour demands of such units could be met by the virtually unpaid labour of large peasant families. The peasantry was constantly eroded by the proletarianisation of those whose holdings were too small to support them, or the emigration of those extra mouths which demographic growth multiplied, and which could not be fed on the family's land. Much of it was always poor, and the sector of smallholders or dwarf peasants undoubtedly tended to increase. But, whatever their importance in economic terms, the number of middling peasant holdings not only maintained itself, but even increased sometimes.*

* In Rhineland and Westphalia, where the number of dwarfholdings fell dramatically and that of smaller holdings (1·25–7·5 hectares) noticeably between 1858 and 1878, the number of large peasants grew a little. Because of the disappearance of so many of the smaller ones – presumably into industry – they now formed more than half of the total, where previously they had formed only a third. In Belgium the number of all holdings increased from 1846 to the crisis of

The growth of the capitalist economy transformed agriculture by its massive demand. It is thus not surprising that our period saw an increase in the amount of land put to agricultural use, not to mention the even greater increase in output through improved productivity. What is not generally recognised is how vast this extension of agricultural land was. Taking the statistically available world as a whole, between 1840 and 1880 the area under crops rose by half, or from *c.* 500 to *c.* 750 million acres.[7] Half of this increase occurred in America, where the farmed area trebled in this period (it quintupled in Australia and grew two-and-a-half times in Canada). There it chiefly took the form of a simple geographical advance of agriculture into the interior. Between 1849 and 1877 wheat production was pushed forward about nine degrees of longitude in the United States, mainly during the 1860s. It is, of course, worth remembering that the region west of the Mississippi was still comparatively un-developed. The very fact that the 'log-cabin' has become the symbol of the pioneer farmer indicates this: on the great prairies timber was not so plentiful.

However, though less immediately visible for being distributed among and around the cultivated area, the figures for Europe are in their way even more startling. Sweden more than doubled its crop area between 1840 and 1880, Italy and Denmark expanded it by more than half, Russia, Germany and Hungary by about a third.[8] Much of this came from the abolition of fallow, much from the farming of what had hitherto been moor, heath or marsh, much, unfortunately, from the destruction of woodlands. In southern Italy and its islands about 600,000 hectares of trees – or about a third of the modest total still standing in those desiccated landscapes – disappeared between 1860 and 1911.[9] In a few favoured regions, including Egypt and India, large-scale irrigation works were also of significance, though a simple and fervent faith in technology produced disastrous and unforeseen side effects, then as now.[10] Only in Britain had the new agriculture already conquered the whole country. There the area under crops grew by less than 5 per cent.

the 1870s, but even in 1880 it was estimated that 60 per cent of the area in agri-cultural use was farmed by peasants (holding from 2 to 50 hectares), while large-scale enterprise and dwarfholdings divided the rest in about equal proportions. In these characteristically industrial countries peasant agriculture plainly held its own.[6]

It would be tedious to multiply the statistics of growing agricultural output and productivity. What is more interesting is to discover how far these were due to industrialisation, and used the same methods and technology as were transforming industry. Before the 1840s the answer would have been: to a very small extent. Even during our period a great part of agriculture was conducted in ways which would have been quite familiar a hundred, even two hundred years earlier, which was natural since striking results could still be achieved by generalising the best methods known to pre-industrial farming. The virgin lands of America were cleared with fire and axe, as in the middle ages; explosives for removing tree-stumps were at best ancillary. The drainage ditches were dug with spades, the ploughs drawn by horses or oxen. For productivity the substitution of the iron for the wooden plough, or even – a neglected but important development – of the scythe for the sickle, were more important than the application of steam power, which never found the basic labours of the farm congenial, since it was largely immobile. Harvesting was the main exception, for it consisted of a series of standardised operations requiring very large temporary inputs of labour – and with the growing shortage of labourers its cost, always high, rose sharply. Threshing machines spread where grain was harvested in developed countries. The major innovation – reaping, harvesting and mowing machines – were confined largely to the United States, where labour was short and fields were large. But in general the application of ingenuity and inventiveness to agriculture did rise strikingly. In 1849–51 an annual average of 191 agriculture patents were taken out in the United States; in 1859–61, 1,282; in 1869–71, no less than 3,217.[11]

Yet, all in all, farming and the farm remained visibly what they had always been in most parts of the world: more prosperous in the developed areas, and hence investing more heavily in improvements, buildings, etc., more businesslike in many places, but not transformed out of recognition. Even industry and its technology were unobtrusive outside the New World. The mass-produced ceramic drainpipes, which were perhaps its most important contribution to agriculture, were buried, the wire-netting and barbed wire which was to take over from walls, hedges and wooden fencing, confined to the ranges of Australia and the United States, corrugated iron hardly yet emancipated from the railroads in connection with which it had been developed. Still, industrial production now contributed seriously to agricultural capital, and so, through the (largely German) science of organic chemistry, did modern science. Artificial fertilisers (potash, nitrates) were not yet used on a large scale: Chilean nitrate imports to Britain had not reached 60,000 tons by 1870. On the other hand, a huge trade developed, to the temporary benefit of the finances of Peru and the permanent profit of some British and French firms, in the natural fertiliser *guano*, of which some 12 million tons were exported between 1850 and 1880, when the *guano* boom collapsed; a trade unthinkable before the era of global mass transportation.[12]*

II

The economic forces moving agriculture in those areas where it was accessible to change were those of expansion. Yet over most of the world it inevitably came up against social and institutional obstacles which prevented or inhibited it, and in so doing also stood in the way of the other great task which capitalist – or indeed any – industrial development set its landed sector. For its function in the modern economy was not merely to supply food and raw material in rapidly growing quantities, but also to provide a – indeed *the* – most important reservoir of labour power for the non-agricultural occupations. Its third great function, that of providing the capital for urban and industrial development itself, it could hardly help fulfilling in agrarian countries, where there were few other sources of revenue for governments and the rich; though it might fulfil it inefficiently and inadequately.

The obstacles came from three sources: the peasants themselves, their social, political and economic superiors, and the entire weight of institutionalised traditional societies, of which pre-industrial agriculture was both the heart and the main body. All three were the predestined victims of capitalism, though, as we have seen, neither the peasantry nor the country-based social hierarchy which rested on its backs were in any immediate danger of collapse. At the very least, all three of these linked phenomena were theoretically

* *Guano* exports began in 1841 and reached £600,000 by 1848. They averaged 2·1 million pounds sterling per year in the 1850s, 2·6 millions in the 1860s, declining thereafter.

incompatible with capitalism, and therefore tended to enter into collision with it.

For capitalism the land was a factor of production and a commodity peculiar only by its immobility and limited quantity, though, as it happens, the great opening of new lands at this period made these limitations appear relatively insignificant for the time being. The problem of what to do about those who happened to own this 'natural monopoly', thus levying a toll on the rest of the economy, therefore seemed relatively manageable. Agriculture was an 'industry' like any other, to be conducted on sound profit-maximising principles, the farmer an entrepreneur. The rural world as a whole was a market, a source of labour, and a source of capital. In so far as its obstinate traditionalism prevented it from doing what political economy required, it had to be made to.

There was no possible way of reconciling such a view with that of peasants or landlords, for whom land was not merely a source of maximisable income but the framework of life; with that of social systems, for which the relations of men to the land and to each other in terms of the land were not, as it were, optional, but obligatory. Even at the level of government and political thinking, where the 'laws of economics' might be increasingly accepted, the conflict was stark. Traditional landlordism might be economically undesirable, but was it not the cement which held together a social structure which might otherwise collapse into anarchy and revolution? (The British land policy in India was to come to grief over this dilemma.) Economically it might be simpler if there was no peasantry, but was not its sturdy conservatism a guarantee of social stability, as its sturdy and numerous progeny were the backbone of most government's armies? At a time when capitalism was evidently ruining its working classes, could a state afford to do without a reservoir of healthy countrymen from which to recruit the towns?*

* 'The . . . peasantry [*Bauernstand*] forms the physically soundest and strongest part of the population, from which the cities, in particular, have constantly to be recruited,' wrote J. Conrad, expressing a widespread continental opinion. 'It forms the core of the army . . . Politically its settled character and attachment to the soil make it the foundation of a prospering rural community . . . The peasantry has at all times been the most conservative element of the state . . . Its appreciation of property, its love of the native soil makes it into the natural enemy of urban revolutionary ideas and a firm bulwark against social-democratic efforts. It has therefore been rightly described as the firmest pillar of every sane state, and with the rapid growth of large cities, its significance as such increases.'[13]

215

Nevertheless, capitalism could not but undermine the agrarian bases of political stability, especially on the margins of, or within the dependent periphery of, the developed west. Economically, as we have seen, the transition to market production, and especially export monoculture, both disrupted traditional social relations and de-stablised the economy. Politically 'modernisation' implied, for those who wanted to undertake it, a frontal collision with the main support of traditionalism, the agrarian society (see chapters 7 and 8 above). The ruling classes of Britain, where pre-capitalist landlords and peasants had disappeared, and of Germany and France, where a *modus vivendi* with the peasantry was established on the basis of a flourishing, and where necessary protected, home market, could rely on the loyalty of the countryside. But elsewhere they could not. In Italy and Spain, in Russia and the United States, in China and Latin America, it was more likely than not to be a region of social ferment and occasional explosion.

For one reason or another three types of agrarian enterprise were under particular pressure: the slave plantation, the serf estate and the traditional non-capitalist peasant economy. The first was liquidated within our period by the abolition of slavery in the United States and in most parts of Latin America, except Brazil and Cuba where its days were numbered. It was officially abolished there in 1889. For practical purposes by the end of our period chattel slavery had retreated to the more backward parts of the Middle East and Asia, where it no longer played a significant agricultural role. The second was formally liquidated in Europe between 1848 and 1868, though the situation of the impoverished and especially the landless peasantry in regions of large estates in southern and eastern Europe often remained semi-servile, in as much as it remained subject to over-whelming non-economic coercion. Where peasants have inferior legal and civil rights to those enjoyed by the rich and powerful, in fact, whatever the theory, they can be coerced non-economically, and on Wallachian, Andalusian or Sicilian estates they were. Compulsory labour services in many Latin-American countries were not abolished, and indeed intensified, so that we can hardly speak of a general liquidation of serfdom there.* However, it seems increasingly to have

* The persistence of such obligations (variously described by local terms such as *yanaconas, huasipungos,* etc.) must not be confused with functionally similar

216

been confined to Indian peasants exploited by non-Indian landlords. The third maintained itself, as we have seen.

The reasons for this wholesale liquidation of pre-capitalist (i.e. non-economic) forms of agrarian dependency are complex. In some cases political factors were obviously decisive. In the Habsburg Empire in 1848, as in Russia in 1861, it was not so much the unpopularity of serfdom among the peasantry which determined emancipation, undoubted though this was, as the fear of a non-peasant revolution which might acquire decisive force by mobilising peasant discontent. Peasant rebellion was a constant possibility, as demonstrated by the agrarian risings in Galicia in 1846, in southern Italy in 1848, in Sicily in 1860, and in Russia in the years after the Crimean War. But it was not the blind peasant rebellions themselves which frightened governments – they were short-lived and would be put down with fire and sword even by liberals, as in Sicily[14] – but the mobilisation of peasant unrest behind a political challenge to the central authority. The Habsburgs thus tried to isolate the various movements of national autonomy from their peasant base, and the Russian tsar did the same in Poland. Without the support of the peasantry the liberal-radical movements were insignificant in agrarian countries, or at least manageable. Both Habsburgs and Romanovs knew this and acted accordingly.

However, insurrection and revolution, whether by peasants or others, explain little more than the timing of some cases of serf emancipation, and nothing about the abolition of slavery. For unlike serf insurrection, slave rebellion was relatively uncommon – nowhere more so than in the United States[15] – and never in the nineteenth century considered a very serious political threat. Was the pressure to abolish serfdom and slavery then economic? Certainly to some extent. It is all very well for modern econometric historians to argue retrospectively that slave or serf agriculture was actually more profitable or even more efficient than agriculture manned by free labour.*

---

arrangements such as debt bondage, any more than the importation of indentured labour must be confused with slavery. Both assume the abolition of formal slavery and serfdom and seek to recreate it within the framework of a technically 'free' contract.

* The argument has been elaborately made for slavery, though not so far to the same extent for serfdom.[16]

This is perfectly possible, and the arguments are indeed strong, though the matter is the subject of impassioned debate among mathematically minded historians as well as among others. However, it is undeniable that contemporaries, operating with contemporary methods and criteria of accountancy, believed that it was inferior, though of course we cannot tell how far the very justified horror of slavery or serfdom biased their calculations. Still, Thomas Brassey the railway entrepreneur, speaking with the voice of business common sense, observed of serfdom that the crop yield in servile Russia was half that in England and Saxony and less than in any other European country, and of slavery that it was 'obviously' less productive than free labour and more expensive than people thought, bearing in mind the cost of purchase or of rearing and maintenance.[17] The British consul in Pernambuco (admittedly reporting to a passionately anti-slavery government) reckoned that the employer of slaves lost 12 per cent in interest which the capital spent on their purchase would otherwise have earned. Mistaken or not, such views were common outside the ranks of slave-owners.

Indeed, slavery was patently on the decline, and not for humanitarian reasons either, though the effective ending of the international slave-trade by British pressure (Brazil resigned itself to abolition in 1850) clearly cut the supply of slaves and raised their price. The import of Africans into Brazil dropped from 54,000 in 1849 to virtually zero in the mid-1850s. The internal slave-trade, though much used in abolitionist arguments, seems to have played no major role. Still, the shift from slave to non-slave labour was striking. By 1872 the free coloured population in Brazil was almost three times as large as the slave population, and even among pure Negroes the two groups were almost equal in number. In Cuba by 1877 the number of slaves had halved, from 400,000 to about 200,000.[18] Possibly even in the most traditional area of slave cultivation, sugar, the mechanisation of sugar-mills from the mid-century diminished the need for labour in processing the product, though in booming sugar economies like Cuba it produced a corresponding rise in the demand for field-hands. However, given the increasing competition of European beet-sugar and the extremely high labour-component in the production of cane-sugar, the pressure to lower labour costs was considerable. Could the slave-plantation economy bear the double cost of investing heavily

218

in both mechanisation and slave workers? Such calculations encouraged the substitution (at least in Cuba) of slaves not so much by free labour as by indentured labour, from among the Maya Indians of Yucatan, victims of the Race War (see chapter 7 above) or from newly opened China. However, there seems no doubt that slavery as a mode of exploitation was on the decline in Latin America, even before it was abolished, and that the economic case against this form of labour appeared increasingly strong after 1850.

As for serfdom, the economic case against it was both general and specific. In general terms it seemed clear that the prevalence of tied peasants inhibited the development of industry, which was regarded as requiring free labour. The abolition of serfdom would therefore be a necessary precondition of free labour mobility. Moreover, how could serf agriculture be economically rational since, to quote a Russian defender of serfdom in the 1850s, it 'precludes the possibility of establishing the cost of production with any accuracy'.[19] It also precluded adequate rational adjustment to the market.

More specifically, both the development of a home market for a variety of foodstuffs and agrarian raw materials, and of an export market – mainly for grain – undermined serfdom. In the northern part of Russia, never very suited to extensive grain farming, peasant farms displaced estate production of hemp, flax and other intensive crops, while handicrafts provided a further market for the peasantry. The number of serfs performing labour services, always a minority, fell. It paid landlords to commute services to market-oriented money-rents. In the empty south, where virgin steppe country turned into livestock ranges and thereafter wheat lands, serfdom was of no great significance. What landlords needed for the booming export economy was better transport, credit, free labour and even machines. Serfdom survived in Russia, as in Rumania, chiefly in areas of grain production with a dense peasant population, where landlords could either compensate for their competitive weakness by raising labour services, or alternatively hope by the same method temporarily to cut themselves in cheaply on the grain export market.

However, the abolition of unfree labour cannot be analysed simply in terms of economic calculation. The forces of bourgeois society were opposed to slavery and serfdom not simply because they believed them to be economically undesirable, nor for moral reasons, but because they seemed incompatible with a market society based on the free pursuit of individual interest. Conversely slave-owners and self-lords on the whole stood by the system because it seemed to them the very foundation of their society and their class. They might actually find it impossible to conceive of themselves without the slaves or serfs who defined their status. The Russian landlords did not and could not revolt against the tsar, who alone provided them with some legitimation against a peasantry profoundly convinced that the land belonged to him who laboured it, but also of their hierarchic subordination to the representatives of God and the emperor. But they opposed emancipation fairly solidly. It was imposed from outside or above and by superior force.

Indeed, had abolition/emancipation been the product of economic forces alone, it would hardly have produced such unsatisfactory results in both Russia and the United States. The areas in which slavery or serfdom had been of marginal importance or genuinely 'uneconomic' – e.g. northern and southern Russia or the border states and the south-west in the United States – adjusted readily to its liquidation. But in the core areas of the old system the problems were much less tractable. Thus in the purely Russian 'black earth' provinces (as distinct from the Ukraine and the steppe frontier) capitalist agriculture was slow to develop, labour dues remained prevalent in the late 1880s, while the expansion of tillage (at the expense of meadows and pastures and at the cost of reinforcing the old three-field system) lagged far behind the southern grain lands.* In short, the purely economic benefits of ending the economy of physical coercion remained debatable.

In the former slave economies this cannot be explained on political grounds, since the South was conquered and the old plantation aristocracy was at least temporarily powerless, though it soon returned. In Russia the interests of the landlord class were, of course, carefully considered and safeguarded. The problem here is rather why emancipation produced an agrarian solution satisfactory to neither gentry, peasantry nor to the prospects of a genuinely capitalist agriculture. In both areas the answer depends on what is the best

* The average increase in arable acreage in the black soil zone between the 1860s and 1880s was about 60 per cent. In the southern Ukraine, the lower Volga, the North Caucasus and Crimea it doubled, but in Kursk, Ryazan, Orel and Voronezh (between 1860 and 1913) it only rose by less than a quarter.[20]

form of agriculture, and especially of large-scale agriculture, under capitalist conditions.

There are two major variants of capitalist agriculture, which Lenin called respectively the 'Prussian' and the 'American' way: large estates operated by capitalist landlord-entrepreneurs with hired labour, and independent commercial farmers of varying sizes also operating with hired labour where necessary, though on a much smaller scale. Both imply a market economy but, whereas even before the triumph of capitalism most large estates operated as productive units exist to sell a large proportion of their output,* most peasant holdings, being primarily self-sustaining, do not. Hence the advantage of large estates and plantations for economic development had lain not so much in their technical superiority, higher productivity, economies of scale, etc., as in their unusual capacity to generate agricultural surpluses for the market. Where the peasantry remained 'pre-commercial,' as in large parts of Russia and among the emancipated slaves of the Americas who returned to subsistence peasant agriculture, the estate retained this advantage, but without the physical compulsions of serfdom or slavery it now found it more difficult to obtain labour, unless the former slaves or serfs were landless or so short of land as to be obliged to become hired labourers – and unless there was no more attractive labour for them to take.

But on the whole the ex-slaves did acquire some land (though not the '40 acres and a mule' of which they dreamed) and the ex-serfs, though losing some of the land to the lords, especially in the regions of expanding commercial agriculture,† remained peasants. Indeed, the survival – even reinforcement – of the old village commune with its arrangements for periodic equitable land-redistribution safeguarded the peasant economy. Hence the increasing tendency for landlords to develop share-cropping tenancies to replace the crops they themselves found it more difficult to produce. Whether the Russian landed aristocracy, landowners like Tolstoi's Count Rostov or Chekhov's Mme Ranevskaya, were more or less likely to transform themselves into agrarian capitalist entrepreneurs than *ante-*

* An estate need not be a productive unit, of course. It may perfectly well collect income in the form of rent in money or in kind or a share of the crop from the landholders on it who constitute the actual units of production.

† But in the central black earth region, the losses were small, or there were even gains.

bellum plantation owners, dreaming of Walter Scott, is quite another question.

But, if the 'Prussian' road was not taken systematically, neither was the 'American' road. This depended on the creation of a large body of enterprising peasant farmers growing essentially cash crops. A minimum size of holding was necessary for this, varying with circumstances. Thus, in the southern United States after the Civil War, 'experience has shown that it is doubtful whether any profit can accrue to a cultivator whose annual crop is less than fifty bales ... The man who cannot make eight or ten bales at least has almost no object in life and nothing to live on.'[21] A large part of the peasantry therefore remained dependent on subsistence farming if their holdings allowed it or, where they did not, depended on labouring to eke out their insufficient (and often cattle-less or cartless) holdings. Within the peasantry a sizeable body of commercial farmers undoubtedly developed – they were of substantial significance in Russia by the 1880s – but class differentiation was inhibited by various factors – racialism in the United States, the persistence of the organised village community in Russia* – and as often as not the fully commercialised and capitalist rural sectors were outside traders or money-lenders (commercial firms and banks).

Neither abolition nor emancipation therefore produced a satisfactory capitalist solution of 'the agrarian problem', and it is doubtful whether this could have been achieved unless the conditions for the development of a capitalist agriculture were already present, as in the areas on the margins of the slave/serf economy such as Texas or (in Europe) Bohemia and parts of Hungary. There we can see the 'Prussian' and/or 'American' process in action. The large noble estates, sometimes helped by injections of finance from the compensation payments for the loss of labour services,† transformed themselves into capitalist undertakings. In the Czech lands they owned 43 per cent of the breweries, 65 per cent of the sugar factories and 60

* Here emancipation produced the result – paradoxical from the liberal point of view – of actually taking the peasants out of the realm of official law and making them formally subject to customary peasant law, which was far from favourable to capitalism.

† In the Czech lands the Schwarzenbergs received 2·2 million Gulden in compensation, the Lobkowitz 1·2 millions, the Waldsteins and Alois Lichtenstein about a million each, the Kinsky, Dietrichstein and Colloredo–Mansfeld around a half-million each.[22]

per cent of the distilleries in the early 1870s. Here, with the concentration on labour-intensive crops, not only large estates with hired labour but large peasant farms also flourished,* and even began to catch up with the estates. In Hungary these remained dominant and the wholly landless serfs got freedom without any land at all.[24] Still, the differentiation of the peasantry into rich and poor or landless was also marked in the advanced Czech lands, as is indicated by the fact that the number of goats – the typical poor man's animal – almost doubled between 1846 and 1869. (On the other hand the output of beef per head of the agricultural population also doubled, a reflection of the growing food market of the cities.)

But in the old core areas of physical coercion, such as Russia and Rumania, where serfdom lasted longest, the peasantry were left as a fairly homogeneous mass (except where divided by race or nationality) and discontented, if not potentially revolutionary. Sheer impotence, due to racial oppression or the dependency of landless men might keep them quiet, like the rural Negroes of the American South or the labourers of the Hungarian plains. On the other hand, the traditional peasantry, especially when communally organised, became if anything more formidable. The Great Depression of the 1870s opened an era of rural unrest and peasant revolution.

Could this have been avoided by a 'more rational' form of emancipation? It is doubtful. For we find very similar results in those regions where the attempt to create the conditions of capitalist agriculture was made not by some global edict abolishing the economy of coercion, but by the more general process of imposing the law of bourgeois liberalism: transforming all landed property into individual property and turning land into a freely saleable commodity like anything else. In theory this process had already been widely applied in the first half of the century (see *The Age of Revolution*, chapter 8) but in practice it was enormously reinforced after 1850 by the triumph of liberalism. This meant, first and foremost, the break-up of old communal organisations and the distribution or alienation of collectively held land, or the land of non-economic institutions such as

* In the last third of the nineteenth century it was estimated, at least for Hungary, that one *Joch* (c. 0·6 hectares) required 1 labour day if under pasture, 6 labour days if under meadows, 8·5 if under cereal crops, 22 if under maize, 23 if under potatoes, 30 if under root crops, 35 if under gardens, 40 if under sugar-beet, 120 if under vineyards and 160 if under tobacco.[23]

the church. This was done most dramatically and ruthlessly in Latin America, e.g. in Mexico under Juarez in the 1860s or in Bolivia under the dictator Melgarejo (1866–71), but it also took place on a large scale in Spain after the revolution of 1854, in Italy after the unification of the country under the liberal institutions of Piedmont, and wherever else economic and legal liberalism triumphed. And liberalism advanced even where governments were by no means unqualified in their crusading zeal for it. The French authorities did something to safeguard communal property among their Moslem subjects in Algeria, even though Napoleon iii (in the Senatus-Consulte of 1863) found it inconceivable that individual property rights in land should not be established formally among the members of Moslem communities 'where possible and opportune', a measure which actually had the effect of permitting Europeans for the first time to buy them out. Still, it was not a charter for wholesale expropriation like the Law of 1873 which (after the great insurrection of 1871) proposed the *immediate* transfer of native property to French legal status, a measure which 'benefited hardly anyone except [European] businessmen and speculators'.[25] With or without official backing, the Moslems lost their lands to white settlers or land companies.

Greed played a part in such expropriations: by governments for the profits from land sales or other income, by landlords, settlers or speculators for estates easily and cheaply acquired. Yet it would be unjust to deny the legislators the sincerity of their conviction that the transformation of land into a freely alienable commodity and the transformation of communal, ecclesiastical, entailed or other historically obsolete relics of an irrational past into private holdings, would alone provide a basis for satisfactory agricultural development. But it did not, at any rate for the peasantry, which on the whole refused to turn itself into a flourishing class of commercial farmers even when it had the chance to do so. (Mostly it had not, since it was unable to acquire the land put on the market, or even to understand the complex legal processes which led to its expropriation.) It may not have strengthened the 'latifundium' as such – the term is ambiguous and deeply encrusted in political mythology – but whoever it strengthened, it was not the subsistence peasant, old or new, the marginal villager who depended on the common lands and, in regions subject to deforestation and erosion, the land itself, no longer protected by communal control of its use.* The main effect of liberalisation was to sharpen the edge of peasant discontent.

The novelty of this discontent was that it could now be mobilised by the political left. In fact, outside parts of southern Europe, it was not yet so mobilised. In Sicily and southern Italy peasant insurrection in 1860 attached itself to Garibaldi, a splendid blond and red-shirted figure who looked every inch the people's liberator, and whose belief in a radical–democratic, secular and even vaguely 'socialist' republic did not seem at all incompatible with their own belief in the saints, the Virgin, the Pope and (outside Sicily) the Bourbon king. In Southern Spain republicanism and the International (in its Bakuninite form) made rapid headway: hardly any Andalusian township between 1870 and 1874 lacked its 'workers' society'.[27] (In France, of course, republicanism, the prevalent form of the left, was already well-established in certain rural regions after 1848 and in a moderate form enjoyed majority support in some after 1871.) Per-haps a rural revolutionary left emerged in Ireland with the Fenians in the 1860s, to burst out in the formidable Land League of the late 1870s and 1880s.

There were admittedly plenty of countries even in Europe – and practically all outside that continent – where the left, revolutionary or otherwise, as yet failed to make any impact on the peasantry; as the Russian populists (see chapter 9 above) discovered when they de-cided to 'go to the people' in the 1870s. Indeed, in so far as the left was urban, secularist or even militantly anti-clerical (see chapter 14 below) and both contemptuous of rural 'backwardness' and unap-preciative of country problems, the peasantry might still be full of suspicion and hostility towards it. The rural success of the militantly anti-Christian anarchists in Spain or republicans in France was exceptional. Yet in this period, at least in Europe, the old-fashioned rural insurrection for church and king against the godless and liberal cities became scarce. Even the second Carlist War in Spain (1872–6) was a much less widespread affair than the first one had been in the 1830s, and virtually confined to the Basque provinces. As the great boom of the 1860s and early 1870s gave way to the agrarian depression of the late 1870s and 1880s, the peasantry could no

* Raymond Carr points out that in Spain from the mid-century 'the forest question begins to be a central theme in regenerationist literature'.[26]

225

longer be taken for granted as a conservative element in politics.

Yet how far was the fabric of life in the countryside torn by the forces of the New World? It is not easy to judge from the vantage-point of the late twentieth century, for in the second half of this century rural life has been more profoundly transformed than at any time since the invention of agriculture. Looking backwards, the ways of the men and women of the countryside in the mid-nineteenth century seem fixed in an ancient tradition changing, if at all, at no more than a snail's pace. Of course this is an illusion, but the exact nature of the change is now difficult to discern, except perhaps among such essentially novel agriculturalists as the settlers in the American West, ready to change farm and crop according to the prospects of prices or speculative profits, equipped with machinery and already buying the city's products through the new-fangled device of the mail-order catalogue.

Yet there were changes in the countryside. There was the railway. There was, with increasing frequency, the elementary school, teaching the national language (a new and second language for most peasant children) and, in conjunction with national administration and national politics, splitting their personality. By 1875, it is reported, the use of those nicknames by which people were known and identified in the villages of the Bray country in Normandy, and even the informal local versions of their first names, had virtually disappeared. This was 'due entirely to the schoolmasters who will not permit that children in their schools use any but the proper names'.[28] Probably they had not so much disappeared as retreated, with the local dialect, into the private and unofficial underworld of non-literate culture. And yet the very division between the literate and the non-literate in the countryside was a powerful force for change. For while, in the oral world of *non-literacy*, ignorance of letters, the national language or national institutions is no handicap, except to those whose business (which is rarely that of agriculture) makes such knowledge necessary, in a literate society the *illiterate* is by definition inferior, and has a strong incentive to remove that inferiority, at least from his or her children. In 1849 it was natural that peasant politics in Moravia should take the form of a rumour that the Hungarian revolutionary leader Kossuth was the son of the 'peasant emperor' Joseph II, close kin of the ancient king Svatopluk, and about to invade the country at the head of a great army.[29] By 1875 politics in the Czech countryside was conducted in more sophisticated terms, and those who expected national salvation from supposed kinsmen of 'people's emperors', ancient or modern, would probably feel a little embarrassed to admit it. That sort of thinking was now increasingly confined to quite non-literate countries which even central European peasants would regard as behind the times, such as Russia, where indeed the populist revolutionaries at this very time attempted – unsuccessfully – to organise a peasant revolution by means of a 'people's pretender' to the tsar's throne.[30]

Relatively few country people were as yet literate, outside parts of western and central Europe (notably the protestant parts) and North America.* But even among the backward and traditional, two kinds of country people were the major pillars of the ancient ways – the old and the women, whose 'old wives' tales' passed them on to new generations, and occasionally, for the benefit of city men, to collectors of folklore and folksong. And yet it is a paradox of the period that change came into country life as often as not through the women. Sometimes, as in England, country girls became more literate than country boys – this seems to have happened in the 1850s. Certainly in the United States it was the women who represented 'civilised ways' – book learning, hygiene, 'nice' houses and furnishings on the city model and sobriety – against the rough, violent and drunken ways of the menfolk; as Huckleberry Finn (1884) found to his cost. Those who pushed sons to 'better themselves' were more likely to be mothers than fathers. But perhaps the most powerful agency of such 'modernisation' was the migration of young peasant girls into domestic service with the urban middle and lower middle classes. Indeed, both for men and women, the great process of uprooting was inevitably a process of undermining ancient ways and learning new ways. To this we must now turn.

* Thus in Spain 75 per cent of all men and 89 per cent of all women were said to be illiterate in 1860, in southern Italy about 90 per cent of all inhabitants and even in the most advanced regions of Lombardy and Piedmont between 57 and 59 per cent (1865), in Dalmatia 99 per cent of conscripts (c. 1870). Conversely in France by 1876 80 per cent of rural men and 67 per cent of rural women were literate, in the Netherlands almost 84 per cent of conscripts – between 89 and 90 per cent in the provinces of Holland and Groningen – and even in the notably undereducated Belgium over 65 per cent of conscripts were able both to read and to write (1869). The standards of literacy applied were doubtless extremely modest.[31]

Chapter Eleven

Men Moving

We asked her where her husband was.
'He's in America.'
'What does he do there?'
'He's got a job as Tsar.'
'But how can a Jew be Tsar?'
'Everything's possible in America', she answered.

Scholem Alejchem, *c.* 1900[1]

The Irish, I am told, are everywhere beginning to drive out the
Negroes from domestic service ... Here it is universal; there is
hardly a servant anywhere who is not Irish.

A. H. Clough to Thomas Carlyle, Boston, 1853[2]

I

The middle of the nineteenth century marks the beginning of the greatest migration of peoples in history. Its exact details can hardly be measured, for the official statistics, such as they were then, fail to capture all the movements of men and women within countries or even between states: the rural exodus towards the cities, the migration between regions and from town to town, the crossing of oceans and the penetration of frontier zones, the flux of men and women moving back and forth in ways even more difficult to specify. Still, one dramatic form of this migration can be approximately documented. Between 1846 and 1875 considerably more than 9 million people left Europe, by far the greater part of these for the United States.[3] This was the equivalent of more than four times the population of London in 1851. In the previous half-century it could not have been more than a million and a half in all.

Population movements and industrialisation go together, for the modern economic development of the world both required substantial shifts of people, made it technically easier and cheaper by means of new and improved communications, and of course enabled the world to maintain a much larger population. The mass uprooting of our period was neither unexpected nor without more modest precedents. It was certainly predictable in the 1830s and 1840s (see *The Age of Revolution*, pp. 169–70). Still, what had previously been an increasingly lively stream, seemed suddenly to become a torrent. Before 1845 only in one year had more than 100,000 foreign passengers arrived in the United States. But between 1846 and 1850 an annual average of more than a quarter of a million left Europe, in the next five years an annual average of almost 350,000; in 1854 alone no less than 428,000 arrived in the United States. And though the numbers fluctuated, according to economic conditions in both the countries of origin and the receiving countries, it continued on a far larger scale than ever before.

However, enormous as these migrations were, they were still modest by later standards. Thus in the 1880s between 700,000 and 800,000 Europeans emigrated on average every year, in the years after 1900 between 1 and 1·4 million a year. Thus between 1900 and 1910 considerably more people migrated to the United States than during the entire period with which this book is concerned.

The most obvious limitation on migration was geographical. Leaving aside the relics of the African slave-trade (now illegal and rather effectively strangled by the British navy), the bulk of international migrants were Europeans, or more accurately in this period western Europeans and Germans. The Chinese were certainly already on the move into the northern and central borderlands of their empire beyond the native region of the Han people, and from the southern coastal regions into the peninsulas and islands of south-east Asia, in what numbers we cannot say. Probably they were modest. In 1871 there were perhaps 120,000 in the Straits Settlements (Malaya).[4] The Indians began after 1852 to migrate in moderate numbers into neighbouring Burma. The void left by the banning of the slave-trade was to some extent being filled by transports of 'indentured' labour, mainly from India and China, whose conditions were scarcely better. One hundred and twenty-five thousand Chinese arrived in Cuba between 1853 and 1874.[5] They were to create the Indian diasporas of Guyana and Trinidad, of the Indian Ocean islands and the Pacific, and the smaller Chinese colonies in Cuba, Peru and the British Caribbean. Adventurous Chinese were already attracted (see chapter 3 above) in some numbers to the pioneer regions of the American

Pacific, to provide local journalists with jokes about laundrymen, cooks (they invented the Chinese restaurant in San Francisco during the gold rush*), and local demagogues during slumps with slogans of racial exclusiveness. The rapidly growing merchant fleets of the world were already largely manned by 'lascar' seamen who left a deposit of small coloured populations in the major international ports. The recruitment of colonial troops, mainly by the French who hoped by this means to offset the demographic superiority of the Germans (a subject anxiously discussed in the 1860s), brought some others for the first time into a European environment.†

Even among the Europeans mass intercontinental migration was confined to the people of relatively few countries, in this period over-whelmingly to the British, the Irish and the Germans, and, from the 1860s on, the Norwegians and Swedes – the Danes never emigrated to the same extent – whose small numbers conceal the enormous relative size of their demographic drain. Thus Norway sent two-thirds of its population increase to the United States, surpassed only by the unfortunate Irish who sent more than their entire increase abroad: the country lost population consistently in every decade after the Great Famine of 1846–7. Still, though the English and the Germans sent hardly more than 10 per cent of their net demographic increase abroad, in absolute numbers this was a very large contingent. Between 1851 and 1880 about 5·3 million left the British Isles (3·5 million of them to the United States, 1 million to Australia, half a million to Canada) – by far the greatest body of trans-oceanic emigrants in the world.

The south Italians and Sicilians, who were to flood into the big cities of the Americas, had hardly yet begun to stir from their native slum villages, the east Europeans, Catholic or Orthodox, remained largely sedentary, only the Jews seeping or flooding into provincial towns from which they had hitherto been excluded and thence into larger cities.‡ The Russian peasants hardly began to migrate into the open spaces of Siberia before 1880, though they moved in large num-

* 'The best restaurants in the place are kept by adventurers from the Flowery Land', observed the Boston *Bankers Magazine*.[6]
† The native troops recruited by the British in this period were overwhelmingly in and for use in India, or such parts of the world as lay within the sphere of the Indian rather than the London offices of the British government.
‡ Hungarian towns were only opened to Jewish settlement in 1840.

bers into the steppes of European Russia, whose settlement was more or less complete by the 1880s. The Poles hardly began to populate the mines of the Ruhr before 1890 though the Czech were moving south into Vienna. The great period of Slav, Jewish and Italian migration to the Americas began in the 1880s. By and large the British Isles, Germany and Scandinavia provided the international migrants, except for specially footloose minorities such as the Galicians and Basques, ubiquitous in the Hispanic world.

Since most Europeans were rural, so were most migrants. The nineteenth century was a gigantic machine for uprooting country-men. Most of them went to the cities, or at any rate out of traditional rural pursuits, to find their way as best they could in strange, fright-ening, but at best boundlessly hopeful new worlds, where the city pavements were said to be paved with gold, though immigrants rarely picked up more than some copper. It is not quite true that the currents of migration and urbanisation were the same. A few groups of migrants, notably among Germans and Scandinavians, who went to the Great Lakes area of the United States, or the earlier Scots settlers in Canada, exchanged a poor agricultural milieu for a better one: only 10 per cent of the foreign immigrants in the United States in 1880 were in agriculture, mostly not as farmers 'possibly', as an observer claimed 'on account of the capital required to purchase and stock a farm',[7] the equipment of which alone was reckoned to cost $900 in the early 1870s.

Still, if the redistribution of countrymen across the face of the globe is not to be neglected, it was less striking than their exodus from agriculture. Migration and urbanisation went together, and in the second half of the nineteenth century the countries chiefly associated with it (the United States, Australia, Argentina) had a rate of urban concentration unsurpassed anywhere except in Britain and the industrial parts of Germany. (By 1890 the twenty largest cities in the western world included five in the Americas and one in Australia.) Men and women moved into cities, though perhaps (in Britain certainly) increasingly from other cities.

If they moved within their own country, this raised no novel prob-lems of technique. In most cases they did not go far or, if they did, the paths from their region to the city had been well-trodden by kinsmen and neighbours, like the hawkers and seasonal building workers who had long been in the habit of coming up to Paris from central France, whose numbers grew with the constructional work of Paris until, after 1870, they turned from seasonal into permanent migrants.[8] New routes were sometimes opened up by technology, such as the railway which brought the Bretons to Paris, to lose their faith (as the proverb had it) at the gates of the Gare Montparnasse, and to supply the brothels of the city with their most characteristic inhabitants. Breton girls replaced those from Lorraine as its most familiar prostitutes.

The women migrants within countries became overwhelmingly domestic servants, until they married some fellow-countryman, or passed into some other urban occupation. The migration of families or even married couples was uncommon. The men followed the traditional trades of their region in the city – the Cardiganshire Welsh became dairymen wherever they went, the Auvergnats dealers in fuel – or, if skilled, their own craft, if enterprising, some form of small commerce, mainly in the food and drink trades. Otherwise they found employment above all in those two great occupations which required no special skills unfamiliar to countrymen, building and transport. In Berlin in 1885 81 per cent of men engaged in food supply, 83·5 per cent of builders, and over 85 per cent of those in transport had been born outside the city.[9] If they rarely had much chance in the more skilled manual jobs, unless apprenticed to some craft at home, they were probably better off than the poorest of the city-born. The worst of the slimy pools of sweated and casual poverty were more likely to be filled by the native than the immigrant. In our period there was not yet much in the way of factory production in most of the major capital cities.

Most of such strictly industrial production was to be found in the middling-sized though rapidly growing cities or even – notably in mining and some kinds of textiles – in villages and small towns. Here there was no comparable demand for women immigrants, except in textiles, and the jobs for immigrant men were, almost by definition, unskilled or low-paid.

Migration across frontiers and oceans raised more complex problems, and not by any means because it was often – though in our period not primarily – entry into a country whose language the migrant did not understand. In fact the largest body of migrants, those from the British Isles, had no significant linguistic difficulties, whereas quite a few internal migrants had, e.g. in the multi-national empires of central and eastern Europe. However, language aside, emigration undoubtedly raised in an acute form the question of where a man or woman belonged (see also chapter 5 above). If one remained in the new country, was one obliged to break one's ties with the old, and if so did one want to? The question did not arise for those settling in their state's colonies, who could continue to remain Englishmen or Frenchmen in New Zealand or Algeria, thinking of the old country as 'home'. It arose most acutely in the United States which welcomed immigrants but also put pressure on them to turn themselves into English-speaking American citizens as soon as possible, since any rational citizen would wish to be an American. In fact, most did so.

A change of citizenship did not of course imply a divorce from the old country. Quite the contrary. The typical emigrant, huddled together with his like in the strange new environment which received him coldly enough – the militant xenophobia of the 'Know-Nothings' was a native American response to the influx of starving Irish in the 1850s – fell back naturally on the only human setting that was familiar and could provide help, the company of his countrymen. The America which taught him, as the first formal sentences of English, 'I hear the whistle. I must hurry'* was not a society but a means of making money. The first-generation immigrant, however zealously he or she tried to learn the techniques of the new life, lived in a self-imposed ghetto, drawing support from the old ways, the men of his kind, the memories of the old country which he had so

* This comes from a brochure of the International Harvester Corporation, designed to teach its Polish labourers English. The subsequent sentences of Lesson One read:

I hear the five-minute whistle.
It is time to go into the shop.
I take my check from the gateboard and hang it on the department board.
I change my clothes and get ready to work.
The starting whistle blows.
I eat my lunch.
It is forbidden to eat until then.
The whistle blows at five minutes of starting time.
I get ready to go to work.
I work until the whistle blows to quit.
I leave my place nice and clean.
I must go home.[10]

readily abandoned. Not for nothing did smiling Irish eyes make the fortunes of the bohemian hacks who were just about to create the modern popular music business in the cities of the United States. Even the wealthy New York Jewish financiers, the Guggenheims, Kuhns, Sachs, Seligmanns and Lehmanns, who had all that money could buy in the United States, which was very nearly everything, were not yet Americans in the way in which the Wertheimsteins in Vienna considered themselves Austrian, the Bleichroeders in Berlin Prussians, even the international Rothschilds in London and Paris, English and French. They remained Germans as well as Americans. They spoke, wrote and thought in German, often sent their children to be educated in the old country, joined and sponsored German associations.[11]

But emigration raised much more elementary material difficulties. Men had to discover where to go and what to do once they got there. They had to get to Minnesota from some remote Norwegian fjord, to Green Lake county, Wisconsin from Pomerania or Brandenburg, to Chicago from some townland in Kerry. Cost itself was not an insuperable difficulty, though the conditions of steerage travel across the ocean were, especially in the years after the Irish famine, notoriously horrible, if not actually murderous. In 1885 the emigrant passage from Hamburg to New York cost $7. (The shipping fares from Southampton to Singapore, which catered to a higher class of trade, had merely been reduced from £110 in the 1850s to £68 in the 1880s.[12] Fares were low, not only because passengers from the lower orders were not believed to require or deserve much better accommodation than cattle and fortunately needed less space, or even because of improvements in communications, but for economic reasons. Emigrants were useful bulk cargo. Probably for most people the cost of the journey to the final port of embarkation – Le Havre, Bremen, Hamburg, above all Liverpool – was far greater than that of the actual crossing.

Even so, the money was not within reach of many of the very poor, though such sums could easily be saved and sent back from America or Australia, with their high wages, to kinsmen in the old country. In fact such payments formed part of the vast sum of remittances from abroad, for emigrants, unused to the high spending of their new countries, were heavy savers. The Irish alone sent back between £1 million and £1·7 million a year in the early 1850s.[13] However, where kinsmen could not help, a variety of intermediary entrepreneurs had a financial interest in doing so. Where there is a large demand for labour (or land*) on one side, a population ignorant of conditions in the receiving country on the other and a long distance between, the agent or contractor will flourish.

Such men earned their profits by steering human cattle into the holds of shipping companies anxious to fill them, towards public authorities and railroad companies interested in populating their empty territories, mine-owners, iron-masters and other employers of raw labour who needed hands. They were paid by these, and by the pennies of helpless men and women who might be forced to cross half of a strange continent before even embarking on the Atlantic crossing: from central Europe to Le Havre, or across the North Sea and via the smoky Pennine valleys to Liverpool. We may assume that very often they exploited ignorance and helplessness, though the extremes of contract labour and debt serfdom were probably uncommon in this period, except among the Indians and Chinese shipped abroad for plantation work. (This does not mean that there were not plenty of Irishmen who paid some 'friend' from the old country unnecessarily for the privilege of finding a job in the New World.) On the whole the entrepreneurs of migration were uncontrolled, except for some supervision of shipping conditions after the terrifying epidemics of the late 1840s. They had the public opinion of the influential behind them. The mid-nineteenth-century bourgeoisie still believed that its continent was grossly overpopulated by the poor. The more of them that were shipped abroad, the better for them (because they would improve their conditions) and for those left behind (because the labour market would be less overstocked). Benevolent societies, even trade unions, arranged to subsidise the emigration of their clients or members as the only practicable means of dealing with pauperism and unemployment. And the fact that during our period the most rapidly industrialising countries, like Britain and Germamy, were also the great exporters of men, seemed to justify them.

The argument was, it is now held, mistaken. On balance the eco-

* Thus a German blacksmith in Princeton, Wisconsin, bought up farmlands and sold them on credit to his immigrant countrymen.[14]

nomy of the dispatching countries would have benefited more by employing its human resources than by expelling them. Conversely, the economies of the New World benefited immeasurably by the exodus from the old. So, of course, did the emigrants themselves. The worst period of their poverty and exploitation in the United States seems to have occurred after the end of our period.

Why did people emigrate? Overwhelmingly for economic reasons, that is to say because they were poor. In spite of the political persecutions after 1848, political or ideological refugees formed only a small fraction of mass emigration, even in 1849–54, though at one time the radicals among them controlled half the German-language press of the United States, which they used to denounce their country of refuge.[15] Their rank-and-file soon settled down abroad like most non-ideological migrants transferring their revolutionary energies to the anti-slavery campaign. The flight of religious sects seeking greater freedom to pursue their often rather peculiar activities was probably less significant than in the previous half-centruy, if only because mid-Victorian governments held no strong views about orthodoxy as such, though probably not displeased to see the heels of the British or Danish Mormons, whose penchant for polygamy created problems. Even in eastern Europe the active anti-semitic campaigns, which were to stimulate the mass emigration of the Jews, still lay in the future.

Did people emigrate to escape bad conditions at home or to seek better ones abroad? There has been a long and rather pointless debate on this question. There is no doubt that poor men were more likely to emigrate than richer ones, and that they were more likely to emigrate if their traditional livelihood had become difficult or impossible. Thus in Norway handicraftsmen migrated more readily than factory workers; later sailors migrated when sail declined before steam, fishermen when oil-driven craft replaced sailing boats. There is equally little doubt that at this period, when the idea of tearing out ancient roots was still strange and terrifying to most people, some kind of cataclysmic force was still required to drive them into the unknown. A Kentish farm-labourer, writing from New Zealand, thanked the farmers for having driven him out by a lockout of the labourers' union, since he now found himself so much better off: he would not have thought of going otherwise.

Nevertheless, as mass migration became part of common people's experience, and every child in County Kildare had some cousin, uncle or brother already in Australia or the United States, uprooting became a common – and not necessarily irreversible – choice based on an assessment of prospects, and not merely a force of destiny. If news came that gold had been found in Australia or jobs were plentiful and well paid in the United States, migration increased. Conversely, it plummeted in the years after 1873, when the economy of the United States was acutely depressed. Still, there can be no doubt that the first great emigration wave of our period (1845–54) was essentially a flight from hunger or pressure of population on land, basically in Ireland and Germany, which supplied 80 per cent of all transatlantic migrants in these years.

Nor was migration necessarily permanent. Emigrants – what proportion of them we do not know – dreamed of making their pile abroad and returning home, rich and respected, to their native villages. A considerable proportion – between 30 and 40 per cent – actually did so, though most commonly for the opposite reason, because they did not like the New World or could not establish themselves there. Some migrated again. As communications were revolutionised, the labour market, especially for men with special skills, expanded until it comprised the entire industrial world. The list of British craft union leaders of this period is filled with men who worked for a spell in the United States or somewhere else overseas, as they might have worked for a spell in Newcastle or Barrow-in-Furness. Indeed, it now became possible for even the temporary and seasonal migrations of Italian or Irish harvesters or railway builders to extend across the oceans.

In fact, the massive increase in migration contained a considerable quantity of impermanent movement – temporary, seasonal or merely nomadic. In itself there was nothing new about such movements. The harvester, the tramping journeymen, the nomadic tinker, hawker, carter and drover were familiar enough before the Industrial Revolution. Nevertheless the rapid and world-wide extension of the new economy was bound to require, and therefore to create, new types of such travellers.

Consider the symbol of this extension, the railway. Its entrepreneurs ranged the globe and with them went the cadre of (mostly British and Irish) foremen, skilled workers and elite labour; sometimes settling down in some foreign country for good, their children becoming the Anglo-Argentines of the next generation,* sometimes moving from country to country like the much less numerous oilmen of our days. Since railways were built anywhere, they could not necessarily rely on a local labour-force, but developed a corps of nomadic labourers (known in Britain as the 'navvies'), such as still characterises the great construction projects all over the world. In most industrial countries these were recruited from marginal and footloose men, ready to work hard for good pay in bad conditions and to drink or gamble away their pay equally hard, with little thought for the future. For, just as for the similar sailors there would always be another ship, so for the mobile diggers there would always be some other great construction project when the present one finished. Free men on the frontiers of industry, shocking the respectable of all classes, the heroes of an unofficial folklore of masculinity, they played the same sort of role as sailors and frontier miners and prospectors, though earning more than the ones, and lacking the others' hope of making their fortune.

In the more traditional agrarian societies these mobile constructors formed an important bridge between rural and industrial life. Organised in regular gangs or teams on the model of seasonal harvesters, led by an elected captain who negotiated terms and shared out the proceeds of the contract, poor peasants from Italy, Croatia or Ireland would criss-cross continents or even oceans to provide labour for the builders of towns, factories or railways. Such migrations developed on the Hungarian plains from the 1850s. The less organised often resented the superior efficiency and greater discipline (or docility), and the readiness to work for lower wages, of these peasants.

Yet it is not enough merely to draw attention to the growth of what Marx called the 'light cavalry' of capitalism, without also observing a significant distinction within the developed countries; or more precisely between the Old and New Worlds. Economic expansion produced a 'frontier' everywhere. In some senses a mining community such as Gelsenkirchen (in Germany), which grew from 3,500 inhabitants to almost 96,000 in half a lifetime (1858–95), was a

* The Indian railways tended to be staffed largely by Eurasians, the children of Indian women and British workers, who were less reluctant to interbreed than the middle and upper classes.

'New World' comparable to Buenos Aires or the Pennsylvanian industrial centres. But in the Old World, on the whole, the need for a mobile population was met without creating more than a comparatively modest and impermanent floating population, except in the great shipping ports and, as it were, in the traditional centres of the shifting and shiftless population, such as the great cities. This may be because its members had, or could soon sink roots into, some sort of community belonging to a structured society. It was in thinly populated regions at or beyond the frontiers of settlement overseas, where shifting bodies of labourers were required, that such groups of genuinely unattached and floating individuals made their presence felt as a group, or were at least more 'visible'. The Old World was full of herdsmen and drovers, but none have attracted as much attention as the American 'cowboys' of our period, though their equivalent in Australia, the itinerant sheep-shearers and other rural labourers of the hinterland, have also produced a locally powerful myth.

II

The characteristic form of travel for the poor was migration. For the middle class and the rich it was increasingly tourism, essentially the product of the railway, the steamship and (in so far as that invention of our period, the picture postcard, is still an essential part of it) of the new scale and speed of postal communications. (These were internationally systematised with the establishment of the International Postal Union in 1869.) Poor men in towns travelled for necessity but rarely for pleasure, except on foot – the autobiographies of self-improving Victorian artisans are full of titanic country walks – and for short periods. Poor men in the country did not travel for pleasure at all, combining enjoyment with business at markets and fairs. The aristocracy travelled much for non-utilitarian purposes, but in ways which have nothing in common with modern tourism. Noble families moved from town house to country house and back again at regular seasons, with a train of servants and baggage vehicles like a small army. (Indeed, the father of Prince Kropotkin issued his wife and serfs proper marching orders in military fashion.) They might establish themselves in some suitable centre of social life for a while, as that Latin-American family did which the *Paris Guide* of 1867 records

239

as arriving with eighteen wagons of baggage. The traditional Grand Tour of the young nobleman had not yet even the Grand Hotel in common with the tourism of the capitalist era, partly because this institution was only now developing – initially as often as not in connection with a railway – partly because noblemen hardly deigned to stop at inns.

Industrial capitalism produced two novel forms of pleasure travel: tourism and summer holidays for the bourgeoisie and mechanised day trips for the masses in some countries such as Britain. Both were the direct results of the application of steam to transport, since for the first time in history this made possible regular and safe journeys for large numbers of people and luggage over any kind of terrain and water. Unlike stage-coaches, which could be readily held up by brigands in remoter regions, railways were immune from the start – except in the American West – even in notoriously unsafe areas such as Spain and the Balkans.

The day trip for the masses, if we except steamer excursions, was the child of the 1850s – to be more precise of the Great Exhibition of 1851, which attracted vast numbers of visitors to its marvels in London, a traffic encouraged by the railways with concession fares, and organised by and for the members of innumerable local societies, chapels and communities. Thomas Cook himself, whose name was to become a by-word for organised tourism in the next twenty-five years, had begun his career arranging such outings and developed it into big business in 1851. The numerous International Expositions (see chapter 2 above) each brought its army of sightseers and the re-building of capital cities encouraged provincials to sample their wonders. Little more need to said about mass tourism in this period. It remained confined to short trips, often quite strenuous by modern standards, bringing in its train a flourishing minor industry of 'souvenirs'. In general the railways, at all events in Britain, took little interest in third-class travel, though the government forced them to provide a minimum of it. Not until 1872 did the British ones earn 50 per cent of their passenger receipts from the common herd. Indeed, as regular third-class traffic increased, the excursion traffic by special train became less important.

The middle class, however, travelled more seriously. The most important form of such journeys, in quantitative terms, was probably that to the family summer holiday or (for the more affluent and over-fed) to the annual cure at some spa. The third quarter of the nineteenth century saw a remarkable development of such resorts – at the seaside in Britain, in the mountains on the continent. (Though Biarritz was already very fashionable in the 1860s, thanks to the patronage of Napoleon III, and Impressionist paintings show a visible interest in the beaches of Normandy, the continental bourgeoisie was as yet uncommitted to salt water and sunshine.) By the mid-1860s a middle-class holiday boom was already transforming parts of the British coastline with seafront promenades, piers and other embellishments, which enabled landed proprietors to draw unsuspected profits from hitherto uneconomic stretches of cliff and beach. These were middle- and lower-middle-class phenomena. On the whole the working-class seaside resort did not become of major significance until the 1880s, and the nobility and gentry would scarcely consider a stay at Bournemouth (where the French poet Verlaine found himself) or Ventnor (where Turgenev and Karl Marx took the air) as a suitable summer activity.

The continental spa (the British ones hardly reached such prominence) were far more stylish, and therefore provided both more luxurious hotels and the entertainments necessary for such a clientele, such as gambling casinos and rather high-class brothels. Vichy, Spa, Baden-Baden, Aix-les-Bains, but above all the great international spas of the Habsburg monarchy, Gastein, Marienbad, Karlsbad, etc., were to nineteenth-century Europe what Bath had been to eighteenth-century England, fashionable gatherings justified by the excuse of drinking some form of disagreeable mineral waters or immersing oneself in some form of liquid under the control of a benevolent medical dictator.* However, the ailing liver was a great leveller, and the mineral spas attracted a cross-section of the non-aristocratic rich and the professional middle classes, whose tendency to eat and drink too much was reinforced by prosperity. After all Dr Kugelmann recommended Karlsbad to so untypical a member of the middle class as Karl Marx, who carefully registered himself as a 'man of private means' to avoid identification, until he discovered that as Dr Marx he

* Their status is indicated by their role in the diplomacy of the period. Napoleon met Bismarck in Biarritz and Cavour in Plombières, and a Convention was actually concluded in Gastein: forerunner of numerous diplomatic conferences held on some lake or riviera in the half-century from 1890 to 1940.

could save some of the rather steep *Kurtaxe*.[16] In the 1840s few such places had emerged from rural simplicity. As late as 1858 *Murray's Guide* described Marienbad as 'comparatively recent' and noted that Gastein had only two hundred guest-rooms. But in the 1860s they were in full flower.

Sommerfrische and *Kurort* were for the normal bourgeois; traditionalist France and Italy still confirm today that annual liverishness was a bourgeois institution. For the delicate, mild sunshine was indicated, that is to say winters on the Mediterranean. The Côte d'Azur had been discovered by Lord Brougham, the radical politician whose statue still presides over Cannes, and, though the Russian nobility and gentry became its most lucrative clients, the name 'Promenade des Anglais' in Nice still indicates who opened this new frontier of moneyed leisure. Monte Carlo built its Hôtel de Paris in 1866. After the opening of the Suez Canal, and especially after the construction of the railway up the Nile, Egypt became the place for those whose health forbade the damp autumns and winters of the north, combining as it did the advantages of climate, exoticism, monuments of ancient culture and (at this stage still informal) European domination. The indefatigable Baedeker produced his first guidebook to this country in 1877.

To go to the Mediterranean in summer, except in search of art and architecture, was still regarded as madness until well into the twentieth century, that era of the novel worship of sun and brown skins. Only a few places, such as the Bay of Naples and Capri, already established thanks to the patronage of the Russian Empress, were regarded as tolerable in the hot season. The modesty of local prices in the 1870s indicates an early stage of tourism. Rich Americans, of course, whether healthy or ill – or more precisely their wives and daughters – made tracks for the centres of European culture, though by the end of our period the millionaires were already beginning to establish their pattern of summer residence in custom-built Xanadus along the stern coasts of New England. The rich in hot countries made for the mountains.

We must, however, begin to distinguish between two kinds of holiday: the longer (summer or winter) residence and the tour which became increasingly practical and rapid. As always the major attractions were romantic landscapes and the monuments of culture, but by the 1860s the British (pioneers as usual) were exporting their passion for physical exercise on to the mountains of Switzerland, where they were later to found skiing as a winter sport. The Alpine Club was founded in 1858 and Edward Whymper climbed the Matterhorn in 1865. For reasons which are obscure, such strenuous activities amid inspiring scenery appealed particularly to Anglo-Saxon intellectuals and professional men of liberal leanings (perhaps the close company of tough and handsome native guides had something to do with it), so that mountaineering joined long country walks as a characteristic activity of Cambridge academics, higher civil servants, public-school-masters, philosophers and economists, to the amazement of Latin, though not entirely of Germanic, intellectuals. As for the less active travellers, their steps were now guided by Thomas Cook and the solid guide-books of the period, the pioneer British *Murray's Guides* being increasingly overshadowed by those bibles of the tourist, the German *Baedekers*, now published in several languages.

Such tours were not cheap. In the early 1870s a six-week round trip for two people from London via Belgium, the Rhine Valley, Switzer-land and France – perhaps still the standard tourist itinerary – cost about £85, or roughly 20 per cent of the income of a man earning £8 a week, which would have been a respectable servant-keeping income in those days.[17] Such a sum would have taken more than three-quarters of the annual income of a well-paid British skilled worker. It is evident that the tourist whom railway companies, hotels and guide-books had in mind belonged to the comfortably-off middle classes. These were the men and women who no doubt complained that in Nice the cost of unfurnished houses had risen between 1858 and 1876 from £64 to £100 per year, and that of women servants from £8–10 to a scandalous £24–30 a year.[18] But these were also the people who, it is safe to say, could afford to pay these prices.

Was the world of the 1870s therefore entirely dominated by migra-tion, travel and demographic flux? It is easy to forget that the maj-ority of the people living on earth still lived and died where they had been born, or, more precisely, that their movements were no greater or no different from what they would have been before the Industrial Revolution. There were certainly more people in the world who resembled the French, 88 per cent of whom in 1861 lived in the *département* of their birth – in the Lot *département* 97 per cent in the *parish* of their birth – than resembled more mobile and migratory populations.[19] And yet, people were gradually torn from their moorings, grew used to lives in which they saw things their fathers had never done and even they had hardly expected to do. By the end of our period immigrants formed a substantial majority not only of countries like Australia, and of cities like New York and Chicago, but of Stockholm, Christiania (the present Oslo), Budapest, Berlin and Rome (between 55 and 60 per cent) of Paris and Vienna (*c.* 65 per cent).[20] Cities and the new industrial areas were, by and large, the magnets which attracted them. What kind of life awaited them there?

Chapter Twelve

City, Industry, The Working Class

Now they even bake our daily bread
With steam and with turbine
And very soon, into our gab,
We'll shove it with a machine.

In Trautenau they have two churchyards,
For the poor and for rich people;
Not even in the grave itself
Is the poor devil their equal.

Poem in *Trautenau Wochenblatt*, 1869[1]

In the old days, if someone had called a journeyman craftsman a
'worker', he would have had a fight on his hands . . . But now they have
told the journeymen the workers are the top rank in the state, they all
insist they want to be workers.

M. May, 1848[2]

The question of poverty is that of death, disease, winter or that of any
other natural phenomenon. I don't know how either is to stop.

William Makepeace Thackeray, 1848[3]

I

To say that new migrants came, or that new generations were now
born, into a world of industry and technology is obvious, but not in
itself very illuminating. What kind of world was it?

It was, in the first place, a world not so much consisting of factories, employers and proletarians as one transformed by the enormous progress of its industrial sector. However striking the changes
produced by the spread of industry itself and by urbanisation, these
in themselves are not the measure of the impact of capitalism. In 1866
Reichenberg (Liberec), the Bohemian textile centre, still produced
half its total output on the looms of artisan weavers, admittedly for
the most part now dependent on a few large factories. It was no doubt
less advanced in its industrial organisation than Lancashire, where

245

the last of the surviving handloom weavers were absorbed into other employment in the 1850s, but it would be unrealistic to claim that it was not industrial. At the peak of the sugar-boom of the early 1870s a mere 40,000 workers were employed in the Czech sugar-factories. But this measures the impact of the new sugar industry less than the fact that the acreage under sugar-beet in the Bohemian countryside had multiplied more than twentyfold between 1853–4 (4,800 hectares) and 1872–3 (123,800 hectares).[4] That the number of railway passengers in Britiain almost doubled between 1848 and 1854 – from *c.* 58 to *c.* 108 million – while the companies' income from freight traffic multiplied almost two-and-a-half times, is more significant than the precise percentage of industrial goods or business travel concealed within these figures.

Still, industrial work itself, in its characteristic structure and setting, and urbanisation – life in the rapidly growing cities – were certainly the most dramatic forms of the new life; new because even the continuity of some local occupation or town concealed far-reaching changes. A few years after the end of our period (1887) the German professor Ferdinand Toennies formulated the distinction between *Gemeinschaft* (community) and *Gesellschaft* (a society of individuals), two twins now familiar to every student of sociology. The distinction is similar to others made by contemporaries between what subsequent jargon would call 'traditional' and 'modern' societies – for instance Sir Henry Maine's formula summarising the progress of society as 'from status to contract'. The point, however, is that Toennies based his analysis not on the difference between peasant community and urbanised society, but between the old-fashioned town and the capitalist city, 'essentially a commercial town and, insofar as commerce dominates its productive labour, a factory town'.[5] This novel environment and its structure is the subject of the present chapter.

The city was indeed the most striking outward symbol of the industrial world, apart from the railway itself. Urbanisation increased rapidly after 1850. In the first half of the century only Britain had an annual rate of urbanisation of more than 0·20 points,* though Belgium almost reached that level. But between 1850 and 1890 even

* This represents the percentage point shift in the level of the urban population between the first and last censuses of the period, divided by the number of years.[6]

Austro-Hungary, Norway and Ireland urbanised at this rate, Belgium and the United States at between 0·30 and 0·40, Prussia, Australia and Argentina at between 0·40 and 0·50, England and Wales (still leading by a short head) and Saxony at over 0·50 per annum. To say that the concentration of people in cities was 'the most remarkable social phenomenon of the present century'[7] was to state the obvious. By our standards it was still modest – by the end of the century hardly more than a dozen countries had achieved the rate of urban concentration of England and Wales in 1801. Still, all (except Scotland and the Netherlands) had achieved this level since 1850.

The typical industrial town was at this period still a medium-sized city, even by contemporary standards, though as it happened in central and eastern Europe some capital cities (which tended to be very large) also became major centres of manufacturing – e.g. Berlin, Vienna and St Petersburg. Oldham had 83,000 inhabitants in 1871, Barmen 75,000, Roubaix 65,000. Indeed, the old pre-industrial cities of repute rarely attracted the new kinds of production, so that the typical new industrial region generally took the form of a sort of growing together of separate villages developing into smaller towns and small towns developing into larger ones. They were hardly yet the vast unbrokenly built-up areas of the twentieth century, though factory chimneys, often strung along river valleys, railway sidings, the monotony of discoloured brick and the pall of smoke which hung above them, gave them a certain coherence. Few of their inhabitants were as yet beyond walking distance from fields. Until the 1870s the larger cities of industrial western Germany, such as Cologne and Düsseldorf, were fed by the peasants of the surrounding region bringing their supplies to the weekly market.[8] In one sense the shock of industrialisation lay precisely in the stark contrast between the black, monotonous, crowded and scarred settlements and the coloured farms and hills immediately adjoining them, as in Sheffield, 'noisy, smoky, loathsome (but) . . . surrounded on all sides by some of the most enchanting countryside to be found on this planet'.[9]

This is what made it still possible – though to a rapidly diminishing extent – for workers in the newly industrialising areas to remain half-agricultural. Until after 1900 the Belgian miners took time off at the right season (if necessary by an annual 'potato strike') to look after their potato patches. Even in northern England the urban unemployed could easily turn to work on nearby farms in the summer: the striking weavers of Padiham (Lancashire) in 1859 supported themselves by hay-making.[10]

The great city – say at this period a settlement of more than 200,000, including a scattering of metropolitan towns of more than half a million* – was not so much industrial (though it might contain a good many factories) as a centre of commerce, transport, administration and the multiplicity of services which a large concentration of people attracts and which in turn swell their number. Most of its inhabitants were indeed workers, of one kind or another, including a large number of domestic servants – almost one in every five Londoners (1851), though surprisingly a considerably smaller proportion in Paris.[12] Still, their very size guaranteed that they also contained a very large number and substantial proportion of the middle and lower middle classes – say between 20 and 23 per cent in both London and Paris.

Such cities grew with extraordinary rapidity. Vienna increased from over 400,000 in 1846 to 700,000 in 1880, Berlin from 378,000 (1849) to almost one million (1875), Paris from 1 to 1·9 million, London from 2·5 to 3·9 million (1851–81), though these figures pale beside some from overseas: Chicago or Melbourne. But the shape, image and structure of the city itself changed, both under pressure of politically motivated building and replanning (notably in Paris and Vienna) and of profit-hungry enterprise. Neither welcomed the presence of the city's poor, the majority of its population, though both recognised their regrettable necessity.

For the city's planners the poor were a public danger, their potentially riotous concentrations to be broken up by avenues and boulevards which would drive the inhabitants of the crowded popular quarters they replaced into some unspecified, but presumably more sanitary and certainly less perilous locations. This was also the view propagated by the railway companies, driving broad belts of lines and sidings into the town centres, preferably through the slums, where

* In the mid-1870s there were thought to be four cities of a million and over in Europe (London, Paris, Berlin, Vienna), six of over half a million (St Petersburg, Constantinople, Moscow, Glasgow, Liverpool, Manchester) and twenty-five of over 200,000. Of these five were in the United Kingdom, four each in Germany and Italy, three in France, two in Spain and one each in Denmark, Hungary, the Netherlands, Belgium, Russian Poland, Rumania and Portugal. Forty-one cities had more than 100,000 inhabitants, nine of these in the United Kingdom and eight in Germany.[11]

real estate costs were low and protests negligible. For building entre-preneurs and property developers the poor were an unprofitable market, compared to the rich pickings from the new specialised business and shopping districts and the solid houses and apartments for the middle class, or the developing suburbs. In so far as the poor did not crowd into the old central districts abandoned by their betters, their dwellings were built by small speculative builders, often little more than artisans, or by the constructors of those gaunt, overflowing tenement blocks expressively known in German as 'rent barracks' (*Mietskasernen*). Of the dwellings built in Glasgow between 1866 and 1874 three-quarters were of one and two rooms only, and even these were soon overfilled.

Who says mid-nineteenth-century city, therefore says 'overcrowd-ing' and 'slum', and the more rapidly the city grew, the worse its overcrowding. In spite of sanitary reform and what little planning there was, urban overcrowding probably increased during this period and neither health nor mortality improved, where they did not actually deteriorate. The major, striking and henceforth continuous improvement in these conditions only began to occur after the end of our period. Cities still devoured their populations, though the British, being the oldest of the industrial era, were coming close to repro-ducing themselves, i.e. to grow without the constant and massive blood transfusion of immigration.

Catering to the needs of the poor would hardly have doubled the number of London architects in twenty years (from just over 1,000 to 2,000 – in the 1830s there had probably been fewer than one hundred), though building and renting slum property could be a very lucrative business, judged by the income per cubic foot of low-cost space.[13] Indeed, the boom in architecture and property development was so great precisely because nothing whatever diverted the flow of capital from what *The Builder* in 1848 called 'one half of the world . . . on the lookout for investment' to 'the other half continually in search of eligible family residences'[14] into serving the urban poor, who clearly did not belong in the world at all. The third quarter of the nineteenth century was the first world-wide era of urban real-estate and con-structional boom – for the bourgeoisie. Its history has been written for Paris by the novelist Zola. It was to see houses on expensive sites rise constantly higher, the consequent birth of the 'lift' or 'elevator', and in the 1880s the construction of the first 'skyscrapers' in the United States. It is worth remembering that, at the moment when Manhattan's business thus began to reach for the skies, New York's Lower East side was probably the most overcrowded slum area in the western world with over 520 persons per acre. Nobody built sky-scrapers for them; perhaps fortunately.

Paradoxically, the more the middle class increased and flourished, diverting resources towards its own housing, offices, the department stores which were so characteristic a development of the era, and its prestige buildings, the less went relatively to the working-class quarters, except in the most general form of social expenditure – streets, sanitation, lighting and public utilities. The only form of private enterprise (including building) which aimed primarily at the mass market, apart from the market and small shop, was the tavern – which became the elaborate 'gin-palace' in the Britain of the 1860s and 1870s – and its offspring the theatre and music-hall. For as the people became urbanised, the ancient ways and practices they brought with them from the countryside or the pre-industrial town became irrelevant or impracticable.

II

The great city was a portent, though it contained only a minority of the population. The great industrial enterprise was as yet less significant. Indeed, by modern standards the size of such enterprises was not unduly impressive, though it tended to increase. In the 1850s a factory of 300 in Britain could still be considered very large, and as late as 1871 the average British cotton factory employed 180 people, the average works manufacturing machinery a mere eighty-five.[15] Admittedly the heavy industry which was so characteristic of our period was much larger, and tended to develop concentrations of capital which controlled entire cities and even regions, and mobilised unusually vast armies of labour under its command.

Railway companies were enormous undertakings, even when constructed and managed entirely under conditions of competitive free enterprise, as normally they were not. By the time the British railway system stabilised itself in the late 1860s, every foot of rail between the Scottish border, the Pennine hills, the sea and the River

Humber was controlled by the North-eastern Railway. Coalmines were still largely individual undertakings and sometimes quite small, though the size of the occasional great mining disasters gives some idea of the scale on which they operated: 145 killed at Risca in 1860, 178 at Ferndale (also South Wales) in 1867, 140 at Swaithe (Yorkshire) and 110 at Mons (Belgium) in 1875, 200 at High Blantyre (Scotland) in 1877. Yet increasingly, especially in Germany, vertical and horizontal combination produced those industrial empires which controlled the lives of thousands. The concern known since 1873 as the *Gutehoffnungshütte A.G.* was by no means the largest in the Ruhr, but by then it had extended from iron-founding into quarrying and mining iron ore and coal – it produced practically all the 215,000 tons of iron ore and half the 415,000 tons of coal it required – and had diversified into transport, rolling and the construction of bridges, ships, and a variety of machinery.[16]

Small wonder that the Krupp works in Essen rose from seventy-two workers in 1848 to almost 12,000 in 1873, or that Schneider in France had multiplied to 12,500 in 1870, so that more than half the population of the town of Creusot worked in their blast furnaces, rolling-mills, power-hammers and engineering workshops.[17] Heavy industry produced not so much the industrial region as such as the company town, in which the fate of men and women depended on the fortunes and goodwill of a single master, behind whom stood the force of law and state power, which regarded his authority as necessary and beneficial.*

For, large or small, the 'master' rather than the impersonal authority of the 'company' ruled the enterprise, and even the company was identified with a man rather than a board of directors. In most people's minds, and in reality, capitalism still meant the one-man, or rather one-family, owner-managed business. Yet this very fact raised two serious problems for the structure of enterprise. They concerned its supply of capital and its management.

By and large the characteristic enterprise of the first half of the

* Art. 414 of the French Penal Code, as modified in 1864, made it a crime for anyone to attempt or actually to bring about or continue a collective stoppage of labour for the purpose of raising or lowering wages or in any way interfering with the free exercise of industry or labour, by means of violence, threats or trickery. Even where this was not actually the model of local legislation, as in Italy, it represented the almost universal attitude of the law.[18]

century had been financed privately – e.g. from family assets – and expanded by reinvesting profits, though this might well mean that, with most of capital tied up in this way, the firm might rely a good deal on credit for its current operations. But the increasing size and cost of such undertakings as railways, metallurgical and other expensive activities requiring heavy initial outlays, made this more difficult, especially in countries newly entering upon industrialisation and lacking large accumulations of private investment capital. It is true that in some countries such reservoirs of capital were already available, amply sufficient not only for their own needs but also anxious to be drawn upon (for a suitable rate of interest) by the rest of the world's economy. The British invested abroad in this period as never before or, relatively speaking – according to some – since. So did the French, probably at the theoretical expense of their own industries, which grew rather more slowly than their rivals'. But even in Britain and France new ways of mobilising these savings, of channelling them into the required enterprises, of organising joint-stock rather than privately financed activities, had to be devised.

The third quarter of the century was therefore a fertile period of experiments in the mobilisation of capital for industrial development. With the notable exception of Britain most of them in one way or another involved the banks, either directly or through the fashionable device of the *crédit mobilier*, a sort of industrial finance company which regarded the orthodox banks as insufficiently suited to or interested in industrial financing and competed with them. The brothers Pereire, those dynamic industrialisers inspired by the ideas of Saint-Simon and enjoying some backing from Napoleon III, developed the prototype model of this device. They spread it all over Europe in competition with their bitter rivals the Rothschilds, who did not like the idea but were obliged to follow suit, and – as so often happens in periods of boom when financiers feel heroic and the money rolls in – it was much imitated, especially in Germany. *Crédits mobiliers* were the rage, at least until the Rothschilds won their battle with the Pereires and – as also often happens in boom periods – some operators ventured a little too far across the always hazy frontier between business optimism and fraud. However, a variety of other devices for similar purposes were also being developed, notably the investment bank or *banque d'affaires*. And of course the stock exchanges, by now trading largely in the shares of industrial and transport undertakings, flourished as never before. In 1856 the Paris *Bourse* alone listed the share of 33 railway and canal companies, 38 mining companies, 22 metallurgical companies, 11 port and shipping companies, 7 omnibus and road transport undertakings, 11 gas companies and 42 assorted industrial undertakings ranging from textiles to galvanised iron and rubber, to the value of about 5½ million gold francs, or rather more than a quarter of all securities traded.[19]

How far were such new ways of mobilising capital required? How far were they effective? Industrialists never liked financiers much, and established industrialists tried to have as little as possible to do with bankers. 'Lille', wrote a local observer in 1869, 'is not a capitalist town, it is first and foremost a great industrial and commercial centre'[20] where men put their profits back into the business, did not play about with them, and hoped they would never have to borrow. No industrialist liked to put himself at the mercy of creditors. Still, he might have to. Krupp grew so fast between 1855 and 1866 that he ran out of capital. There is an elegant historical model, according to which the more backward an economy and the later it started upon industrialisation, the greater its reliance on the new large-scale methods of mobilising and directing savings. In the developed western countries private resources and the capital market were quite adequate. In central Europe the banks and similar institutions had to act much more systematically as 'developers' of history. Further east, south and overseas, governments had to step in themselves, generally with the aid of foreign investment, either to secure capital at all or, more likely, to see that investors were guaranteed – or at least *thought* they were guaranteed – the dividends that would alone mobilise their money, or alternatively to undertake economic activities themselves. Whatever the validity of this theory, there is no doubt that in our period the banks (and similar institutions) played a much greater role as developers and directors of industry in Germany, the great industrial newcomer, than in the west. Whether they meant to – as the *crédits mobiliers* did – or whether they were much good at it, is a more obscure question. Probably they were not particularly expert until big industrialists, now recognizing the need for much more elaborate financing than in the simple old days, colonised the big banks themselves, as they increasingly did in Germany after 1870.

Finance did not much affect the organisation of businesses, though it might influence their policy. The problem of management was more difficult. For the basic model of the individually or family-owned and managed enterprise, the patriarchal family autocracy, was increasingly irrelevant to the industries of the second half of the nineteenth century. 'The best instruction', wrote a German handbook of 1868, 'is by word of mouth. Let it be given by the entrepreneur himself, all-seeing, omnipresent and ever available, whose personal orders are reinforced by the personal example which his employees have constantly before their eyes.'[21] This advice, suited to small craft-masters or farmers, might still make some sense in the moderately small counting houses of even quite large bankers and merchants, and remained valid in as much as *instruction* was an essential aspect of management in newly industrialising countries. There even men with the basic training of craft workers (preferably in metals) had still to be taught the specific skills of the skilled factory worker. The great majority of Krupp's skilled men, and indeed of all German machine-building enterprises, seem to have been trained on the job in this way. Only in Britain could employers already rely on a ready-made, indeed on a largely self-made, supply of skilled men with industrial experience. The paternalism of so many large continental undertakings owed something to this long association of workers with the firm with which they, as it were, grew up and on which they depended. But the lords of rail, mine and steel-mill cannot really have expected to look paternally over their workers' shoulders at all times, and they certainly did not do so.

The alternative and complement to instruction was command. But neither the autocracy of the family nor the small-scale operations of craft industry and merchant business provided much guidance for really large capitalist organisation. So, paradoxically, private enterprise in its most unrestricted and anarchic period tended to fall back on the only available models of large-scale management, the military and bureaucratic. The railway companies, with their pyramid of uniformed and disciplined workers, possessing job security, often promotion by seniority and even pensions, are an extreme example. The appeal of military titles, which occur freely among the early British railway executives and managers of large port undertakings, did not rest on pride in the hierarchies of soldiers and officials, such as the Germans felt, but on the inability of private enterprise as yet to devise a specific form of management for big business. It clearly had advantages from the organisational point of view. Yet it did not generally solve the problem of keeping labour itself at work, loyally, diligently and modestly. It was all very well for countries where uniforms were fashionable – as they certainly were not in Britain and the United States – to encourage among the labourers the soldierly virtues, not the least of which was to be poorly paid.

> I am a soldier a soldier of industry
> And like you, I have my flag.
> My labour has enriched the fatherland.
> I'd have you know, my destiny is glorious.[22]

Thus sang a poetaster in Lille (France). But even there patriotism was hardly enough.

The age of capital found it difficult to come to terms with this problem. The bourgeoisie's insistence on loyalty, discipline and modest contentment could not really conceal that its real views about what made workers labour were quite different. But what were they? In theory they should labour in order to stop being workers as soon as possible, thus entering the bourgeois universe. As 'E.B.' put it in the *Songs for English Workmen to Sing* in 1867:

> Work, boys, work and be contented
> So long as you've enough to buy a meal;
>   The man you may rely
>   Will be wealthy by and by
> If he'll only put his shoulder to the wheel.[23]

But though this hope might be enough for some who were actually to lift themselves out of the working class, and perhaps also for a greater number who never got beyond dreaming of success as they read Samuel Smiles's *Self-Help* (1859) or similar handbooks, it was perfectly evident that most workers would remain workers all their lives, and indeed that the economic system required them to do so. The promise of the field-marshal's baton in every private's knapsack was never intended as a programme for promoting all soldiers to field-marshals.

If promotion was not an adequate incentive, was money? But it was an axiom of mid-nineteenth-century employers that wages must be kept as low as possible, though intelligent entrepreneurs with international experience, like Thomas Brassey, the railway builder, were beginning to point out that the labour of the well-paid British workman was in fact cheaper than that of the abysmally paid coolie, because his productivity was so much higher. But such paradoxes were unlikely to convince businessmen brought up on the economic theory of the 'wage-fund', which they believed to be a scientific demonstration that raising wages was impossible and trade unions were therefore doomed to failure. 'Science' became rather more flexible around 1870, when organised labour looked like becoming a permanent actor on the industrial scene, rather than appearing in an occasional brief walk-on part. The great pundit of economics, John Stuart Mill (1806–73) (he happened personally to sympathise with labour), modified his position on the question in 1869, after which the 'wage-fund' theory no longer enjoyed canonical authority. Still, there was no change in business principles. Few employers were willing to pay more than they had to.

Moreover, economics apart, in the countries of the Old World the middle class believed that workers should be poor, not only because they had always been, but also because economic inferiority was a proper index of class inferiority. If, as happened very occasionally – for instance in the great boom of 1872–3 – some workers actually earned enough to afford for a brief moment the luxuries which employers regarded as their right, indignation was sincere and heartfelt. What business had coal-miners with grand pianos and champagne? In countries of labour shortage, undeveloped social hierarchy and a truculent and democratic working population, things might be different; but in Britain and Germany, France and the Habsburg Empire, unlike Australia or the United States, the suitable maximum for the labouring class was a sufficiency of good decent food (preferably with less than a sufficiency of strong drink), a modestly crowded dwelling, and clothing adequate to protect morals, health and comfort without risking improper emulation of the costume of their betters. It was to be hoped that capitalist progress would eventually bring the labourers nearer to this maximum, and regrettable (though not inconvenient for keeping wages down) that so many were still so far below it. However, it was unnecessary, undesirable and dangerous for wages to rise beyond this.

In fact, the economic theories and the social assumptions of middle-class liberalism were at odds with each other. In one sense the theories triumphed. Increasingly, during our period, the wage-relationship was transformed into a pure market-relationship, a cash nexus. Thus we have seen that British capitalism in the 1860s abandoned non-economic compulsion of labour (such as the Master and Servant Acts which punished breaches of contract by workers with jail), long-term hiring contracts (such as the 'annual bond' of the northern coal-miners), and truck payments, while the average length of hiring was shortened, the average period of payment gradually reduced to a week, or even a day or an hour, thus making the market bargain more sensitive and flexible. On the other hand, the middle classes would have been shocked and appalled if the workers had actually asked for the sort of life they themselves took for granted, and even more if they had looked like achieving it. Inequality of life and expectations was built into the system.

This limited the economic incentives they were prepared to provide. They were willing to tie wages to output by various systems of 'piecework', which seem to have spread during our period, and to point out that the workers had best be thankful to have work at all, since there was a large reserve army outside, waiting for their jobs.

Payment by results had some obvious advantages: Marx called it the most suitable form of wage-payment for capitalism. It provided a genuine incentive for the worker to intensify his labour and thus raise his productivity, a guarantee against slacking, an automatic device for reducing the wage-bill in times of depression, as well as a convenient method – by the cutting of piece-rates – to reduce labour costs and to prevent wages from rising higher than was thought necessary or proper. It divided workers from one another, since their earnings might vary widely even within the same establishment, or different types of labour might be paid in entirely different ways. Sometimes the skilled were actually a species of sub-contractor, paid by output, who hired their unskilled assistants at a flat time-wage and saw to it that they kept up the pace. The trouble was that (where it was not already part of tradition) the introduction of piece-work was often resisted, especially by the skilled men, and that it was complex and obscure not only for the workers, but for employers who often had only the haziest idea of what production-norms to set. Also, it was not easily applicable in certain occupations. The workers attempted to remove these disadvantages by reintroducing the concept of an incompressible and predictable basic wage of 'standard rate', through trade unions or through informal practices. The employers were about to remove theirs by what its American champions were to call 'scientific management', but in our period they were still groping for this solution.

Perhaps this led to a greater emphasis on the other economic incentive. If any single factor dominated the lives of nineteenth-century workers it was *insecurity*. They did not know at the beginning of the week how much they would bring home at the end. They did not know how long their present work would last or, if they lost it, when they would get another job or under what conditions. They did not know when accident or sickness would hit them, and though they knew that some time in middle age – perhaps in the forties for un-skilled labourers, perhaps in the fifties for the more skilled – they would become incapable of doing a full measure of adult physical labour, they did not know what would happen to them between then and death. Theirs was not the insecurity of peasants, at the mercy of periodic – and to be honest, often more murderous – catastrophes such as drought and famine, but capable of predicting with some accuracy how a poor man or woman would spend most days of their lives from birth to the graveyard. It was a more profound unpredict-ability, in spite of the fact that probably a good proportion of workers were employed for long periods of their lives by a single employer. There was no certainty of work even for the most skilled: during the slump of 1857–8 the number of workers in the Berlin engineering industry fell by almost a third.[24] There was nothing that corresponds to modern social security, except charity and relief from actual destitution, and sometimes little of either.

For the world of liberalism insecurity was the price paid for both progress and freedom, not to mention wealth, and was made tolerable by continuous economic expansion. Security was to be bought – at least sometimes – but not for free men and women but, as the English terminology put it clearly, for 'servants' – whose liberty was strictly constrained: domestic servants, 'railway servants', even 'civil ser-vants' (or public officials). In fact, the greatest body even of these, the urban domestic servants, did not enjoy the security of the favoured family retainers of the traditional nobility and gentry, but constantly faced insecurity in its most terrible form: instant dismissal 'without a character', i.e. a recommendation to future employers from the former master, or more likely mistress. For the world of the established bourgeois was also considered to be basically insecure, a state of war in which they might at any moment become the casualties of competition, fraud or economic slump, though in practice the businessmen who were thus vulnerable probably formed only a minority of the middle classes, and the penalty of failure was rarely manual labour, let alone the workhouse. The most serious risk which faced them was that to their involuntarily parasitic women-folk – the unexpected death of the male breadwinner.

Economic expansion mitigated this constant insecurity. There is not much evidence that real wages in Europe began to go up significantly until the later part of the 1860s, but even before then the general feeling that times were improving was unmistakable in the developed countries, the contrast with the disturbed and desperate 1830s and 1840s was palpable. Neither the continent-wide surge in the cost of living in 1853–4 nor the dramatic and world-wide slump of 1858 brought any serious social unrest. The truth is that the great economic boom provided employment – at home and for emigrants abroad – on a quite unprecedented scale. Bad though they were, dramatic cyclical slumps in the developed countries now looked less like proofs of economic breakdown than as temporary interruptions of growth. There was evidently no absolute labour shortage, if only because the reserve armies of the rural population (at home and abroad) were now for the first time advancing *en masse* upon the industrial labour markets. Yet the fact that their competition did not reverse what all scholars agree to be a distinct, if modest, improvement in all but the environmental conditions of the working classes suggests the scale and impetus of economic expansion.

Yet, unlike the middle class, the worker was rarely more than a hair's breadth removed from the pauper, and insecurity was therefore constant and real. He had no significant reserves. Those who could live on savings for a few weeks or months were 'that rare class'.[25] The wages of even the skilled were at best modest. In normal times that overlooker in a Preston spinning mill who, with his seven employed children, earned £4 a week in a week of full employment, would have been the envy of his neighbours. But it did not take many weeks of the Lancashire cotton famine (due to the interruption of raw material supplies by the American Civil War) to reduce even such a family to charity. The normal or even inevitable road of life passed across chasms into which the worker and his family might and probably would fall: the birth of children, old age and retirement. In Preston, 52 per cent of all working-class families with children below working age, working full-time in a year of memorably good trade (1851), could be expected to live below the poverty line.[26] As for old age, it was a catastrophe to be stoically expected, a decline in earning power from the forties as physical strength ebbed – especially for the less skilled – followed by poverty, and as like as not charity and poor relief. For the middle class the mid-nineteenth century was the golden era of the middle-aged, when men reached the peak of their careers, earnings and activity and physiological decline had not yet become obvious. Only for the oppressed – labouring people of both sexes and women of all classes – did the flower of life bloom in youth.

Neither economic incentives nor insecurity therefore provided a really effective *general* mechanism for keeping labour hard at work; the former, because their scope was limited, the latter because much of it was or seemed as unavoidable as the weather. The middle class found this hard to understand. Why should the best, soberest and ablest workers be the ones most likely to form trade unions, since they were the very ones who were worth the highest wages and the most regular employment? But unions were in fact composed of and certainly led by such men, though the bourgeois mythology saw them as mobs of the stupid and misled, instigated by agitators who could not otherwise have earned a comfortable living. There was of course no mystery. The workers for whom employers competed were not merely the ones with the bargaining strength to make unions practicable, but also those most aware that 'the market' alone guaranteed them neither security nor what they thought they had a right to.

Nevertheless, so long as they did not organise – and sometimes even when they did – the workers themselves provided their employers with a solution to the problem of labour management: by and large they liked to work, and their expectations were remarkably modest. The unskilled or raw immigrants from the countryside were proud of their strength, and came from an environment where hard labour was the criterion of a person's worth and wives were chosen not for their looks but for their work-potential. 'My experience has shown', said an American steelmill superintendent in 1875, 'that Germans, Irish, Swedes and what I denominate "Buckwheats" – young American country boys – judiciously mixed, make the most effective and tractable force you can find'; in fact, anything was better than 'Englishmen, who are great sticklers for high wages, small production and strikes'.[27]

On the other hand, the skilled were moved by the uncapitalist incentive of craft knowledge and craft pride. The very machines of this period, iron and brass filed and polished with the hand of love, in perfect working order after a century (in so far as they still survive), are a visual demonstration of this. The endless catalogue of objects displayed in the international expositions, however awful aesthetically, are monuments to the pride of those who made them. Such men did not take kindly to orders and supervision, and were indeed often beyond effective control, except by the collective of their workshop. They also often resented piece-wages or any other method of speeding up complex and difficult tasks, and thereby lowering the quality of self-respecting work. But if they would work no more and no faster than the job required, they would work no slower and no less: nobody had to give them a special incentive to give of their best. 'A fair day's work for a fair day's pay' was their motto and, if they expected the pay to satisfy them, they also confidently expected the work to satisfy everybody, including themselves.

In fact, of course, this essentially non-capitalist approach to work benefited employers rather than workers. For the buyers in the labour market operated on the principle of buying in the cheapest market and selling in the dearest, though sometimes ignorant of proper cost-accounting methods. But the sellers were not normally asking the maximum wage which the traffic would bear and offering in return the minimum quantity of labour they could get away with. They were trying to earn a decent living as human beings. They were perhaps trying to 'better themselves'. In brief, though naturally not insensitive to the difference between lower and higher wages, they were engaged in human life rather than in an economic transaction.*

* The extreme example of this contrast occurred in the field of professional spectator sports, though the modern forms of these were barely in their infancy

But can we speak of 'the workers' as a single category or class at all? What was there in common between groups of people often so distinct in their environment, their social origins, their formation, their economic situation, and sometimes even their language and customs? Not even poverty, for though by the standards of the middle classes all of them had modest incomes – except in such a paradise of labour as Australia in the 1850s where newspaper compositors could earn up to £18 a week[28] – by the standards of the poor there was a vast difference between the well-paid and more or less regularly employed skilled 'artisan', who wore a copy of respectable middle-class costume on Sundays or even on the way to and from work, and the ragged starveling who hardly ever knew where his, still less his family's, next meal was to come from. They were indeed all united by a common sense of manual labour and exploitation, and increasingly by the common fate of wage-earning. They were united by their growing segregation from a bourgeoisie whose wealth increased dramatically while their own situation remained precarious, a bourgeoisie which became increasingly self-contained and impervious to would-be entrants from below.* For there was all the difference between the modest hillocks of comfort which the successful worker or ex-worker might reasonably hope to climb and the really impressive accumulations of wealth. The workers were pushed into a common consciousness not only by this social polarisation but, in the cities at least, by a common style of life – in which the tavern ('the workman's church' as a bourgeois liberal called it) played a central role – and by a common style of thought. The least conscious tended to be tacitly

---

in our period. The British professional footballer, who appeared in the late 1870s, was to work – until after the Second World War – essentially for a straight wage plus glory and an occasional windfall, though his cash value on the transfer market would soon reach thousands of pounds. The moment when the football star himself expected to be paid for his market value marks a fundamental transformation in the sport; one achieved much earlier in the United States than in Europe.

* In Lille the (bourgeois) 'upper class' rose from 7 to 9 per cent of the population between 1820 and 1873–5, but its share of the wealth left in wills grew from 58 to 90 per cent. The 'popular classes' who rose from 62 to 68 per cent left only 0·23 per cent of testamentary wealth. Modest though this figure had been in 1821, it was then still 1·4 per cent.[29]

secularised, the most conscious were radicalised, the supporters of the International in the 1860s and 1870s, the future followers of the socialists. The two phenomena were linked, for traditional religion had always been a bond of social unity through the ritual assertion of community. But the common processions and ceremonies atrophied in Lille during the Second Empire. The small craft workers of Vienna, whose simple piety and naïve joy in Catholic pomp and spectacle Le Play noted in the 1850s, became indifferent to these things. Within less than two generations they had transferred their faith to socialism.[30]

The heterogeneous groups of 'the labouring poor' undoubtedly tended to become part of a 'proletariat' in cities and industrial regions. The growing importance of trade unions in the 1860s registered this, the very existence – not to mention the strength – of the International would have been impossible without it. Yet 'the labouring poor' had not been a mere assembly of disparate groups. They had, especially in the hard hopeless times of the first half of the century, been fused into a homogeneous mass of the discontented and the oppressed. This homogeneity was now being lost. The era of a flourishing and stable liberal capitalism offered 'the working class' the possibility of improving its collective lot through collective organisation. But those who merely remained the miscellaneous 'poor' could make little use of the trade unions and even less use of Mutual Aid Societies. Unions were, by and large, organisations of favoured minorities, though mass strikes could occasionally mobilise the masses. Moreover, liberal capitalism offered the individual worker distinct prospects of improvement on bourgeois terms, which large bodies of the labouring population were unable or unwilling to seize.

A fissure therefore ran through what was increasingly becoming 'the working class'. It separated 'the workers' from 'the poor', or alternatively 'the respectable' from the 'unrespectable'. In political terms (see chapter 6 above) it separated people like 'the intelligent artisan', to whom British middle-class radicals were anxious to give the vote, from the dangerous and ragged masses whom they were still determined to exclude.

No term is harder to analyse than 'respectability' in the mid-nineteenth-century working class, for it expressed simultaneously the penetration of middle-class values and standards, and also the attitudes without which working-class self-respect would have been difficult to achieve, and a movement of collective struggle impossible to build: sobriety, sacrifice, the postponement of gratification. If the movement of the workers had been clearly revolutionary, or at least sharply segregated from the middle-class world (as it had been before 1848 and was to be again in the era of the second International), the distinction would have been clear enough. Yet in the third quarter of the nineteenth century the line between personal and collective improvement, between imitating the middle class and, as it were, defeating it with its own weapons, was often impossible to draw. Where do we place William Marcroft (1822–94)? He could easily be presented as a modest example of Samuel Smiles's self-help – the illegitimate son of a farm-servant and a weaver, totally lacking in formal education, who advanced from Oldham textile-worker to foreman in an engineering works, until in 1861 he set up independently as a dentist, dying worth almost £15,000, which was by no means negligible: a lifelong radical Liberal and temperance advocate. And yet his modest place in history is due to an equally lifelong passion for co-operative production (i.e. socialism through self-help), to which he devoted his days. Conversely, William Allan (1813–74) was unquestionably a believer in the class struggle and, in the words of his obituary, 'on social questions he inclined to Robert Owen's school'. Yet this radical worker, formed in the revolutionary school of before 1848, was to make his mark on labour history as the cautious, moderate and above all efficient administrator of the greatest of the 'new model' skilled unions, the Amalgamated Society of Engineers; and was both a practising Anglican churchman and 'in politics a sound and consistent liberal, not given to political quackery in any form'.[31]

The fact is that the capable and intelligent workman, especially if skilled, at this time provided both the main prop of middle-class social control and industrial discipline and also the most active cadres of the workers' collective self-defence. He provided the first, because a stable, prosperous and expanding capitalism needed him, offered him prospects of modest improvement, and in any case now seemed inescapable. It no longer looked provisional and temporary. Conversely, the great revolution seemed less a first instalment of an even greater change than the last instalment of a past era: at best a splendid highly coloured memory, at worst a proof that there were no

264

dramatic shortcuts to progress. But he also provided the second, because – with the possible exception of the United States, that land which appeared to promise the poor a personal way out of lifelong poverty, the worker a private exit from the working class, and every citizen equality with every other – the working classes knew that the liberal free market alone would not give them their rights and their needs. They had to organise and fight. The British 'aristocracy of labour', a stratum peculiar to that country where the class of independent small producers, shopkeepers, etc., was relatively insignificant, as was the lower middle class of white-collar workers and minor bureaucrats, helped to turn the Liberal Party into a party with genuine mass appeal. At the same time it formed the core of the unusually powerful organised trade-union movement. In Germany even the most 'respectable' workers were pressed into the ranks of the proletariat by the distance which separated them from the bourgeoisie, and the strength of intermediate classes. Here the men who streamed into the new 'self-improvement' associations (*Bildungsvereine*) in the 1860s – there were 1,000 such clubs in 1863, no less than 2,000 in Bavaria alone by 1872 – rapidly drifted away from the middle-class liberalism of these bodies, though perhaps not sufficiently from the middle-class culture they inculcated.[32] They were to become the cadres of the new social-democratic movement, especially after the end of our period. But they were self-improving workmen none the less, 'respectable' because self-respecting, and carried the bad as well as the good sides of their respectability into the parties of Lassalle and Marx. Only where revolution still seemed the *only* plausible solution for the conditions of the labouring poor, or where – as in France – the tradition of insurrection and the revolutionary social republic was the dominant political tradition of the working people, was 'respectability' a relatively insignificant factor, or confined to the middle classes and those who wished to be identified with them.

What of the others? Though they were the subjects of much more inquiry than the 'respectable' working classes (but in this generation distinctly less so than before 1848 or after 1880), we really know very little about anything except their poverty and squalor. They did not express public opinions and were rarely touched by even those organisations, trade unionist, political or otherwise, which bothered to appeal to them. Even the Salvation Army, formed specifically with the 'unrespectable' poor in mind, hardly succeeded in becoming more than a welcome addition to free public entertainment (with its uniforms, bands and lively hymns), and a useful source of charity. Indeed, for many of the unskilled or sweated trades the sort of organisations which were beginning to make the strength of labour movements were quite impracticable. Great surges of political movement, such as Chartism in the 1840s, could recruit them: the London costermongers (small market traders) described by Henry Mayhew were all Chartists. Great revolutions could, though perhaps only briefly, inspire even the most oppressed and a-political: the prostitutes of Paris were strong supporters of the Commune of 1871. But the age of bourgeois triumph was precisely not one of revolutions nor even popular mass political movements. Bakunin was perhaps not entirely wrong in supposing that in such a time the spirit of at least potential insurrection was most likely to smoulder among the marginal and sub-proletariat, though he was quite mistaken in believing that they would be the base of revolutionary movements. The miscellaneous poor supported the Paris Commune, but its activists were the more skilled workers and craftsmen; and that most marginal section of the poor – the adolescents – were under-represented among them. Adult men, especially those old enough still to have a memory, however faint, of 1848, were the characteristic insurrectionaries of 1871.

The line which divided the labouring poor into the potential militants of labour movement and the rest was not sharp, and yet it existed. 'Association' – the free and conscious formation of voluntary democratic societies for social defence and improvement – was the magic formula of the liberal era; through it even the labour movements which were to abandon liberalism were to develop.[33] Those who wanted to and could effectively 'associate' might at best shrug their shoulders at, and at worst despise, those who neither could nor wanted to, not least the women, who were virtually excluded from the world of club formalities, points-of-order and proposals for membership. The boundaries of that part of the working classes – it might overlap with the independent craftsmen, shopkeeper and even the small entrepreneur – which was coming to be recognised as a social and political force pretty well coincided with those of the world

266

of clubs – Mutual Aid Societies, fraternal benevolent orders (generally with strong rituals), choirs, gymnastic or sports clubs, even voluntary religious organisations at one extreme, labour unions and political associations at the other. That covered a varying, though substantial, part of the working class – perhaps by the end of our period some 40 per cent in Britain. But it left a great many out. They were the objects and not the subjects of the liberal era. The others expected and got little enough: they got even less.

It is difficult, looking back, to form a balanced view of the condition of all these working people. For one thing, the range of countries in which there were modern cities and modern industry was now much wider, and so was the range of stages in industrial development which they represented. Generalisation is therefore not easy, and its value is limited, even if we confine it – as we must – to the relatively developed countries as distinct from the backward, to the urban working classes as distinct from the agrarian and peasant sectors. The problem is to strike a balance between, on the one hand, the harsh poverty which still dominated the lives of most working folk, the repulsive physical environment and the moral void which surrounded so many of them, and, on the other, the undoubted general improvement of their conditions and prospects since the 1840s. Self-satisfied spokesmen for the bourgeoisie were inclined to overstress the improvement, though none would deny what Sir Robert Giffen (1837–1900), looking back on the British half-century before 1883, tactfully called 'a residuum still unimproved', nor that the improvement 'even when measured by a low ideal, is far too small', nor that 'no one can contemplate the condition of the masses of the people without desiring something like a revolution for the better'.[34] Less self-satisfied social reformers, while not denying improvement – in the case of the elite of workers whose relative scarcity of qualifications put them into a fairly continuous sellers' market, the substantial improvement – gave a less rose-tinted picture:

'There remain [wrote Miss Edith Simcox, again in the early 1880s], . . . some ten millions of town workers, including all mechanics and labourers whose life is not normally overshadowed by the fear of "coming on the parish". No hard and fast line can be drawn between the workers who are and those who are not to be counted amongst "the poor"; there is a constant flux, and besides those who suffer from chronic underpayment, artisans, as well as tradesmen and rustics, are constantly sinking, with or without their own fault, into the depth of misery. It is not easy to judge how many of the ten millions do or might belong to the prosperous aristocracy of the working classes, that section with which politicians come into contact, and from whence come those whom society is rather over-hasty to welcome as "representative working men" . . . I confess I should hardly venture to hope that more than two millions of skilled workers, representing a population of five millions, are living habitually in a state of ease and comparative security of the modest sort . . . The other five millions include the labourers and less skilled workers, male and female, whose maximum wages only suffice for the necessities and barest decencies of existence, and for whom therefore any mischance means penury, passing swiftly into pauperism.'[35]

But even such informed and well-meaning impressions were somewhat too sanguine, for two reasons. First, because (as the social surveys which become available from the late 1880s make clear) the poor workers – who formed almost 40 per cent of the London working class – hardly enjoyed the 'barest decencies of existence', even by the austere standards then applied to the lower orders. Second, because the 'state of ease and comparative security of the modest sort' amounted to little enough. The young Beatrice Potter, anonymously living among the textile workers of Bacup, had no doubt that she shared the lives of the 'comfortable working class' – dissenters and co-operators, a tight community without the casual, marginal or 'unrespectable', surrounded by 'the general well-being of well-earned and well-paid work', 'the cottages comfortable and well-furnished, and the teas excellent'. And yet this acute observer would describe the very same people – almost unaware of what she was observing – as physically overworked during times of busy trade, as eating and sleeping too little, as too physically exhausted for intellectual effort, at the mercy of 'the many chances of breakdown and failure meaning absence of physical comfort'. The deep and simple puritan piety of these men and women was, she saw, a response to the fear of 'worn-out and failed lives'.

> 'Life in Christ' and hope in another world bring ease and refinement into a mere struggle for existence, calming the restless craving after the good things of this world by an 'other worldliness' and making failure a 'means of grace' instead of a despicable want of success.[36]

This is not the picture of starvelings about to arise from their slumbers, but neither is it a picture of men and women 'better, immensely better, than they were fifty years ago', still less of a class that 'had almost all the material benefit of the last fifty years' (Giffen)[37] as self-satisfied and ignorant liberal economists maintained. It is a picture of self-respecting and self-reliant people whose expectations were pitifully modest, who knew they could be worse off, who perhaps remembered times when they had been even poorer, but who were always haunted by the spectre of poverty (as they understood the term). The standards of the middle-class life would never be for such as these, but pauperism was always near. 'One mustn't take too much of a good thing, for money is easily spent', said one of Beatrice Potter's hosts, putting the cigarette she had offered him on the mantelpiece after one or two puffs, for the next night. Anyone who forgets that this is how men and women thought of the goods of life in those days will never be competent to judge the small but genuine improvement which the great capitalist expansion brought to a substantial part of the working classes in the third quarter of the ninteenth century. And the gap which separated them from the bourgeois world was wide – and unbridgeable.

Chapter Thirteen

The Bourgeois World

*You know that we belong to a century when men are only valued for
what is in them. Every day some master, insufficiently energetic or
serious, is forced to descend from the ranks in society which seemed to
be permanently his, and some intelligent and plucky clerk takes his
place.*

Mme Motte-Bossut to her son, 1856[1]

Behold his little ones *around him, they bask in the warmth of his smile.
And* infant innocence *and joy lighten their happy faces.
He is* holy *and they* honour *him, he is* loving, *and they* love *him,
He is* consistent *and they* esteem *him, he is* firm *and they* fear *him
His friends are the* excellent *among men
He goeth to the* well-ordered *home.*

Martin Tupper, 1876[2]

I

We must now look at that bourgeois society. The most superficial
phenomena are sometimes the most profound. Let us begin our
analysis of that society, which reached its apogee at this period, with
the appearance of the clothes its members wore, the interiors which
surrounded them. 'Clothes make man' said the German proverb, and
no age was more aware of it than one in which social mobility could
actually place numerous people into the historically novel situation
of playing new (and superior) social roles and therefore having to
wear the appropriate costumes. It was not long since the Austrian
Nestroy had written his entertaining and embittered farce *The Talis-
man* (1840), in which the fortunes of a poor red-haired man are
dramatically changed by the acquisition, and subsequent loss, of a
black wig. The home was the quintessential bourgeois world, for in
it, and only in it, could the problems and contradictions of his society
be forgotten or artificially eliminated. Here and here alone the bourgeois and even more the petty bourgeois family could maintain
the illusion of a harmonious, hierarchic happiness, surrounded by the

material artefacts which demonstrated it and made it possible, the dream-life which found its culminating expression in the domestic ritual systematically developed for this purpose, the celebration of Christmas. The Christmas dinner (celebrated by Dickens), the Christmas tree (invented in Germany, but rapidly acclimatised through royal patronage in England), the Christmas song – best known through the Germanic *Stille Nacht* – symbolised at one and the same time the cold of the outside world, the warmth of the family circle within, and the contrast between the two.

The most immediate impression of the bourgeois interior of the mid-century is overcrowding and concealment, a mass of objects, more often than not disguised by drapes, cushions, cloths and wall-papers, and always, whatever their nature, elaborated. No picture without a gilded, a fretted, a chased, even a velvet-covered frame, no seat without upholstery or cover, no piece of textile without tassel, no piece of wood without some touch of the lathe, no surface without some cloth or object on it. This was no doubt a sign of wealth and status: the beautiful austerity of Biedermayer interiors had reflected the straitness of Germanic provincial bourgeois finances more than their innate taste, and the furnishings of servants' rooms in the bour-geois houses were bleak enough. Objects express their cost and, at a time when most domestic ones were still produced largely by manual crafts, elaboration was largely an index of cost together with expen-sive materials. Cost also bought comfort, which was therefore visible as well as experienced. Yet objects were more than merely utilitarian or symbols of status and achievement. They had value in themselves as expressions of personality, as both the programme and the reality of bourgeois life, even as *transformers* of man. In the home all these were expressed and concentrated. Hence its internal accumulations.

Its objects, like the houses which contained them, were *solid*, a term used, characteristically, as the highest praise for a business enterprise. They were made to last, and they did. At the same time they must express the higher and spiritual aspirations of life through their beauty, unless they represented these aspirations by their very existence, as did books and musical instruments, which remained surprisingly functional in design, apart from fairly minor surface flourishes, or unless they belonged to the realm of pure utility such as kitchenware and luggage. Beauty meant decoration, since the mere construction of the houses of the bourgeoisie or the objects which furnished them was seldom sufficiently grandiose to offer spiritual and moral sustenance in itself, as the great railways and steamships did. *Their* outsides remained functional; it was only their insides, in so far as they belonged to the bourgeois world like the newly devised Pullman sleeping-cars (1865) and the first-class steamer saloons and state-rooms, which had *décor*. Beauty therefore meant decoration, something applied to the surface of objects.

This duality between solidity and beauty thus expressed a sharp division between the material and the ideal, the bodily and the spiritual, highly typical of the bourgeois world; yet spirit and ideal in it depended on matter, and could be expressed only through matter, or at least through the money which could buy it. Nothing was more spiritual than music, but the characteristic form in which it entered the bourgeois home was the piano, an exceedingly large, elaborate and expensive apparatus, even when reduced, for the benefit of a more modest stratum aspiring to true bourgeois values, to the more manageable dimensions of the upright (*pianino*). No bourgeois interior was complete without it; no bourgeois daughter, but was obliged to practise endless scales upon it.

The link between morality, spirituality and poverty, so obvious to non-bourgeois societies, was not entirely snapped. It was recognised that the exclusive pursuit of higher things was very likely to be unremunerative except in certain of the more saleable arts, and even then prosperity would come only in mature years: the poor student or young artist, as private tutor or guest at the Sunday dinner-table, was a recognised subaltern part of the bourgeois family, at any rate in those parts of the world in which culture was highly respected. But the conclusion drawn was not that there was a certain contradiction between the pursuit of material and mental achievement, but that one was the necessary basis for the other. As the novelist E. M. Forster was to put it in the Indian summer of the bourgeoisie: 'In came the dividends, up went the lofty thoughts.' The most suitable fate for a philosopher was to be born the son of a banker, like George Lukacs. The glory of German learning, the *Privatgelehrter* (or private scholar) rested on the private income. It was right that the poor Jewish scholar should marry the daughter of the richest local merchant, because it was unthinkable that a community which respected

272

16   India from above: British officer relaxing, c. 1870

The last of the Herd.

17   India from below: Madras famine, 1876-8

18 Men moving: emigrants arriving at Cork for the voyage to America, 1851

19 Pioneers: settlers' cabin

20 Railway builders: Indian coolies laying the track

21 Devil's Gate Bridge during the construction of the Union Pacific Railroad

22   A slave auction in Virginia, *c.* 1860

23   Henry Morton Stanley arrives in an African village (from his own sketch)

24   1848: the overthrow of the French monarchy on the barricades

25   Paris Commune 1871: attack on the barricade at the corner of rue de la Huchette in the Latin Quarter

26   The world of capital – the factory: Iron and Steel Works, Barrow

27   Industrial relations: emblem of the Amalgamated Society of Engineers

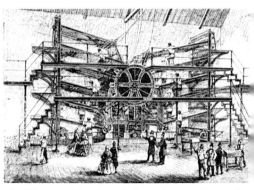

28   The world of capital – the machine: *Daily Telegraph*'s ten-feeder printing machine

29   The reality of war: The American Civil War from one of the first on-the-spot war photographers

30   Seventh Cavalry attacking Indian village: print from *Harper's Weekly*, 1868

THE HOMELESS POOR.

"AH! WE'RE BADLY OFF BUT JUST THINK OF THE POOR MIDDLE CLASSES, WHO ARE OBLIGED TO EAT ROAST MUTTON AND BOILED FOWL EVERY DAY!"

31   Coda: cartoon from *Punch*, 1859

learning should reward its luminaries with nothing more tangible than praise.

This duality of matter and spirit implied a hypocrisy which unsympathetic observers considered to be not merely all-pervasive but a fundamental characteristic of the bourgeois world. Nowhere was this more obvious, in the literal sense of being visible, than in the matter of sex. This is not to imply that the mid-nineteenth-century (male) bourgeois (or those who aspired to be like him) was merely dishonest, preaching one morality while deliberately practising another, though patently the conscious hypocrite is more often to be found where the gap between official morality and the demands of human nature is unbridgeable, as in this period it often was. Plainly Henry Ward Beecher, the great New York preacher of puritanism, should either have avoided having tumultuous extra-marital love-affairs or chosen a career which did not require him to be quite such a prominent advocate of sexual restraint; though one cannot entirely fail to sympathise with the bad luck which linked him in the mid-1870s with the beautiful feminist and advocate of free love, Victoria Woodhull, a lady whose convictions made privacy difficult.* But it is pure anachronism to suppose, as several recent writers on 'The Other Victorians' have done, that the official sexual morality of the age was mere window-dressing.

In the first place, its hypocrisy was not simply a lie, except perhaps among those whose sexual tastes were as powerful as they were publicly inadmissible, e.g. prominent politicians depending on puritan voters or respectable homosexual businessmen in provincial cities. It was hardly hypocritical at all in the countries (e.g. most Roman Catholic ones) in which a frankly dual standard was accepted: chastity for unmarried bourgeois women and fidelity for married ones, the free pursuit of all women (except perhaps marriageable daughters of the middle and upper classes) by all young bourgeois men, and a tolerated infidelity for the married ones. Here the rules of the game were perfectly understood, including the need for a certain discretion

* This splendid woman, one of two equally attractive and emancipated sisters, caused Marx some moments of irritation because of her efforts to convert the American section of the International into an organ for the propagation of free love and spiritualism. The two sisters did very well out of their relations with Commodore Vanderbilt, who looked after their financial interests. Eventually she married well and died in the odour of respectability in England, in Bredon's Norton, Worcestershire.[3]

in cases where the stability of the bourgeois family or property would otherwise have been threatened: passion, as every Italian of the middle class still knows, is one thing, 'the mother of my children' quite another. Hypocrisy entered this pattern of behaviour only in so far as the bourgeois women were supposed to remain entirely outside the game, and therefore in ignorance of what the men, and women other than themselves, were up to. In Protestant countries the morality of sexual restraint and fidelity was supposed to be binding on both sexes, but the very fact that it was felt to be so even by those who broke it, led them not so much into hypocrisy as into personal torment. It is quite illegitimate to treat a person in such a situation as a mere swindler.

Moreover, to a very great extent bourgeois morality was actually applied; indeed it may have become increasingly effective as the masses of the 'respectable' working classes adopted the values of the hegemonic culture, and the lower middle classes, which followed it by definition, grew in numbers. Such matters resisted even the intense interest of the bourgeois world in 'moral statistics', as a late-nineteenth-century reference book sadly admitted, dismissing all the attempts to measure the extent of prostitution as failures. The only comprehensive attempt to measure venereal infection, which plainly had a strong connection with some kinds of extra-marital sex, revealed little except that in Prussia, not unexpectedly, it was much higher in the megalopolis Berlin than in any other province (tending normally to diminish with the size of cities and villages), and that it reached its maximum in towns with ports, garrisons and institutes of higher education, i.e. with heavy concentrations of unmarried young men away from their homes.* There is no reason to suppose that the average Victorian member of the middle class, lower middle class or 'respectable' working class in, say, Victorian England and the United States failed to live up to his or her standards of sexual morality. The young American girls who surprised cynical men-about-town in the Paris of Napoleon III by the freedom with which they were allowed by their parents to go about alone and in the company of young American men are as strong evidence about sexual morals as journalistic

* The doctors of Prussia were asked to give the numbers of all venereal patients treated in April 1900. There is no reason to believe that the relative figures would have been very different thirty years earlier.[4]

274

exposés of haunts of vice in mid-Victorian London: probably stronger.[5] It is entirely illegitimate to read post-Freudian standards into a pre-Freudian world or to assume that sexual behaviour then must have been like ours. By modern standards those lay monasteries, the Oxford and Cambridge colleges, look like case books of sexual pathology. What would we think today of a Lewis Carroll whose passion was to photograph little girls naked? By Victorian standards their worst vices were almost certainly gluttony rather than lust, and the sentimental taste of so many dons for young men – almost certainly (the very term is revealing) 'platonic' – among the natural crotchets of inveterate bachelors. It is our age which has turned the phrase 'to make love' (in the English language) into a simple synonym for sexual intercourse. The bourgeois world was haunted by sex, but not necessarily sexual promiscuity: the characteristic nemesis of the bourgeois folk-myth, as the novelist Thomas Mann saw so clearly, followed a *single* fall from grace, like the tertiary syphilis of the composer Adrian Leverkuehn in *Dr Faustus*. The very extremism of its fears reflects a prevailing naivety, or innocence.*

This very innocence, however, allows us to see the powerful sexual element in the bourgeois world very clearly in its costume, an extraordinary combination of temptation and prohibition. The mid-Victorian bourgeois was swathed in garments, leaving little publicly visible except the face, even in the tropics. In extreme cases (as in the United States) even objects reminiscent of the body (the legs of tables) might be hidden away. At the same time, and never more so than in the 1860s and 1870s, every secondary sexual characteristic was grotesquely overemphasised: men's hair and beards, women's hair, breasts, hips and buttocks, swelled to enormous size by means of false chignons, *culs-de-Paris*, etc.† The shock effect of Manet's famous *Déjeuner sur l'Herbe* (1863) derives precisely from the contrast between the utter respectability of the dress of the men and the

---

* The strength of prevailing moral standards in Protestant countries has been revealed in the behaviour of North American slave-owners towards their female slaves. Contrary to what might have been expected, and to the prevalent ethos in Catholic-Mediterranean countries – 'there is no such thing as a sweet tamarind or a mulatto virgin' went a Cuban proverb – it seems that the amount of miscegenation, or indeed illegitimacy, in the rural slave South was rather small.[6]

† The fashion for the crinoline, which totally obscured the lower parts while over-emphasising the waist's contrast with the vaguely suggested hips, was a transitional phase of the 1850s.

nakedness of the woman. The very shrillness with which bourgeois civilisation insisted that woman was essentially a spiritual being implied both that men were not, and that the obvious physical attraction between the sexes could not be fitted into the system of values. Achievement was incompatible with enjoyment, as the folklore of championship sport still assumes by sentencing sportsmen to temporary celibacy before the big match or fight. More generally, civilisation rested on the repression of instinctive urges. The greatest of bourgeois psychologists, Sigmund Freud, made this proposition the cornerstone of his theories, though later generations read into him a call for the abolition of repression.

But why was an in itself not implausible view held with a passionate, indeed a pathological, extremism which contrasted so notably (as Bernard Shaw was to observe with his usual wit) with the ideal of moderation and the *juste milieu* which had traditionally defined middle-class social ambitions and roles?[7] On the lower rungs of the ladder of middle-class aspiration, the answer is easy. Heroic efforts alone could lift a poor man and woman, or even their children, out of the slough of demoralisation on to the firm plateau of respectability and, above all, define his position there. As for the member of Alcoholics Anonymous, there could be no compromise solution: it was either total abstinence or total relapse. Indeed, the movement for total abstinence from alcohol, which also flourished at this time in Protestant and puritan countries, illustrates this clearly. It was not effectively designed as a movement to abolish, still less to limit, mass alcoholism, but to define and set apart the class of those individuals who had demonstrated by their personal force of character that they were distinct from the unrespectable poor. Sexual puritanism fulfilled the same function. But this was a 'bourgeois' phenomenon only in so far as it reflected the hegemony of bourgeois respectability. Like the reading of Samuel Smiles or the practice of other forms of 'self-help' and 'self-improvement' it replaced bourgeois success more often than it prepared for it. At the level of the 'respectable' artisan or clerk, abstinence had often to be its own reward. In material terms it gave only modest returns.

The problem of bourgeois sexual puritanism is more complex. The belief that mid-nineteenth-century bourgeois were unusually full-blooded and therefore obliged to build unusually impenetrable defences against physical temptation is unconvincing: what made the temptations so great was precisely the extremism of the accepted moral standards, which also made the fall correspondingly more dramatic, as in the case of the Catholic-puritan Count Muffat in Emile Zola's *Nana*, the novel of prostitution in the Paris of the 1860s. Of course the problem was to some extent economic, as we shall see. The 'family' was not merely the basic social unit of bourgeois society but its basic unit of property and business enterprise, linked with other such units through a system of exchanges of women-plus-property (the 'marriage portion') in which the women were by strict convention deriving from pre-bourgeois tradition *virgines intactae*. Anything which weakened this family unit was impermissible, and nothing more obviously weakened it than uncontrolled physical passion, which introduced 'unsuitable' (i.e. economically undesirable) suitors and brides, split husbands from wives, and wasted common resources.

But the tensions were more than economic. They were particularly great during our period, when the morality of abstinence, moderation and restraint conflicted dramatically with the realities of bourgeois success. The bourgeois no longer lived either in a family economy of scarcity or in a rank of society remote from the temptations of high society. Their problem was spending rather than saving. Not only did the non-working bourgeois become increasingly frequent – in Cologne the number of *rentiers* paying income tax grew from 162 in 1854 to almost 600 in 1874[8] – but how else except by spending was the successful bourgeois, whether or not he held political power as a class, to demonstrate his conquest? The word *parvenu* (newly-rich) automatically became a synonym of the lavish spender. Whether these bourgeois tried to ape the life style of the aristocracy or, like class-conscious Krupp and his fellow-magnates of the Ruhr, built themselves castles and industrial-feudal empires parallel to and more impressive than those of the Junkers whose titles they refused, they had to spend, and in a manner which inevitably brought their life style closer to that of the unpuritan aristocracy, and that of their womenfolk even more so. Before the 1850s this had been a problem of a relatively few families; in some countries, such as Germany, of hardly any. Now it became the problem of a class.

The bourgeoisie as a class found enormous difficulty in combining getting and spending in a morally satisfactory manner, just as it failed to solve the equivalent material problem, how to secure a succession of equally dynamic and capable businessmen within the same family, a fact which increased the role of daughters, who could introduce new blood into the business complex. Of the four sons of the banker Friedrich Wichelhaus in Wuppertal (1810–86) only Robert (b. 1836) remained a banker. The other three (b. 1831, 1842 and 1846) ended as landowners and an academic, but both daughters (b. 1829 and 1838) married industrialists, including a member of the Engels family.[9] The very thing for which the bourgeoisie strove, profit, ceased to be an adequate motivation once it had brought sufficient wealth. Towards the end of the century the bourgeoisie discovered at least a temporary formula for combining getting and spending, cushioned by the acquisitions of the past. These final decades before the catastrophe of 1914 were to be the 'Indian summer', the *belle époque* of bourgeois life, retrospectively lamented by its survivors. But in the third quarter of the nineteenth century the contradictions were perhaps at their most acute: effort and enjoyment coexisted, but clashed. And sexuality was one of the victims of the conflict, hypocrisy the victor.

II

Buttressed by clothes, walls and objects, there was the bourgeois family, the most mysterious institution of the age. For, if it is easy to discover or to devise connections between puritanism and capitalism, as a large literature bears witness, those between nineteenth-century family structure and bourgeois society remain obscure. Indeed the apparent conflict between the two has rarely even been noticed. Why should a society dedicated to an economy of profit-making competitive enterprise, to the efforts of the isolated individual, to equality of rights and opportunities and freedom, rest on an institution which so totally denied all of these?

Its basic unit, the one-family household, was both a patriarchal autocracy and a microcosm of the sort of society which the bourgeoisie as a class (or its theoretical spokesmen) denounced and destroyed: a hierarchy of personal dependence.

> 'There in firm wisdom ruleth well the father, husband, master.
> Heaping it with prosperities, as guardian, guide and judge.'[10]

Below him – to continue quoting the Proverbial Philosopher Martin Tupper, there flitted 'the good angel of the house, the mother, wife and mistress'[11] whose work, according to the great Ruskin, was:

'I To please people
II To feed them in dainty ways
III To clothe them
IV To keep them orderly
V To teach them,'[12]

a task for which, curiously, she was required to show, or to possess, neither intelligence nor knowledge ('Be good sweet maid and let who will be clever', as Charles Kingsley put it). This was not merely because the new function of the bourgeois wife, to show off the capacity of the bourgeois husband to keep her in leisure and luxury, conflicted with the old functions of actually running a household, but also because her inferiority to the man must be demonstrable:

'Hath she wisdom? It is precious, but beware that thou exceed:
For woman must be subject and the true mastery is of the mind.'[13]

However, this pretty, ignorant and idiotic slave was also required to exercise mastery; not so much over the children, whose lord was once again the *pater familias*,* as over the servants, whose presence distinguished the bourgeois from his social inferiors. A 'lady' was definable as someone who did no work, hence who ordered someone else to do it,[15] her superiority being established by this relationship. Sociologically the difference between working and middle classes was that between servant-keepers and potential servants, and was so used in Seebohm Rowntree's pioneer social survey of York at the end of the century. The servants themselves were increasingly and overwhelmingly women – between 1841 and 1881 the percentage of men in domestic offices and personal services in Britain fell from about 20 to about 12 – so that the ideal bourgeois household consisted of a male lord dominating a number of hierarchically graded females, all the more so as male children tended to leave the home as they grew up, or even – among the British upper classes – as soon as they reached the age of boarding school.

* 'The children again did all they could to make their dear adored father happy; they drew, worked, recited, wrote compositions, played the piano.' This to celebrate the birthday of Albert, Prince Consort of Queen Victoria.[14]

But the servant, though receiving wages, and therefore a domestic analogue to the worker whose employment defined the male bourgeois in the economy, was essentially quite different, since her (or more rarely his) main link with the employer was not the cash nexus, but personal, and indeed for practical purposes total, dependence. Everything about her life was strictly prescribed, and, because she lived in some meagrely furnished attic of the household, controllable. From the apron or uniform she wore to the testimonial of good behaviour or 'character', without which she became unemployable, everything about her symbolised a relation of power and subjection. This did not exclude close if unequal personal relations any more than it did in slave societies. Indeed it probably encouraged them, though it must never be forgotten that for every nursemaid or gardener who lived out their lives in the service of one family there were a hundred country girls who passed briefly through the household to pregnancy, marriage or another job, being treated merely as yet another instance of that 'servant problem' which filled the conversations of their mistresses. The crucial point is that the structure of the bourgeois family flatly contradicted that of bourgeois society. Within it freedom, opportunity, the cash nexus and the pursuit of individual profit did not rule.

It could be argued that this was so because the individualist Hobbesian anarchism which formed the theoretical model of the bourgeois economy provided no basis for any form of social organisation, including that of the family. And indeed, in one respect, it was a deliberate contrast to the outside world, an oasis of peace in a world of battle, *le repos du guerrier*.

'You know [wrote a French industrialist's wife to her sons in 1856] that we live in a century when men have value only by their own efforts. Every day the brave and clever assistant takes over from the master, whose slackness and lack of seriousness demotes him from the rank which seemed to be permanently his.'

'What a battle,' wrote her husband, locked in competition with British textile manufacturers. 'Many will die in the struggle, even more will be cruelly wounded.'[16] The metaphor of war came as naturally to the lips of men who discussed their 'struggle for existence' or the 'survival of the fittest', as the metaphor of peace came to

280

them when they described the home: 'the dwelling place of joy', the place where 'the satisfied ambition of the heart rejoiced', as it could never rejoice outside, since it could never be satisfied, or afford to admit itself satisfied.[17]

But it may also be that in the bourgeois family the essential inegalitarianism on which capitalism rested found a necessary expression. Precisely because it was not based on collective, institutionalised, traditional inequalities, dependence had to be an individual relationship. Because superiority was so uncertain for the individual, it had to have one form that was permanent and secure. Because its essential expression was money, which merely expresses the relationship of exchange, other forms of expression which demonstrated the domination of persons over persons had to supplement it. There was of course nothing new in a patriarchal family structure based on the subordination of women and children. But where we might have expected a bourgeois society logically to break it up or transform it – as indeed it was to be disintegrated later – the classic phase of bourgeois society reinforced and exaggerated it.

How far this 'ideal' bourgeois patriarchy actually represented reality is quite another matter. An observer summed up the typical bourgeois of Lille as a man who 'fears God, but above all his wife, and reads the *Echo du Nord*',[18] and this is at least as likely a reading of the facts of bourgeois family life as the male-formulated theory of female helplessness and dependence, sometimes pathologically exaggerated into the masculine dream, and occasional practice, of the child-wife selected and formed by the future husband. Still, the existence and even reinforcement of the ideal-type bourgeois family in this period is significant. It is sufficient to explain the beginnings of a systematic feminist movement among middle-class women in this period, at all events in the Anglo-Saxon or Protestant countries.

The bourgeois household, however, was merely the nucleus of the larger family connection within which the individual operated: 'the Rothschilds', 'the Krupps', or for that matter 'the Forsytes', who make so much of nineteenth-century social and economic history an essentially dynastic affair. But though an enormous amount of material about such families has been accumulated over the past century, neither the social anthropologists nor the compilers of genealogical handbooks (an aristocratic occupation) have taken

281

sufficient interest in them to make it easy to generalise with any confidence about such family groups.

How far were they newly promoted from the lower social ranks? Not to any substantial extent, it would seem, though in theory nothing prevented social ascent. Out of the British steelmasters in 1865, 89 per cent came from middle-class families, 7 per cent from the lower middle class (including small shopkeepers, independent artisans, etc.) and a mere 4 per cent from workers, skilled or – more improbably – unskilled.[19] The bulk of the textile manufacturers in northern France at the same period were similarly children of what could already be considered the middle strata; the bulk of the mid-nineteenth-century Nottingham hosiery manufacturers had similar origins, two-thirds of them actually coming from the hosiery trade. The founding fathers of capitalist enterprise in south-western Germany were not always rich, but the number of those with long family experience in business, and often in the industries they were to develop, is significant: Swiss-Alsatian Protestants like the Koechlin, Geigy or Sarrasin, Jews grown up in the finance of small princelings, rather than technically innovating craftsmen-entrepreneurs. Educated men – notably sons of Protestant pastors or civil servants – modified but did not change their middle-class status by capitalist enterprise.[20] The careers of the bourgeois world were indeed open to talent, but the family with a modest amount of education, property and social connections among others of the middle rank undoubtedly started with a relatively enormous advantage; not least the capacity to intermarry with others of the same social status, in the same line of business or with resources which could be combined with their own.

The economic advantages of a large family or an interlocking connection of families were of course still substantial. Within the business it guaranteed capital, perhaps useful business contacts, and above all reliable managers. The Lefebvres of Lille in 1851 financed the woolcombing enterprise of a brother-in-law, Amedée Prouvost. Siemens and Halske, the famous electrical firm set up in 1847, got its first capital from a cousin; a brother was the first salaried employee and nothing was more natural than that the three brothers Werner, Carl and William should take charge respectively of the Berlin, St Petersburg and London branches. The famous Protestant clans of Mulhouse relied on one another: André Koechlin, son-in-law of the Dollfus

282

who founded Dollfus-Mieg (both he and his father had married into the Miegs), took over the firm until his four brothers-in-law were old enough to manage it, while his uncle Nicholas ran the Koechlin family firm 'with which he associated exclusively his brothers and brothers-in-law as well as his old father'.[21] Meanwhile another Dollfus, great-grandson of the founder, entered another local family firm, Schlumberger et Cie. The business history of the nineteenth century is full of such family alliances and interpenetrations. They required a large number of available sons and daughters, but there was no shortage of these, and hence – unlike among the French peasantry which required one and only one heir to take over the family holding – no strong incentive to birth control, except among the poor and struggling lower middle class.

But how were such clans organised? How did they operate? At what point did they cease to represent family groups and turn into a coherent social group, a local bourgeoisie, or even (as perhaps in the case of Protestant and Jewish bankers) a more widespread network, of which family alliances form merely one aspect? We cannot answer such questions as yet.

III

What, in other words, do we mean by the 'bourgeoisie' as a class in this period? Its economic, political and social definitions differed somewhat, but were still sufficiently close to each other to cause relatively little difficulty.

Thus, economically, the quintessential bourgeois was a 'capitalist' (i.e. either the possessor of capital, or the receiver of an income derived from such a source, or a profit-making entrepreneur, or all of these things). And, in fact, the characteristic 'bourgeois' or member of the middle class in our period included few people who did not fit into one or other of these pigeon-holes. The top 150 families of Bordeaux in 1848 included ninety businessmen (merchants, bankers, shopowners, etc., though in this town as yet few industrialists), forty-five owners of property and *rentiers* and fifteen members of the liberal professions, which were, of course, in those days, varieties of private enterprise. There was among them a total absence of the higher and (at least nominally) salaried business executive who formed the largest single group in the top 450 Bordeaux families in 1960.[22] We might add that, though proprety from land or, more commonly, from urban real-estate, remained an important source of bourgeois income, especially among the middle and lower bourgeoisie in areas of lagging industrialisation, it was already diminishing somewhat in importance. Even in non-industrial Bordeaux (1873) it formed only 40 per cent of the wealth left at death in 1873 (23 per cent of the biggest fortunes), while in industrial Lille at the same time it formed only 31 per cent.[23]

The personnel of bourgeois politics was naturally somewhat different, if only because politics is a specialised and time-consuming activity which does not attract all equally, or for which not all are equally fitted. Nevertheless during this period the extent to which bourgeois politics was actually conducted by practising (or retired) bourgeois was quite striking. Thus in the second half of the nineteenth century between 25 and 40 per cent of the members of the Swiss Federal Council consisted of entrepreneurs and *rentiers* (20–30 per cent of the Council members being the 'federal barons' who ran the banks, railways and industries), a rather larger percentage than in the twentieth century. Another 15–25 per cent consisted of practising members of the liberal professions, i.e. lawyers – though 50 per cent of all members had law degrees, this being the standard educational qualification for public life and administration in most countries. Another 20–30 per cent consisted of professional 'public figures' (prefects, rural judges, and other so-called Magistrates).[24] The Liberal group in the Belgian Chamber at mid-century had an 83 per cent bourgeois membership: 16 per cent of its members were businessmen, 16 per cent *proprietaires*, 15 per cent *rentiers*, 18 per cent professional administrators and 42 per cent liberal professions, i.e. lawyers and a few medical men.[25] This was equally, and perhaps more, marked in local politics in the cities, dominated as these naturally were by the bourgeois (i.e. normally Liberal) notables of the place. If the upper echelons of power were largely occupied by older groups, traditionally established there, from 1830 (in France), from 1848 (in Germany) the bourgeoisie 'assaulted and conquered the lower levels of political power', such as municipal councils, mayoralties, district councils, etc., and kept them under control until the rise of mass politics in the last decades of the century. From 1830 Lille was run by mayors who were prominent businessmen.[26] In Britain the big cities were notoriously in the hands of the oligarchy of local businessmen.

Socially the definitions were not so clear, though the 'middle class' obviously included all the above groups, provided they were wealthy and established enough: businessmen, property-owners, liberal professions and the upper echelons of administration, which were, of course, numerically quite a small group outside the capital cities. The difficulty lay both in defining the 'upper' and 'lower' limits of the stratum within the hierarchy of social status, and in allowing for the marked heterogeneity of its membership within those limits: there was always, at least, an accepted internal stratification into *grande moyenne* and *petite* bourgeoisie, the latter shading off into strata which would be *de facto* outside the class.

At the top end the bourgeoisie was more or less distinct from the aristocracy (high or low), depending partly on the legal and social exclusiveness of that group or on its own class-consciousness. No bourgeois could become a real aristocrat in, say, Russia or Prussia, and even where patents of low nobility were freely distributed, as in the Habsburg Empire, no Count Chotek or Auersperg, however ready to join the board of directors of a business enterprise, would consider a Baron von Wertheimstein as anything except a middle-class banker and a Jew. Britain was almost alone in systematically, though at this period still modestly, absorbing businessmen into the aristocracy – bankers and financiers rather than industrialists.

On the other hand, until 1870, and even thereafter, there were still German industrialists who refused to allow their nephews to become reserve-officers, as being unsuitable for young men of their class, or whose sons insisted on doing their military service in the infantry or engineers rather than the socially more exclusive cavalry. But it must be added that as the profits rolled in – and they were very substantial in our period – the temptation of decorations, titles, intermarriage with the nobility and in general an aristocratic life style was not often resisted by the rich. English non-conformist manufacturers would transfer to the Church of England, and in the north of France the 'barely concealed Voltaireanism' of before 1850 turned into increasingly fervent Catholicism after 1870.[27]

At the bottom the dividing-line was much more clearly economic, though businessmen – at least in Britain – might draw a sharp qualita-

285

tive line between themselves and those social outcasts who actually sold goods directly to the public, such as shopkeepers; at least until retail trade had shown that it could also make millions for its practitioners. The independent artisan and small shopkeeper clearly belonged to a lower middle class or *Mittelstand* which had little in common with the bourgeoisie except aspiration to its social status. The rich peasant was not a bourgeois, and neither was the white-collar employee. Nevertheless, there was in the mid-nineteenth century a sufficiently large reservoir of the older type of economically independent petty commodity producer or seller, and even of the skilled worker and foreman (who still often took the place of the modern technological cadre), for the dividing-line to be hazy: some would prosper and, at least in their localities, become accepted bourgeois.

For the main characteristic of the bourgeoisie as a class was that it was a body of persons of power and influence, independent of the power and influence of traditional birth and status. To belong to it a man had to be 'someone'; a person who counted *as an individual*, because of his wealth, his capacity to command other men, or otherwise to influence them. Hence the classical form of bourgeois politics was, as we have seen, entirely different from the mass politics of those below them, including the petty-bourgeoisie. The classical recourse of the bourgeois in trouble or with cause for complaint was to exercise or ask for personal influence: to have a word with the mayor, the deputy, the minister, the old school or college comrade, the kinsman or business contact. Bourgeois Europe was or grew full of more or less informal systems for protection or mutual advancement, old-boy networks, or mafias ('friends of friends'), among which those arising from common attendance at the same educational institutions were naturally very important, especially the institutions of higher learning, which produced national rather than merely local linkages.* One among these types of network, freemasonry, served an even more important purpose in certain countries, notably Roman Catholic Latin ones, for it could actually serve as the ideological cement for the liberal bourgeoisie in its political dimension, or indeed, as in

* In Britain, however, the so-called 'public schools', which developed rapidly in this period, brought the sons of the bourgeoisie from different parts of the country together at an even earlier age. In France some of the great *lycées* in Paris may have served a similar purpose, at all events for intellectuals.

Italy, as virtually the only permanent and national organisation of the class.[28] The individual bourgeois who felt called upon to comment on public matters knew that a letter to *The Times* or the *Neue Freie Presse* would not merely reach a large part of his class and the decision makers, but, what was more important, that it would be printed on the strength of his standing *as an individual*. The bourgeoisie as a class did not organise mass movements but pressure groups. Its model in politics was not Chartism but the Anti-Corn-Law League.

Of course the degree to which the bourgeois was a 'notable' varied enormously, from the *grande bourgeoisie* whose range of action was national or even international, to the more modest figures who were persons of importance in Aussig (Ustí nad Labem) or Groningen. Krupp expected and received more consideration than Theodor Boeninger of Duisburg, whom the regional administration merely recommended for the title of Commercial Counsellor (*Kommerzienrat*) because he was wealthy, a capable industrialist, active in public and church life and had supported the government in elections and on both municipal and district councils. Yet both in their various ways were people 'who counted'. If armour-plates of internal snobbishness divided millionaires from the rich, and these in turn from the merely comfortable, which was natural enough in a class whose very essence was to climb higher by individual effort, it did not destroy that sense of group consciousness which turned the 'middle rank' of society into the 'middle class' or 'bourgeoisie'.

It rested on common assumptions, common beliefs, common forms of action. The bourgeoisie of the third quarter of the nineteenth century was overwhelmingly 'liberal', not necessarily in a party sense (though as we have seen Liberal parties were prevalent), as in an ideological sense. They believed in capitalism, in competitive private enterprise, technology, science and reason. They believed in progress, in a certain amount of representative government, a certain amount of civil rights and liberties, so long as these were compatible with the rule of law and with the kind of order which kept the poor in their place. They believed in culture in addition to, and sometimes as an alternative to religion, in extreme cases substituting the ritual attendance at opera, theatre or concert for that at church. They believed in the career open to enterprise and talent, and that their own lives

287

proved its merits. As we have seen, by this time the traditional and often puritan belief in the virtues of abstemiousness and moderation was finding it hard to resist the reality of achievement, but they were still regretted. If ever German society was to collapse, argued a writer in 1855, it would be because the middle classes had begun to pursue appearance and luxury 'without seeking to counterbalance it with the simple and hard-working (competent) sense of the bourgeois [*Buergersinn*], with respect for the spiritual forces of life, with the effort to identify science, ideas and talent with the progressive development of the Third Estate'.[29] Perhaps that pervasive sense of a struggle for existence, a natural selection in which, after all, victory or even survival proved both fitness and the essentially moral qualities which could alone achieve fitness, reflects an adaptation of the old bourgeois ethic to the new situation. Darwinism, social or otherwise, was not merely science but ideology, even before it was formulated as such. To be a bourgeois was not merely to be superior, but also to have demonstrated moral qualities equivalent to the old puritan ones.

But more than anything else, it meant superiority. The bourgeois was not merely independent, a man to whom no one (save the state or God) gave orders, but one who gave orders himself. He was not merely an employer, entrepreneur or capitalist but socially a 'master', a 'lord' (*Fabrikherr*), a '*patron*' or '*chef*'. The monopoly of command – in his house, in his business, in his factory – was crucial to his self-definition, and its formal assertion, whether nominal or real, is an essential element in all industrial disputes of the period: 'But I am also the Director of the Mines, that is to say the head [*chef*] of a large population of workers ... I represent the principle of authority and am bound to make it respected in my person: such has always been the conscious object of my relations with the working class.'[30] Only the member of the liberal professions, or the artist and intellectual who was not essentially an employer or someone with subordinates, was not primarily a 'master'. Even here the 'principle of authority' was far from absent, whether from the comportment of the traditional continental university professor, the autocratic medical man, the orchestral conductor or the capricious painter. If Krupp commanded his armies of workers, Richard Wagner expected total subservience from his audience.

Dominance implies inferiority. But the mid-nineteenth-century bourgeoisie was divided on the nature of that inferiority of the lower classes about which there was no substantial disagreement, though attempts had to be made to distinguish, within the subaltern mass, between those who might be expected to rise into, at least, the respectable lower middle class and those who were beyond redemption. Since success was due to personal merit, failure was clearly due to personal lack of merit. The traditional bourgeois ethic, puritan or secular, had ascribed this to moral or spiritual feebleness rather than to lack of intellect, for it was evident that not much in the way of brains was needed for success in business, and conversely that mere brains did not guarantee wealth and still less 'sound' views. This did not necessarily imply anti-intellectualism, though in Britain and the United States it was pervasive, because the triumphs of business were pre-eminently those of poorly educated men using empiricism and common sense. Even Ruskin reflected the common view when he argued that 'busy metaphysicians are always entangling *good* and *active* people, and weaving cobwebs among the finest wheels of the world's business'. Samuel Smiles put the matter more simply:

'The experience to be gathered from books, though often valuable, is but of the nature of *learning*; whereas the experience gained from actual life is of the nature of *wisdom*; and a small store of the latter is worth vastly more than a stock of the former.'[31]

But a simple classification into the morally superior and inferior, though adequate to distinguish the 'respectable' from the drunken and licentious labouring mass, was plainly no longer adequate, except for the striving lower middle class, if only because the ancient virtues were no longer visibly applicable to the successful and wealthy bourgeoisie. The ethic of abstinence and effort could hardly be applied to the success of the American millionaires of the 1860s and 1870s, or even to the wealthy manufacturer, retired to a life of country-house leisure, still less to his *rentier* relatives; to those whose ideal was, in Ruskin's words:

'that [life] should be passed in a *pleasant undulating world* with iron and coal everywhere beneath it. On each *pleasant bank* of this world is to be a *beautiful mansion* ... a *moderately sized park*; a large garden and hothouses; and *pleasant carriage* drives through the shrubberies. In this mansion are to live ...

the English gentleman with his *gracious wife* and his *beautiful family*; he always able to have the boudoir and the jewels for the wife, and the *beautiful ball dresses* for the daughters, and hunters for the sons, and a shooting in the Highlands for himself.'[32]

Hence the growing importance of the alternative theories of *biological* class superiority, which pervade so much of the nineteenth-century bourgeois *Weltanschauung*. Superiority was the result of natural selection, genetically transmitted (see chapter 14 below). The bourgeois was, if not a different species, then at least the member of a superior race, a higher stage in human evolution, distinct from the lower orders who remained in the historical or cultural equivalent of childhood or at most adolescence.

From master to master-race was thus only a short step. Yet the right to dominate, the unquestioned superiority of the bourgeois as a species, implied not only inferiority but ideally an accepted, willing inferiority, as in the relation between man and woman (which once again symbolises much about the bourgeois world view). The workers, like women, *ought* to be loyal and contented. If they were not, it must be due to that crucial figure in the social universe of the bourgeoisie, the 'outside agitator'. Though nothing was more obvious to the naked eye than that the members of craft unions were likely to be the best, the most intelligent, the most skilled workers, the myth of the work-shy outsider exploiting simple-minded but basically sturdy operatives was indestructible. 'The conduct of the workers is deplorable,' wrote a French mining manager in 1869, in the process of ferociously repressing the sort of strike of which Zola's *Germinal* has given us a vivid picture, 'but one must recognise that they have been merely the savage instruments of agitators'.[33] To be more precise: the active working-class militant or potential leader *must* be by definition an 'agitator', since he could not be fitted into the stereotype of obedience, dullness and stupidity. When in 1859 nine of the most upright miners from Seaton Delaval – 'every man a teetotaller, six of them Primitive Methodists, and two of the six local preachers' – were sent to jail for two months after a strike *which they had opposed*, the mine manager was quite clear on this point. 'I know they are respectable men, and that is why I put them in prison. It is no use sending to jail those who cannot feel.'[34]

Such an attitude reflected the determination to decapitate the lower classes, in so far as they did not shed their potential leaders spontaneously by absorption into the lower middle class. But it also reflected a considerable degree of confidence. We are a long way from those factory-owners of the 1830s, living in constant fear of something like slave insurrections (see *The Age of Revolution*, epigraph to chapter 11). When master-manufacturers talked of the danger of communism which lurked behind any limitation of the absolute right of employers to hire and fire at will, they meant not social revolution but merely that the right of property and the right of domination were indistinguishable, and a bourgeois society must go to the dogs once interference with property rights was permitted.[35] Hence the reaction of fear and hatred was all the more hysterical when the spectre of social revolution once again irrupted into a confident capitalist world. The massacres of the Paris Communards (see chapter 9 above) testify to its force.

IV

A class of masters: yes. A ruling class? The answer is more complex. The bourgeoisie was evidently not a ruling class in the sense in which the old-style landowner was, whose position gave him, *de jure* or *de facto*, the effective state power over the inhabitants of his territory. He normally operated within a functioning framework of state power and administration which was not his own, at least outside the actual buildings he occupied ('my home is my castle'). Only in areas remote from this authority, as in isolated mining settlements, or where the state was itself weak, as in the United States, could bourgeois masters exercise that sort of direct rule, whether by command over the local forces of public authority, by private armies of Pinkerton men, or by banding together in armed groups of 'vigilantes' to maintain 'order'. Moreover, in our period the case of states in which the bourgeoisie had won formal political control, or did not have to share it with older political elites, was still quite exceptional. In most countries the bourgeoisie, however defined, plainly did not control or exercise political power, except perhaps at the subaltern or municipal level.

What it did exercise was hegemony, and what it increasingly determined was policy. There was no alternative to capitalism as a method of economic development, and at this period this implied both the

291

realisation of the economic and institutional programme of the liberal bourgeoisie (with local variations), and the crucial position in the state of that bourgeoisie itself. Even for the socialists the road to proletarian triumph ran through a fully developed capitalism. Before 1848 it had seemed for a moment that its crisis of transition (see *The Age of Revolution*, p. 304) might also prove to be its final crisis, at least in England, but in the 1850s it became clear that its major period of growth was only just beginning. It was unshakable in its main bastion, Britain, and elsewhere the prospects of social revolution paradoxically seemed to depend more than ever on the prospect of the bourgeoisie, domestic or foreign, creating that triumphant capitalism which would make possible its own overthrow. In a sense both Marx, who hailed the British conquest of India and the American conquest of half Mexico as historically progressive at this time, and the progressive elements in Mexico or India, who looked to alliance with the United States or the British Raj against their own traditionalists (see chapter 7 above), were recognising the same global situation. As for the rulers of conservative, anti-bourgeois and anti-liberal regimes in Europe, whether in Vienna, Berlin or St Petersburg, they recognised, however reluctantly, that the alternative to capitalist economic development was backwardness, and consequent weakness. Their problem was how to foster capitalism and with it the bourgeoisie without also acquiring bourgeois-liberal political regimes. The simple rejection of bourgeois society and its ideas was no longer viable. The only organisation which frankly undertook to resist it without qualification, the Catholic Church, merely isolated itself. The *Syllabus of Errors* of 1864 (see p. 131 above) and the Vatican Council demonstrated, by the very extremism of their rejection of everything that characterised the mid-nineteenth century, that they were entirely on the defensive.

From the 1870s on this virtual monopoly of the bourgeois programme (in its 'liberal' forms) began to crumble. But, by and large, in the third quarter of the nineteenth century it was pretty well unchallengeable. In economic affairs even the absolutist rulers of central and eastern Europe found themselves abolishing serfdom and dismantling the traditional apparatus of economic state controls and corporate privileges. In political affairs they found themselves calling upon, or at least coming to terms with, bourgeois liberals of the more moderate sort and, however nominally, their kind of representative institutions. Culturally it was the bourgeois life style which prevailed over the aristocratic, if only by a fairly general withdrawal of the old aristocracy from the world of culture (as that word was now understood): they became, in so far as they were not already, the 'barbarians' of Matthew Arnold (1822–88). After 1850 it is difficult to think of any kings who were great patrons of the arts, except mad ones like Ludwig II of Bavaria (1864–86), any noble magnates who were great collectors of art, except eccentrics.* Before 1848 the certainties of the bourgeoisie had still been qualified by the fear of social revolution. After 1870 they were once again to be undermined, not least by the fear of the growing movements of the working classes. But in the intervening period their triumph seemed beyond doubt or challenge. The age, judged Bismarck, who had no sympathy for a bourgeois society, was one of 'material interests'. Economic interests were an 'elementary force'. 'I believe that the advance of economic questions in domestic development is progressing and cannot be halted.'[36] But what represented that elementary force at this period, if not capitalism and the world made by and for the bourgeoisie?

* The imperial Russian ballet is perhaps an exception; but the relationships between members of ruling houses and their dancers traditionally went beyond the purely cultural.

Chapter Fourteen

Science, Religion, Ideology

Our aristocracy is handsomer (more hideous according to Chinese or Negro) than the middle classes, from [having the] pick of the women; but oh, what a shame is primogeniture for destroying Natural Selection!
Charles Darwin, 1864[1]

It is almost as though people want to show how intelligent they think they are by the degree of their emancipation from Bible and Catechism.
F. Schaubach on popular literature, 1863[2]

John Stuart Mill cannot help claiming the suffrage for the Negro – and the woman. Such conclusions are the inevitable results of the premises whence he started . . . [and their] reductio ad absurdum.
Anthropological Review, 1866[3]

I

The bourgeois society of the third quarter of the nineteenth century was self-confident and proud of its achievements. In no field of human endeavour was this more so than in the advancement of knowledge, in 'science'. Educated men of this period were not merely proud of their sciences, but prepared to subordinate all other forms of intellectual activity to them. In 1861 the statistician and economist Cournot observed that 'the belief in philosophic truth has cooled off to such an extent that neither the public nor the academies any longer like to receive or to welcome works of this kind, except as products of pure scholarship or historical curiosity.'[4] It was not, indeed, a happy period for the philosophers. Even in their traditional home, Germany, there was nobody of comparable stature to succeed the great figures of the past. Hegel himself, regarded as one of the 'deflated balloons' of German philosophy by his former French admirer, Hippolyte Taine (1828–93), went out of fashion in his native country, and the way in which 'the tiresome, conceited and mediocre epigones who set the tone among the educated German public' treated him moved Marx in the 1860s 'to declare myself publicly a disciple of that great thinker'.[5] The two dominant trends in philosophy subordinated themselves to science: French positivism, associated with the school of the curious Auguste Comte, and British empiricism, associated with John Stuart Mill, not to mention the mediocre thinker whose influence was then greater than any other anywhere in the world, Herbert Spencer (1820–1903). The double base of Comte's 'positive philosophy' was the immutability of the laws of nature and the impossibility of all infinite and absolute knowledge. In so far as it reached out beyond the rather eccentric sect of the Comtist 'Religion of Humanity', positivism became little more than a philosophical justification of the conventional method of the experimental sciences, and similarly for most contemporaries Mill was, again in the words of Taine, the man who had opened up 'the good old road of induction and experiment'. Yet this view implied, or rather was explicitly based in Comte and Spencer, on a historical view of evolutionary progress. The positive or scientific method was (or would be) the triumph of the last of the stages through which mankind must pass – in Comte's terms, the theological, the metaphysical and the scientific; each with its own institutions, of which Mill and Spencer at least agreed that liberalism (in the broadest sense) was the suitable expression. One might say with little exaggeration that in this view the progress of science made philosophy redundant, except as a sort of intellectual laboratory assistant to the scientist.

Moreover, with such confidence in the methods of science it is not surprising that educated men of the second half of the century were immensely impressed with its achievements. Indeed, they sometimes came close to thinking that these achievements were not merely impressive but final. William Thompson, Lord Kelvin, the celebrated physicist, thought that all the basic problems of physics had been solved, though a number of relatively minor problems remained to be cleared up. He was, as we know, quite startlingly mistaken.

Nevertheless, the mistake was both significant and comprehensible. In science as in society there are revolutionary and non-revolutionary periods and, whereas the twentieth century is revolutionary in both, to an extent even greater than the 'age of revolution' (1789–1848), the period with which this book deals was (with certain exceptions) revolutionary in neither. This does not mean that conventional men of intelligence and ability thought that either science or society had solved all problems, though in some respects, such as those which concerned the basic pattern of an economy and the basic pattern of the physical universe, some very able ones felt that all substantial ones had been solved. It does, however, mean that such men had no serious doubts about the direction in which they were going and ought to go, and the methods, intellectual or practical, of getting there. Nobody doubted the fact of progress, both material and intellectual, since it seemed too obvious to be denied. It was, indeed, the dominant concept of the age, though there was a rather fundamental division between those who thought that progress would be more or less continuous and linear, and those (like Marx) who knew that it must and would be discontinuous and contradictory. Doubts could arise only about matters of, as it were, taste, such as manners and morals, where simple quantitative accumulation provided no guidance There could be no question that men in 1860 knew more than ever before, but whether they were 'better' could not be demonstrated in the same way. But these were matters which preoccupied theologians (whose intellectual reputation was not high), philosophers and artists (who were admired but somewhat in the manner in which wealthy men admire the diamonds they can afford to buy their women) and social critics, of the left or right, who did not like the kind of society they lived in or found themselves forced into. Among articulate and educated persons in 1860 these were a distinct minority.

Though massive progress was visible in all branches of knowledge, it seemed evident that some were further advanced, some more fully formed, than others. Thus it seemed that physics was more mature then chemistry, and had already left behind the stage of effervescent and explosive progress in which that science was still so visibly engaged. Chemistry in turn, even 'organic chemistry', was considerably more advanced than the life-sciences, which just seemed to be taking off into an era of exciting progress. Indeed, if any single scientific theory is to represent the advances of natural science in our period, and was recognised as crucial, it was the theory of evolution, and if any one figure dominated the public image of science it was the craggy and somewhat ape-like one of Charles Darwin (1809–82). The strange, abstract and logically fantastic world of the mathematicians remained somewhat isolated both from the general and the scientific public, perhaps more so than before, since its main contact with both, physics (through physical technology), appeared at this stage to have less use for its most advanced and adventurous abstractions than in the great days of the construction of a celestial mechanics. The calculus, without which the achievements of engineering and communications of the period would have been impossible, was by now far behind the moving frontier of mathematics. This was perhaps best represented by the greatest mathematician of the period, Georg Bernhard Riemann (1826–66), whose university teacher's thesis of 1854 'On the hypotheses which underlie geometry' (published 1868) can no more be omitted from a discussion of nineteenth-century science than Newton's *Principia* can from that of the seventeenth century. It laid the foundations of topology, the differential geometry of manifolds and the theory of space-time and gravitation. Riemann even envisaged a theory of physics compatible with modern quantum theory. Yet these and other highly original mathematical developments did not come into their own until the new revolutionary age of physics which began at the end of the century.

However, in none of the natural sciences did there seem to be serious uncertainty about the general direction in which knowledge was advancing, or the basic conceptual or methodological framework of its advance. Discoveries were plentiful, theories sometimes novel but not, as it were, unexpected. Even the Darwinian theory of evolution was impressive, not because the *concept* of evolution was new – it had been familiar for decades – but because it provided for the first time a satisfactory explanatory model for the origin of species, and did so in terms which were entirely familiar even to non-scientists, since they echoed the most familiar concept of the liberal economy, competition. Indeed, an unusual number of great scientists wrote in terms which allowed them to be readily popularised – sometimes excessively so – Darwin, Pasteur, the physiologists Claude Bernard (1813–78) and Rudolf Virchow (1821–1902) and Helmholtz (1821–94) (see p. 315), not to mention physicists like William Thompson, Lord Kelvin. The basic models or 'paradigms' of scientific theories seemed firm, though great scientists like James Clerk Maxwell (1831–79) formulated their versions with the instinctive caution which made them compatible with later theories based on very different models.

Within the natural sciences there was little of that passionate and puzzled confrontation which occurs when there is a clash, not of different hypotheses, but of different ways of looking at the same problem, i.e. when one party proposes not merely a different answer, but one which the other party considers to be impermissible or 'unthinkable'. Such a clash occurred in the remote little world of mathematics when H. Kronecker (1839–1914) savaged K. Weierstrass (1815–97), R. Dedekind (1831–1916) and G. Cantor (1845–1918) on the issue of the mathematics of infinity. Such *Methodenstreite* (battles of methods) divided the world of the social scientists, but in so far as they entered the natural sciences – even the biological ones on the sensitive issue of evolution – they reflected an intrusion of ideological preferences rather than professional debate. There is no convincing scientific reason why they did not occur. Thus that most typical mid-Victorian scientist William Thompson, Lord Kelvin (typical in his combination of great if conventional theoretical power, quite enormous technological fertility* and consequent business success), was clearly not happy about the mathematics of Clerk Maxwell's electromagnetic theory of light, which is regarded by many as the point of departure for modern physics. However, as he found it possible to reformulate it in terms of his own engineering type of mathematics (which is not), he did not challenge it. Again, Thompson demonstrated to his satisfaction that, on the basis of known physical laws, the sun could not be older than 500 million years, and that therefore the time-scale required for geological and biological evolution on the earth was impossible. (As he was an orthodox Christian, he welcomed this conclusion.) In fact, according to the physics of 1864, he was correct: it was only the discovery of then unknown sources of nuclear energy which allowed physicists to suppose a much longer life-span for the sun and consequently the earth. But Thompson did not wonder whether his physics might be incomplete, if they conflicted with accepted geology, and the geologists merely went ahead irrespective of physics. The debate might as well not have taken place, so far as the further development of both sciences is concerned.

So the world of science moved along its intellectual railway tracks, and its further progress seemed, like that of the railways themselves, to offer the prospect of the laying-down of more tracks of the same

* I am reminded by Dr S. Zienau that 'there is not an electrical measuring instrument in the pre-electronic era, in telegraphy and railway signalling cabins, post-office stations and power-supply companies, which does not owe something to Thompson'.

kind through new territory. The skies appeared to contain little that would have startled older astronomers, apart from a host of new observations by means of more powerful telescopes and measuring instruments (both largely German developments)* and the use of the new technique of photography, as well as spectroscopic analysis, first applied to the light of the stars in 1861, which was to turn out to be an enormously powerful tool of research.

The physical sciences had developed quite dramatically in the previous half-century, when such apparently disparate phenomena as heat and energy were unified by the laws of thermodynamics, while electricity, magnetism and even light itself converged towards a single analytical model. Thermodynamics made no major advances during our period, though Thompson completed the process of reconciling the new doctrines of heat with the older ones of mechanics in 1851 (*The Dynamical Equivalent of Heat*). The remarkable mathematical model of the electromagnetic theory of light, formulated by that ancestor of modern theoretical physics, James Clerk Maxwell, in 1862, was indeed both profound and open-ended. It left the way open for the discovery of the electron. Yet Maxwell, perhaps because he never achieved an adequate exposition of what he described as his 'somewhat awkward theory' (this was not made until 1941!)[6] failed to convince such leading contemporaries as Thompson and Helmholtz, or even the brilliant Austrian Ludwig Boltzmann (1844–1906), whose memoir of 1868 virtually launched statistical mechanics as a subject. Probably the physics of the mid-nineteenth century was not as spectacular as that of the preceding and following period, but its theoretical advances were indeed very impressive. And yet, the electromagnetic theory and the laws of thermodynamics between them seemed, to quote Bernal, 'to imply a certain finality'.[7] At all events the British (headed by Thompson), and indeed other physicists who had done their creative work in thermodynamics, were strongly tempted by the view that man had now acquired a definitive understanding of the laws of nature (though a Helmholtz or Boltzmann was

* Until the 1890s Joseph Fraunhofer's (1787–1826) telescope model remained the prototype of the giant refractors which were then installed in the American observatories. British astronomy now lagged behind the continent in quality, but made up for it by a long and unbroken record of observations. 'Greenwich could be compared with an old-established firm of conservative routine, solid reputation and a guaranteed clientele, viz. all the world's navigation' (S. Zienau).

rightly unconvinced). Perhaps the remarkable technological fertility of the physics of mechanical model-building made the illusion of finality more tempting.

There was evidently no such finality about the second great natural science, perhaps the most flourishing of all in the nineteenth century, chemistry. Its expansion was dramatic, especially in Germany, not least because its industrial uses were so multifarious: from bleaches, dye-stuffs and fertilisers to medical products and explosives. Chemists were well on the way to forming over half the total of persons professionally engaged in science.[8] The foundations of chemistry as a mature science had been laid in the last third of the eighteenth century. It had blossomed ever since, and went on developing in an exciting overflowing fountain of ideas and discoveries during our period.

The basic elementary processes of chemistry were understood and the essential analytical tools were already available; the existence of a limited number of chemical elements, composed of different numbers of basic units (atoms), and compounds of elements composed of basic multi-atomic units of molecules, and some idea of the rules of these combinations was familiar, as indeed it had to be for the great advances in the essential activity of chemists, the analysis and synthesis of various substances. The special field of organic chemistry was already flourishing, though this was still confined to the properties – mainly the properties useful in production – of materials derived from sources that had once been alive, such as coal. It was still a long way from biochemistry, i.e. the understanding of how these substances functioned in the living organism. Nevertheless, the models of chemistry remained rather imperfect, and substantial advances in understanding them were made in the third quarter of the nineteenth century. They illuminated the *structure* of chemical compounds, which had hitherto been seen simply in quantitative terms (i.e. the number of atoms in a molecule).

It became possible to determine the correct numbers of each kind of atom in a molecule by means of the already available Avogadro's Law of 1811, which a patriotic Italian chemist drew to the attention of an international symposium on the question in 1860, the year of Italian unity. Moreover – another fruitful borrowing from physics – Pasteur discovered in 1848 that chemically identical substances could be physically distinct, e.g. rotating or not rotating the plane of polarised light. From this it followed, among other things, that molecules had a shape in three-dimensional space, and the brilliant German chemist Kekulé (1829–96), in the very Victorian situation of a passenger sitting on top of a London bus in 1865, imagined the first of the complex structural molecular models, the famous benzene ring of six carbon atoms to each of which a hydrogen atom was attached. One might say that the architect's or engineer's conception of a model replaced what had hitherto been the accountant's model – C_6H_6, the mere counting of atoms – in the chemical formula.

Perhaps even more remarkable was the major generalisation in the field of chemistry produced by this period, Mendeleev's (1834–1907) Periodic Table of Elements (1869). Thanks to the solution of the problems of atomic weight and valency (the number of links the atom of an element possesses with other atoms), the atomic theory, somewhat neglected after its flowering in the early nineteenth century, came into its own again after 1860, and simultaneously technology in the shape of the spectroscope (1859) allowed various new elements to be discovered. Moreover, the 1860s were a great period of standardisation and measurement. (They saw, among other things, the fixing of the familiar units of electrical measurement, the volt, ampère, watt and ohm.) Various attempts to reclassify the chemical elements according to valency and atomic weight were therefore made. That by Mendeleev and the German Lothar Meyer (1830–95) rested on the fact that the properties of elements varied in a periodic manner with their atomic weights. Its brilliance lay in the assumption that, according to this principle, certain places in the periodic table of all the ninety-two elements were still empty, and in predicting the properties of the as yet undiscovered elements which were to fill them. The Mendeleev Table appeared at first sight to conclude the study of the atomic theory by setting a limit to the existence of fundamentally different kinds of matter. In actual fact 'it was to find its full interpretation in a new concept of matter no longer made of immutable atoms but by relatively impermanent associations of a few fundamental particles, themselves liable to change and transformation'. But at the time Mendeleev, like Clerk Maxwell, looked like the last word in an old discussion rather than the first in a new one.

Biology remained a long way behind the physical sciences, held back not least by the conservatism of the two major bodies of men concerned with its practical application, the farmers and especially the doctors. Retrospectively the greatest of the early physiologists is Claude Bernard, whose work provides the basis of all modern physiology and biochemistry, and who, moreover, wrote one of the finest analyses of the processes of science ever written in his *Introduction to the Study of Experimental Medicine* (1865). However, though honoured, especially in his native France, his discoveries were not immediately applicable and his contemporary influence therefore less than that of his fellow-countryman Louis Pasteur, who became, with Darwin, perhaps the mid-nineteenth-century scientist most widely known to the general public. Pasteur was drawn into the field of bacteriology, of which he became the great pioneer (together with Robert Koch [1843–1910], a German country doctor), through industrial chemistry, more precisely the analysis of why beer and vinegar sometimes go bad, for reasons which chemical analysis could not reveal. Both the techniques of bacteriology – the microscope, the preparation of cultures and slides, etc. – and its immediate applicability – the eradication of the diseases of animals and humans – made the new discipline accessible, understandable and appealing. Techniques like antisepsis (developed by Lister [1827–1912] around 1865), 'pasteurisation' or other methods of safeguarding organic products from the intrusions of microbes, and inoculation were at hand, and the arguments and results sufficiently palpable to break down even the entrenched hostility of the medical profession. The study of bacteria was to provide biology with an enormously useful approach to the nature of life, but at this period it raised no theoretical questions which the most conventional scientist would not immediately recognise.

The most significant and dramatic advance in biology was one which had only marginal relevance at the time to the study of the physical and chemical structure and mechanism of life. The theory of evolution by natural selection reached out far beyond biology, and therein lies its significance. It ratified the triumph of history over all the sciences, though 'history' in this connection was generally confused by contemporaries with 'progress'. Moreover, by bringing man himself into a scheme of biological evolution, it abolished the sharp line between natural and human or social sciences. Henceforth the

302

whole cosmos or at least the whole solar system must be conceived as a process of constant historical change. The sun and the planets were in the midst of such a history and so, as the geologists had already established (see *The Age of Revolution*, chapter 15), was the earth. Living things were now also included in this process, though the question whether life itself had evolved from non-life still remained unsolved and, mainly for ideological reasons, extremely sensitive. (The great Pasteur believed that he had shown that it could not so evolve.) Darwin brought not only animals but man himself into the evolutionary scheme.

The difficulty for mid-nineteenth-century science lay not so much in admitting such a historisation of the universe – nothing was easier to conceive in an era of such overwhelmingly obvious and massive historic changes – as to combine it with uniform, continuous and non-revolutionary operations of unchanging natural laws. A distrust of social revolutions was not absent from their considerations, any more than a distrust of traditional religion whose sacred texts committed it to discontinuous change ('creation') and interference with the regularity of nature ('miracles'). However, it also seemed at this stage that science depended on uniformity and invariance. Reductionism seemed essential to it. Only revolutionary thinkers like Marx found it easy to conceive of situations in which, as it were, 2 + 2 no longer equalled 4 but might equal something else instead or also.* It had been the great achievement of the geologists to explain how, given enough time, the operation of exactly the same forces visible today could explain the enormous variety of what could be observed on the inanimate earth, past and present. It was the great achievement of natural selection to explain the even greater variety of living species, including man. This success was to tempt, and still tempts, thinkers to deny or underestimate the very different and novel processes which govern historic change and reduce the changes in human societies to the rules of biological evolution – with important political consequences and, sometimes, intentions ('social-Darwinism'). The society in which western scientists lived – and all scientists belonged to the western world, even those situated on its margins as in Russia –

* This was the issue, in the mathematicians' discussion of infinity, which was so shocking precisely because the rules of arithmetic simply no longer gave the expected results.

combined stability and change, and so did their evolutionary theories.

They were, nevertheless, dramatic or rather traumatic, because for the first time they came into deliberate and militant confrontation with the forces of tradition, conservatism and especially religion. They abolished the special status of man as hitherto conceived. The violence with which evolution was resisted was ideological. How could man, created in God's image, be no more than a modified monkey? Given the choice between apes and angels, the opponents of Darwin took the side of the angels. The strength of this resistance demonstrates the force of traditionalism and organised religion even among the most emancipated and educated groups of the western populations, for the discussion was confined to the highly literate. Yet what is equally, and perhaps more, striking is the readiness of the evolutionists publicly to challenge the forces of tradition – and their comparatively rapid triumph. There had been plenty of evolutionists in the first half of the century, but the biologists among them had handled the subject with caution and some personal fear. Darwin himself held back the views he had already formed until 1859.

This was not due to the fact that the evidence for the descent of man from animals now became too overwhelming to resist, though, as it happened, it accumulated rapidly in the 1850s. The ape-like skull of Neanderthal man (1856) could no longer be argued away. Still the evidence had been strong enough before 1848. It was due to the happy conjuncture of two facts, the rapid advance of a liberal and 'progressive' bourgeoisie and the absence of revolution. The challenge to the forces of tradition grew stronger, but it no longer seemed to imply social upheaval. Darwin himself illustrates this combination. A bourgeois, a man of the moderate liberal left, and unquestionably ready to confront the forces of conservatism and religion from the late 1850s (though not before), he politely rejected the offer of Karl Marx to dedicate the second volume of *Capital* to him.[8a] He was not, after all, a revolutionary.

The fortunes of Darwinism thus depended, not so much on its success in convincing the scientific public, i.e. on the evident merits of *The Origin of Species*, but on the political and ideological conjuncture of time and country. It was, of course, immediately adopted by the extreme left, which had, indeed, long provided a powerful component of evolutionary thinking. Alfred Russel Wallace (1823–1913), who actually discovered the theory of natural selection independently of Darwin and shared its glory with him, came from that tradition of artisan science and radicalism which played so important a part in the early nineteenth century and which found 'natural history' so congenial. Formed in the milieu of Chartism and Owenite 'Halls of Science', he remained a man of the extreme left who returned late in life to a militant support of land nationalisation and even socialism, while maintaining his belief in those other characteristic theories of heterodox and plebeian ideology, phrenology and spiritualism (see p. 319 below). Marx immediately hailed the *Origin* as 'the basis in natural science for our views',[9] and social democracy became strongly – and with some of Marx's disciples such as Kautsky excessively – Darwinian.

This evident affinity of the socialists for biological Darwinism did not prevent dynamic and progressive liberal middle classes from welcoming, indeed championing, it. It triumphed rapidly in England and in the self-confident liberal atmosphere of Germany during the decade of unification. In France, where the middle class preferred the stability of the Napoleonic Empire and intellectuals of the left felt no need of ideas imported from non-French and therefore backward foreigners, Darwinism did not advance rapidly until after the end of the Empire and the defeat of the Paris Commune. In Italy its champions were more nervous of its social-revolutionary implications than of papal thunderbolts, but nevertheless confident enough. In the United States it not only triumphed rapidly, but was very soon turned into an ideology of militant capitalism. Conversely, opposition to Darwinian evolution, even among scientists, came from the socially conservative.

II

Evolution links the natural sciences to the human or social sciences, though the latter term is anachronistic. Still, the need for a specific and general science of society (as distinct from the various relevant special disciplines already dealing with human affairs) was for the first time seriously felt. The British Association for the Promotion of Social Science (1857) merely had the modest object of applying scientific methods to social reforms. However, sociology, a term invented by Auguste Comte in 1839 and popularised by Herbert Spencer (who wrote a premature book on the principles of this as of numerous other sciences [1876]), was much talked about. At the end of our period it had produced neither a recognised discipline nor an academic teaching subject. On the other hand, the wider but cognate field of anthropology was emerging rapidly as a recognised science out of law, philosophy, ethnology and travel literature, the study of language and folklore and the medical sciences (via the then popular subject of 'physical anthropology' which led to a fashion for measuring and collecting the skulls of various peoples). The first person to teach it officially was probably Quatrefages in 1855, in the professorship which existed in this subject at the Musée National in Paris. The foundation of the Paris Anthropological Society (1859) was followed by a remarkable outburst of interest in the 1860s, when similar associations were formed in London, Madrid, Moscow, Florence and Berlin. Psychology (another recent coinage, this time by John Stuart Mill) was still linked with philosophy – A. Bain's *Mental and Moral Science* (1868) still combined it with ethics – but was increasingly given an experimental orientation with W. Wundt (1832–1920), who had been assistant to the great Helmholtz. It was unquestionably an accepted discipline by the 1870s, at all events in German universities. It also reached out into the social and anthropological fields, and indeed a special journal linking it with linguistics was founded as early as 1859.[10]

By the standards of the 'positive' and especially the experimental sciences, the record of these new social sciences was not impressive, though three could already claim genuine and systematic achievement as sciences before 1848: economics, statistics and linguistics (see *The Age of Revolution*, chapter 15, pp. 283–7). The link between economics and mathematics now became close and direct (with A. A. Cournot [1801–77] and L. Walras [1834–1910], both Frenchmen), and the application of statistics to social phenomena was already sufficiently advanced to stimulate their application to the physical sciences. At least so it has been held by students of the origins of the statistical mechanics pioneered by Clerk Maxwell. Certainly social statistics flourished as never before, their practitioners finding plentiful public employment. International statistical congresses came to be held at intervals from 1853 on, and the scientific standing of the subject was recognised by the election of the celebrated and admirable Dr William Farr (1807–83) to the Royal Society. Linguistics, as we shall see, followed a different line of development.

And yet, on the whole, except methodologically, these results were not outstanding. The marginal utility school of economics, developed simultaneously in Britain, Austria and France around 1870, was formally elegant and sophisticated, but unquestionably considerably narrower than the old 'political economy' (or even the recalcitrant Germans' 'historical school of economics'), and to this extent a less realistic approach to economic problems. Unlike the natural sciences, in a liberal society the social ones did not even have the stimulus of technological progress. Since the basic model of the economy seemed perfectly satisfactory, it left no great problems to solve, such as those of growth, possible economic breakdown or the distribution of incomes. In so far as these matters were not already solved, the automatic operations of market economics (on which the analysis therefore concentrated henceforward) would solve them, to the extent that they were not beyond human solution. In any case, things were obviously improving and progressing, a situation which was unlikely to concentrate the minds of economists on the more profound aspects of their science.

The reservations bourgeois thinkers had about their world were social and political rather than economic, especially where the danger of revolution was unforgotten, as in France, or emerging with the rise of a labour movement, as in Germany. But if the German thinkers, who never swallowed extreme liberal theory wholesale, were, like conservatives everywhere, worried that the society produced by liberal capitalism would prove dangerous and unstable, they had little to propose except preventive social reforms. The basic image of the sociologist was the biological one of the 'social organism', the functional co-operation of all groups in society, so different from the class struggle. It was ancient conservatism dressed up in nineteenth-century costume and, incidentally, hard to combine with that other biological image of the century which stood for change and progress, namely 'evolution'. It was in fact a better basis for propaganda than for science.

Hence the only thinker of the period who developed a comprehensive theory of social structure and social change which still commands respect was the social-revolutionary Karl Marx, who enjoys the admiration, or at least the respect, of economists, historians and sociologists. This is a remarkable achievement, for his contemporaries (except for some economists) are now forgotten, even by highly educated men and women, or else they have weathered the intervening century so badly that intellectual archaeologists can once more discover forgotten merits in their writings. But what is striking is not so much the fact that Auguste Comte or Herbert Spencer were, after all, persons of some intellectual stature, than that men who were once regarded as the Aristotles of the modern world have practically vanished from sight. They were in their time incomparably more famous and influential than Marx, whose *Capital* was described in 1875 by an anonymous German expert as the work of a self-educated man ignorant of the progress of the past twenty-five years.[11] For at this time in the west Marx was taken seriously only within the international labour movement and especially the growing socialist movement of his own country, and his intellectual influence even there was as yet slight. However, the intellectuals of an increasingly revolutionary Russia immediately read him avidly. The first German edition of *Capital* (1867) – a thousand copies – took five years to sell out, but in 1872 the first thousand copies of the Russian edition sold out in less than two months.

The problem Marx set himself was the same as that which other social scientists tried to confront: the nature and mechanics of the transition from a pre-capitalist to a capitalist society and its specific modes of operation and tendencies of future development. Since his answers are relatively familiar, we need not recapitulate them here, though it is worth noting that Marx resisted the tendency, which elsewhere grew constantly more powerful, to separate economic analysis from its historic social contexts. The problem of the historic development of nineteenth-century society led both theorists and even practical men deep into the remoter past. For, both within capitalist countries and at the points where expanding bourgeois society encountered – and destroyed – other societies, the living past and the emerging present came into open conflict. German thinkers saw the hierarchical order of 'estates' in their own country give way to a society of conflicting classes. British lawyers, especially those with experience in India, contrasted the ancient society of 'status'

308

with the new one of 'contract' and saw the transition from the first to the second as the principal pattern of historical development. Russian writers actually lived simultaneously in the two worlds – the ancient communalism of the peasantry, which so many of them knew from the long summers on their seignorial estates, and the world of the westernised and much-travelled intellectual. For the mid-nineteenth-century observer all history coexisted at the same time, except for that of the ancient civilisations and empires such as classical antiquity, which had been (literally) buried, awaiting the spades of H. Schliemann (1822–90) in Troy and Mycenae or Flinders Petrie (1853–1942) in Egypt.

One might have expected the discipline most closely connected with the past to make a peculiarly important contribution to the development of the social sciences, but in fact history as an academic specialisation was of peculiarly little help to them. Its practitioners were overwhelmingly concerned with rulers, battles, treaties, political events or politico-legal institutions, in a word with retrospective politics, if not actually with current politics in historical fancy-dress. They elaborated the methodology of research on the basis of the documents in the now admirably ordered and preserved public archives, and they increasingly (following the lead of the Germans) organised their publications round the two poles of the academic thesis and the specialist scholarly journal: the *Historische Zeitschrift* was first published in 1858, the *Revue Historique* in 1876, the English *Historical Review* in 1886 and the *American Historical Review* in 1895. But what they produced were at best permanent monuments of erudition on which we still draw, and at worst giant-sized pamphlets which are now read, if at all, only for their interest as literature. Academic history, in spite of the moderate liberalism of some of its practitioners, had a natural bias towards preserving the past and suspecting, if not deploring, the future. The social sciences at this stage had the opposite bias.

Nevertheless, if the academic historians followed their by-way of scholarship, history remained the main constituent of the new social sciences. This was particularly obvious in the enormously flourishing – and like so many other scientific disciplines, pre-eminently German – field of linguistics, or rather, to use the contemporary term, philology. Its main interest lay in the reconstruction of the historical

309

evolution of the Indo-European languages which, perhaps because in Germany they were known as 'Indo-German', attracted national, if not nationalist, attention in that country. Efforts to establish a much broader evolutionary typology of languages, i.e. to discover the origins and historic development of speech and language, were also made – e.g. by H. Steinthal (1823–99) and A. Schleicher (1821–68) – but the family trees of language thus constructed remained highly speculative and the relations between the various 'genera' and 'species' extremely doubtful. In fact, with the exception of Hebrew and cognate semitic languages which attracted Jewish or biblical scholars and some work on Finno-Ugrian languages (which happened to have a central-European representative in Hungary), not much outside the Indo-European languages had been systematically studied in the countries in which mid-nineteenth-century philology flourished.* On the other hand, the fundamental insights of the first half of the century were now systematically applied and developed in Indo-European evolutionary linguistics. The regular patterns of sound change discovered by Grimm for German were now investigated and specified more closely, methods of reconstructing earlier unwritten forms of words and constructing models of linguistic 'family trees' were established, other models of evolutionary change (like Schmidt's 'wave-theory') were suggested and the use of analogy – especially grammatical analogy – were developed; for philology was nothing if not comparative. By the 1870s the leading school of the *Junggrammatiker* (Young Grammarians) believed itself capable of actually reconstructing the original Indo-European from which so many languages between Sanskrit in the east and Celtic in the west were descended, and the redoubtable Schleicher actually wrote texts in this reconstructed language. Modern linguistics has taken an entirely different road, rejecting the historicist and evolutionist interests of the mid-nineteenth century perhaps with excessive violence, and to this extent the main development of philology in our period worked out known principles rather than anticipating new ones. But it was very typically an evolutionist social science, and by contemporary standards a highly successful one, both among scholars and the general public. Unfortunately, among the latter (and in spite of the

* The American school of linguistics, based on the study of Amer-Indian languages, had not yet developed.

310

specific disclaimers of scholars like F. Max-Muller [1823–1900] of Oxford), it encouraged the belief in racism, the speakers of Indo-European languages (a purely linguistic concept) being identified with 'the Aryan race'.

Racism played a distinctly central role in another rapidly developing social science, anthropology, a merger of two originally quite distinct disciplines, 'physical anthropology' (chiefly deriving from anatomical and similar interests) and 'ethnography' or the description of various – generally backward or primitive – communities. Both inevitably confronted, and were indeed dominated by, the problem of the differences between different human groups and (as they were drawn into the evolutionist model), the problem of the descent of man and of different types of society, of which the bourgeois world appeared unquestionably the highest. Physical anthropology automatically led to the concept of 'race', since the physical differences between white, yellow or black peoples, Negroes, Mongols, Caucasians (or whatever other classifications might be used) were undeniable. This did not in itself imply any belief in racial inequality, superiority or inferiority, though when married to the study of the evolution of man on the basis of the pre-historic fossil record, it did. For man's earliest identifiable ancestors – notably Neanderthal man – were clearly both more ape-like and culturally inferior to their discoverers. But if some existing races could be shown to be closer to the apes than others, would this not prove their inferiority?

The argument is feeble, but made a natural appeal to those who wanted to prove racial inferiority, e.g. of blacks to whites – or for that matter of anyone to whites. (The shape of the monkey could be discerned by the eye of prejudice even in the Chinese and Japanese, as witness many a modern cartoon.) But if Darwinian biological evolution suggested a hierarchy of races, so did the comparative method as applied in 'cultural anthropology', of which E. B. Tylor's *Primitive Culture* (1871) was the leading landmark. For E. B. Tylor (1832–1917), as for so many believers in 'progress' who observed communities and cultures which, unlike fossil man, had not died out these were not so much inferior by nature as representatives of an earlier stage of evolution on the road to modern civilisation. They were analogous to infancy or childhood in the life of individual man. This implied a theory of stages – Tylor was influenced by Comte's – which

311

he applied (with the usual caution of respectable men touching on this still explosive subject) to religion. From the primitive 'animism' (a word invented by him) the road led to the higher monotheistic religions, and eventually the triumph of science which, capable of explaining increasingly large areas of experience without reference to spirit, would 'in one department after another substitute for independent voluntary action the working out of systematic law'.[12] Meanwhile, however, historically modified 'survivals' of earlier stages of civilisation could be discerned everywhere, even in the evidently 'backward' parts of civilised nations, e.g. in the superstitions and customs of the countryside. Thus the peasant became a link between savage man and civilised society. Tylor, who thought of anthropology as 'essentially a reformer's science', did not, of course, believe that this indicated any incapacity of peasants to become fully paid-up members of civilised society. But what was easier than to assume that those who represented the stage of childhood or adolescence in the development of civilisation were themselves 'child-like' and had to be treated like children by their mature 'parents'?

> As the type of the Negro [wrote the *Anthropological Review*] is foetal, so that of the Mongol is infantile. And in strict accordance with this, we find that their government, literature and art are infantile also. They are beardless children whose life is a task and whose chief virtue consists in unquestioning obedience.[13]

Or, as a Captain Osborn put it in a bluff naval way in 1860: 'Treat them as children. Make them do what we know is for their benefit as well as our own, and all difficulties in China are at an end.'[14]

Other races were therefore 'inferior', either because they represented an earlier stage of biological evolution or of socio-cultural evolution, or both. And their inferiority was proved because in fact the 'superior race' was superior by the criteria of its own society: technologically more advanced, militarily more powerful, richer and more 'successful'. The argument was both flattering and convenient – so convenient that the middle classes were inclined to take it over from the aristocrats (who had long fancied themselves a superior race) for internal as well as international purposes: the poor were poor because they were biologically inferior and conversely, if citizens belonged to 'lower races', it was no wonder that they stayed poor and backward. The argument was not yet clothed in the garments of modern genetics, which had virtually not yet been invented: the now celebrated experiments of the monk Gregor Mendel (1822–84) on the sweet peas in his Moravian monastery garden (1865) passed completely unnoticed until they were rediscovered about 1900. But in a primitive way the view that the upper classes were a higher type of humanity, developing its superiority by endogamy, and threatened by mixture with the lower orders and even more by the more rapid increase of the inferior, was widely held. Conversely, as the (mainly Italian) school of 'criminal anthropology' purported to prove, the criminal, the anti-social, the socially underprivileged, belonged to a different and inferior human strain from the 'respectable', and could be recognised as such by measuring the skull or in other simple ways.

Racism pervades the thought of our period to an extent hard to appreciate today, and not always easy to understand. (Why, for instance, the widespread horror of miscegenation and the almost universal belief among whites that 'half-breeds' inherited precisely the *worst* features of their parents' races?) Apart from its convenience as a legitimation of the rule of white over coloured, rich over poor, it is perhaps best explained as a mechanism by means of which a fundamentally inegalitarian society based upon a fundamentally egalitarian ideology rationalised its inequalities, and attempted to justify and defend those privileges which the democracy implicit in its institutions must inevitably challenge. Liberalism had no logical defence against equality and democracy, so the illogical barrier of race was erected: science itself, liberalism's trump card, could prove that men were *not* equal.

But of course the science of our period did not prove this, though some scientists might wish it to. The Darwinian tautology ('survival of the fittest', the proof of fitness being survival) could not prove that men were superior to earthworms, since both survived successfully. 'Superiority' was read into the record by means of the assumption of equating evolutionary history with 'progress'. And even though the evolutionary history of man quite correctly discerned progress in certain important matters – notably science and technology – though paying no attention to others, it did not, and indeed could not, make 'backwardness' permanent and irreparable. For it was based on the assumption that human beings, at least since the emergence of homo sapiens, were the same, their behaviour obeying the same uniform

313

laws, though in different historical circumstances. English was different from the original Indo-European, but not because modern Englishmen operated in a linguistically different manner from the ancestral tribes in, as was then commonly believed, central Asia. The basic paradigm of the 'family tree', which appears both in philology and anthropology, implies the opposite of genetic or other permanent forms of inequality. The kinship systems of Australian aborigines, Pacific islanders and Iroquois Indians, which the ancestors of modern social anthropology like Lewis Morgan (1818–81) now began to study seriously – though the subject was still primarily studied in the library rather than in the field – were seen as 'survivals' of earlier stages in the evolution of what had become the nineteenth-century family. But the point about them was that they were comparable: different, but not necessarily inferior.* 'Social Darwinism' and racist anthropology or biology belong not to the science of the nineteenth century but to its politics.

If we look back upon both the natural and social sciences of the period we shall be struck most vividly with their self-confidence. It was less obviously unjustified in the natural than in the social sciences, but equally marked. The physicists who felt they had left their successors with little more to do than to clean up a few minor problems expressed the same mood as August Schleicher, who was sure that ancient Aryans had talked exactly the putative language which he had reconstructed for them. This sentiment was not so much based on results – those of the evolutionist disciplines were hardly capable of experimental falsification – as on a belief in the infallibility of the 'scientific method'. 'Positive' science, operating on objective and ascertained facts, connected by rigid links of cause and effect, and producing uniform, invariant general 'laws' beyond query or wilful modification, was the master-key to the universe, and the nineteenth century possessed it. More than this: with the rise of the world of the nineteenth century the early and infantile stages of man characterised by superstition, theology and speculation were over, Comte's 'third stage' of positive science had arrived. It is now easy to make fun of that confidence, both in the adequacy of the method and the

* This was of course accepted for the peoples of classical antiquity, whose kinship systems formed the basis of the pioneer studies of the historical evolution of the family, e.g. J. J. Bachofen's *Mutterrecht* (Matriarchal Law) in 1861.

permanence of the theoretical models, but it was no less powerful for being, as some of the old philosophers might have pointed out, misplaced. And if the scientists felt that they could speak with certainty, how much more so the lesser publicists and ideologists who were all the more certain of the experts' certainties, because they could understand most of what the experts said, at least in so far as it could still be said without the use of higher mathematics. Even in physics and chemistry they still appeared to be within the grasp of the 'practical man' – say a civil engineer. Darwin's *Origin of Species* was totally accessible to the educated laymen. Never again was it to be so easy for blunt common sense, which knew in any case that the triumphant world of liberal capitalist progress was the best of all possible worlds, to mobilise the universe on behalf of its prejudices.

The publicists, popularisers and ideologists were now to be found throughout the western world and wherever there was a local elite attracted by 'modernisation'. The original scientists and scholars – at any rate those who enjoyed, and still enjoy, a reputation outside their own countries – were more unevenly distributed. In fact, they were virtually confined to parts of Europe and North America.* Work of considerable quality and international interest was now produced in significant quantities in central and eastern Europe, and most notably in Russia, and this was probably the most striking change in the 'academic' map of the western world in our period, though no history of science in this period can be written without reference to some eminent North Americans, notably the physicist Willard Gibbs (1839–1903). Still, it would be hard to deny that in, say, 1875 what went on in the university of Kazan and Kiev was more significant than what went on in Yale and Princeton.

But mere geographical distribution cannot sufficiently bring out what was increasingly the dominant fact about the academic life of our period, namely the hegemony of the Germans, backed as it was by the numerous universities using their language (which included those in most of Switzerland, most of the Habsburg Empire and the Baltic regions of Russia), and by the powerful attraction exercised by German culture in Scandinavia, eastern and south-eastern Europe. Outside the Latin world and Britain, and even to some extent within

* In Europe the Iberian and Balkan peninsulas remained rather backward in this respect.

both, the German model of the university was generally adopted. The German predominance was above all quantitative: in our period probably more new scientific journals were published in this language than in French and English combined. Outside certain fields of natural science like chemistry and probably mathematics, which they clearly dominated, their extremely high qualitative achievement was perhaps less obvious, because (unlike the early nineteenth century) there was not at this time a specifically German genre of natural philosophy. While the French, probably for nationalist reasons, stuck to their own style – with a consequent isolation of French natural science (though not of French mathematics) – except for a few celebrated individuals, the Germans did not. Perhaps their own style, which became dominant in the twentieth century, did not emerge as such until sciences moved into the phase of theory and systematising which (for rather obscure reasons) suited them admirably. At all events the much more narrowly based British natural sciences – which admittedly enjoyed the benefit of an impressive public forum of both specialists and lay bourgeois, and even artisans – continued to produce scientists of enormous renown, like Thompson and Darwin.

Except in academic history and linguistics, there was no such German dominance in the social sciences. Economics was still largely British, though in retrospect we may detect major analytical work in France, Italy and Austria. (The Habsburg Empire, though in some senses part of the German cultural area, followed a very different intellectual trajectory.) Sociology, for what little that is worth, was primarily associated with France and Britain, and enthusiastically taken up in the Latin world. In anthropology the world-wide connections of the British gave them a notable advantage. 'Evolution' in general – that bridge between the natural and social sciences – had its centre of gravity in Britain. The truth is that the social sciences reflected the pre-conceptions and problems of bourgeois liberalism in its classic form, which was not found in Germany, where bourgeois society inserted itself into the Bismarckian framework of aristocrats and bureaucrats. The most eminent social scientist of the period, Karl Marx, worked in Britain, derived the framework of his concrete analysis from the un-German science of economics, and the empirical basis of his work from the 'classic' though by this time no longer unchallenged form of bourgeois society – the British.

316

'Science' was the core of that secular ideology of progress, whether liberal or, to a small but growing extent, socialist, which requires no special discussion, since its general nature should have by now clearly emerged from this history.

Compared to secular ideology, religion in our period is of comparatively slight interest, and does not deserve extended treatment. Nevertheless it deserves some attention, not only because it still formed the idiom in which the overwhelming majority of the world's population thought, but also because bourgeois society itself, in spite of its growing secularisation, was plainly worried about the possible consequences of its own daring. A public disbelief in God became relatively easy in the mid-nineteenth century, at all events in the western world, since so much of the verifiable statements in the Judeo–Christian holy scriptures had been undermined or actually disproved by the sciences, historical, social and above all natural. If Lyell (1797–1875) and Darwin were right, then the book of Genesis was simply wrong in its literal meaning; and the intellectual opponents of Darwin and Lyell were being visibly routed. Upper-class free thought had long been familiar, at least among gentlemen. Middle-class and intellectual atheism was not novel either and became militant with the growing political importance of anti-clericalism. Working-class free thought, though already associated with revolutionary ideologies, took specific shape, both as older revolutionary ideologies declined, leaving only their less directly political aspects behind, and as new ideologies of the kind, firmly based on a materialist philosophy, gained ground. The 'secularist' movement in Britain derived directly from the old working-class radical, Chartist and Owenite movements, but it now existed as an independent body, particularly attractive to men and women who reacted against an unusually intensive religious background. God was not merely dismissed, but actively under attack.

This militant attack on religion coincided, but was not quite identical with, the equally militant current of anti-clericalism which embraced all intellectual currents from the moderate liberals to the Marxists and anarchists. The attack on churches, and most obviously official state churches and the international Roman Catholic Church – which claimed the right to define truth or the monopoly of certain functions affecting the citizen (such as marriage, burial and education) – did not in itself imply atheism. In countries containing more than one religion it could be conducted by the members of one religious denomination against another. In Britain it was primarily fought by members of the non-conformist sects against the Anglican Church; in Germany Bismarck, who entered into a bitter *Kulturkampf* against the Roman Catholic Church in 1870–71, certainly did not, as an official Lutheran, intend the existence of God or the divinity of Jesus to be at stake. On the other hand, in countries of a single monolithic faith, most obviously the Catholic ones, anti-clericalism normally implied the rejection of all religion. There was indeed a weak 'liberal' current within Catholicism which resisted the increasingly rigid ultra-conservatism of the Roman hierarchy, formulated in the 1860s (see p. 131 above for the *Syllabus of Errors*) and officially triumphant at the Vatican Council of 1870, with its declaration of papal infallibility. However, it was easily routed in the church, even though supported by some ecclesiastics who wished to preserve a relative autonomy of their national Catholic Church, and who were probably strongest in France. But 'Gallicanism' cannot really be called 'liberal' in the accepted sense, even though it was more prepared, on pragmatic as well as anti-Roman grounds, to come to terms with modern secular and liberal governments.

Anti-clericalism was militantly secularist, in as much as it wanted to deprive religion of any official status in society ('disestablishment of the church', 'separation of church and state'), leaving it as a purely private matter. It was to be transformed into one or several purely voluntary organisations, analogous to clubs of stamp-collectors only doubtless larger. But this was based not so much on the falsity of the belief in God or any particular version of such belief, but on the growing administrative capacity, scope and ambition of the secular state – even in its most liberal and *laissez-faire* form – which was bound to expel private organisations from what was now considered its field of action. However, basically anti-clericalism was political, because the chief passion behind it was the belief that established religions were hostile to progress. And so indeed they were, being both sociologically and politically very conservative institutions. The Roman Catholic Church, indeed, had nailed hostility to all that the mid-nineteenth century stood for firmly to its mast. Sects or the heterodox might be liberal or even revolutionary, religious minorities might be attracted by liberal toleration, but churches and orthodoxies were not. And, in so far as the masses – especially the rural masses – were still in the hands of these forces of obscurantism, traditionalism and political reaction, their power had to be broken, if progress was not to be in jeopardy. Hence anti-clericalism was more militant and passionate in proportion to the 'backwardness' of the country. Politicians argued about the status of Catholic schools in France, but in Mexico much more was at stake in the struggle of lay governments against the priests.

'Progress', emancipation from tradition – both for society and for individuals – therefore seemed to imply a militant break with ancient beliefs which found passionate expression in the behaviour of the militants of popular movements, as well as of middle-class intellectuals. A book named *Moses or Darwin* was to be more widely read in the libraries of German social democratic workers than the writings of Marx himself. Standing at the head of progress – even of socialist progress – there stood, in the minds of common men, the great educators and emancipators, and science (developed logically into 'scientific socialism') was the key to intellectual emancipation from the shackles of a superstitious past and an oppressive present. The west-European anarchists, who reflected the spontaneous instincts of such militants with great accuracy, were savagely anti-clerical. It was no accident that a radical blacksmith in the Italian Romagna named his son Benito Mussolini after the anti-clerical president of Mexico, Benito Juarez.

Nevertheless, even among free-thinkers, a nostalgia for religion remained. Middle-class ideologists, who appreciated the role of religion as an institution maintaining a state of suitable modesty among the poor and a guarantee of order, sometimes experimented with neo-religions, such as Auguste Comte's 'religion of humanity' which substituted a selection of great men for the Pantheon or calendar of saints, though such experiments were not notably successful. But there was also a genuine tendency to rescue the consolations of religion into the age of science. 'Christian Science', founded by Mary Baker Eddy (1821–1910) who published her scriptures in 1875, indicates one such attempt. The remarkable popularity of spiritualism, which first acquired its vogue in the 1850s, is probably due to this.

319

Its political and ideological affinities were with progress, reform and the radical left, and not least with women's emancipation, especially in the United States which was its main centre of diffusion. But apart from its other attractions, it had the considerable advantage of appearing to place survival after death on the sound basis of experimental science, perhaps even (as the new art of photography purported to prove) on that of the objective image. When miracles can no longer be accepted, para-psychology expands its potential public. Sometimes, however, it probably indicated nothing but that general human thirst for colourful ritual which traditional religion normally slakes so efficiently. The mid-nineteenth century is full of invented secular rituals, especially in the Anglo-Saxon countries, where trade unions devised elaborate allegorical banners and certificates, Mutual Aid Societies ('Friendly Societies') surrounded themselves with the paraphernalia of mythology and ritual in their 'lodges', and Klu-Klux-Klanners, Orangemen and less political 'secret' orders displayed their vestments. The oldest, or at any rate the most influential, of these secret, ritualised and hierarchical bodies was actually committed to free-thought and anti-clericalism, at any rate outside the Anglo-Saxon countries: the freemasons. Whether their membership increased in this period, we do not know, though it is likely; certainly their political significance did (cf. p. 286 above).

But if even the free-thinkers hankered after at least some spiritual consolations of the traditional kind, they nevertheless seemed to be pursuing a retreating enemy. For – as the Victorian writings of the 1860s eloquently witness – the faithful had 'doubts', especially if they were intellectuals. Religion was undoubtedly on the decline, not merely among intellectuals but in the rapidly growing great cities, where the provision for religious worship, like sanitation, lagged behind population and the communal pressures to conform to religious practice and morality were only faintly felt.

And yet the mid-nineteenth century decades did not see any decline of mass religion comparable to the intellectual rout of theology. The bulk of the Anglo-Saxon middle classes remained believers, and in general practising believers, or at any rate hypocrites. Of the great American millionaires only one (Andrew Carnegie) advertised unbelief. The rate of expansion of unofficial Protestant sects slackened, but – at least in Britain – the 'non-conformist conscience' which they represented became politically much more influential as they became more middle class. Religion did not decline among the new emigrant communities overseas: in Australia the percentage of church attendance among the population of fifteen years and over rose from 36·5 in 1850 to almost 59 in 1870, and settled down in the middle 40s in the last decades of the century.[15] The United States, in spite of Col. Ingersoll the celebrated atheist (1833–99), was a much less godless country than France.

So far as the middle classes were concerned, the decline of religion was, as we have seen, inhibited not only by tradition and the striking failure of liberal rationalism to provide any emotional substitute for collective religious worship and ritual (except perhaps through art – see chapter 15 below), but also by the reluctance to abandon so valuable, perhaps so indispensable, a pillar of stability, morality and social order. So far as the masses were concerned, its expansion may well have been chiefly due to those demographic factors on which the Catholic Church increasingly liked to rely for its ultimate triumph: the mass migration of men and women from more traditional, i.e. pious, environments, into new cities, regions and continents and the higher fertility of the godly poor compared with the unbelievers corrupted by progress (including birth control). There is no evidence that the Irish became more religious in our period and some that migration weakened the hold of the faith on them: but their dispersion and their birth-rate undoubtedly made the Catholic Church grow relatively and absolutely throughout Christendom. And yet, were there no forces within religion to revive and spread it?

Certainly at this stage Christian missionary endeavour was not notably successful, whether directed towards recuperating the lost proletariat at home or the heathen, still less the believer in rival world religions, abroad. Considering the very substantial expenditures – between 1871 and 1877 the British alone contributed £8 million to the missions[16] – the results were extremely modest. Christianity of any and all denominations failed to become a serious competitor to the only genuinely expanding religion, Islam. This continued to spread irresistibly, without benefit of missionary organisation, money or the support of great powers, through the backlands of Africa and parts of Asia, assisted doubtless, not only by its egalitarianism, but also by a consciousness of superiority to the values of the conquering

321

Europeans. No missionaries ever made a dent into a Mohammedan population. They made only slight dents into non-Islamic ones, since they still generally lacked the main weapon of Christian penetration, namely actual colonial conquest, or at least the official conversion of rulers who dragged their subjects behind them, as happened in Madagascar which declared itself a Christian island in 1869. Christianity made some advances in south India (mostly among the lowest strata of the caste system) in spite of the lack of enthusiasm of the government, and in Indochina following the French conquest, but no significant ones in Africa, until imperialism multiplied the number of missionaries (from perhaps 3,000 Protestant ones in the mid-1880s to perhaps 18,000 in 1900) and put a great deal more material power behind the spiritual power of the Redeemer.[17] Indeed, during the heyday of liberalism missionary endeavour may actually have lost some impetus. Only about three or four new Catholic missionary centres were opened in Africa in each of the decades between 1850 and 1880, compared with six in the 1840s, fourteen in the 1880s and seventeen in the 1890s.[18] Christianity was most effective when elements of it were absorbed into local religious ideology in the form of 'nativist' syncretist cults. The Taiping movement in China (see chapter 7 above) was by far the greatest and most influential of such phenomena.

And yet within Christianity there were signs of a counter-attack against the advance of secularisation. Not so much in the Protestant world, where the formation and expansion of new unofficial sects seem to have lost much of the dynamism they had before 1848 – with the possible exception of the blacks in Anglo-Saxon America – as among the Catholics. The miracle cult at Lourdes in France, which began with a shepherd girl's vision in 1858, expanded with enormous rapidity; perhaps spontaneously to begin with, but certainly soon with active ecclesiastical support. By 1875 a branch establishment of Lourdes was actually opened in Belgium. Less dramatically, anti-clericalism provoked a substantial movement of evangelisation among the faithful, and a major reinforcement of clerical influence. In Latin America the rural population had been largely Christians without priests: until after 1860 most of the Mexican clergy was urban. Against official anti-clericalism the Church systematically captured or reproselytised the countryside. In a sense, faced with the threat of secular reform, it reacted as it had done in the sixteenth century with a counter-reformation. Catholicism, now totally intransigent, ultramontane, refusing any intellectual accommodation with the forces of progress, industrialisation and liberalism, became a more formidable force after the Vatican Council of 1870 than before – but at the cost of abandoning much ground to its adversaries.

Outside Christianity religions relied mainly on the force of traditionalism to resist the erosion of the liberal era, or of confrontation with the west. Attempts to 'liberalise' them appealed to the semi-assimilated bourgeoisie (like the Reform Judaism which emerged in the late 1860s), were execrated by the orthodox and despised by the agnostics. The forces of tradition were still overwhelmingly powerful, and often reinforced by resistance to 'progress' and European expansion. As we have seen, Japan even created a new state religion, Shintoism, out of traditional elements, largely for anti-European purposes (see chapter 8 above). Even the westernisers and revolutionaries in the Third World were to learn that the easiest way to success as a politician among the masses was to acquire the role, or at least the prestige, of the Buddhist monk or the Hindu holy man. And yet, though the number of frank unbelievers in our period remained relatively small (after all, even in Europe the female half of the human race was hardly yet affected by agnosticism), they dominated an essentially secular world. All that religion could do against them was to retire within its admittedly vast and powerful fortifications and prepare for a very long siege.

Chapter Fifteen

The Arts

We have only to convince ourselves thoroughly that our history today is made by the same human beings *who once also made the works of Greek art. But having done so, our task is to discover* what *it is that has changed these human beings so fundamentally, that* we *now produce merely the output of luxury industries, whereas they created works of art.*

Richard Wagner[1]

Why do you write in verse? No one cares for it now . . . In our age of sceptical maturity and republican independence, verse is a super-annuated form. We prefer prose, which, by virtue of its freedom of movement, accords more truly with the instincts of democracy.

Eugene Pelletan, French deputy, *c.* 1877[2]

I

If the triumph of bourgeois society seemed congenial to science, it was much less so to the arts. Assessments of value in the creative arts are always highly subjective, but it can hardly be denied that the era of the dual revolution (1789–1848) had seen amazingly distinguished and widespread achievement by men and women of quite extraordinary gifts. The second half of the nineteenth century, and especially the decades which are the subject of this book, do not make an equally overpowering impression, except in one or two relatively backward countries, the most notable of which by far was Russia. This is not to say that the creative achievements of this period were mediocre, though, in surveying those whose greatest work or public acclaim falls between 1848 and the 1870s, we should not forget that many were already mature people with an impressive production before 1848. After all – and to take merely three of the most unquestionably great – by then Charles Dickens (1812–70) was almost halfway through his *oeuvre*, Honoré Daumier (1808–79) had been an active graphic artist since the 1830 revolution, and even Richard Wagner

(1813–83) had several operas behind him: *Lohengrin* was produced as early as 1851. Still, there is no doubt that prose literature, and especially the novel, flourished remarkably, thanks mainly to the continued glory of the French and the British and the new glory of the Russians. In the history of painting this was clearly a remarkable and indeed an outstanding period, thanks almost entirely to the French. In music the era of Wagner and Brahms is inferior only in comparison with the preceding era of Mozart, Beethoven and Schubert.

Still, if we take a closer look at the creative scene, it becomes a shade less inspiring. We have already noted its geographic patchiness. For Russia this was an astonishingly triumphant era, both in music and above all in literature, not to mention the natural and social sciences. A decade like the 1870s, which saw the simultaneous peak of Dostoievsky and Tolstoi, P. Tchaikovsky (1840–93), M. Mussorgsky (1835–81) and the classic Imperial Ballet, has little to fear from any competition. France and Britain, as we have seen, maintained a very distinguished level, the one mainly in prose literature, the other also in painting and poetry.* The United States, though still insignificant in the visual arts and in highbrow music, was beginning to establish itself as a literary force with Melville (1819–91), Hawthorne (1804–64) and Whitman (1819–91) in the east, and with a new crop of populist writers emerging from the journalism of the west, among whom Mark Twain (1835–1910) was to be the most impressive. Still, by global standards this was a provincial achievement and in many respects less impressive, and internationally less influential, than the creative work which now came out of some small nations asserting a national identity. (Curiously enough several less distinguished American writers of the first half of the century had made more of a stir abroad.) The composers of the Czechs (A. Dvořák [1841–1904], B. Smetana [1824–84]) found it easier to win international acceptance than their writers, isolated by a language which few outside their people could read or be bothered to learn. Linguistic difficulties also localised the reputation of writers from other regions, some of whom occupy a key position in the literary history of their peoples – e.g. the Dutch and the Flemings. Only the Scandinavians began to cap-

* In English poetry the achievement of Tennyson, Browning *et al.* is somewhat less impressive than that of the great romantics of the age of revolution; in France that of Baudelaire and Rimbaud is not.

ture a wider public, perhaps due to the fact that their most celebrated representative – Henrik Ibsen (1828–1906) who reached maturity just as our period ends – chose to write plays for the theatre.

Against this we must set a distinct and in some ways spectacular decline in the quality of the highest work from those two great centres of creative activity, the German-speaking peoples and the Italians. There may be argument about music, though in Italy there is little but G. Verdi (1813–1901), whose career was well launched before 1848, and in Austro-Germany among the acknowledged great composers only Brahms (1833–97) and Bruckner (1824–96) emerged essentially during this period, Wagner being already virtually mature. Still, these names are impressive enough, especially Wagner, a towering genius though a very nasty man and cultural phenomenon. But the case for the creative arts among these two people must rest pretty well entirely on music. There can be no serious argument about the inferiority of their literature and visual arts to those of the period before 1848.

Taking the various arts separately, the general lowering of the level is equally obvious in some, their superiority over the preceding period undeniable in none. Literature, as we have seen, flourished, mainly through the suitable medium of the novel. It can be regarded as the one genre which found it possible to adapt itself to that bourgeois society whose rise and crises formed its chief subject matter. Attempts have been made to salvage the reputation of mid-nineteenth century architecture, and no doubt there were distinguished achievements. However, when one considers the orgy of building into which a prosperous bourgeois society threw itself from the 1850s, these are neither outstanding nor particularly numerous. The Paris rebuilt by Haussman is impressive for its planning, but not for the buildings which lined its new squares and boulevards. Vienna, which aimed at masterpieces more single-mindedly, achieved only a rather doubtful success. The Rome of King Victor Emmanuel, whose name is probably associated with more pieces of bad architecture than that of any other sovereign, is a disaster. Compared to the admirable achievements of, say, neo-classicism – the last unified style of architecture before the triumph of twentieth-century 'modern' orthodoxy – the buildings of the second half of the nineteenth century are still more likely to stimulate apologia rather than universal admiration. This does not, of course, apply to the work of the brilliant and imaginative engineers, though this tended to be increasingly hidden behind 'fine art' façades.

Even apologists have until recently found it hard to say much in favour of most of the painting of this period. The work that has become a permanent part of the imaginary museum of twentieth-century men is, almost without exception, French: survivors of the age of revolution like Daumier and G. Courbet (1819–77), the Barbizon school and the *avant-garde* group of the Impressionists (an indiscriminate label which we need not analyse more closely at the moment), who emerged in the 1860s. This achievement is indeed deeply impressive, and a period which saw the emergence of E. Manet (1832–83), E. Degas (1834–1917) and the young P. Cézanne (1839–1906), need not worry about its reputation. Nevertheless, these painters were not merely untypical of what was put on canvas in increasingly vast quantities at this time, but deeply suspect to respectable art and public taste. About the official academic or popular art of the period in all countries, the most that can be reasonably said is that it was not all uniform in character, that its standards of craftsmanship were high, and that some modest merits can be rediscovered here and there. Most of it was and is terrible.

It may be that mid- and late-nineteenth-century sculpture, amply displayed in innumerable monumental works, deserves to be a little less neglected than it has been – after all it produced the young Rodin (1840–1917). However, any collection of Victorian plastic work *en masse*, such as may still be seen in the houses of wealthy Bengalis who bought the stuff up by the boatload, is an acutely depressing sight.

II

This was in some ways a tragi-comic situation. Few societies have cherished the works of creative genius (itself virtually a bourgeois invention as a social phenomenon – see *The Age of Revolution*, chapter 14) more than that of the nineteenth-century bourgeoisie. Few have been prepared to spend money so freely on the arts and, in purely quantitative terms, no previous society bought anything like the actual amount of old and new books, material objects, pictures, sculptures, decorated structures of masonry and tickets to musical or theatrical performances. (The growth of population alone would put this statement beyond challenge.) Above all, and paradoxically, few societies have been so convinced that they lived in a golden age of the creative arts.

The taste of the period was nothing if not contemporary, as was indeed natural for a generation which believed in universal and constant progress. Herr Ahrens (1805–81), a north German industrialist who settled in the culturally more congenial climate of Vienna and began to collect in his fifties, naturally bought modern pictures rather than old masters, and he was typical of his kind.[3] The Bolckow (iron), Holloway (patent pills), Mendel 'the merchant prince' (cotton), who competed with one another to raise the price of oil-paintings in Britain, made the fortunes of contemporary academic painters.[4] The journalists and city fathers, who proudly recorded the opening and full cost of those mammoth public buildings which began to disfigure the northern townscapes after 1848, only incompletely concealed by the soot and fog which immediately enveloped them, genuinely believed themselves to be celebrating a new renaissance, financed by businessmen-princes comparable to the Medici. Alas, the most evident conclusion which historians can draw from the later nineteenth century is that the mere expenditure of money does not guarantee a golden age of the arts.

Still, the amounts of money spent were impressive by any standards except those of the unprecedented productive capacity of capitalism. However, they were no longer spent by the same people. The bourgeois revolution was victorious even in the characteristic field of activity of princes and nobility. None of the great rebuildings of cities between 1850 and 1875 any longer makes a royal or imperial palace, even a complex of aristocratic palaces, into the dominating feature of the townscape. Where the bourgeoisie was weak, as in Russia, tsar and grand-dukes might still be the chief individual patrons, but in fact their role even in such countries seems far less central than it had been before the French Revolution. Elsewhere an occasional eccentric minor prince like Ludwig II of Bavaria, or scarcely less eccentric aristocrat like the Marquess of Hertford, might put all their passion into buying art and artists, but on the whole horses, gambling and women were more likely to put them into debt than the patronage of the arts.

Who then paid for the arts? Governments and other public entities, the bourgeoisie and – the point deserves notice – an increasingly significant section of the 'lower orders', to whom technological and industrial processes made the products of creative minds available in increasing quantities and at diminishing prices.

Secular public authorities were almost the only customers for those gigantic and monumental buildings whose purpose was to testify to the wealth and splendour of the age in general and the city in particular. Their purpose was rarely utilitarian. In the era of *laissez-faire*, government buildings were not unduly conspicuous. They were not normally religious, except in very Catholic countries and when constructed for internal use by such (minority) religious groups as the Jews and the British non-conformists, who wished to record their rapidly growing wealth and self-satisfaction. The passion for 'restoring' and completing the great churches and cathedrals of the middle ages, which swept mid-nineteenth-century Europe like a contagious disease, was civic rather than spiritual. Even in the most splendid monarchies they belonged increasingly to 'the public' rather than the court: imperial collections were now museums, operas opened their box-offices. They were, in fact, characteristic symbols of glory and culture, for even the titanic town halls which city fathers competed to construct were far larger than the modest needs of municipal administration required. The hard-headed businessmen of Leeds deliberately rejected utilitarian calculations in the construction of theirs. What were a few thousands more, when the point was to assert that 'in the ardour of mercantile pursuits the inhabitants of Leeds have not omitted to cultivate the perception of the beautiful and a taste for the fine arts'? (In fact it cost £122,000 or about three times its original estimate, equivalent to rather over 1 per cent of the *total* yield of the income tax for the *entire* United Kingdom in the year of its opening, 1858.)[5]

An example may illustrate the general character of such building. The city of Vienna razed its old fortifications in the 1850s and filled the empty space in subsequent decades with a magnificent circular boulevard flanked by public buildings. What were they? One represented business (the stock exchange), one religion (the Votivkirche), three higher education, three civic dignity and public affairs (the town hall, palace of justice and parliament) and no less than eight the arts: theatres, museums, academies, etc.

The demands of the bourgeoisie were individually more modest, collectively far greater. Their patronage as individuals was probably not yet as important in this period as it was to become in the last generation before 1914, when the millionaires of the United States raised prices for certain works of art to a higher peak than ever before or since. (Even at the end of our period the robber barons were still too busy robbing to throw themselves wholeheartedly into displaying proceeds of their brigandage.) Still it was evident, particularly from 1860 on, that there was plenty of money about. The 1850s produced only one article of French eighteenth-century furniture (the international status symbol of the wealthy interior) which made over £1,000 at an auction, the 1860s eight, the 1870s fourteen, including one lot which actually fetched £30,000; such articles as large Sèvres vases (a very similar status symbol) made £1,000 or more three times in the 1850s, seven times in the 1860s, eleven times in the 1870s.[6] A handful of competing merchant-princes is enough to make the fortunes of a handful of painters and art-dealers, but even a numerically modest public is enough to maintain a substantial artistic output if it is comfortably off. The theatre, and to some extent classical music concerts, prove this, for both prosper on the basis of quite small numbers. (Opera and classical ballet then as now relied on subsidies by government or the status-seeking rich, not always unmindful of the facility of access to beautiful ballerinas and singers which this brought.) The theatre flourished, at least financially. So did the publishers of solid and expensive books for a limited market, whose dimensions are perhaps indicated by the circulation of the London *Times*, which moved between 50,000 and 60,000 in the 1850s and 1860s, though reaching 100,000 on a few special occasions. Who could complain when Livingstone's *Travels* (1857) sold 30,000 in a guinea edition in six years?[7] At all events the business and domestic needs of the bourgeoisie made the fortunes of plenty of architects who built and rebuilt substantial areas of the cities for them.

The bourgeois market was new only in so far as it was now unusually large and increasingly prosperous. On the other hand, the mid-century produced a really revolutionary phenomenon: for the first time, thanks to technology and science, some kinds of creative work became technically reproducible cheaply, and on an unprecedented scale. Only one of these processes actually competed with the act of artistic creation itself, namely photography, which came of age in the 1850s. As we shall see, its effect on painting was immediate and profound. The rest merely brought lower-quality versions of individual products within the reach of a mass public: writing, through the multiplication of cheap paperbacks, stimulated notably by the railways (the leading series were typically called 'railway' or 'travellers' libraries), pictures through the steel engravings which the new process of electro-typing (1845) made it possible to reproduce in vast quantities without loss of detail or refinement, both through the development of journalism, literature or self-education by instalments, etc.*

The sheer economic significance of this early mass market is commonly underrated. The incomes of leading painters, impressive even by modern standards – Millais averaged £20–25,000 a year of mid-Victorian pounds sterling between 1868 and 1874 – were based largely on the 2 guineas engravings in 5 shilling frames which Gambart, Flatou or similar entrepreneurs launched. Frith's *Railway Station* (1860) fetched £4,500 in such subsidiary rights plus £750 for exhibition rights.[8] Such impresarios took Mlle Rosa Bonheur (1822–99) to the Scottish highlands in order to persuade her to add the stags and crags which Landseer had demonstrated to be so saleable to the horses and cattle which had already made her fortune among the animal-loving British public. Similarly in the 1860s they drew the attention of L. Alma-Tadema (1836–1912) to ancient Rome, with its historic nudity and orgies, to considerable mutual benefit. As early as 1853 E. Bulwer-Lytton (1803–73), never a writer to neglect economics, sold ten years' paperback rights, in the novels he had already written, to Routledge's Railway Library for £20,000, £5,000 down.[9] Except for the unique Harriet Beecher Stowe's *Uncle Tom's Cabin* (1852), which may have sold 1·5 million in a year in the British Empire in forty, mostly pirated, editions, the mass market for the arts cannot compare with our own times. Yet it existed and its importance was undeniable.

Two observations must be made about it. The first is to note the marked devaluation of the traditional crafts, which were most directly affected by the advance of mechanical reproduction. Within a generation this was to produce especially in Britain, the home of industrialisation, the politico-ideological reaction of the (largely socialist)

* That these developments had been pioneered in the 1830s and 1840s does not diminish the significance of the quantitative expansion from the 1850s.

331

arts-and-crafts movement, whose anti-industrialist, implicitly anti-capitalist, roots can be traced through William Morris's designing firm of 1860 to the Pre-Raphaelite painters of the 1850s. The second concerns the nature of the public which influenced the artists. It was, plainly, not only an aristocratic or bourgeois clientele, such as that which evidently determined the content of the London West End or Paris boulevard theatre. It was, at the very least, also a mass public of the modest lower middle class and others, including skilled workers, who aspired to respectability and culture. The arts of the third quarter of the nineteenth century were in every sense *popular*, as the new mass advertisers of the 1880s knew when they bought up some of the more regrettable and expensive paintings to put on their posters.

The arts were prosperous, and so were the creative talents which appealed to the public – and they were by no means typically the worst. It is a myth that the leading talents of the period were normally left to starve in some bohemia by unappreciative philistines. We can certainly discover those who, for various reasons, resisted or tried to shock a bourgeois public, or simply failed to attract purchasers, mostly in France (G. Flaubert [1821–80], the early Symbolists, the Impressionists), but also elsewhere. However, more often than not the men and women whose reputations have stood the test of the subsequent century were people whose contemporary reputation ranged from the highly respected to the idolised, and whose professional income ranged from the comfortably middle class to the fabulous. Tolstoi's family was to live comfortably on the proceeds of a bare handful of novels when the great man had given up his estates. Charles Dickens, about whose finances we happen to be unusually well informed, could reckon on £10,000 a year in most years from 1848 on, while in the 1860s his annual income rose, reaching some £33,000 in 1868 (most of which came from the already enormously profitable American lecture circuit).[10] $150,000 would be a very substantial income today, but around 1870 it put a man in the class of the very rich. By and large, then, the artist had come to terms with the market. And even those who did not become wealthy, were respected. Dickens, W. Thackeray (1811–63), George Eliot (1819–80), Tennyson (1809–92), Victor Hugo (1802–85), Zola (1840–1902), Tolstoi, Dostoievsky, Turgenev, Wagner, Verdi, Brahms, Liszt (1811–86), Dvořák, Tchaikovsky, Mark Twain, Henrik Ibsen: these are not names of men who in their lifetime lacked public success and appreciation.

What is more, he (and in this period much more rarely than in the first half of the nineteenth century, she) enjoyed not merely the possibility of material comfort, but special esteem. In monarchical and aristocratic society the artist had been at best an ornamenter or an ornament of court and palazzo, a valued piece of property, and at worst one of those expensive and perhaps moody suppliers of luxury services and articles like hair-stylists and couturiers, which the fashionable life requires. For bourgeois society he represented 'genius', which was a non-financial version of individual enterprise, 'the ideal', which complemented and crowned material success and, more generally, the spiritual values of life.

There is no understanding the arts in the later nineteenth century without a sense of this social demand that they should act as all-purpose suppliers of spiritual contents to the most materialist of civilisations. One might almost say that they took the place of traditional religion among the educated and emancipated, i.e. the successful middle classes, supplemented of course by the inspiring spectacles of 'nature', i.e. landscape. This was most evident among the German-speaking peoples, who had come to regard culture as their special monopoly in the days when the British had cornered economic, the French political success. Here operas and theatres became temples in which men and women worshipped, all the more devoutly for not always *enjoying* the works of the classic repertoire, and in which children were formally initiated at primary-school by, say, Schiller's *Wilhelm Tell* to advance eventually to the adult mysteries of Goethe's *Faust*. That unpleasant genius Richard Wagner had a sound understanding of this function when he constructed his cathedral at Bayreuth (1872–6) where the faithful pilgrims came to listen, in pious exaltation, for long hours and several days, and prohibited from the frivolities of untimely applause, to the master's Germanic neo-paganism. Sound not only in appreciating the connection between sacrifice and religious exaltation, but also in grasping the importance of the arts as bearers of the new secular religion of nationalism. For what, other than armies, could express that elusive concept of the nation better than the symbols of art – primitive, as in flags and anthems, elaborate and profound, as in those 'national' schools of music which became so closely identified with the nations of our period in their moment of acquiring collective consciousness, independence or unification, a Verdi in the Italian *risorgimento*, a Dvořák and Smetana among the Czechs?

Not all countries pushed the worship of the arts to the point it reached in central Europe, and more specifically among the assimilated and – over most of Europe and the United States culturally German or Germanised – Jewish middle class.* In general capitalists of the first generation were philistines, though their wives did their best to take an interest in higher things. The only gentile American tycoon who had a genuine passion for the things of the spirit – he happened also to be the only freethinking anti-clerical among them – was Andrew Carnegie, who could not wholly forget the tradition of his rebellious and cultured handloom-weaver father. Outside Germany, and perhaps even more Austria, there were few bankers who would wish to see their sons become composers or conductors, perhaps because there they had not the alternative prospect of hoping to see them as cabinet ministers or premiers. The replacement of religion by self-cultivation and the combined worship of nature and the arts was characteristic only of sections of the intellectual middle classes, such as those who were later to form the English 'Bloomsbury', men and women of comfortable inherited private means, rarely involved in business themselves.

Nevertheless, even in the more philistine bourgeois societies, perhaps with the exception of the United States, the arts occupied a special place of respect and esteem. The great collective status symbols of theatre and opera arose in the centres of capital cities – the focus of town-planning as in Paris (1860) and Vienna (1869), visible as cathedrals as in Dresden (1869), invariably gigantic and monumentally elaborate as in Barcelona (from 1862) or Palermo (from 1875). The museums and public galleries of art arose, or were amplified, reconstructed and transformed, as were great national libraries –

* What the arts, and notably classical music, owe to the patronage of this small, wealthy and profoundly culture-imbued community in the later nineteenth century is incalculable.

the reading-room of the British Museum was constructed in 1852-7, the Bibliothèque Nationale reconstructed in 1854-75. More generally, the number of large libraries (unlike universities) multiplied phenomenally in Europe, though as yet modestly in the philistine United States. In 1848 there had been about four hundred, with perhaps 17 million volumes in Europe; by 1880 there were almost twelve times as many with almost twice the number of books. Austria, Russia, Italy, Belgium, Holland and Italy multiplied the numbers of their libraries more than tenfold, Britain almost as much, even Spain and Portugal almost fourfold, though the United States less than threefold. (On the other hand the United States almost quadrupled the number of its books, a rate surpassed only by Switzerland.)[11]

The shelves of bourgeois households filled with the elaborately bound works of the national and international classics. The visitors to galleries and museums multiplied: the Royal Academy exhibition in 1848 attracted perhaps 90,000 visitors, but by the end of the 1870s almost 400,000. By that time its 'private views' had become fashionable occasions for the upper classes, as sure a sign of the rising social status of painting as the social glitter of theatrical 'first nights', in which London began to compete with Paris after 1870; in both cases with disastrous effect on the arts concerned. The bourgeois tourists now could hardly avoid that endless and footsore pilgrimage to the shrines of the arts, which is still in progress along the hard floors of Louvre, Uffizi and San Marco. The artists themselves, down to the hitherto dubious theatrical and operatic performers, became respected and respectable, suitable candidates for knighthood or peerage.* They did not even have to conform to the mores of the normal bourgeois, so long as their cravats, velvet berets and cloaks were of sufficiently expensive material. (Here again Richard Wagner showed a faultless sense of the bourgeois public: even his scandals became part of the creative image.) Gladstone at the end of the 1860s was the first prime minister to invite luminaries of the arts and intellectual life to his official dinners.

Did the bourgeois public actually *enjoy* the arts which it patronised

---

* In Britain painters had long been knighted, but Henry Irving, who established his reputation in our period, was to become the first actor to win this status, and Tennyson was the first poet – or artist of any kind – to be made a peer. However, in spite of the cultural influence of the (German) Prince-Consort, such honours were still rare in our period.

and cherished with such growing lavishness? The question is anachronistic. It is true that there were certain kinds of artistic creation which maintained a straightforward relationship with a public that they merely sought to entertain. Chief among these was 'light music', which, perhaps alone among the arts, had its golden age in our period. The word 'operetta' appears for the first time in 1856 and the decade from 1865 to 1875 was to see the peak of achievement of Jacques Offenbach (1819–80), Johann Strauss jr. (1825–99) – the 'Blue Danube Waltz' dates from 1867, *Die Fledermaus* from 1874 – Suppé's (1820–95) 'Light Cavalry' and the early successes of Gilbert and Sullivan (1836–1911, 1842–1900). Until the weight of high art fell too heavily on it, even opera maintained its *rapport* with a public which sought straightforward enjoyment (*Rigoletto, Il Trovatore, La Traviata* – admittedly works barely posterior to 1848) and the commercial stage multiplied its well-carpentered dramas and intricate farces, of which only the latter have just survived the landslide of time (Labiche [1815–88], Meilhac [1831–97] and Halévy [1834–1908]). But such entertainments were accepted as culturally inferior, like the various girl-shows which Paris pioneered in the 1850s, with which they clearly had much in common.* Real high art was not a matter for mere enjoyment or even for something that could be isolated as 'aesthetic appreciation'.

'Art for art's sake' was still a minority phenomenon among late romantic artists themselves, a reaction against the ardent political and social commitment of the era of revolutions, intensified by the bitter disappointments of 1848, the movement which had swept so many creative spirits with it. Aestheticism did not become a bourgeois fashion until the late 1870s and 1880s. Creative artists were sages, prophets, teachers, moralists, sources of *truth*. Effort was the price paid for their rewards by a bourgeoisie only too ready to believe that everything of value (financial or spiritual) required initial abstention from enjoyment. The arts were part of this human endeavour. Their cultivation crowned it.

* The takings of the Folies Bergère were second only to the Opéra and well ahead of the Comédie Française.[12]

What was the nature of this truth? Here we must single out architecture from the other arts, because it lacked the theme which gave them a semblance of unity. Indeed the most characteristic thing about it is the absence of any single accepted, moral-ideological-aesthetic 'style' such as had always impressed their stamp on past epochs. Eclecticism ruled. As Pietro Selvatico observed as early as the 1850s in his *Storia dell'Arte del Disegno*, there was no one style or beauty. Each style was adapted to its purpose. Thus of the new buildings along the Viennese Ringstrasse the church was naturally gothic, the parliament Grecian, the city hall a combination of renaissance and gothic, the stock exchange (like most others of its kind during this period) a modestly opulent classicism, the museums and university high renaissance, the Burgtheater and Opera what can be best described as Second Empire operatic, in which eclectic elements of the renaissance predominate.

The requirements of pomp and splendour normally found the high renaissance and late gothic most suitable as an idiom. (Baroque and rococo were despised until the twentieth century). The renaissance, age of merchant princes, was naturally the most congenial style to men who saw themselves as their successors, but other suitably reminiscent styles were freely available. Thus the landed noblemen of Silesia, who turned themselves into capitalist millionaires thanks to the coal on their estates, and their more bourgeois colleagues, raided the entire architectural history of centuries. The 'Schloss' of the banker von Eichborn (1857) remains clearly Prussian-neo-classical, a style still favoured by the more bourgeois rich at the end of our period. Gothic, with its joint suggestion of medieval burgher glory and knightly fame, next tempted the more aristocratic and affluent, as in Koppitz (1859) and Miechowitz (1858). The experience of Napoleon III's Paris, on which well-known Silesian tycoons like Prince Henckel von Donnersmarck had left their mark, if only by marrying one of its leading courtesans, La Païva, naturally suggested further models of splendour, at least to the princes of Donnersmarck, Hohenlohe and Pless. The Italian, Dutch and north German renaissance provided equally acceptable models for the less grandiose, either singly or in combination.[13] Even the least expected motifs appear. Thus the wealthy Jews in our period adopted for preference a Moorish-Islamic style for their increasingly opulent synagogues, an assertion (echoed in Disraeli's novels) of oriental aristocracy which did not have to compete with the occidental,[14] and very nearly the only example of a deliberate use of non-western models in the arts of the western bourgeoisie, until the fashion for Japanese motifs of the later 1870s and 1880s.

In brief, architecture expressed no kind of 'truth' in the literal sense, though this did not exclude moral conviction and aspiration. What it chiefly expressed was the confidence and self-confidence of the society that built it, and this sense of the immense and unquestioned faith in bourgeois destiny is what makes its best examples impressive, if only by sheer bulk. It was a language of social symbols. Hence the deliberate concealment of what was really novel and interesting in it, the magnificent technology and engineering which showed their face in public only on the rare occasions when what was to be symbolised was to be technical progress itself: in the Crystal Palace of 1851, the Rotunda of the Vienna exhibition of 1873, later the Eiffel Tower (1889). Otherwise even the glorious functionalism of utilitarian buildings was increasingly disguised, as in railway stations – crazily eclectic like London Bridge (1862), baronial-gothic like St Pancras, London (1868), renaissance like the Südbahnhof, Vienna (1869–73). (However, several important stations fortunately resisted the lush tastes of the new era.) Only the bridges gloried in their engineering beauty – even this perhaps rather heavy now, thanks to the abundance and cheapness of iron – though that curious phenomenon, the gothic suspension bridge (Tower Bridge, London), was already on the horizon. And yet technically, behind those renaissance and baronial façades, the most enterprising, original, *modern* things were happening. The decorations of the Second Empire apartment house in Paris already began to conceal that original and remarkably advanced invention, the passenger lift or elevator. Perhaps the only piece of justified technical braggadocio which architects rarely resisted, even in buildings with 'artistic' public faces, was that of the giant span or cupola – as in the market halls, library reading-rooms, and such vast public shopping arcades as the Victor Emmanuel Gallery in Milan. Otherwise no age has hidden its merits so persistently.

Architecture had no 'truth' of its own, because it had no meaning that could be expressed in words. The other arts had, because theirs could. Nothing is more surprising to mid-twentieth-century generations, educated in a very different critical dogma, than the mid-nineteenth-century belief that in the arts form was unimportant, content paramount. It would be wrong to think of this simply as the subordination of the other arts to literature, though their content was believed to be expressible in words, with varying degrees of adequacy, and though literature was certainly the key art of the period. If 'every picture told a story' and even music did surprisingly often – this was, after all, the characteristic age of operas, ballet-music and descriptive suites* – the programme note was bound to be prominent. It would be truer to claim that each art was supposed to be expressible in terms of others, so that the ideal 'total work of art' (the *Gesamtkunstwerk* of which Wagner, as usual, made himself the spokesman) united them all. Still, the arts in which meaning could be expressed precisely, i.e. in word or representational image, had the advantage over those in which it could not. It was easier to turn a story into an opera (e.g. *Carmen*) or even pictures into a composition (Mussorgsky's *Pictures from an Exhibition* [1874]), than to turn a musical composition into a picture, or even lyric poetry.

The question 'what is it about?' was therefore not only legitimate but fundamental to any judgment of the mid-century arts. The answer in general was: 'reality' and 'life'. 'Realism' is the term which has come most naturally to the lips of contemporary and later observers about this period, at all events when dealing with literature and the visual arts. No term is more ambiguous. It implies the attempt to describe, to represent, or at all events to find a precise equivalent, of facts, images, ideas, sentiments, passions – in the extreme case Wagner's specific musical *Leitmotive*, each of which stood for a person, situation or action, or his musical recreations of sexual ecstasy (*Tristan and Isolde* [1865]). But what is the reality so represented, the life 'like which' art is to be? The bourgeoisie of the mid-

* The literary inspiration of music was particularly marked. Goethe inspired works by Liszt, Gounod, Boito and Ambroise Thomas, not to mention Berlioz; Schiller works by Verdi; Shakespeare Mendelssohn, Tchaikovsky, Berlioz and Verdi. Wagner, who invented his own poetic drama, regarded his music as subordinate to it, though his flatulent pseudo-medieval verse is clearly dead without the music, which has become part of the concert repertoire even without the words.

century was torn by a dilemma which its triumph made even more acute. The image of itself which it desired could not represent *all* reality in so far as that reality was one of poverty, exploitation and squalor, of materialism, of passions and aspirations whose existence threatened a stability which, in spite of all self-confidence, was felt to be precarious. There was, to quote the journalistic motto of the *New York Times*, a difference between the news and 'all the news that's fit to print'. Conversely, in a dynamic and progressive society reality was, after all, not static. Was it not realism to represent, not the necessarily imperfect present, but the better situation to which men aspired and which was already, surely, being created? Art had a future dimension (Wagner, as usual, claimed to represent it). In brief, 'real' and 'lifelike' images in art diverged increasingly from the stylised and sentimentalised ones. At best the bourgeois version of 'realism' was a socially suitable selection, as in the famous *Angelus* of J.-F. Millet (1814–75), where poverty and hard labour seemed to be made acceptable by the obedient piety of the poor; at worst it turned into the sentimental flattery of the family portrait.

In the representational arts there were three ways of escape from this dilemma. One was to insist on representing all reality, including the unpleasant or dangerous. 'Realism' turned into 'naturalism' or '*verismo*'. This normally implied a conscious political critique of bourgeois society, as with Courbet in painting, Zola and Flaubert in literature, though even works which lacked any such deliberately critical intention, like Bizet's (1838–75) masterpiece, the low-life opera *Carmen* (1875), were resented by the public and the critics as though they had been political. The alternative was to abandon contemporary or any reality entirely, either by cutting the links between art and life, or more specifically contemporary life ('art for art's sake') or by deliberately choosing the approach of the visionary (as in the revolutionary young Rimbaud's *Bateau Ivre* [1871]) or, in a different mode, the evasive fantasy of humorists like Edward Lear (1812–88) and Lewis Carroll (1832–98) in Britain, Wilhelm Busch (1832–1908) in Germany. But, in so far as the artist did not retreat (or advance) into deliberate fantasy, the basic images were still supposed to be 'lifelike'. And at this point the visual ones encountered a profound, traumatic shock: the competition of technology through the photograph.

340

Photography, invented in the 1820s, publicly fostered in France from the 1830s, became a workable medium for the mass reproduction of reality in our period, and was rapidly developed as a commercial business in the France of the 1850s, largely by unsuccessful members of the artistic *bohéme* like Nadar (1820–1911), for whom it replaced artistic and established financial success, and by all manner of other petty entrepreneurs who entered an open and relatively cheap trade. The insatiable demands of the bourgeoisie, and especially the aspiring petty-bourgeoisie, for cheap portraits provided the basis of its success. (English photography remained much longer in the hands of comfortable ladies and gentlemen who practised it for experimental purposes and as a hobby.) It was immediately obvious that it destroyed the monopoly of the representational artist. A conservative critic observed as early as 1850 that it must seriously jeopardise the existence of 'entire branches of art, such as engravings, lithography, the genre-picture and portraiture'.[15] How could these compete in the sheer reproduction of nature (except in colour) with a method which translated 'the facts' themselves into an image directly and, as it were, scientifically? Did photography then replace art? Neo-classicists and the (by now) reactionary romantics inclined to believe that it did, and that this was undesirable. J. A. D. Ingres (1780–1867) saw it as an improper invasion of the realm of art by industrial progress. Ch. Baudelaire (1821–67), from his very different point of view, thought the same: 'What man, worthy of the name of artist, what genuine lover of art, has ever confused industry with art?'[16] The correct role of photography for both was that of a subordinate and neutral technique, analogous to printing or shorthand in literature.

Curiously enough the realists, who were more directly threatened by it, were not so uniformly hostile. They accepted progress and science. Was not – as Zola observed – Manet's painting, like his own novels, inspired by the scientific method of Claude Bernard (see chapter 14 above)?[17] And yet, even as they defended photography, they resisted the simple identification of art with exact and naturalistic reproduction which their theory appeared to imply. 'Neither drawing nor colour nor the exactitude of representation', argued the naturalist critic Francis Wey, 'constitute the artist: it is the *mens divina*, the divine inspiration ... What makes the painter is not the hand but the brain: the hand merely obeys.'[18] Photography was useful, because it could help the painter to rise above a mere mechanical copy of objects. Torn between the idealism and the realism of the bourgeois world, the realists also rejected photography but with a certain embarrassment.

The debate was passionate, but it was settled by that most characteristic device of bourgeois society, property-right. The law of France, which protected 'artistic property' specifically against plagiarism or copying under a law of the Great Revolution (1793), left industrial products to the much vaguer protection of Article 1382 of the Civil Code. All photographers argued strongly that the modest customers who acquired their products were buying not merely cheap and recognisable images, but also the spiritual values of art. At the same time those photographers who did not know celebrities well enough to take their highly marketable portraits could not resist the temptation to pirate copies of them, which implied that the original photographs were not legally protected as art. The courts were called upon to decide when Messrs Mayer and Pierson sued a rival firm for pirating its pictures of Count Cavour and Lord Palmerston. In the course of 1862 the case went through all tribunals up to the Court of Cassation, which decided that photography was, after all, an art, since this was the only means of effectively protecting its copyright. And yet – such are the complexities which technology introduced into the world of the arts – could even the law in its majesty speak with a single voice? What if the requirements of property conflicted with those of morality, as happened when, inevitably, the photographers discovered the commercial possibilities of the female body, especially in the form of the readily portable 'visiting-card' format?

That such 'nude photographs in female shape, whether in an upright or prone position, but provocative to the eye in their total nakedness'[19] were obscene, admitted of no doubt: a law had declared them so in the 1850s. But, like their considerably more daring successors, the girlie photographers of the mid-nineteenth century could – at this period vainly – rebut the arguments of morality with those of art: the radical art of realism. Technology, commerce and the *avant garde* formed an underground alliance, mirroring the official alliance of money and spiritual value. The official view could hardly not prevail. Condemning one such photographer, the public prosecutor also condemned 'that school of painting which calls itself realist and suppresses beauty . . . which substitutes for those gracious nymphs of Greece and Italy, the nymphs of a hitherto unknown race, sadly notorious on the banks of the Seine'.[20] His speech was reported in *Le Moniteur de la Photographie* in 1863, the year of Manet's *Déjeuner sur l'Herbe*.

Realism was therefore both ambiguous and contradictory. Its problems could be avoided only at the price of trivialisation by the 'academic' artist who painted what was acceptable and saleable, and let the relations between science and imagination, fact and ideal, progress and eternal values and the rest look after themselves. The serious artist, whether critical of bourgeois society or sufficiently logical to take its claims seriously, was in a more difficult position, and the 1860s initiated a phase of development which showed it to be not only difficult but insoluble. With the programmatic, i.e. naturalistic, 'realism' of Courbet the history of western painting, complex but coherent since the Italian renaissance, comes to an end. The German art-historian Hildebrand characteristically concluded his study of nineteenth-century painting with him in this decade. What came after – or rather what was already appearing simultaneously with the Impressionists – could no longer be so readily attached to the past: it anticipated the future.

The fundamental dilemma of realism was simultaneously one of subject matter and technique, and also of the relations between both. So far as subject matter went, the problem was not simply whether to choose the common subject against the 'noble' and 'distinguished', the topics untouched by the 'respectable' artists against those which formed the staple of the academies, as the frankly political artists of the left – e.g. the revolutionary and Communard Courbet – were inclined to do.[21] So, of course, in a sense were all artists who took naturalistic realism seriously, since they had to paint what the eye could really see, which was things or rather sense-impressions and not ideas, qualities or value judgments. *Olympia* was clearly not an idealised Venus but – in Zola's words – 'doubtless some model whom Edouard Manet has quietly copied just as she was . . . in her youthful slightly tarnished nakedness',[22] and all the more shocking for formally echoing a famous Venus of Titian. But whether or not a political manifesto was intended, realism *could not* paint Venus but only naked

343

girls, just as it could not paint majesty, but only people with crowns; which is why Kaulbach on the proclamation of William I as German Emperor in 1871 is considerably less effective than David's or Ingres's *ikons* of Napoleon I.

But though realism thus seemed politically radical, because it was more at ease with contemporary and popular subject matter,* in fact it limited, perhaps made impossible, the art of political and ideological commitment which had dominated the period before 1848, for political painting cannot do without ideas and judgments. It certainly almost eliminated from serious art the most common form of political painting of the first half of the century, namely the historical picture, in rapid decline from the middle of the century. The naturalistic realism of Courbet, the republican, democrat and socialist, did not provide the basis of politically revolutionary art, not even in Russia, where a naturalistic technique was subordinated to storytelling by the *Peredvizhniki*, pupils of the revolutionary theorist Chernishevski, and therefore became indistinguishable, except in subject matter, from academic painting. It marked the end of one tradition, not the beginning of another.

Revolution in art and the art of revolution thus began to diverge, in spite of the efforts of theorists and propagandists like the '48'er Théophile Thoré (1807–69) and the radical Emile Zola to hold them together. The Impressionists are important not for their popular subject matter – Sunday outings, popular dances, the townscapes and street scenes of cities, the theatres, race-courses and brothels of the bourgeois society's half-world – but for their innovations of method. But these were simply the attempt to pursue further the representation of reality, 'what the eye sees', by means of techniques analogous to and borrowed from photography and the ever-progressing natural sciences. This implied abandoning the conventional codes of past painting. What did the eye 'really' see as light fell on objects? Certainly not the accepted code signals for a blue sky, white clouds or facial features. Yet the attempt to make realism more 'scientific' inevitably removed it from common sense, until in due course the new techniques were themselves to become a conventional code. As

* 'When other artists correct nature by painting Venus, they lie. Manet asked himself why he should lie. Why not tell the truth? He has introduced us to Olympia, a girl of our own times, whom we have met in the streets, pulling a thin shawl of faded wool over her narrow shoulders', and more in this vein (Zola).[23]

it happens, we now read it without difficulty as we admire Manet, A. Renoir (1841–1919), Degas, C. Monet (1840–1926) or C. Pissaro (1830–1903). At the time they were incomprehensible, 'a pot of paint flung in the public's face' as Ruskin was to exclaim about James MacNeill Whistler (1834–1903).

This problem was to prove temporary, but two other aspects of the new art were to be less manageable. First, it brought painting up against the inevitable limits on its 'scientific' character. For instance, logically Impressionism implied not single paintings but a coloured and preferably three-dimensional film, capable of reproducing the constant change of light on objects. Claude Monet's series of pictures of the façade of Rouen cathedral went as far as it was possible to do by means of paint and canvas, which was not very far. But if the search for science in art produced no finite solution, then all it had achieved was the destruction of a conventional and generally accepted code of visual communication, which was not replaced by 'reality' or any other single such code, but by a multiplicity of equally possible conventions. In the last analysis – but the 1860s and 1870s were still a long way from this conclusion – there might be no way of choosing between the subjective visions of any individual; and when that point was to be reached the search for a perfect objectivity of visual statement was transformed into the triumph of perfect subjectivity. The road was a tempting one, for if science was one basic value of bourgeois society, individualism and competition were others. The very strongholds of academic training and standards in the arts were, sometimes unconsciously, substituting the new criterion of 'originality' for the ancient ones of 'perfection' and 'correctness' at this period, opening the way to their own eventual supersession.

Second, if art was analogous to science, then it also shared with it the characteristic of *progress* which (with some qualifications) makes 'new' or 'later' equal 'superior'. This raised no difficulties in science, for its most pedestrian practitioner in 1875 evidently understood physics better than Newton or Faraday. This is not true in the arts: Courbet was better than, say, the Baron Gros, not because he came later or was a realist, but because he had more talent. Moreover, the word progress itself was ambiguous, since it could be and was applied equally to any historically observed change, which was (or was believed to be) improvement, but also to attempts to bring about desirable changes in the future. Progress might or might not be a fact, but 'progressive' was a statement of political intention. The revolutionary in art could easily be confused with the revolutionary in politics, especially by muddled minds like P-J. Proudhon, and both could be equally easily confused with something very different, namely 'modernity' – a word which is first recorded around 1849.*

To be 'contemporary' in this sense also had implications of change and technical innovation, as well as of subject matter. For if, as Baudelaire perceptively observed, the pleasure of representing the present comes not only from its possible beauty, but also from its 'essential character of being the present', then each succeeding 'present' must find its specific form of expression, since no other could express it adequately, if at all. This might or might not be 'progress' in the sense of objective amelioration, but it certainly was 'progress' in as much as the ways of apprehending all the pasts must inevitably give way to those of apprehending our time, which were better just because they were contemporary. The arts must constantly renew themselves. And in doing so, inevitably, each succession of innovators would – at least temporarily – lose the mass of the traditionalists, the philistines, those who lacked what the young Arthur Rimbaud (1854–91) – who formulated so much of the elements of this future for the arts – called 'the vision'. In short, we begin to find ourselves in the now familiar world of the *avant garde* – though the term was not yet current. It is no accident that the retrospective genealogy of the *avant-garde* arts, normally takes us back no further than the Second Empire in France – to Baudelaire and Flaubert in literature, to the Impressionists in painting. Historically it is largely a myth, but the dating is significant. It marks the collapse of the attempt to produce an art intellectually consistent with (though often critical of) bourgeois society – an art embodying the physical realities of the capitalist world, progress and natural science as conceived by positivism.

* 'In summary, Courbet . . . is an expression of the times. His work coincides with the *Positive Philosophy* of Auguste Comte, the *Positive Metaphysics* of Vacherot, my own *Human Right* or *Immanent Justice*; the right to work and the right of the worker, announcing the end of capitalism and the sovereignty of the producers; the phrenology of Gale and Spurzheim; the physiognomy of Lavater' (P-J. Proudhon).[24]

This breakdown affected the marginal strata of the bourgeois world more than its central core: students and young intellectuals, aspiring writers and artists, the general *bohème* of those who refused (however temporarily) to adopt the ways of bourgeois respectability, and mixed readily with those who were unable to, or whose way of life precluded it. The increasingly specialised districts of the great cities where all these met – the Latin Quarter or Montmartre* – became the centres of such *'avant gardes'*, and young provincial rebels like the boy Rimbaud, avidly reading little magazines or heterodox poetry in places like Charleville, gravitated towards them. They provided both the producers and the consumers of what would, a century later, be called an 'underground' or 'counter-culture', and by no means a negligible market, though not yet solvent enough to provide the *avant-garde* producer with a living. The growing desire of the bourgeoisie to clasp the arts to its bosom multiplied the candidates for its embrace – art students, aspiring writers, etc. Henry Murger's *Scenes of Bohemian Life* (1851) produced an enormous vogue for what might be called bourgeois society's urban equivalent for the eighteenth-century *fête champêtre* – playing at not belonging to it, in what was now the secular paradise of the western world and an art-centre with which Italy could no longer compete. There were in the second half of the century perhaps between ten and twenty thousand people in Paris calling themselves 'artists'.[25]

Though some revolutionary movements in this period were almost entirely confined to the Latin Quarter milieu – e.g. the Blanquists – and though the anarchists were to identify the mere membership of the counter-culture with revolution, the *avant garde* as such had no specific politics, or no politics at all. Among the painters the ultra-leftists Pissaro and Monet fled to London in 1870 to avoid taking part in the Franco–Prussian War, but Cézanne, in his provincial refuge, plainly took no real interest in the political views of his closest friend, the radical novelist Zola. Manet and Degas – bourgeois of private means – and Renoir quietly went to war and avoided the Paris

* The turn to realistic – i.e. open-air – painting also created those curious little, often temporary, colonies of artists in the countryside round Paris, the Norman coast or – rather later – Provence, which seem not to occur much before the middle of the nineteenth century.

Commune; Courbet took only too public a part in it. A passion for Japanese prints – one of the most significant cultural by-products of the opening of the world to capitalism – united the Impressionists, the ferociously Republican Clemenceau – mayor of Montmartre under the Commune – and the brothers Goncourt who were hysterically anti-Communard. They were united, like the Romantics before 1848, only by a common dislike of the bourgeoisie and its political regimes – in this instance the Second Empire – the reign of mediocrity, hypocrisy and profit.

Until 1848 these spiritual Latin Quarters of bourgeois society had hope – of a republic and social revolution – and perhaps even, with all their hatred, a certain grudging admiration for the dynamism of the more dynamic robber barons of capitalism, cutting their way through the barriers of traditional aristocratic society. Flaubert's *Sentimental Education* (1869) is the story of that hope in the hearts of the world-storming young men of the 1840s and its double disappointment, by the 1848 revolution itself and by the subsequent era in which the bourgeoisie triumphed at the cost of abandoning even the ideals of its own revolution, 'Liberty, Equality and Fraternity'. In a sense the Romanticism of 1830–48 was the chief victim of this disillusion. Its visionary realism turned into 'scientific' or positivistic realism, retaining – perhaps developing – the element of social criticism* or at least scandal but losing the vision. This in turn transformed itself into 'art for art's sake', or into the preoccupation with the formalities of language, style and technique. 'Everybody has inspiration', the old poet Gautier (1811–72) told a young man. 'Every bourgeois is moved by sunrise and sunset. The poet has craftsmanship.'[26] When a new form of visionary art was to emerge among the generation who had been children or unborn in 1848 – Arthur Rimbaud's main work appeared in 1871–3, Isidore Ducasse, the 'Comte de Lautréamont' (1846–70) published his *Chants de Maldoror* in 1869 – it was to be esoteric, irrationalist and, whatever the intentions of its practitioners, unpolitical.

With the collapse of the dream of 1848 and the victory of the reality of Second Empire France, Bismarckian Germany, Palmerstonian and Gladstonian Britain and the Italy of Victor Emmanuel,

* Mgr Dupanloup observed that any priest with experience of provincial confessionals recognised the accuracy of Flaubert's *Madame Bovary*.

the western bourgeois arts starting with painting and poetry therefore bifurcated into those appealing to the mass public and those appealing to a self-defined minority. They were not quite as outlawed by bourgeois society as the mythological history of the *avant-garde* arts has it, but on the whole it remains undeniable that the painters and poets who came to maturity between 1848 and the end of our period, and whom we still admire, appealed indifferently to the contemporary market and were famous, if at all, for causing scandal: Courbet and the Impressionists, Baudelaire and Rimbaud, the early Pre-Raphaelites, A. C. Swinburne (1837–1909), Dante Gabriel Rossetti (1828–82). But this is clearly not the case with all the arts, not even with all those which depended entirely on bourgeois patronage, with the exception of the spoken drama of the period, about which the less said the better. This is perhaps due to the fact that the difficulties which beset 'realism' in the visual arts were less unmanageable in some others.

VI

They hardly affected music at all, since no representational realism is seriously possible in that art, and the very attempt to introduce it must be either metaphorical or dependent on words or drama. Unless fused into the Wagnerian *Gesamtkunstwerk* (the all-embracing art of his operas) or the modest song, realism in music meant the representation of identifiable emotions: including – as in Wagner's *Tristan* (1865) – the recognisable emotions of sex. More commonly, as in the flourishing national schools of composers – Smetana and Dvořák in Bohemia, Tchaikovsky, N. Rimsky Korsakov (1844–1908), Mussorgsky, etc., in Russia, E. Grieg (1843–1907) in Norway and, of course, the Germans (but not the Austrians) – they were the emotions of nationalism for which convenient symbols existed, in the form of motifs from folk music, etc. But, as has already been suggested, serious music flourished not so much because it suggested the real world, but because it suggested the things of the spirit and thus provided among other things a surrogate for religion, as it had always provided a powerful adjunct to it. If it wanted to be performed at all, it had to appeal to patrons or the market. To that extent it could oppose the bourgeois world only from within, an easy task, since the bourgeois himself was unlikely to recognise when he was being criticised. He might well feel that his own aspirations and the glory of his culture were being expressed. So music flourished, in a more or less traditional romantic idiom. Its most militant *avant gardist*, Richard Wagner, was also its most celebrated public figure, since he actually succeeded (admittedly thanks to the patronage of the mad king Ludwig of Bavaria) in convincing the most financially solvent cultural authorities and members of the bourgeois public that they themselves belonged to that spiritual élite, high above the philistine masses, which alone deserved the art of the future.

Prose literature, and especially that characteristic art form of the bourgeois era the novel, flourished for exactly the opposite reason. Words could, unlike notes, represent 'real life' as well as ideas, and unlike the visual arts their technique made no claim actually to imitate it. 'Realism' in the novel therefore held no immediate and insoluble contradictions such as those which photography introduced into painting. Some novels might aim at a more rigorous documentary truth than others, some might wish to extend their subject matter to fields regarded as improper or not fit for respectable attention (the French Naturalists favoured both), but who could deny that even the least literally-minded, the most subjective, wrote stories about the actual world, and most often actual contemporary society? There is no novelist of this period who cannot be transformed into dramatised television serials. Hence the popularity and flexibility of the novel as a *genre*, and its amazing achievements. With comparatively rare exceptions – Wagner in music, some French painters and perhaps some poetry – the supreme achievements in the arts of our period were novels: Russian, English, French, perhaps even (if we include Melville's *Moby Dick*) American. And (with the exception of Melville) the greatest novels of the greatest novelists won fairly immediate recognition, if not always understanding.

The great potential of the novel lay in its scope: the most vast and ambitious themes lay within the novelist's grasp: *War and Peace* (1869) tempted Tolstoi, *Crime and Punishment* (1866) Dostoievsky, *Fathers and Sons* (1862) Turgenev. The novel attempted to seize the reality of an entire society, though curiously enough the deliberate attempts to do so in our period, through connected series of such narratives on the model of Scott and Balzac, did not attract the

350

greatest talents: even Zola only began his retrospective giant portrait of the Second Empire (the Rougon–Macquart series) in 1871, Pérez Galdós (1843–1920) his *Episodios Nacionales* in 1873, Gustav Freytag (1816–95) – to descend rather lower – his *Die Ahnen* (*The Ancestors*) in 1872. The success of these titanic efforts varied outside Russia, where they were almost uniformly successful; though no era which contains the mature Dickens, Flaubert, George Eliot, Thackeray and Gottfried Keller (1819–90) need fear much competition. But what is characteristic of the novel and made it so much the typical art form of our period was that its most ambitious efforts were achieved not through myth and technique (as in Wagner's *Ring*) but through the pedestrian description of everyday reality. It did not so much storm the heavens of creation as plod inexorably into them. For this reason it also lent itself, with minimal loss, to translation. At least one major novelist in our period became a genuinely international figure: Charles Dickens.

However, it would be unfair to confine the discussion of the arts in the age of bourgeois triumph to masters and masterpieces, especially those confined to a minority public. It was, as we have seen, a period of art for the masses by means of the technology of reproduction which made the unlimited multiplication of still images possible, the marriage between technology and communications which produced the mass newspaper and periodical – especially the illustrated magazine – and the mass education which made all these accessible to a new public. The contemporary works of art which were really widely known during this period – that is, known beyond the 'cultured' minority – were, with very rare exceptions, of which Charles Dickens is probably the outstanding,* not those we admire most today. The literature which sold most widely was the popular newspaper, which reached unprecedented circulations of a quarter or even half a million in Britain and the United States. The secular pictures which were to be found on the walls of pioneer cabins in the American West or artisan cottages in Europe were prints of Landseer's *Monarch of the Glen* (or their national equivalents), or portraits of Lincoln, Garibaldi or Gladstone. The compositions from 'high

---

* But Dickens wrote as a journalist – his novels were published in instalments – and behaved as a performer, known to many thousands thanks to his stage readings of dramatic scenes from his works.

culture' which entered mass consciousness were Verdi tunes performed by the ubiquitous Italian organ-grinders or those bits of Wagner which could be adapted as music for weddings: but not the operas themselves.

But this in itself implied a cultural revolution. With the triumph of city and industry an increasingly sharp division grew up between the 'modern' sectors of the masses, i.e. the urbanised, the literate, and those who accepted the content of the hegemonic culture – that of the bourgeois society – and the increasingly undermined 'traditional' ones. Increasingly sharp, because the heritage of the rural past became increasingly irrelevant to the pattern of urban working-class life: in the 1860s and 1870s the industrial workers in Bohemia stopped expressing themselves through folksong and took to music-hall song, doggerel ballads about a life which had little left in common with their fathers'. This was the void which the ancestors of the modern popular music and entertainment business began to fill for those of modest cultural ambitions, and which collective self-help and organisation – from the end of our period increasingly through political movements – filled for the more active, conscious and ambitious. In Britain the era when music-halls multiplied in the cities was also the era when choral societies and working-class brass bands, with a repertoire of popular 'classics' from high culture, multiplied in the industrial communities. But it is characteristic that during these decades the flow of culture ran in one direction – from the middle class downwards, at least in Europe. Even in what was to become the most characteristic form of proletarian culture, mass spectator sports, the pattern in our period was set – as in Association Football – by the young men of the middle class who founded its clubs and organised its competitions. Not until the late 1870s and early 1880s were these captured and held by the working class.*

But even the most traditional rural patterns of culture were undermined, not so much by migration as by education. For once primary education becomes available to the masses, traditional culture inevitably ceases to be basically oral and face-to-face, and splits into a superior or dominant culture of the literate and an inferior or reces-

* In Britain, the 'sporting country' *par excellence*, the period actually saw a decline of the pattern of purely professional plebeian sport which had begun to develop earlier, e.g. in cricket. Several activities which were then quite prominent, virtually disappeared, e.g. professional foot-races, walking and rowing contests.

sive one of the non-literate. Education and national bureaucracy turned even the village into a schizophrenic assembly of people, split between the pet names and nicknames by which they were known to their neighbours and kin ('Crippled Paquito') and the official names of school and state by which they were known to authority ('Francisco Gonzalez Lopez'). The new generations became in effect bilingual. The increasingly numerous attempts to save the old language for literacy in the form of a 'dialect literature' (as in Ludwig Anzengruber's [1839–89] peasant dramas, William Barnes's [1800–86] poems in the Dorset dialect, Fritz Reuter's [1810–74] *plattdeutsch* autobiographies or – a little later – the attempt to revive a provençal literature in the *Félibrige* movement [1854]) appealed either to middle-class romantic nostalgia, populism or 'naturalism'.*

By our standards, this decline was as yet modest. But it was significant because during these years it was not yet visibly offset by the development of what might be called a new proletarian or urban counter-culture. (In the countryside there was never to be such a phenomenon.) The hegemony of the official culture, inevitably identified with the triumphant middle class, was asserted over the subaltern masses. In this period there was little to mitigate that subalternity.

* The major exception was the populist-democratic counter-attack on high (i.e. in this instance 'foreign') culture by the humorist-journalist writers of the Western and Southern United States, which systematically used the actual spoken language as its base; its greatest monument is Mark Twain's *Huckleberry Finn* (1884).

Chapter Sixteen

Conclusion

Do what you like, destiny has the last word in human affairs. There's real tyranny for you. According to the principles of Progress, destiny should have been abolished long ago.

Johann Nestroy, Viennese comic playwright, 1850[1]

The era of liberal triumph began with a defeated revolution and ended in a prolonged depression. The first forms a more convenient signpost for marking the beginning or end of a historical period than the second, but history does not consult the convenience of historians, though some of them are not always aware of it. The requirements of drama might suggest concluding this book with a suitably spectacular event – the proclamation of German Unity and the Paris Commune in 1871 perhaps, or even the great stock-exchange crash of 1873 – but the demands of drama and reality are, as so often, not the same. The path ends not with the view of a peak or a cataract, but of the less easily identifiable landscape of a watershed: some time between 1871 and 1879. If we have to put a date to it, let us choose one which symbolises 'the middle 1870s' without being associated with any event sufficiently outstanding to obtrude itself unnecessarily, say 1875.

The new era which follows the age of liberal triumph was to be very different. Economically it was to move away rapidly from unrestrained competitive private enterprise, government abstention from interference and what the Germans called *Manchesterismus* (the free trade orthodoxy of Victorian Britain), to large industrial corporations (cartels, trusts, monopolies), to very considerable government interference, to very different orthodoxies of policy, though not necessarily of economic theory. The age of individualism ended in 1870, complained the British lawyer A. V. Dicey, the age of 'collectivism' began; and though most of what he gloomily noted as the advances of 'collectivism' strike us as insignificant, he was in a sense right.

The capitalist economy changed in four significant ways. In the first place, we now enter a new technological era, no longer determined by the inventions and methods of the first Industrial Revolution: an era of new sources of power (electricity and oil, turbines and the internal combustion engine), of new machinery based on new materials (steel, alloys, non-ferrous metals), of new science-based industries, such as the expanding organic chemical industry. In the second place, we now increasingly enter the economy of the domestic consumer market, pioneered in the United States, fostered not only (and as yet, in Europe, modestly) by rising mass incomes, but above all by the sheer demographic growth of the developed countries. From 1870 to 1910 the population of Europe rose from 290 to 435 million, that of the United States from 38·5 to 92 million. In other words, we enter the period of mass production, including that of some consumer durables.

In the third place – and in some ways this was the most decisive development – a paradoxical reversal now took place. The era of liberal triumph had been that of a *de facto* British industrial monopoly internationally, within which (with some notable exceptions) profits were assured with little difficulty by the competition of small- and medium-sized enterprises. The post-liberal era was one of international competition between rival national industrial economies – the British, the German, the North American; a competition sharpened by the difficulties which firms within each of these economies now discovered, during the period of depression, in making adequate profits. Competition thus led towards economic concentration, market control and manipulation. To quote an excellent historian:

Economic growth was now also economic struggle – struggle that served to separate the strong from the weak, to discourage some and to toughen others, to favour the new, hungry nations at the expense of the old. Optimism about a future of indefinite progress gave way to uncertainty and a sense of agony, in the classical meaning of the word. All of which strengthened and was in turn strengthened by sharpening political rivalries, the two forms of competition merging in that final surge of land hunger and that chase for 'spheres of influence' that have been called the New Imperialism.[2]

The world entered the period of imperialism, in the broad sense of the word (which includes the changes in the structure of economic organisation, e.g. 'monopoly-capitalism') but also in the narrower sense of the word: a new integration of the 'underdeveloped' countries as dependencies into a world economy dominated by the 'developed' countries. Apart from the impulse of rivalry (which led powers to divide the globe into formal or informal reservations for their own businessmen), of markets and of capital exports, this was also due to the increased significance of raw materials not available in most of the developed countries themselves, for climatic and geological reasons. The new technological industries required such materials: oil, rubber, non-ferrous metals. By the end of the century Malaya was a known producer of tin, Russia, India and Chile in manganese, New Caledonia of nickel. The new consumer economy required rapidly growing quantities not only of materials also produced in the developed countries (e.g. grain and meat) but of those which could not be (e.g. tropical or sub-tropical beverages and fruit, or overseas vegetable oil for soap). The 'banana republic' became as much part of the capitalist world economy as the tin and rubber or the cocoa colony.

On a global scale this dichotomy between developed and (theoretically complementary) underdeveloped areas, though not in itself new, began to take a recognisably modern shape. The development of the new pattern of development/dependence was to continue with only brief interruptions until the slump of the 1930s, and forms the fourth major change in the world economy.

Politically the end of the liberal era meant literally what the words imply. In Britain the Whig/Liberals (in the broad sense of those who were not Tory/Conservatives) had been in office, with two brief exceptions, throughout the period from 1848 to 1874. In the last quarter of the century they were to be in office for no more than eight years. In Germany and Austria the Liberals ceased, in the 1870s, to be the main parliamentary base of governments, in so far as governments required such a base. They were undermined not only by the defeat of their ideology of free trade and cheap (i.e. relatively inactive) government, but by the democratisation of electoral politics (see chapter 6 above), which destroyed the illusion that their policy represented the masses. On the one hand, the depression added to the force of protectionist pressure by some industries and the national agrarian interests. The trend towards freer trade was reversed in Russia and Austria in 1874–5, in Spain in 1877, in Germany in 1879, and practically everywhere else except Britain – and even here free trade was under pressure from the 1880s. On the other, the demand from below for protection against the 'capitalists' by the 'little men', for social security, public measures against unemployment and a wage-minimum from the workers, became vocal and politically effective. The 'better classes', whether the ancient hierarchical nobility or the new bourgeoisie, could no longer speak for the 'lower orders' or, what is more to the point, rely on their uncompensated support.

A new, increasingly powerful and intrusive state and within it a new pattern of politics therefore developed, foreseen with gloom by anti-democratic thinkers. 'The modern version of the Rights of Man', thought the historian Jacob Burckhardt in 1870, 'includes the right to work and subsistence. For men are no longer willing to leave the most vital matters to society, because they want the impossible and imagine that it can only be secured under compulsion of the state.'[3] What troubled them was not only the allegedly utopian demand of the poor for the right to live decently, but the capacity of the poor to impose it. 'The masses want their peace and their pay. If they get it from a republic or a monarchy, they will cling to either. If not, without much ado they will support the first constitution to promise them what they want.'[4] And the state, no longer controlled by the moral autonomy and legitimacy which tradition gave it or the belief that economic laws could not be broken, would become increasingly an all-powerful Leviathan in practice, though a mere tool for achieving the aims of the masses in theory.

By modern standards the increase in the role and functions of the state remained modest enough, though its expenditure (i.e. its activities) had increased almost everywhere in our period *per capita*, largely as a result of the sharp rise in the public debt (except in those strongholds of liberalism, peace and unsubsidised private enterprise, Britain, Holland, Belgium and Denmark).* In any case social expenditure, except perhaps on education, remained fairly negligible. On the other hand, in politics three new tendencies emerged out of the confused tensions of the new era of economic depression, which

* This increase in expenditure was much more marked in the developing countries overseas, which were in the process of building the infrastructure of their economies – the United States, Canada, Australia and Argentina – by means of capital imports.

357

almost everywhere became one of social agitation and discontent.

The first, and most apparently novel, was the emergence of independent working-class parties and movements, generally with a socialist (i.e. increasingly a Marxist) orientation, of which the German Social Democratic Party was both the pioneer and the most impressive example. Though the governments and middle classes of the time regarded them as the most dangerous, in fact they shared the values and assumptions of the rationalist enlightenment on which liberalism rested. The second tendency did not share this heritage, and was indeed flatly opposed to it. Demagogic anti-liberal and anti-socialist parties emerged in the 1880s and 1890s, either from under the shadow of their formerly liberal affiliation – like the anti-semitic and pan-German nationalists who became the ancestors of Hitlerism – or under the wing of the hitherto politically inactive churches, like the 'Christian-Social' movement in Austria.* The third tendency was the emancipation of mass nationalist parties and movements from their former ideological identification with liberal-radicalism. Some movements for national autonomy or independence tended to shift, at least theoretically, towards socialism, especially when the working class played a significant role in their country; but it was a national rather than an international socialism (as among the so-called Czech People's Socialists or the Polish Socialist Party) and the national element tended to prevail over the socialist. Others moved towards an ideology based on blood, soil, language, what was conceived to be the ethnic tradition and little else.

This did not disrupt the basic political pattern of the developed states which had emerged in the 1860s: a more or less gradual and reluctant approach to a democratic constitutionalism. Nevertheless the emergence of non-liberal mass politics, however theoretically acceptable, frightened governments. Before they learned to operate the new system, they were – notably during the 'Great Depression' – sometimes inclined to relapse into panic or coercion. The Third Republic did not re-admit the survivors of the massacre among the Communards into politics until the early 1880s. Bismarck, who knew

* For various reasons, among which the self-sealing ultrareactionary position of the Vatican under Pius ix (1846–78) was perhaps the most important, the Catholic Church failed to use its enormous potential in mass politics effectively, except in a few western countries in which it was a minority and obliged to organise as a pressure group – as in the 'Centre Party' in Germany from the 1870s.

how to manage bourgeois liberals but neither a mass socialist party nor a mass Catholic party, made the Social Democrats illegal in 1879. Gladstone lapsed into coercion in Ireland. However this proved to be a temporary phase, rather than a permanent tendency. The framework of bourgeois politics (where it existed) was not stretched to breaking-point until well into the twentieth century.

Indeed, though our period subsides into the troubled time of the 'Great Depression', it would be misleading to paint too highly coloured a picture of it. Unlike the slump of the 1930s, the economic difficulties themselves were so complex and qualified that historians have even doubted whether the term 'depression' is justifiable as a description of the twenty years after this volume ends. They are wrong, but their doubts are enough to warn us against excessively dramatic treatment. Neither economically nor politically did the structure of the mid-nineteenth-century capitalist world collapse. It entered a new phase but, even in the form of a slowly modified economic and political liberalism, it had plenty of scope left. It was different in the dominated, the underdeveloped, the backward and poor countries, or those situated, like Russia, both in the world of the victors and the victims. There the 'Great Depression' opened an era of imminent revolution. But for a generation or two after 1875 the world of the triumphant bourgeoisie appeared to remain firm enough. Perhaps it was a little less self-confident than before, and its assertions of self-confidence therefore a little shriller, perhaps a little more worried about its future. Perhaps it became rather more puzzled by the breakdown of its old intellectual certainties, which (especially after the 1880s) thinkers, artists and scientists underlined with their ventures into new and troubling territories of the mind. But surely 'progress' still continued, inevitably, and in the form of bourgeois, capitalist and in a general sense liberal societies. The 'Great Depression' was only an interlude. Was there not economic growth, technical and scientific advance, improvement and peace? Would not the twentieth century be a more glorious, more successful version of the nineteenth?

We now know that it would not be.

TABLE 1

EUROPE AND THE USA: STATES AND RESOURCES

	1847–50		1876–80			
	popu-lation (*millions*)	steam power (000 HP)	number of towns, 50,000 and over	popu-lation (*millions*)	steam power (000 HP)	post units per capita
United Kingdom	27	1,290	32	32·7	7,600	48·2
France	34·1	370	14	36·9†	3,070	29·5
Germany	—	—	17	42·7	5,120	28·7
Prussia	11·7	92				
Bavaria	4·8					
Saxony	1·8					
Hanover	1·8					
Würtemberg	1·7					
Baden	1·3					
32 other states between 0·02 and 0·9 (Austria)	*					
Russia	66·0	70	8	85·7	1,740	2·6
Austria with Hungary	37·0	100	13	37·1†	1,560	12·0
Italy	—	—		27·8	500	13·4
2 Sicilies	8·0		4			
Sardinia	4·0		2			
Papal States	2·9		1			
Tuscany	1·5		2			
3 other states between 0·1 and 0·5 (Austria)						

* Parts of the Austrian Empire counted in 'Germanic Confederation' until 1866.

TABLE 1 *(cont.)*

	1847–50			1876–80		
	popu- lation (*millions*)	steam power (000 HP)	number of towns, 50,000 and over	popu- lation (*millions*)	steam power (000 HP)	post units *per* *capita*
Spain	12·3	20	8	16·6	470	7·1
Portugal	3·7	0	2	4·1	60	5·4
Sweden (inc. Norway)	3·5	0	1	4·3	310	12·5
Denmark	1·4	0	1	1·9†	90	26·6
Netherlands	3·0	10	5	3·9	130	29·5
Belgium	4·3	70	5	5·3	610	35·5
Switzerland	2·4	0	0	2·8	230	46·1
Ottoman Empire	*c.* 30‡	0	7	28 (1877)†	—	?
Greece	*c.* 1·0	0	—	1·9	0	2·3
Serbia	*c.* 0·5	0	—	1·4	0	0·7
Rumania	—	—	—	5·0	0	1·5
United States	23·2	1,680	7	50·2†	9,110	47·7

† Significant loss or gain of territory/population, 1847–76.
‡ European territory only.

TABLE 2

I DENSITY OF RAILWAY NETWORK, 1880*

km^2 (per 10,000)	country
over 1,000	Belgium
over 750	United Kingdom
over 500	Switzerland, Germany, Netherlands
250–499	France, Denmark, Austria–Hungary, Italy
100–249	Sweden, Spain, Portugal, Rumania, United States, Cuba
50–99	Turkey, Chile, New Zealand, Trinidad, Victoria, Java
10–49	Norway, Finland, Russia, Canada, Uruguay, Argentina, Peru, Costa Rica, Jamaica, India, Ceylon, Tasmania, N.S. Wales, S. Australia, Cape Colony, Algeria, Egypt, Tunis

II RAILWAYS AND STEAMSHIPS, 1830–76*

	km of railways	tons of steamships
1831	332	32,000
1841	8,591	105,121
1846	17,424	139,973
1851	38,022	263,679
1856	68,148	575,928
1861	106,886	803,003
1866	145,114	1,423,232
1871	235,375	1,939,089
1876	309,641	3,293,072

* F. X. von Neumann Spallart, *Übersichten der Weltwirtschaft* (Stuttgart 1880), pp. 335 ff.

III SEA TRAFFIC OF THE WORLD. GEOGRAPHICAL DISTRIBUTION OF TONNAGE, 1879*

area	total tonnage (000)	area	total tonnage (000)
Europe		*Rest of the World*	
Arctic Sea	61	North America	3,783
North Sea	5,536	South America	138
Baltic	1,275	Asia	700
Atlantic, inc. Irish Sea and Channel	4,553	Australia and Pacific	359
Western Mediterranean	1,356		
E. Mediterranean, inc. Adriatic	604		
Black Sea	188		

*A. N. Kiaer, *Statistique Internationale de la Navigation Maritime* (Christiania 1880, 1881).

TABLE 3

WORLD GOLD AND SILVER PRODUCTION, 1830–75
(000 KILOGRAMMES)*

	gold	silver
1831–40	20·3	596·4
1841–50	54·8	780·4
1851–55	197·5	886·1
1851–60	206·1	905·0
1861–65	198·2	1,101·1
1866–70	191·9	1,339·1
1871–75	170·7	1,969·4

* Neumann-Spallart, *op. cit.* (1880), p. 250.

TABLE 4
WORLD AGRICULTURE, 1840–87*

	value of output (£ mill)		number employed (000)	
	1840	1887	1840	1887
Britain	218	251	3,400	2,460
France	269	460	6,950	6,450
Germany	170	424	6,400	8,120
Russia	248	563	15,000	22,700
Austria	205	331	7,500	10,680
Italy	114	204	3,600	5,390
Spain	102	173	2,000	2,720
Portugal	18	31	700	870
Sweden	16	49	550	850
Norway	8	17	250	380
Denmark	16	35	280	420
Holland	20	39	600	840
Belgium	30	55	900	980
Switzerland	12	19	300	440
Turkey, etc.	98	194	2,000	2,900
Europe	1,544	2,845	50,430	66,320
United States	184	776	2,550	9,000
Canada	12	56	300	800
Australia	6	62	100	630
Argentina	5	42	200	600
Uruguay	1	10	50	100

* M. Mulhall, *A Dictionary of Statistics* (London 1892), p. 11.

The World in 1847

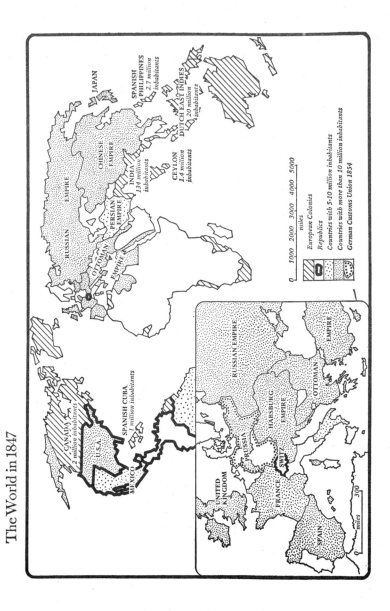

CANADA
2 million inhabitants

U.S.A.

SPANISH CUBA
1 million inhabitants

MEXICO

JAPAN

SPANISH
PHILIPPINES
2.7 million
inhabitants

DUTCH EAST INDIES
20 million
inhabitants

RUSSIAN
EMPIRE

CHINESE
EMPIRE

PERSIAN
EMPIRE

OTTOMAN
EMPIRE

INDIA
134 million
inhabitants

CEYLON
1.4 million
inhabitants

miles
0   1000 2000 3000 4000 5000

European Colonies
Republics
Countries with 5-10 million inhabitants
Countries with more than 10 million inhabitants
German Customs Union 1854

RUSSIAN EMPIRE

HABSBURG
EMPIRE

OTTOMAN
EMPIRE

PRUSSIA

UNITED
KINGDOM

FRANCE

SWITZ.

SPAIN

miles
0   300

366

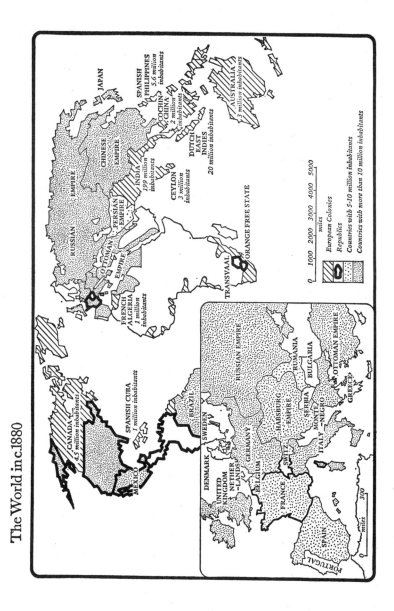

The World in c.1880

JAPAN

SPANISH
PHILIPPINES
5.6 million
inhabitants

CHINESE
EMPIRE

COCHIN
CHINA
2 million
inhabitants

AUSTRALIA
3 million inhabitants

RUSSIAN
EMPIRE

INDIA
199 million
inhabitants

DUTCH
EAST
INDIES
20 million inhabitants

PERSIAN
EMPIRE

OTTOMAN
EMPIRE

CEYLON
3 million
inhabitants

FRENCH
ALGERIA
1 million
inhabitants

ORANGE FREE STATE

TRANSVAAL

miles

0   1000 2000 3000 4000 5000

European Colonies

Republics

Countries with 5-10 million inhabitants

Countries with more than 10 million inhabitants

CANADA
4.5 million inhabitants

SPANISH CUBA
1 million inhabitants

MEXICO

BRAZIL

RUSSIAN EMPIRE

RUMANIA

BULGARIA

SWEDEN

HABSBURG
EMPIRE

SERBIA

MONTE-
NEGRO

OTTOMAN EMPIRE

GREECE

DENMARK

UNITED
KINGDOM

NETHER-
LANDS

GERMANY

BELGIUM

SWITZ.

FRANCE

ITALY

SPAIN

PORTUGAL

miles

0   300

367

1847 Slavery and Serfdom in the Western World

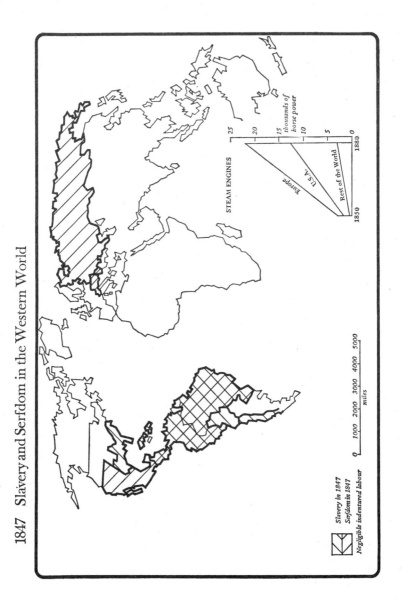

STEAM ENGINES

25
20
15 thousands of
10 horse power
5
0
1880   1850

Europe
U.S.A.
Rest of the World

0 1000 2000 3000 4000 5000
miles

Slavery in 1847
Serfdom in 1847
Negligible indentured labour

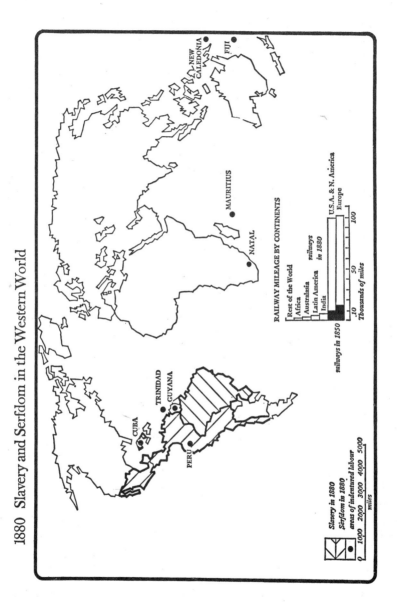

1880 Slavery and Serfdom in the Western World

RAILWAY MILEAGE BY CONTINENTS

Rest of the World
Africa
Australasia
Latin America
India

U.S.A. & N. America
Europe

railways in 1880
railways in 1850

10   50   100
Thousands of miles

NEW CALEDONIA
FIJI
MAURITIUS
NATAL
CUBA
TRINIDAD
GUYANA
PERU

Slavery in 1880
Serfdom in 1880
areas of indentured labour

0   1000 2000 3000 4000 5000
miles

A World on the Move

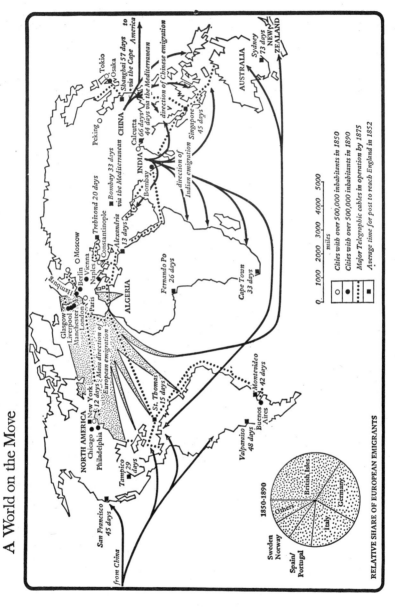

NORTH AMERICA
San Francisco 45 days
Chicago
Philadelphia
New York 12 days: Main direction of
European emigration
Tampico 29 days
St. Thomas 15 days
Valparaiso 48 days
Montevideo 42 days
Buenos Aires
from China

Glasgow
Liverpool
Manchester
London
Paris
Berlin
Vienna
Moscow
Naples
Constantinople
Trebizond 20 days
Alexandria 13 days
ALGERIA
Fernando Po 26 days
Cape Town 33 days

Peking
CHINA
Tokio
Osaka
Shanghai 57 days to via the Cape America
Bombay 33 days via the Mediterranean
Bombay
INDIA
Calcutta 66 days 44 days via the Mediterranean
direction of Chinese emigration
direction of Indian emigration
Singapore 45 days

AUSTRALIA
Sydney 73 days
NEW ZEALAND

miles
0   1000   2000   3000   4000   5000

○ Cities with over 500,000 inhabitants in 1850
● Cities with over 500,000 inhabitants in 1890
⋯ Major Telegraphic cables in operation by 1875
■ Average time for post to reach England in 1852

1850-1890
British Isles
Germany
Italy
Others
Sweden Norway
Spain/ Portugal

RELATIVE SHARE OF EUROPEAN EMIGRANTS

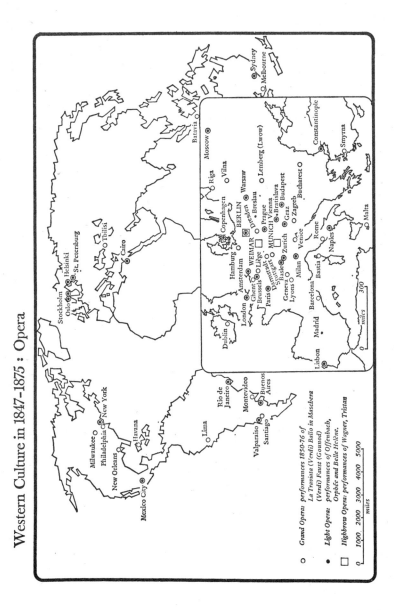

Western Culture in 1847–1875 : Opera

Grand Opera: performances 1850–76 of
    La Traviata (Verdi) Ballo in Maschera
    (Verdi) Faust (Gounod)

Light Opera: performances of Offenbach,
    Orphée and Belle Hélène.

Highbrow Opera: performances of Wagner, Tristan

Notes

INTRODUCTION

1 See J. Dubois, *Le Vocabulaire politique et social en France de 1869 à 1872* (Paris 1963).
2 D. A. Wells, *Recent Economic Changes* (New York 1889), p. 1.

CHAPTER 1: 'THE SPRINGTIME OF PEOPLES'

1 P. Goldammer (ed.), *1848, Augenzeugen der Revolution* (East Berlin 1973), p. 58.
2 Goldammer, *op. cit.*, p. 666.
3 K. Repgen, *Märzbewegung und Maiwahlen des Revolutionsjahres 1848 im Rheinland* (Bonn 1955), p. 118.
4 *Rinascità, Il 1848, Raccolta di Saggi e Testimonianze* (Rome 1948).
5 R. Hoppe and J. Kuczynski, 'Eine . . . Analyse der Märzgefallenen 1848 in Berlin', *Jahrbuch für Wirtschaftgeschichte* (1964), IV, pp. 200–276; D. Cantimori in F. Fejtö, ed., *1848 – Opening of an Era* (1948).
6 Roger Ikor, *Insurrection ouvrière de juin 1848* (Paris 1936).
7 K. Marx and F. Engels, Address to the Communist League (March 1850) (*Werke* VII, p. 247).
8 Paul Gerbod, *La Condition universitaire en France au 19e siècle* (Paris 1965).
9 Karl Marx, *Class Struggles in France 1848–1850* (*Werke*, VII, pp. 30–31).
10 Franz Grillparzer, *Werke* (Munich 1960), I, p. 137.
11 Marx, *Class Struggles in France* (*Werke*, VII, p. 44).

CHAPTER 2: THE GREAT BOOM

1 Cited in *Ideas and Beliefs of the Victorians* (London 1949), p. 51.
2 I owe this reference to Prof. Sanford Elwitt.
3 'Philoponos', *The Great Exhibition of 1851; or the Wealth of the World in its Workshops* (London 1850), p. 120.

4   T. Ellison, *The Cotton Trade of Great Britain* (London 1886), pp. 63 and 66.

5   Horst Thieme, 'Statistische Materialien zur Konzessionierung der Aktiengesellschaften in Preussen bis 1867', *Jahrbuch für Wirtschafts-geschichte* (1960), II, p. 285.

6   J. Bouvier, F. Furet and M. Gilet, *Le Mouvement du profit en France au 19e siècle* (Hague 1955), p. 444.

7   Engels to Marx (5 November 1857) (*Werke*, XXIX, p. 211).

8   Marx to Danielson (10 April 1879) (*Werke*, XXXIV, pp. 370–75).

9   Calculated from Ellison, *op. cit.*, Table II, using the multiplier on p. 111.

10   F. S. Turner, *British Opium Policy and its Results to India and China* (London 1876), p. 305.

11   B. R. Mitchell and P. Deane, *Abstract of Historical Statistics* (Cambridge 1962), pp. 146–7.

12   C. M. Cipolla, *Literacy and Development in the West* (Harmondsworth 1969), Table I, Appendix II, III.

13   F. Zunkel, 'Industriebürgertum in Westdeutschland' in H. U. Wehler (ed.), *Moderne Deutsche Sozialgeschichte* (Cologne–Berlin 1966), p. 323.

14   L. Simonin, *Mines and Miners or Underground Life* (London 1868), p. 290.

15   Daniel Spitzer, *Gesammelte Schriften* (Munich and Leipzig 1912), II, p. 60.

16   J. Kuczynski, *Geschichte der Lage der Arbeiter unter dem Kapitalismus* (East Berlin 1961), XII, p. 29.

CHAPTER 3: THE WORLD UNIFIED

1   K. Marx and F. Engels, *Manifesto of the Communist Party* (London 1848).

2   U.S. Grant, Inaugural Message to Congress (1873).

3   I. Goncharov, *Oblomov* (1859).

4   J. Laffey, 'Racines de l'imperialisme français en Extrême-Orient', *Revue d'Histoire Modern et Contemporaine* XVI (April–June 1969), p. 285.

5   Many of these data are taken from W. S. Lindsay, *History of Merchant Shipping*, 4 vols (London 1876).

6   M. Mulhall, *A Dictionary of Statistics* (London 1892), p. 495.

7 F. X. von Neumann-Spallart, *Ubersichten der Weltwirtschaft* (Stutt-gart 1880), p. 336; 'Eisenbahnstatistik', *Handwörterbuch der Staats-wissenschaften* (2nd ed.) (Jena 1900).

8 L. de Rosa, *Iniziativa e capitale straneiro nell' Industria metalmeccanica del Mezzogiorno, 1840–1904* (Naples 1968), p. 67.

9 Sir James Anderson, *Statistics of Telegraphy* (London 1872).

10 Engels to Marx (24 August 1852) (*Werke*, XXVIII, p. 118).

11 *Bankers Magazine*, V (Boston 1850–51), p. 11.

12 *Bankers Magazine*, IX (London 1849), p. 545.

13 *Bankers Magazine*, V (Boston 1850–51), p. 11.

14 Neumann–Spallart, *op. cit.*, p. 7.

CHAPTER 4: CONFLICTS AND WAR

1 Prince Napoléon Louis Bonaparte, *Fragments Historiques, 1688 et 1830* (Paris 1841), p. 125.

2 Jules Verne, *From the Earth to the Moon* (1865).

CHAPTER 5: BUILDING NATIONS

1 Ernest Renan, 'What is a Nation' in A. Zimmern (ed.), *Modern Political Doctrines* (Oxford 1939), pp. 191–2.

2 Johann Nestroy, *Häuptling Abendwind* (1862).

3 Shatov in F. Dostoievsky, *The Possessed* (1871–2).

4 Gustave Flaubert, *Dictionnaire des idées reçues* (*c.* 1852).

5 Walter Bagehot, *Physics and Politics* (London 1873), pp. 20–21.

6 Cited in D. Mack Smith, *Il Risorgimento Italiano* (Bari 1968), p. 422.

7 Tullio de Mauro, *Storia linguistica dell'Italia unita* (Bari 1963).

8 J. Kořalka, 'Social problems in the Czech and Slovak national move-ments' in: Commission Internationale d'Histoire des Mouvements Sociaux et des Structures Sociales, *Mouvements Nationaux d'Indépen-dance et Classes Populaires* (Paris 1971), I, p. 62.

9 J. Conrad, 'Die Frequenzverhältnisse der Universitäten der hauptsäch-lichsten Kulturländer' *Jahrbücher für Nationalökonomie und Statistik* (1891) 3rd ser. I, pp. 376 ff.

10 I am obliged to Dr R. Anderson for these data.

CHAPTER 6: THE FORCES OF DEMOCRACY

1 H. A. Targé, *Les Déficits* (Paris 1868), p. 25.
2 Sir T. Erskine May, *Democracy in Europe* (London 1877), I, p. lxxi.
3 Karl Marx, *The Eighteenth Brumaire of Louis Bonaparte* (*Werke*, VIII, pp. 198–9).
4 G. Procacci, *Le elezioni del 1874 e l'opposizione meridionale* (Milan 1956) p. 60; W. Gagel, *Die Wahlrechtsfrage in der Geschichte der deutschen, liberalen Parteien 1848–1918* (Düsseldorf 1958), p. 28.
5 J. Ward, *Workmen and Wages at Home and Abroad* (London 1868), p. 284.
6 J. Deutsch, *Geschichte der österreichischen Gewerkschaftsbewegung* (Vienna 1908), pp. 73–4; Herbert Steiner, 'Die internationale Arbeiterassoziation und die österr. Arbeiterbewegung), *Weg und Ziel* (Vienna, Sondernummer, Jänner 1965), pp. 89–90.

CHAPTER 7: LOSERS

1 Erskine May, *op. cit.*, I, p. 29.
2 J. W. Kaye, *A History of the Sepoy War in India* (1870), II, pp. 402–3.
3 Bipan Chandra, *Rise and Growth of Economic Nationalism in India* (Delhi 1966), p. 2.
4 Chandra, *op. cit.*
5 E. R. J. Owen, *Cotton and the Egyptian Economy 1820–1914* (Oxford 1969), p. 156.
6 Nikki Keddie, *An Islamic Response to Imperialism* (Los Angeles 1968), p. 18.
7 Hu Sheng, *Imperialism and Chinese Politics* (Peking 1955), p. 92.
8 Jean A. Meyer in *Annales E.S.C.* 25, 3 (1970), pp. 796–7.
9 Karl Marx, 'British Rule in India', *New York Daily Tribune* (June 25 1853) (*Werke*, IX, p. 129).
10 B. M. Bhatia, *Famines in India* (London 1967), pp. 68–97.
11 Ta Chen, *Chinese Migration with Special Reference to Labour Conditions* (US Bureau of Labor Statistics, Washington 1923).
12 N. Sanchez Albornoz, 'Le Cycle vital annuel en Espagne 1863–1900', *Annales E.S.C.* 24, 6 (November–December 1969); M. Emerit, 'Le Maroc et l'Europe jusqu'en 1885', *Annales E.S.C.* 20, 3 (May–June 1965).
13 P. Leroy-Beaulieu, *L'Algérie et la Tunisie*, 2nd ed. (Paris 1897), p. 53.
14 *Almanach de Gotha* 1876.

1   Jakob Burckhardt, *Reflections on History* (London 1943), p. 170.
2   Erskine May, *op. cit.*, I, p. 25.
3   Cited in Henry Nash Smith, *Virgin Land* (New York 1957 ed.), p. 191. I am indebted to this valuable study of the agrarian-utopian strain in the United States as well as to Eric Foner, *Free Soil, Free Labor, Free Men* (Oxford 1970).
4   Herbert G. Gutman, 'Social Status and Social Mobility in Nineteenth Century America: The Industrial City. Paterson, New Jersey' (mimeo) (1964).
5   Martin J. Primack, 'Farm construction as a use of farm labor in the United States 1850–1910', *Journal of Economic History*, XXV (1965), p. 114 ff.
6   Rodman Wilson Paul, *Mining Frontiers of the Far West* (New York 1963), pp. 57–81.
7   Joseph G. McCoy, *Historic Sketches of the Cattle Trade of the West and South-west* (Kansas City 1874; Glendale, California 1940). The author founded Abilene as a cattle centre and became its mayor in 1871.
8   Charles Howard Shinn in *Mining Camps, A Study in American Frontier Government* ed. R. W. Paul (New York, Evanston and London 1965), chapter XXIV, pp. 45–6.
9   Hugh Davis Graham and Ted Gurr (eds.), *The History of Violence in America* (New York 1969), chapter 5, especially p. 175.
10 W. Miller (ed.), *Men in Business* (Cambridge [Mass.] 1952), p. 202.
11 I am obliged to Dr William Rubinstein for the data on which this guess is based.
12 Herbert G. Gutman, 'Work, Culture and Society in Industrializing America 1815–1919', *American Historical Review*, 78, 3 (1973), p. 569.
13 John Whitney Hall, *Das Japanische Kaiserreich* (Frankfurt 1968), p. 282.
14 Nakagawa, Keiichiro and Henry Rosovsky, 'The Case of the Dying Kimono', *Business History Review*, XXXVII (1963), pp. 59–80.
15 V. G. Kiernan, *The Lords of Human Kind* (London 1972), p. 188.
16 Horace Capron, 'Agriculture in Japan' in *Report of the Commissioner for Agriculture, 1873* (Washington 1874), pp. 364–74.
17 Kiernan, *op. cit.*, p. 193.

CHAPTER 9: CHANGING SOCIETY

1 Erskine May, *op. cit.*, I, pp. lxv-vi.
2 *Journaux des Frères Goncourt* (Paris 1956), II, p. 753.
3 *Werke*, XXXIV, pp. 510–11.
4 *Werke*, XXXII, p. 669.
5 *Werke*, XIX, p. 296.
6 *Werke*, XXXIV, p. 512.
7 M. Pushkin, 'The professions and the intelligentsia in nineteenth-century Russia', *University of Birmingham Historical Journal*, XII, I (1969), pp. 72 ff.
8 Hugh Seton Watson, *Imperial Russia 1861–1917* (Oxford 1967), pp. 422–3.
9 A. Ardao, 'Positivism in Latin America', *Journal of the History of Ideas* XXIV, 4 (1963), p. 519, notes that Comte's actual Constitution was imposed on the state of Rio Grande do Sul (Brazil).
10 G. Haupt, 'La Commune comme symbole et comme exemple', *Mouvement Social*, 79 (April–June 1972), pp. 205–26.
11 Samuel Bernstein, *Essays in Political and Intellectual History* (New York 1955), chapter XX, 'The First International and a New Holy Alliance', especially pp. 194–5 and 197.
12 J. Rougerie, *Paris Libre 1871* (Paris 1971), pp. 256–63.

CHAPTER 10: THE LAND

1 Cited in Jean Meyer, *Problemas campesinos y revueltas agrarias (1821–1910)* (Mexico 1973), p. 93.
2 Cited in R. Giusti, 'L'agricoltura e i contadini nel Mantovano (1848–1866)', *Movimento Operaio* VII, 3–4 (1955), p. 386.
3 Neumann-Spallart, *op. cit.*, p. 65.
4 Mitchell and Deane, *op. cit.*, pp. 356–7.
5 M. Hroch, *Die Vorkämpfer der nationalen Bewegung bei den kleinen Völkern Europas* (Prague 1968), p. 168.
6 'Bauerngut', *Handwörterbuch der Staatswissenschaften* (2nd ed.), II, pp. 441 and 444.
7 'Agriculture' in Mulhall, *op. cit.*, p. 7.
8 I. Wellman, 'Histoire rurale de la Hongrie', *Annales E.S.C.*, 23, 6 (1968), p. 1203; Mulhall, *loc. cit.*
9 E. Sereni, *Storia del paesaggio agrario italiano* (Bari 1962), pp. 351–2. Industrial deforestation should not be neglected either. 'The large

amount of fuel required by [the furnaces of Lake Superior, USA] has already made a very decided impression on the surrounding timber,' wrote H. Bauermann in 1868 (*A Treatise on the Metallurgy of Iron* [London 1872], p. 227); daily supply of a single furnace required the clearing of an acre of forest.

10 Elizabeth Whitcombe, *Agrarian Conditions in Northern India, I, 1860–1900* (Berkeley, Los Angeles and London 1972), pp. 75–85, discusses the consequences of large-scale irrigation engineering in the United Provinces critically.

11 Irwin Feller, 'Inventive activity in agriculture, 1837–1900', *Journal of Economic History*, xxii (1962), p. 576.

12 Charles McQueen, *Peruvian Public Finance* (Washington 1926), pp. 5–6. *Guano* supplied 75 per cent of Peruvian government income of all kinds in 1861–6, 80 per cent in 1869–75. (Heraclio Bonilla, *Guano y burguesia en el Peru* [Lima 1974], pp. 138–9, citing Shane Hunt.)

13 'Bauerngut', *Handwörterbuch der Staatswissenschaften* (2nd ed.), ii, p. 439.

14 See G. Verga's short story 'Liberty', based on the rising at Bronte, which is among those discussed in D. Mack Smith, 'The peasants' revolt in Sicily in 1860' in *Studi in Onore di Gino Luzzatto* (Milan 1950), pp. 201–240.

15 E. D. Genovese, *In Red and Black, Marxian Explorations in Southern and Afro-American History* (Harmondsworth 1971), pp. 131–4.

16 For the most elaborate version of this argument see R. W. Fogel and S. Engermann, *Time on the Cross* (Boston and London 1974).

17 Th. Brassey, *Work and Wages Practically Illustrated* (London 1872).

18 H. Klein, 'The Coloured Freedmen in Brazilian Slave Society', *Journal of Social History* 3, i (1969), pp. 36; Julio Le Riverend, *Historia economica de Cuba* (Havana 1956), p. 160.

19 P. Lyashchenko, *A History of the Russian National Economy* (New York 1949), p. 365.

20 Lyashchenko, *op. cit.*, pp. 440 and 450.

21 D. Wells, *Recent Economic Changes* (New York 1889), p. 100.

22 Jaroslav Purš, 'Die Entwicklung des Kapitalismus in der Landwirtschaft der böhmischen Länder 1849–1879', *Jahrbuch für Wirtschaftsgeschichte* (1963), iii, p. 38.

23 I. Orosz, 'Arbeitskräfte in der ungarischen Landwirtschaft,' *Jahrbuch für Wirtschaftsgeschichte* (1972) ii, p. 199.

24 J. Varga, *Typen und Probleme des bäuerlichen Grundbesitzes 1767–1849* (Budapest 1965), cited in *Annales E.S.C.* 23, 5 (1968), p. 1165.

25 A. Girault and L. Milliot, *Principes de Colonisation et de Législation Coloniale. L'Algérie* (Paris 1938), pp. 383 and 386.

26 Raymond Carr, *Spain 1808–1939* (Oxford 1966), p. 273.

27 José Termes Ardevol, *El Movimiento Obrero en Espana. La Primera Internacional (1864–1881)* (Barcelona 1965), unpag. Appendix: Sociedades Obreras creadas en 1870–1874.

28 A. Dubuc, 'Les sobriquets dans le Pays de Bray en 1875', *Annales de Normandie* (August 1952), pp. 281–2.

29 Purš, *op. cit.*, p. 40.

30 Franco Venturi, *Les Intellectuels, le peuple et la revolution. Histoiré du populisme russe au XIX siècle* (Paris 1972), ii, pp. 946–8. This magnificent book, an earlier edition of which exists in English translation (*Roots of Revolution* [London 1960]), is the standard work on its subject.

31 M. Fleury and P. Valmary, 'Les Progrès d'instruction élementaire de Louis xiv à Napoléon iii', *Population* xii (1957), pp. 69 ff; E. de Laveleye, *L'Instruction du Peuple* (Paris 1872), pp, 174, 188, 196, 227–8 and 481.

CHAPTER 11: MEN MOVING

1 Scholem Alejchem, *Aus dem nahen Osten* (Berlin 1922).

2 F. Mulhauser, *Correspondence of Arthur Clough* (Oxford 1957), ii, p. 396.

3 I. Ferenczi, ed. F. Willcox, *International Migrations*; Vol. 1 *Statistics*, National Bureau of Economic Research (New York 1929).

4 Ta Chen, *Chinese Migration with Special Reference to Labor Conditions*, United States Bureau of Labour Statistics (Washington 1923), p. 82.

5 S. W. Mintz, 'Cuba: Terre et Esclaves', *Etudes Rurales*, 48 (1972), p. 143.

6 *Bankers Magazine*, v (Boston 1850–51), p. 12.

7 R. Mayo Smith, *Emigration and Immigration, A Study in Social Science* (London 1890), p. 94.

8 M-A. Carron, 'Prélude a l'exode rural en France: les migrations anciennes des travailleurs creusois', *Revue d'histoire économique et sociale*, 43, (1965), p. 320.

9 A. F. Weber, *The Growth of Cities in the Nineteenth Century* (New York 1899), p. 374.

10 Herbert Gutman, 'Work, Culture and Society in industrializing America, 1815–1919', *American History Review*, 78 (3 June 1973), p. 533.

11 Barry E. Supple, 'A Business Elite: German-Jewish Financiers in Nineteenth Century New York', *Business History Review*, XXXI (1957), pp. 143–78.

12 Mayo Smith, *op. cit.*, p. 47; C. M. Turnbull, 'The European Mercantile Community in Singapore, 1819–1867', *Journal of South East Asian History*, X, I (1969), p. 33.

13 Ferenczi, ed. Willcox, *op. cit.*, Vol. II, p. 270 n.

14 K. E. Levi, 'Geographical Origin of German Immigration to Wisconsin', *Collections of the State Historical Society of Wisconsin*, XIV (1898), p. 354.

15 Carl F .Wittke, *We who built America* (New York 1939), p. 193.

16 Egon Erwin Kisch, *Karl Marx in Karlsbad* (East Berlin 1968).

17 C. T. Bidwell, *The Cost of Living Abroad* (London 1876), Appendix. Switzerland was the main objective of this tour.

18 Bidwell, *op. cit.*, p. 16.

19 Georg v.Mayr, *Statistik und Gesellschaftslehre*; II, *Bevoelkerungsstatistik*, 2. Lieferung (Tübingen 1922), p. 176.

20 E. G. Ravenstein, 'The Laws of Migration', *Journal of the Royal Statistical Society*, 52 (1889), p. 285.

CHAPTER 12: CITY, INDUSTRY, THE WORKING CLASS

1 J. Purš, 'The working class movement in the Czech lands', *Historica*, X (1965), p. 70.

2 M. May, *Die Arbeitsfrage* (1848) cited in R. Engelsing, 'Zur politischen Bildung der deutschen Unterschichten, 1789–1863' *Hist. Ztschr.* 206, 2 (April 1968), p. 356.

3 *Letters and Private Papers of W. M. Thackeray*, ed. Gordon N. Ray, II, 356 (London 1945).

4 J. Purš, 'The industrial revolution in the Czech Lands', *Historica*, II (1960), pp. 210 and 220.

5 Cited in H. J. Dyos and M. Wolff (eds.) *The Victorian City* (London and Boston 1973), I, p. 110.

6 Dyos and Wolff, *op. cit.*, I, p. 5.

7 A. F. Weber (1898) cited in Dyos and Wolff, *op. cit.*, I, p. 7.

8 H. Croon, 'Die Versorgung der Staedte des Ruhrgebietes im 19. u. 20. Jahrhundert' (mimeo) (International Congress of Economic History 1965), p. 2.

9 Dyos and Wolff, *op. cit.*, I, p. 341.

10 L. Henneaux-Depooter, *Misères et Luttes Sociales dans le Hainaut 1860–96* (Brussels 1959), p. 117; Dyos and Wolff, *op. cit.*, p. 134.

11 G. Fr. Kolb, *Handbuch der vergleichenden Statistik* (Leipzig 1879).
12 Dyos and Wolff, *op. cit.*, I, p. 424.
13 Dyos and Wolff, *op. cit.*, I, p. 326.
14 Dyos and Wolff, *op. cit.*, I, p. 379.
15 J. H. Clapham, *An Economic History of Modern Britain* (Cambridge 1932), II, pp. 116–17.
16 Erich Maschke, *Es entsteht ein Konzern* (Tübingen 1969).
17 R. Ehrenberg, *Krupp-Studien* (Thünen-Archiv II, Jena, 1906–9), p. 203; C. Fohlen, *The Fontana Economic History of Europe, 4: The Emergence of Industrial Societies* (London 1973), I, p. 60; J. P. Rioux, *La Révolution Industrielle* (Paris 1971), p. 163.
18 G. Neppi Modona, *Sciopero, potere politico e magistratura 1870–1922* (Bari 1969), p. 51.
19 P. J. Proudhon, *Manuel du Spéculateur à la Bourse* (Paris 1857), pp. 429 ff.
20 B. Gille, *The Fontana Economic History of Europe, 3: The Industrial Revolution* (London 1973), p. 278.
21 J. Kocka, 'Industrielles Management: Konzeptionen und Modelle vor 1914', *Vierteljahrschrift für Sozial – und Wirtschaftsgesch.* 65/3 (October 1969), p. 336, quoting from Emminghaus, *Allgemeine Gewerbslehre*.
22 P. Pierrard, 'Poesie et chanson . . . à Lille sous le 2e Empire', *Revue du Nord*, 46 (1964), p. 400.
23 G. D. H. Cole and Raymond Postgate, *The Common People* (London 1946), p. 368.
24 H. Mottek, *Wirtschaftsgeschichte Deutschlands* (East Berlin 1973), II, p. 235.
25 E. Waugh, *Home Life of the Lancashire Factory Folk during the Cotton Famine* (London 1867), p. 13.
26 M. Anderson, *Family Structure in Nineteenth Century Lancashire* (Cambridge 1973), p. 31.
27 O. Handlin (ed.) *Immigration as a Factor in American History* (Englewood Cliffs 1959), pp. 66–7.
28 J. Hagan and C. Fisher, 'Piece-work and some of its consequences in the printing and coal mining industries in Australia, 1850–1930', *Labour History*, 25 (November 1973), p. 26.
29 A. Plessis, *De la fête impériale au mur des Fédérés* (Paris 1973), p. 157.
30 E. Schwiedland, *Kleingewerbe und Hausindustrie in Österreich* (Leipzig 1894), II, pp. 264–5 and 284–5.
31 J. Saville and J. Bellamy (eds.), *Dictionary of Labour Biography*, I, p. 17.
32 Engelsing, *op. cit.*, p. 364.

33 Rudolf Braun, *Sozialer und kultureller Wandel in einem ländlichen Industriegebiet im 19. u. 20. Jahrhundert* (Erlenbach-Zürich and Stuttgart 1965), p. 139, uses this term specifically for the period. His invaluable books (see also *Industrialisierung und Volksleben* [1960]) cannot be recommended too highly.

34 *Industrial Remuneration Conference* (London 1885), p. 27.

35 *Industrial Remuneration Conference*, pp. 89–90.

36 Beatrice Webb, *My Apprenticeship* (Harmondsworth 1938), pp. 189 and 195.

37 *Industrial Remuneration Conference*, pp. 27 and 30.

CHAPTER 13: THE BOURGEOIS WORLD

1 Cited in L. Trénard, 'Un Industriel roubaisien du xix siècle', *Revue du Nord*, 50 (1968), p. 38.

2 Martin Tupper, *Proverbial Philosophy* (1876).

3 See Emanie Sachs, *The Terrible Siren* (New York 1928), especially pp. 174–5.

4 G. von Mayr, *Statistik und Gesellschatslehre III Sozialstatistik*, Erste Lieferung (Tübingen 1909), pp. 43–5. For the unreliability of statistics on prostitution, *ibid.* (5. Lieferung), p. 988. For the strong relationship of prostitution and venereal infection, Gunilla Johansson, 'Prostitution in Stockholm in the latter part of the 19th century' (mimeo) (1974). For estimates of the prevalence and mortality from syphilis in France, see T. Zeldin, *France 1848–1945* (Oxford 1974), I, pp. 304–6.

5 The freedom of visiting American girls is noted in the relevant section of the chapter on foreigners in Paris in the superb *Paris Guide 1867* (2 vols).

6 For Cuba, Verena Martinez Alier, 'Elopement and seduction in 19th century Cuba', *Past and Present*, 55 (May 1972); for the American South E. Genovese, *Roll Jordan Roll* (New York 1974), pp. 413–30 and R. W. Fogel and Stanley Engermann, *op. cit.*

7 From the 'Maxims for Revolutionists' in *Man and Superman*: 'A moderately honest man with a moderately faithful wife, moderate drinkers both, in a moderately healthy house: that is the true middle class unit'.

8 Zunkel, *op. cit.*, p. 320.

9 Zunkel, *op. cit.*, p. 526 n. 59.

10 Tupper, *op. cit.*: 'Of Home', p. 361.

11 Tupper, *loc. cit.*, p. 362.

12 John Ruskin, 'Fors Clavigera', in E. T. Cook and A. Wedderburn (eds.), *Collected Works* (London and New York 1903–12), vol. 27, letter 34.

13 Tupper, *op. cit.*: 'Of Marriage', p. 118.

14 H. Bolitho (ed.), *Further Letters of Queen Victoria* (London 1938), p. 49.

15 'My opinion is that if a woman is obliged to work, at once (although she may be a Christian and well bred) she loses the peculiar position which the word *lady* conventionally designates' (Letter to the *English-woman's Journal*, VIII (1866), p. 59).

16 Trénard, *op. cit.*, pp. 38 and 42.

17 Tupper, *op. cit.*: 'Of Joy', p. 133.

18 J. Lambert-Dansette, 'Le Patronat du Nord. Sa période triomphante', in *Bulletin de la Société d'histoire moderne et contemporaine*, 14, Série 18 (1971), p. 12.

19 Charlotte Erickson, *British Industrialists: Steel and Hosiery, 1850–1950* (Cambridge 1959).

20 H. Kellenbenz, 'Unternehmertum in Südwestdeutschland', *Tradition*, 10, 4 (August 1965), pp. 183 ff.

21 *Nouvelle Biographie Générale* (1861); articles: Koechlin, p. 954.

22 C. Pucheu, 'Les Grands notables de l'Agglomération Bordelaise du milieu du XIXe siècle à nos jours', *Revue d'histoire et sociale*, 45 (1967), p. 493.

23 P. Guillaume, 'La Fortune Bordelaise au milieu du XIX siècle', *Revue d histoire économique et sociale*, 43 (1965), pp. 331, 332, and 351.

24 E. Gruner, 'Quelques reflexions sur l'élite politique dans la Confédération Helvetique depuis 1848', *Revue d'histoire économique et sociale*, 44 (1966), pp. 145 ff.

25 B. Verhaegen, 'Le groupe Libéral à la Chambre Belge (1847–1852)', *Revue Belge de Philologie et d'histoire*, 47 (1969), 3–4, pp. 1176 ff.

26 Lambert-Dansette, *op. cit.*, p. 9.

27 Lambert-Dansette, *op. cit.*, p. 8; V. E. Chancellor (ed.), *Master and Artisan in Victorian England* (London 1969), p. 7.

28 Serge Hutin, *Les Francs-Maçons* (Paris 1960), pp. 103 ff. and 114 ff.; P. Chevallier, *Histoire de la Francmaçonnerie française*, II (Paris 1974). For the Iberian world, the judgment: 'The Freemasonry of that period was nothing but the universal conspiracy of the revolutionary middle class against feudal, monarchical and divine tyranny. It was the International of that class', cited in Iris M. Zavala, *Masones, Comuneros y Carbonarios* (Madrid 1971), p. 192.

29 T. Mundt, *Die neuen Bestrebungen zu einer wirtschaftlichen Reform der unteren Volksklassen* (1855), cited in Zunkel, *op. cit.*, p. 327.
30 Rolande Trempé, 'Contribution à l'étude de la psychologie patronale: le comportement des administrateurs de la Societé des Mines de Carmaux (1856–1914)', *Mouvement Social*, 43 (1963), p. 66.
31 John Ruskin, *Modern Painters*, cited in W. E. Houghton, *The Victorian Frame of Mind* (Newhaven 1957), p. 116. Samuel Smiles, *Self Help* (1859), chapter 11, pp. 359–60.
32 John Ruskin, 'Traffic', *The Crown of Wild Olives*, (1866) *Works* 18, p. 453.
33 Trempé, *op. cit.*, p. 73.
34 W. L. Burn, *The Age of Equipoise* (London 1964), p. 244 n.
35 H. Ashworth in 1953–4, cited in Burn, *op. cit.*, p. 243.
36 H. U. Wehler, *Bismarck und der Imperialismus* (Cologne–Berlin 1969), p. 431.

CHAPTER 14: SCIENCE, RELIGION, IDEOLOGY

1 Francis Darwin and A. Seward (eds.), *More Letters of Charles Darwin* (New York 1903), II, p. 34.
2 Cited in Engelsing, *op. cit.*, p. 361.
3 *Anthropological Review*, IV (1866), p. 115.
4 P. Benaerts *et. al.*, *Nationalité et Nationalisme* (Paris 1968), p. 623.
5 Karl Marx, *Capital*, I, postscript to second edition.
6 In the *Electromagnetic Theory* of Julius Stratton of the MIT. Dr S. Zienau, to whom my references to physical sciences are enormously indebted, tells me that this came at a fortunate moment for the Anglo-Saxon war-effort in the field of radar.
7 J. D. Bernal, *Science in History* (London 1969), II, p. 568.
8 Bernal, *op. cit.*
8a Lewis Feuer has lately suggested that it was not Marx but Edward Aveling who approached Darwin, but this does not affect the argument.
9 Marx to Engels (19 December 1860) (*Werke*, XXX, p. 131).
10 H. Steinthal and M. Lazarus, *Zeitschrift für Völkerpsychologie und Sprachwissenschaft.*
11 F. Mehring, *Karl Marx, The Story of his Life* (London 1936), p. 383
12 E. B. Tylor, 'The Religion of Savages', *Fortnightly Review* VI (1866), p. 83.
13 *Anthropological Review* IV (1866), p. 120.

14 Kiernan, *op. cit.*, p. 159.
15 W. Philips, 'Religious profession and practice in New South Wales 1850–1900', *Historical Studies* (October 1972), p. 388.
16 *Haydn's Dictionary of Dates* (1889 ed.): Missions.
17 Eugene Stock, *A Short Handbook of Missions* (London 1904), p. 97. The statistics in this biased and influential manual are taken from J. S. Dennis, *Centennial Survey of Foreign Missions* (New York and Chicago 1902).
18 *Catholic Encyclopedia*; artice: Missions, Africa.

CHAPTER 15: THE ARTS

1 R. Wagner, 'Kunst und Klima', *Gesammelte Schriften* (Leipzig 1907), III, p. 214.
2 Cited in E. Dowden, *Studies in Literature 1789–1877* (London 1892), p. 404.
3 Th. v. Frimmel, *Lexicon der Wiener Gemäldesammlungen* (A–L 1913–14); article: Ahrens.
4 G. Reitlinger, *The Economics of Taste* (London 1961), chapter 6. I have relied much on this valuable work, which brings to the study of art a hard-headed financial realism suitable to our period.
5 Asa Briggs, *Victorian Cities* (London 1963), pp. 164 and 183.
6 Reitlinger, *op. cit.*
7 R. D. Altick, *The English Common Reader* (Chicago 1963), pp. 355 and 388.
8 Reitlinger, *op. cit.*
9 F. A. Mumby, *The House of Routledge* (London 1934).
10 M. V. Stokes, 'Charles Dickens: A Customer of Coutts & Co.', *The Dickensian*, 68 (1972), pp. 17–30. I am indebted to Michael Slater for this reference.
11 Mulhall, *op. cit.*; article: Libraries. A special note should be made of the British public-library movement. Nineteen cities installed such free libraries in the 1850s, eleven in the 1860s, fifty-one in the 1870s (W. A. Munford, *Edward Edwards* [London 1963]).
12 T. Zeldin, *France 1848–1945* (Oxford 1974), I, p. 310.
13 G. Grundmann, 'Schlösser und Villen des 19. Jahrhunderts von Unternehmern in Schlesien', *Tradition*, 10, 4 (August 1965), pp. 149–62.
14 R. Wischnitzer, *The Architecture of the European Synagogue* (Philadelphia 1964), chapter x, especially pp. 196 and 202–6.

15 Gisèle Freund, *Photographic und bürgerliche Gesellschaft* (Munich 1968), p. 92.
16 Freund, *op. cit.*, pp. 94–6.
17 Cited in Linda Nochlin (ed.), *Realism and Tradition in Art* (Englewood Cliffs 1966), pp. 71 and 74.
18 Gisèle Freund, *Photographie et Société* (Paris 1974), p. 77.
19 Freund, *op. cit.* (1968), p. 111.
20 Freund, *op. cit.* (1968), pp. 112–13.
21 For the question of artists and revolution in this period, see T. J. Clark, *The Absolute Bourgeois* (London 1973) and *Image of the People: Gustave Courbet* (London 1973).
22 Nochlin, *op. cit.*, p. 77.
23 Nochlin, *op. cit.*, p. 77.
24 Nochlin, *op. cit.*, p. 53.
25 Even in that lesser centre of Bohemia, Munich, the Münchner Kunstverein had about 4,500 members in the mid-1870s. P. Drey, *Die wirtschaftlichen Grundlagen der Malkunst. Versuch einer Kunstökonomie* (Stuttgart and Berlin 1910).
26 'In art the handicraft is almost everything. Inspiration – yes, inspiration is a very pretty thing, but a little *banale*; it is so universal. Every bourgeois is more or less affected by a sunrise or sunset. He has a certain measure of inspiration.' Cited in Dowden, *op. cit.*, p. 405.

CHAPTER 16: CONCLUSION

1 Johann Nestroy, *Sie Sollen Ihn Nicht Haben* (1850).
2 D. S. Landes, *The Unbound Prometheus* (Cambridge 1969), pp. 240–41.
3 Burckhardt, *op. cit.*, p. 116.
4 Burckhardt, *op. cit.*, p. 171.

Further Reading

With very few exceptions the following notes refer only to books, and books in the English language. This does not mean that they are the best available, though often they are. It is a concession to the ignorance of foreign languages of most readers in the English-speaking world.

The bibliography of the period is so vast that no attempt can be made to cover all aspects of it, even selectively, and the choices suggested are personal, and sometimes fortuitous. Guides to reading on most topics are contained in the American Historical Association's periodically revised *A Guide to Historical Literature*. The bibliography in the *Cambridge Economic History of Europe*, vol. VI, is wider than its title suggests. J. Roach (ed.), *A Bibliography of Modern History* (1968), may also be consulted, with caution. Most of the books listed below contain bibliographical references either in footnotes or separately.

Among general works of historical reference W. Langer's *Encyclopedia of World History* gives the main dates, as does Neville Williams, *Chronology of the Modern World* (1966). Alfred Mayer, *Annals of European Civilization 1500–1900* (1949), deals with the arts and sciences. M. Mulhall, *A Dictionary of Statistics* (1892), remains the best compendium of figures. For general nineteenth-century reference the eleventh edition of the *Encyclopaedia Britannica*, still available in good university libraries, is far superior to its successors, as the *Encyclopaedia of the Social Sciences* (1931) is – for our purposes – to its successor of 1968. Biographical compendia and reference works on special subjects are too numerous to mention. Among historical atlases J. Engel *et. al.*, *Grosser Historischer Weltatlas* (1957), the Rand–McNally *Atlas of World History* (1957) and the *Penguin Historical Atlas* (1974–) are recommended.

G. Barraclough, *An Introduction to Contemporary History* (1967) and C. Morazé, *The Triumph of the Middle Classes* (1966) – the latter with brilliantly designed maps – may serve as an introduction to global history. V. G. Kiernan's elegant and erudite *The Lords of Human Kind* (1969, 1972) surveys European attitudes to the outside world. Both the *New Cambridge Modern History*, vol. X (J. P. T. Bury [ed.], *The Zenith of European Power 1839–1870*), and the two parts of the *Cambridge Economic History*, vol. VI (*The Industrial Revolutions and After*) range beyond Europe. Both may be constantly consulted with profit. As for more strictly European surveys,

M. S. Anderson, *The Ascendancy of Europe 1815–1914* (1972), and E. J. Hobsbawm, *The Age of Revolution, Europe 1789–1848* (1962), range beyond the continent. W. E. Mosse, *Liberal Europe 1848–1875* (1974), covers exactly the same period as the present book. William L. Langer, *Political and Social Upheaval 1832–1852* (1969) – useful bibliography – is much the best of the chronologically relevant volumes in the series *The Rise of Modern Europe* edited by the same author.

Of general works on more specialised fields, C. Cipolla (ed.), *The Fontana Economic History of Europe* (1973, vols. 3, 4i and 4ii) are extremely convenient, but by far the best introduction to the economic history of the period is D. S. Landes' superb *The Unbound Prometheus* (1969), an expansion of this author's contribution to the *Cambridge Economic History*. The relevant volumes of C. Singer *et al.*, *A History of Technology*, are for reference. G. L. Mosse, *The Culture of Western Europe: the nineteenth and twentieth centuries* (1963), is a convenient introduction to its subject. J. D. Bernal, *Science in History* (1965), is brilliant, but its sections on our period should not be taken uncritically. Neither should those of A. Hauser, *The Social History of Art* (1952). Various volumes of the *Penguin History of Art* cover the nineteenth century. Peter Stearns, *European Society in Upheaval* (1975 ed.), is an attempt, perhaps premature, to survey the social history of the continent. Two works by C. Cipolla, *The Economic History of World Population* (1962) and *Literacy and Development in the West* (1969), are useful brief introductions. A. F. Weber, *The Growth of Cities in the 19th century* (1899 and reissues), has been an invaluable compendium since its original publication.

Not all countries possess modern, conveniently sized comprehensive national histories in English for our period. Britain does not, though H. Perkin, *The Origin of Modern English Society 1780–1880* (1969), and Geoffrey Best, *Midvictorian Britain 1850–75* (1971), are good on social history and J. H. Clapham, *An Economic History of Modern Britain*, ii (*1850–1880*) (1932), is still remarkable. The best history by far of France is the (untranslated) *Nouvelle Histoire de la France Contemporaine*, vols. 8 and 9, by M. Agulhon (*1848 ou l'apprentissage de la Republique*) and Alain Plessis (*De la fête imperiale au mur des fédérés*) (both 1973). Hajo Holborn, *A History of Modern Germany 1840–1945* (1970) is good, but for our period T. S. Hamerow's *Restoration, Revolution, Reaction, Economics and Politics in Germany 1815–1871* (1958) and *Social Foundations of German Unification* (1969) are highly relevant. C. A. Macartney, *The Habsburg Empire 1790–1918* (1969), and the impressive Raymond Carr, *Spain 1808–1939* (1966), contain all most of us need to know about their countries, B. J. Hovde, *The Scandinavian Countries 1720–1865*, 2 vols. (1943), more than this.

Histories of Russia reflect strongly-held opinions. Hugh Seton Watson, *Imperial Russia 1801–1917* (1967), is full of information; so is P. Lyashchenko, *A History of the Russian National Economy* (1949). G. Procacci, *History of the Italian People*, II (1973) is a good but very compressed introduction; D. Mack Smith, *Italy, A Modern History* (1959), an early work by the leading specialist on this period in Italian history. L. S. Stavrianos, *The Balkans since 1453* (1958), is an excellent survey.

For the non-European world most readers will require not histories of the period, but general introductions to unfamiliar milieus. For China this may be found in China Readings 1, Franz Schurmann and O. Schell (eds.) *Imperial China* (1967): for Japan, in The Japan Reader 1, J Livingston, J. Moore and F. Oldfather (eds.), *Imperial Japan 1800–1945* (1973); for the Islamic world G. von Grunebaum (ed.), *Unity and Variety in Muslim Civilization* (1955); for Latin America, some of Lewis Hanke (ed.), *Readings in Latin American History II: Since 1810* (1966); for India, Elizabeth Whitcombe, *Agrarian Conditions in Northern India, I: The United Provinces under British Rule* (1972); for Egypt, E. R. J. Owen, *Cotton and the Egyptian Economy 1820–1914* (1969). For the leading events in their respective countries, M. Franz, *The Taiping Rebellion* (1966), and W. G. Beasley, *The Meiji Restoration* (1972).

The bibliography of American history is limitless. Any general history will do for those totally unfamiliar with that country, e.g. E. C. Rozwenc, *The Making of American Society I; to 1877* (1972), supplemented by R. B. Morris, *Encyclopaedia of American History* (1965). All lag behind the progress of research.

The main theme of the present book is the creation of a single world under capitalist hegemony. For the process of exploration see J. N. L. Baker, *A History of Geographical Discovery and Exploration* (1931); for mapping, Cdr L. S. Dawson RN, *Memoirs of Hydrography II* (covers 1830–80) (reprinted 1969); for transport, a brief introduction by M. Robbins, *The Railway Age* (1962), and a bulky and triumphant chronicle W. S. Lindsay, *History of Merchant Shipping*, 4 vols. (1876). The expansion of settlement and enterprise is inseparable from the history of migration (see chapter 11); see Brinley Thomas, *Migration and Economic Growth* (1954); for the human side, M. Hansen, *The Immigrant in American History* (1940) and C. Erickson, *Invisible Immigrants: The Adaptation of English and Scottish immigrants in 19th century America* (1972) while Hugh Tinker, *A New System of Slavery* (1974) deals with the export of indentured labour. For the moving frontier R. A. Billington *Westward Expansion* (1949), and Rodman Wilson Paul, *Mining Frontiers of the Far West* (1963). For capitalist enterprise abroad, D. S. Landes' splendid *Bankers and Pashas: Inter-*

national Finance and Modern Imperialism in Egypt (1958), L. H. Jenks, *The Migration of British Capital to 1875* (1927), H. Feis, *Europe, The World's Banker* (1930), A. T. Helps, *The Life and Labours of Mr Brassey* (1872, reprinted 1969) and W. Stewart, *Henry Meiggs, A Yankee Pizarro* (1946). The last two deal with titans of railway construction. An interesting glimpse into contemporary attitudes is Jean Chesneaux, *The Political and Social Ideas of Jules Verne* (1972), author of *Round the World in Eighty Days*.

The history of the bourgeoisie, key class of our period, remains to be adequately written, certainly in English and in generally accessible form. Asa Briggs, *Victorian People* (1955) is a useful introduction, but the best guide is to be found in the Rougon-Macquart series of novels by Emile Zola, which analyse the society of the French Second Empire, and whose documentary reliability is high. See also Mario Praz's introduction to G. S. Métraux and F. Crouzet (eds.), *The Nineteenth-Century World* (1968). Among the monographs one must mention Adeline Daumard, *La Bourgeoisie parisienne 1815–1848* (short version 1970), A. Tudesq, *Les Grands Notables en France*, 2 vols. (1964), good on the formation of political consciousness during the 1848 revolution, and F. Zunkel, 'Industriebürgertum in Westdeutschland' in H. U. Wehler's (ed.), *Moderne Deutsche Sozialgeschichte* (1966). For the aspirations of the lower middle class and deemed suitable for all, Samuel Smiles, *Self Help* (1859 and numerous editions). W. L. Burn, *The Age of Equipoise* (1964), is an excellent cross-section of (English) bourgeois society, and T. Zeldin, *France 1848–1945*, vol. 1 (1974), a very good guide to French bourgeois society, including family and sex. J. R. Vincent. *The Formation of the British Liberal Party 1857–68* (1972) is stimulating.

Though there are excellent books on the nineteenth-century city in addition to A. F. Weber (e.g. Asa Briggs, *Victorian Cities* [1963], and the encyclopaedic H. J. Dyos and M. Wolff [ed.] *The Victorian City*, 2 vols. [1973]), general guides to the world of the manual workers – as distinct from histories of their organisations – are scarce. John Burnett (ed.), *Useful Toil* (1974), collects British workers' autobiographies, with convenient introductions, and Henry Mayhew's *London Labour and the London Poor*, 4 vols. (originally 1861–2) is reportage of genius about the greatest of western cities. E. J. Hobsbawm, *Labouring Men* (1964), contains some relevant studies. Numerous valuable studies for particular countries, especially France, are unfortunately untranslated. One might single out Michelle Perrot, *Les Ouvriers en grève, 1871–90*, vol. 2 (1974), Rolande Trempé, *Les Mineurs de Carmaux* (1971) and Rudolf Braun, *Sozialer und kultureller Wandel in einem landlichen Industriegebiet* (1965), whose significance is far greater than the narrow local basis (in Switzerland) would suggest. J. Kuczynski's massive *Geschichte der Lage der Arbeiter unter dem Kapitalismus*, 40 vols. (1960–72) must be mentioned. Vols. 2, 3 and 18–20 deal with German workers during this period.

In addition to general works already mentioned, land, agriculture and agrarian society can be studied in T. Shanin (ed.), *Peasants and Peasant Societies* (1971), Jerome Blum, *Lord and Peasant in Russia* (1961), Geroid T. Robinson, *Rural Russia under the Old Regime* (1932), F. M. L. Thompson, *English Landed Society in the 19th Century* (1963) and F. A. Shannon, *The Farmer's Last Frontier* (1945). For the much-debated question of the last era of slavery, see Eugene G. Genovese, *The World the Slaveholders made* (1969) and *Roll, Jordan Roll: the World the Slaves Made* (1974) and R. W. Fogel and S. Engermann, *Time on the Cross*, 2 vols. (1974), a controversial work. For the less-known economy of indentured labour, Alan Adamson, *Sugar without Slaves* (1972). Zola's *La Terre* combines accuracy and urban prejudice about peasants. For uprooted peasants, O. Handlin (ed.), *Immigration as a Factor in American History* (1959).

A. J. P. Taylor, *The Struggle for Mastery in Europe, 1848–1918* (1954) and W. E. Mosse, *The European Powers and the German Question 1848–1871* (1969), will serve to introduce the history of international relations; A. Vagts, *A History of Militarism* (1938), E. A. Pratt, *The Rise of Rail Power in War and Conquest* (1915), and H. Nickerson, 'Nineteenth Century Military Techniques', *Journal of World History*, IV (1957–8), that of wars. Michael Howard, *The Franco-Prussian War* (1962), is a model monograph.

For contemporary attitudes on the two great issues of national and popular government, see Walter Bagehot, *Physics and Politics* (1873), and *The British Constitution* (1872: numerous editions). The historiography and discussion of nationalism is unsatisfactory. Ernest Renan, 'What is a Nation?' in A. Zimmern (ed.), *Modern Political Doctrines* (1939) is a starting-point. The best book is M. Hroch, *Die Vorkämpfer der nationalen Bewegung bei den kleinen Völkern Europas* (Prague 1968); cf. also Commission Internationale d'Histoire des Mouvements Sociaux et des Structures Sociales, *Mouvements Nationaux d'Indépendance et Classes Populaires aux 19e et 20e siècles*, vol. 1 (1971). On the extension of the vote in Britain in 1867, Royden Harrison, *Before the Socialists* (1965), chapters III–IV; for Germany, G. Mayer, 'Die Trennung der proletarischen von der bürgerlichen Demokratie in Deutschland 1863–70' in *Grünberg's Archiv*, II (1911), pp. 1–67. See also the works of J. R. Vincent, T. S. Hamerow and T. Zeldin, *The Political System of Napoleon III* (1958). For the revolutions of the period, V. G. Kiernan, *The Revolution of 1854 in Spanish History* (1966), C. A. M. Hennessy, *The Federal Republic in Spain 1868–74* (1962), and, among a vast literature on the Paris Commune including Marx's famous *Civil War in France*, J. Rougerie, *Paris Libre 1871* (1971). W. L. Langer, *Political and Social Upheaval 1832-52* (1969), and Peter Stearns, *The 1848 Revolution* (1974), may introduce readers to the greatest revolution of our period, about which Marx wrote two contemporary booklets (*Class Struggles in France*, and *The Eighteenth Brumaire of Louis Bonaparte*), Engels one (*Revolution and Counter Revolution in Germany*), and A. de Tocqueville some memorable passages in his *Memoirs*. The greatest freedom-fighter of the period is the subject of J. Ridley, *Garibaldi* (1974), the Russian revolutionaries of a classic work, F. Venturi's *Roots of Revolution* (1960).

H. K. Girvetz, *From Wealth to Welfare: The Evolution of Liberalism* (1963), describes the changing meanings of the prevalent bourgeois ideology; Henry Nash Smith, *Virgin Land* (1957) is an excellent guide to the ideology of radicalism, which found its purest expression on the frontier (see also Eric Foner, *Free Soil, Free Labor, Free Men* [1970]). G. Lichtheim, *The Origins of Socialism* (1969), is the best introduction to its subject. G. D. H. Cole, *A History of Socialist Thought, II: Marxism and Anarchism 1850–1890* (1954), is still the most comprehensive general account. For non-socialist criticism of capitalism, see perhaps the greatest of contemporary ones, J. Burckhardt, *Reflexions on World History* (1945). E. Roll, *A History of Economic Thought*, is concise and intelligent, moving away between editions from the author's earlier radical positions. W. M. Simon, *European Positivism in the 19th Century* (1963) is about a rather central ideological current of this period. Franz Mehring, *Karl Marx, The Story of His Life* (1936) is preferable to later introductions to life and thought, since the author reflects what Marx meant to the generation of his immediate disciples and followers. A. D. White, *A History of the Warfare of Science and Theology* (1896) is worth consulting for the same reasons. On Darwinism, J. Burrow, *Evolution and Society: A Study in Victorian Social Theory* (1966), the same author's introduction to the Penguin edition of *The Origin of Species* (1968), R. Hofstadter, *Social Darwinism in American Thought* (1955), and W. Bagehot, *Physics and Politics* (1873).

J. T. Merz, *A History of European Thought in the 19th Century* (4 vols. 1896–1914) remains essential for a study of 19th century science. S. P. Thompson, *The Life of William Thompson* (2 vols, 1910) deals with a central figure. J. D. Bernal, *Science and Industry in the 19th Century* (1953) is a brilliant monograph. The same author's *Science in History* has been mentioned above. A. Findlay, *A Hundred Years of Chemistry* (1948) is a convenient treatment of a crucial science. For the arts, in addition to the general works mentioned, G. Reitlinger, *The Economics of Taste* I and II (1961, 1963) discusses the nature of the art market, T. J. Clark, *The Absolute Bourgeois* and *Image of the People* (1973) art and revolution, Linda Nochlin, *Realism* (1971) is self-explanatory (see also her 'The invention of the Avant-Garde: France 1830–1880' in *Art News Annual* 34), as is Gisèle Freund, *Photographie und bürgerliche Gesellschaft* (1968). Walter Benjamin, 'Paris–Capital of the 19th Century' (in *New Left Review* 48, 1968) is brief but profound. G. Lukacs, *Studies in European Realism* (1950) is the work of a notable critic of prose, Georg Brandes, *Main Currents in Nineteenth Century Literature* (6 vols. 1901–5) gives the near-contemporary view. Bryan Magee, *Aspects of Wagner* (1972) defends a great but disagreeable composer. Cyril Ehrlich, *The Piano: A History* (1976) is quite excellent on the social as well as the technical aspects of the central musical instrument of the period.

On the crisis which concludes our period, Hans Rosenberg, *Grosse Depression und Bismarckzeit* (1967) and David Wells, *Recent Economic Changes* (1889).

A general work of very considerable interest may be mentioned in conclusion: Barrington Moore, *Social Origins of Dictatorship and Democracy* (1967, Penguin 1973).

394

Index

Australia (*contd.*)
immigration, 82, 143, 230, 231, 234, 237, 244; railways, 70, 72, 74, 362; religion, 321; shipping, 363; trade unions, 134, 135, 139; unexplored, 65, 68; urbanisation, 231, 247

Austria, 89, 94, 131; agriculture, 365; Christian-Social movement, 385; education, 117, 120; exclusion from Germany, 92, 97; freedom to practise any trade, 51; industrialisation, 55; liberal politics, 129, 356; libraries, 335; military and political importance in Europe, 100; suffrage, 128; telegraph system, 76, 77; trade, 66, 356; trade unions, 138; *see also* Habsburg Empire

Bach, Alexander, 33
Bachofen, J. J., 314n
bacteriology, 302
Baden, population, 360
Baden-Baden, 241
Baedeker, Karl, 242, 243
Bagehot, Walter, 16, 105, 133
Bain, A., 306
Baker, S. W., 67
Bakunin, Michael, 37, 114n, 136, 191, 192, 193, 194, 198, 225, 266
Balkans, 93, 104, 107, 112, 210
Baltic, trading in, 53; shipping, 363
Balzac, Honoré de, 350
Bank of California, 82
Bankers Magazine, 80, 230n
Barbizon school, 327
Barcelona, 334
Barmen, 138, 247
Barnes, William, 353
Barth, H., 67
Bateau Ivre (Rimbaud), 340
Baudelaire, Charles, 325n, 341, 346, 349
Bavaria, population, 360; revolution, 22; 'self-improvement' associations, 265

Bayreuth, 333
Bebel, August, 117, 137
Beeches, Henry Ward, 273
Beethoven, Ludwig van, 325
Belgium, 52, 251, 322, 357; agriculture, 365; Belgian Chamber, 284; foreign trade, 66; higher education, 58; industrialisation, 56, 247; iron exports, 44; iron production, 56, 57; labour unrest, 138; laws against usury, 51; libraries, 335; literacy, 227n; politics, 128, 130; population, 205, 361; railways, 362; revolution, 22n, 23; steam power, 56, 361; suffrage, 127; telegraph system, 76, 77; trade cycle, 85; urbanisation, 246, 247
Belinsky, V., 199
Bengal, 207
Bengal army, 152
Benthamites, 140
Berbers, 144, 149
Berlin, 22, 27, 28, 29, 35, 234, 237, 248, 258, 282
Berlioz, Hector, 339n
Bernal, J. D., 299
Bernard, Claude, 297, 302, 341
Bessemer, converter, 57
Biarritz, 241
Bildungsvereine, 265
biology, 301–3
Birmingham, 67
Bismarck, Count Otto von, 16, 98, 201, 348; alliance with National Liberals, 129; and the bourgeoisie, 39, 132–3, 293; and formation of the Three Emperors' League, 201; and Hungary, 93; and Napoleon III, 124, 241n; opposition to Roman Catholic Church, 318; prohibits socialist activity, 142, 358–9; and unification of Germany, 90–2, 97; universal suffrage in Germany, 138
Bizet, Georges, 340
Black Sea, shipping, 74, 363
Blanc, Louis, 37, 134

Chekhov, Anton, 221
chemical industry, 57, 59n
chemistry, 296, 300–1, 315
Chernishevsky, N., 199, 344
Chicago, 16, 166, 169, 208, 244, 248
Chile, 80, 356; nitrate exports, 214; railways, 70, 362; shipping, 146
China, 65, 80, 144, 216, 219; Anglo-French military expeditions, 95; Chinese immigration to California, 80; famines, 162, 163; imperialism, 144; Manchu dynasty, 156, 157, 159; migrations, 229–30, 235; Ming dynasty, 156, 157; opium trade, 49; relations with West, 156–7, 158–9, 160–1, 179, 180; revolutions, 155–9; *see also* Opium War; Taiping Rebellion
Chinese People's Republic, 200
Chotek, Count, 285
Christian Science, 319–20
Church of England, 285
cities *see* urbanisation
The Civil War in France (Marx), 140
Clemenceau, Georges, 348
Clough, A. H., 228
Cluseret, Gustave Paul, 116
coal, 55, 57, 61, 251
Cobden, Richard, 46
Cologne, 29, 247, 277
Colombia, 22, 53, 130, 148, 166, 200, 207
Colorado, 165, 169
Columbus, Christopher, 48
Communist League, 21, 36, 134
Communist Manifesto, 21, 28, 79, 116, 135, 189, 190
Comte, Auguste, 306, 308, 314; E. B. Tyler influenced by, 311; and influence in Brazil, 148, 199; and positivism, 295, 314, 346n; 'religion of humanity', 319; and Saint-Simonianism, 191
Connemara, 70
Conrad, J. 215n

Cook, Thomas, 240, 243
Cooke, Sir William Fothergill, 75
Copenhagen, 53
Corn Laws, abolition of, 46, 53, 287
Cortes, Hernando, 48
Costa Rica railways, 362
Côte d'Azur, 242
Courbet, Gustave, 327, 340, 343, 344, 345, 346n, 348, 349
Cournot, A. A., 294, 306
Court of Cassation, 342
crédit mobilier, 45, 252, 253
Creusot, 251
Crime and Punishment (Dostoievsky), 350
Crimean War, 16, 89, 96–7, 99, 101, 162, 217
Croat nationalism, 109n, 113, 119
Crocker, Charles, 175
Crystal Palace, 47, 338
Cuba, Chinese immigration, 229; European immigration, 147; exports, 147; railways, 70, 362; slavery, 171, 216, 218–19; as Spanish colony, 165
Custer, George, 170
Custozza, battle of, 31, 32
Czech People's Socialists, 358
Czechs, arts, 325, 334, 349; changes in country life, 227; estates, 222–3; nationalism, 106, 109 &n, 110, 113, 119, 120; peasant farms, 223; Prague insurrection (1848), 26; sugar factories, 246; trade unions, 138; *see also* Habsburg Empire

Dalhousie, Lord, 152
Danube, 51, 74
Darwin, Charles, 148, 185, 294; as dominant figure in science, 296, 302, 316; *Origin of Species*, 304–5, 315; and theory of evolution, 297, 302–5, 311, 313, 317
Daumier, Honoré, 324, 337
David, Jacques Louis, 344

Davitt, Michael, 115
day trips, 240
Dedekind, R., 298
Degas, Edgar, 327, 345, 347
Déjeuner sur l'Herbe (Manet), 275, 343
Denmark, 89n, 230, 235, 357; abolition of gilds, 51; agriculture, 212, 365; colonialism, 165; and 1848 revolutions, 22n; political systems, 129; population, 361; and railways, 362; telegraph system, 76; trade unions, 140; and towns, 361
Diaz, Porfirio, 166
Dicey, A. V., 354
Dickens, Charles, 84, 271, 324, 332, 351 &n
Disraeli, Benjamin, 91, 133, 139, 338
Dobrolyubov, N., 199
Dr Faustus (Mann), 275
Dollfus-Mieg, 283
Dominican Republic, 164
Donnersmarck, Prince Henckel von, 337
Dostoievsky, Fyodor, 103, 194, 325, 332, 350
Dresden, 334
Dual Revolution (1780–1840), 66
Ducasse, Isidor, 348
Dupanloup, Mgr, 348n
Düsseldorf, 247
Dutt, R. C., 153n
Dvořák, Antonin, 325, 332, 334, 349
The Dynamical Equivalent of Heat (Thompson), 299

East India Company, 151
'Eastern Question', 95, 96, 104
Echo du Nord, 281
economics, 306, 307, 316
Eddy, Mary Baker, 319
Edison, Thomas Alva, 58
education, 58–9, 117–20, 226, 352–3
Egypt, 101; cotton exports, 207; irrigation, 212; railways, 70, 71, 362; relations with West, 153–5,

160–1; tourism, 242
Eichborn, von, 337
Eichendorff, Joseph von, 21
Eiffel Tower, 338
Eliot, George, 332, 351
emigration *see* migration
Engels, Freidrich, 37, 38, 64, 138, 188, 208; *Communist Manifesto*, 21, 79; expects political crisis in United States, 190; on gold rushes, 50, 79; and nationalism, 109n
Engels family, 278
Episodios Nacionales (Galdos), 351
Esperanto, 84
Europe, agriculture, 365; population, 360–1; railways, 70–1, 362; sea traffic, 363; states and resources, 360–1; telegraph system, 76; *see also individual countries*
evolution, theory of, 302–5, 311, 313
exploration, 67–8, 78

famines, 104, 162–3
Faraday, Michael, 75, 345
Farr, William, 307
Fathers and Sons (Turgenev), 350
Faust (Goethe), 333
Favre, Jules, 125
Félibrige movement, 353
Fenians, 104, 114–16, 141, 189, 225; *see also* Ireland
Ferry, Jules, 125
Finland, nationalism, 106; railways, 362
firearms, mass production of, 60, 61, 99
Fischhof, Adolf, 34
Fisk, Jim, 73, 174, 175–6
Flatou, 331
Flaubert, Gustave, 103, 332, 340, 346, 348 &n, 351
Die Fledermaus (Strauss), 336
Flemings, 130
Florence, Uffizi, 335
food production *see* agriculture
Forster, E. M., 272
Fourier, François, 191

France, 164; agriculture, 216, 226, 365; anthropology, 306; anarchism, 193; the arts, 325 &n, 326, 330, 341, 346, 347–8, 350; Bourbon dynasty, 133; bourgeoisie in, 282, 283–5, 290; business expansion, 164; Catholicism, 285; colonialism, 153, 165; Crimean War, 96; Darwinism, 305; education, 35, 58–9, 117, 118, 226; elections, 33–4, 39, 90; foreign investment, 49; and foreign policy, 94 95–6; and foreign trade, 66, 146; gold coinage, 49; in Indochina, 165 322; industrialisation, 56, 61, 100–1; investment, 252; iron production, 55, 56, 251; Japan and, 184–5; July monarchy, 125; labour unrest, 138; literacy/illiteracy, 58n., 227n; as a major power, 95–6, 100, 101; migration of workers, 210, 231–2; nationalism, 108, 111; painting, 330; Penal Code, 251n; philosophy, 295; photography, 340, 341; politics, 123–6, 129; population, 205, 243–4, 360; railways, 74, 362; redistribution of land in Algeria, 224; religion in, 318, 322; republicanism, 225; Second Empire, 39–40, 46, 74, 95, 97, 124, 263, 346, 348, 351; steam power, 56, 360; telegraph system, 76; textile industry, 282; Third Republic, 118, 125, 133; tourism and holidays, 241, 242, 243; trade unions, 36, 52, 135, 136; urbanisation, 231–2, 360; viticulture, 58; wars, 97; workers, 256, 290; *see also* French Revolution; Paris Commune

Franco-Prussian War, 92, 97, 99–100, 101, 116, 153, 347

Frankfurt Assembly, 25

Fraunhofer, Joseph, 299n

Frederick William IV, King of Prussia, 27

Freemasonry, 148, 286–7

Freiligrath, F., 34

French Revolution, 14, 15, 21–34, 36–38, 105, 191

Freud, Sigmund, 276

Freytag, Gustav, 351

Friendly Societies, 134

Frith, William Powell, 351

Gaj, 32

Galdós, Benito Pérez, 361

Gale, Franz Joseph, 346n

Galicia, 28, 217, 231

Gama, Vasco da, 48

Gambart, 331

Gambetta, Léon Michel, 125

Garcia Marquez, 130

Garibaldi, Giuseppe, 16, 38, 116, 136, 351; ideology, 192; Sicilian campaign, 93, 188, 200, 225

Gastein, 241, 242

Gautier, Théopile, 348

Geigy family, 282

Gelsenkirchen, 238–9

General German Workers Association, 137

Geneva Convention, 99

German Customs Union (*Zollverein*), 89n

Germany, agriculture, 212, 214, 216, 365; arts and culture, 315–16, 326, 333, 340, 349; *Bildungsvereine*, 265; bourgeoisie in, 282, 284, 285, 287, 288; Chemical industry, 59n, 300; Communist League, 21; Darwinism, 305; economic growth, 62; education, 59, 117, 118, 272, 315–16; elections, 33; emigration, 81, 229, 230, 231, 232, 234, 235, 237, 238; foreign trade, 66; Frankfurt Assembly, 25; freedom to practise any trade, 51; *Gründerjahre*, 62; industrial enterprise, 48, 282; industrialisation, 56, 100–1, 247, 251, 253; iron and steel production, 55, 56, 57, 251; labour relations, 52; and labour unrest, 138; laws against usury, 51;

Germany (*contd.*)

music, 326, 349; nationalism, 30n, 106, 108, 109, 110, 111–12, 113, 116–117; philosophy, 294; political systems, 128, 129, 131, 356; population, 24n, 89, 360; psychology, 306; radicalism, 33; railways, 362; Reichstag, 127; religion, 318; and revolutions of 1848, 22, 23, 27; slumps, 62, 85, 258; socialism, 137–8, 139, 141, 142; steam power, 56, 360; suffrage, 127, 138; telegraph system, 76; trade, 356; trade unions, 36, 138; unification, 15–16, 24, 25, 46, 89 &n, 90–1, 92, 97, 104, 305; urbanisation, 231, 232, 360; workers, 254, 256, 265; *see also* Prussia; Social Democratic Party

Germinal (Zola), 290

Gewerbeordnung, 52

Gibbs, Willard, 315

Giffen, Sir Robert, 267, 269

Gilbert, Sir William Schenk, 336

Gilchrist-Thomas 'basic' process (steel production), 58

gilds, abolition of, 51

Gintl, 75

Gladstone, William Ewart, 91, 335, 348, 351, 359

Glasgow, 249

Goethe, Johann Wolfgang, 333, 339n

gold, 49–50, 78–82, 170, 180, 230, 364

Goncharov, I., 64

Goncourt brothers, 187, 348

Görgei, 32

Gould, Jay, 73, 174, 175, 176

Gounod, Charles François, 339n

Grant, Ulysses S., 64

Gravelotte, battle of, 100

Great Britain, agriculture, 212, 214, 216, 365; aristocracy, 285; the arts, 325 &n, 328, 329, 331–2, 335 &n, 338, 340, 341, 350, 351; bourgeoisie, 282, 285–6, 289, 292; Chartism, 27, 45; coal production,

55, 61, 251; colonialism, 164, 165, 292; consumption of tea and sugar, 209; control of cities, 284; cotton industry, 44, 48n, 53, 61, 134, 259–260; Crimean War, 96; Darwinism, 305; education, 58, 59, 118, 227, 286n; electorate, 90; emigration, 81, 82, 230, 231, 232, 233, 235, 236, 237; exploration, 67; exports, 44, 48 &n, 54, 66, 68; foreign policy, 94; foreign trade, 53–4, 66, 146; free trade, 51, 53, 357; gold coinage, 49; and India, 95, 144, 150–3, 161, 215; Indochina, 145; industrial revolution, 61; industrialisation, 13, 56, 245–6, 250; investment, 252; and Irish nationalism, 115; iron and steel production, 54, 55, 56, 61; labour relations, 52; labour unrest, 138; laws against usury, 51; Liberal Party, 264, 265, 356; libraries, 335; as a major power, 95, 100; 'Master and Servant' Acts, 52, 257; merchant navy, 75; nationalism, 111; Ordnance Survey maps, 68; philosophy, 295; politics, 23, 128, 129; population, 205, 360; possibility of socialist revolution, 189; railways, 54, 246, 250–1, 254, 362; religion, 131, 318, 320–1; repeal of Corn Laws, 46, 53; rubber imports, 60; seaside holidays, 241; socialism, 134, 137, 139, 141; sport, 262n, 352n; state expenditure, 357; steam power, 55, 360; steelmasters, 282; suffrage, 127–8; telegraph system, 75, 76–7; tourism, 240, 243; trade cycle, 85; trade unions, 52, 134–6, 139, 265; urbanisation, 231, 246, 247–8, 360; war with China, 156–7, 180; workers, 254–5, 256, 257, 259–60, 265, 267

Great Depression, 62–3, 223, 358, 359

Great Eastern, 76

Great Exhibition, 1851, 47, 240

Greece, 23; independence, 104; pop-

India (*contd.*)
162, 163; irrigation, 212; manganese production, 356; opium trade, 49; population, 143; railways, 70, 72, 238n, 362
Indian Mutiny, 151–2, 153
Indian National Congress, 153
Indochina, 322
Indonesia, 143, 165, 207
industrial revolution, 14, 15, 48, 57, 61, 209, 237
inflation, 49–50
Ingersoll, Robert Green, 321
Ingres, J. A. D., 341, 344
International, First, 18, 135–7, 138, 140, 189, 190, 193, 201, 225, 262, 273n
International, Second, 264
International Meteorological Organisation, 84
International Postal Union, 239
International Red Cross, 84n, 99
International Signals Code, 84
international standardisation and unification, 84
International Telegraph Union, 84
International Workers' Association, 140
International Workingmen's Association (IWMA) *see* International, First
Introduction to the Study of Experimental Medicine, 302
Ireland, 359; Agrarian Depression, 115; emigration, 81, 230, 234–5, 237, 238; Great Famine, 230; Land League, 225; nationalism, 104, 106, 109; religion, 320, 321; urbanisation, 247; *see also* Fenians
Irish Republican Army, 114
Irish Republican Brotherhood *see* Fenians
iron and steel industry, 54–5, 56, 57, 58, 61
Irving, Sir Henry, 335n

Islam, 78, 87, 144, 155, 163, 321
Ismail Pasha, Khedive of Egypt, 154
Italy, 52, 136; agriculture, 212, 365; anarchism, 193; Darwinism, 305; democracy, 89; education, 117, 118; emigration, 230, 231, 237, 238; freemasonry, 287; labour unrest, 138; libraries, 335; literacy, 227n; as a major power, 101; music, 326, 334; Mutual Aid Societies, 134; nationalism, 106, 109, 110–11, 113, 192; peasant rebellions, 216, 217, 225; political systems, 129, 131; population, 360; railways, 362; redistribution of land, 224; revolution, 22, 23, 30–1, 45; science, 300; suffrage, 127, 132; telegraph system, 76; tourism, 242; unification, 24, 25, 28, 46, 89, 91–3, 97, 104; wars, 97, 100

Jacoby, C. G., 34
Jamaica railways, 362
Japan, 65, 80, 144, 160, 338; development, 177–86; imperialism, 144; industrialisation, 100, 101; Meiji Restoration, 101, 105, 180, 181, 182; railways, 71; religion, 323; Shinto cult, 185
Japan Herald, 186
Java, famine, 162; railways, 71, 362
Jellacic, Baron, 32
Jesuits, 98
Jews, 198, 272, 282–3, 285, 329; the arts and, 334 &n, 338; emigration, 230, 231, 235; nationalism, 119 &n; in Russia, 51; synagogues, 338; in United States, 234
Jones, Ernest, 45–6
Joseph ii, Emperor, 226
Juarez, Benito, 148, 224, 319
Juglar, Clement, 62
Junggrammatiker, 310

Kagoshima, 178, 181
Kansas, 165, 168

Moses or Darwin, 319
Motte-Bossut, 270
Mozart, Wolfgang Amadeus, 325
Mughal Empire, 152
Mukherjee's Magazine, 151
Mulhouse, 282
Murger, Henry, 347
Murray's Guide, 242, 243
museums and art galleries, 334–5
music, 325, 326, 330, 333–4, 336, 339
&n, 340, 349–50
Mussorgsky, Modest, 325, 339, 349
Mussolini, Benito, 319
Mutterrecht (Bachofen), 314
Mutual Aid Societies, 263, 267, 320

Nadar, 341
Nana (Zola), 277
Nanking, 157, 158
Naples, 132, 242
Napoleon I, Emperor of France, 16,
94, 95, 100, 104, 197, 344
Napoleon III, Emperor of France, 74,
88, 241, 252, 337; and attempts to
liberalise the imperial system, 90;
and Cavour, 92–3; character, 124–6;
collapse of Second Empire, 97, 202;
design of Paris, 154, 155, 338;
foreign policy, 95–6; meets Bis-
marck, 241n; and Napoleon I, 16;
as President of Second Empire, 39–
40, 46, 91, 124; property rights in
Algeria, 224; and Proudhon, 134;
and trade unions, 52, 136, 139
Napoleonic Wars, 85, 100
National Labor Reform Party (United
States), 137
National Labor Tribune, 177
National Labor Union (United States),
137
nationalism, 103–21, 358
Nebraska, 165, 168
Nechaev, Sergei Gennadevich, 194, 198
Nestroy, Johann, N., 103, 270, 354
Netherlands *see* Holland

Neue Freie Presse, 287
Neue Rheinische Zeitung, 34
Nevada, 165, 169
New Caledonia, 356
New Granada (Colombia), 53
New Mexico, 165
New York, 62, 69, 77, 81, 82, 136, 234,
244, 250
New York Herald, 67, 77
New York Times, 340
New Zealand, British exports to, 66;
colonisation, 143, 149, 233, 236;
railways, 70, 362
Newton, Isaac, 297, 345
Nice, 242, 243
Nicholas I, Tsar of Russia, 97, 195
Nihilists, 194
Normandy, 226
North America, railways, 70, 71; ship-
ping, 363; unexplored, 65; *see also*
Canada, United States
North German Federation, 51
North Sea shipping, 363
Norway, 349; agriculture, 365; emi-
gration, 230, 236; nationalism, 106,
112; political systems, 129; pop-
ulation, 361; railways, 362; tele-
graph system, 76; urbanisation, 247–
361
Novara, 31

Odessa, 210
Offenbach, Jacques, 336
oil, 59
Oldham, 247, 264
Olympia (Manet), 343, 344n
Opium Wars, 99, 156, 159, 180
Orangemen, 320
Ordnance Survey maps, 68
Oregon, 82, 165
The Origin of Species (Darwin), 304–5,
315
Osborn, Captain, 312
Ottoman Empire, 23, 65, 144; as an
autocracy, 127; and Balkan revolts,

407

408

Social Darwinism, 176, 184, 288, 303, 314; *see also* Darwin
Social Democratic Party of Germany (SPD), 137, 188–9, 190, 358, 359
social sciences, 305–14, 316, 325
Society for Social Policy (Germany), 139
sociology, 305–6, 316
Solferino, battle of, 100
Songs for English Workmen to Sing, 255
South Africa, colonisation, 149; railways, 70, 362
South America, 78, 206, 208; British exports to, 66; railways, 70, 71, 362; rubber industry, 60; shipping, 363; slumps, 86; unexplored, 65; *see also* Latin America *and individual countries*
Southampton, 82
Spa, 241
Spain, agriculture, 199, 210, 216, 365; anarchism, 193, 194, 225; Bourbons, 141; Carlist War, 225; colonialism, 96, 145, 146, 147, 165; and free trade movement, 52, 356; hunger-riots, 45; labour unrest, 138; libraries, 335; literacy/illiteracy, 58n, 227n; population, 361; railways, 362; redistribution of land, 224; revolutions, 23, 93, 141, 200, 224, 225; steam power, 361; telegraph system, 76; urbanisation, 361
Speke, John Hanning, 67, 78
Spencer, Herbert, 185, 193, 194, 295, 306, 308
sport, 262n, 352 &n
Spurzheim, Johann Caspar, 346n
Standard Oil Company, 59
Stanford, Leland, 175
Stanley, Henry Morton, 67, 78
Stark, 75
statistics, 306–7
steam power, 55–6, 74–5, 360–1
steamships, 362

Steinthal, H., 310
Stephenson, George, 57
Storia dell'Arte del Disegno (Selvatico), 337
Stowe, Harriet Beecher, 331
Strauss, Johann, jr., 336
Strousberg, Barthel, 73
submarine cables, 68, 76, 77
Suez Canal, 16, 69, 74, 75, 81, 154, 242
suffrage, 127, 132, 138, 192 &n
Sullivan, Sir Arthur, 336
Sumitomo, 178–9
summer holidays, 240, 241
Suppé, Franz von, 336
Sutter's Mill, 78–9
Svatopluk, King, 226
Sweden, abolition of gilds, 51; agriculture, 212, 365; education, 58 &n; emigration, 230; industrialisation, 56; political systems, 129; population, 361; railways, 362; and revolutions of, 1848, 23; suffrage, 128; telegraph system, 76; urbanisation, 361
Swift, 208
Swinburne, A. C., 349
Switzerland, 52, 315, 335; agriculture, 365; anarchism, 193; Federal Council, 284; illiteracy, 58n; industrialisation, 55; mountaineering, 243; population, 361; railways, 362; and revolutions of 1848, 22n, 23; suffrage, 126 &n; telegraph system, 76
Sydney, 82
Syllabus of Errors (Pius IX), 131, 292, 318
Symbolists, 332
Syria, 95

Tafilelt, 86
Tahiti, 71
Taine, Hippolyte, 294, 295
Taiping Rebellion, 94, 98, 99, 155–9, 173, 200, 322
Talabot, P. F., 74

United States (*contd.*)
147, 161, 292; Wild West, 168–70, 173, 208; workers, 261; *see also* American Civil War
Universal Postal Union, 84
urbanisation, 205, 211, 231–2, 244, 245–50
Uruguay, 98, 147n; agriculture, 365; railways, 362
Utah, 165, 168

Vacherot, Etienne, 346n
Vanderbilt, Cornelius, 73, 82, 174, 175, 273n
Vanderbilt family, 176
Vatican Council, 292, 318, 323
Venezuela, 207
Venice, Venetians, 27, 31; San Marco, 335
Ventnor, 241
Verdi, Giuseppe, 154, 326, 332, 334, 339n, 352
Verein für Sozialpolitik, 139
Verlaine, Paul, 241
Verne, Jules, 58, 68–9, 88
Vichy, 241
Victor Emmanuel II, King of Italy, 92, 110, 326, 348
Victoria, Queen of England, 279n
Vienna, 234; architecture and town planning, 326, 329, 334, 337, 338; as centre of manufacturing, 247, 248; railways, 71; revolutions, 22, 27; Rotunda, 47, 338; slump of 1873, 86; socialism, 138, 263; Südbahnhof, 338
Vienna International Exhibition, 60
Vietnam, 144
Vinogradov, P., 200
Virchow, Rudolf, 297
Virginia City, 169, 170
Volapük, 84

wages, 255–62

Wagner, Richard, 288, 324–5, 326, 332, 333, 335, 339 &n, 340, 349, 350, 351, 352
Wallace, Alfred Russel, 304–5
Walras, L., 306
War and Peace (Tolstoi), 197, 350
wars and warfare, 88–102
Weerth, Georg, 21
Weierstrass, K., 298
Welsh nationalism, 108, 110, 111
Wertheimstein, Baron von, 285
Wertheimstein family, 234
Westphalia, 211n
Wey, Francis, 341–2
Wheatstone, C., 58, 75
Whewell, William, 43
Whistler, James McNeill, 345
White Star line, 69
Whitman, Walt, 325
Whymper, Edward, 243
Wichelhaus, Friedrich, 278
Wilde, Oscar, 70
Wilde, Sir William, 70
Wilhelm Tell (Schiller), 333
William I, Emperor of Prussia, 344
Wilson, Thomas Woodrow, 107
Wisconsin, 81, 165
Wo Jen, 158
Woodhull, Victoria, 192n, 273 &n
working classes, 254–69; and bourgeoisie, 290, 352
Wundt, W., 306
Württemberg, population, 360

Yucatan, 145, 219
Yugoslavia, 107

Zeiss, 58
Zienau, Dr S., 298n, 299n
Zionism, 111n
Zola, Emile, 249, 277, 290, 332, 340, 341, 343, 344 &n, 347, 351
Zulus, 144, 149

THE AGE OF REVOLUTION
1789–1848

Eric Hobsbawm

'A brilliant account of Europe in its revolutionary
age . . . No one could ask for more.'
A.J.P. Taylor

'A harsh, brilliant, powerful, fascinating book.'
Peter Laslett, Guardian

'The work is challenging, learned, brilliant in its
analytical power, wide-ranging in its lucid exposition of
literary, aesthetic and scientific achievements and packed
with novel insight.'
English Historical Review

'Brilliant.'
Times Literary Supplement

Eric Hobsbawm traces with brilliant analytical clarity
the transformation brought about in every sphere of
European life by the Dual Revolution – the 1789 French
Revolution and the Industrial Revolution that originated
in Britain. This enthralling and original account
highlights the significant sixty years when industrial
capitalism established itself in Western Europe and when
Europe established the domination of the rest of the
world it was to hold for a century.

Abacus
0 349 10484 0

THE AGE OF EMPIRE
1875–1914
Eric Hobsbawm

'This is history writing grand in ambition, excellently
and wittily written . . . its sheer synoptic power and
eloquence will make this book a classic.'
Observer

'A superbly rich and erudite portrait of a society which
was evolving rapidly under a variety of pressures –
economic, technological and political.'
Times Literary Supplement

'It takes far grreater gifts – and far greater nerve – to
simplify and to scintillate than to criticise and to
complicate. This outstanding book displays both these
admirable qualities in abundance. As in the previous
volumes, the prodigious learning is lightly and lucidly
borne, the range of example and breadth of allusion
could not be bettered, and the illustrations have been
admirably selected in order to complement the text.'
New Society

The splendid finale to Eric Hobsbawm's study of the
nineteenth century, *The Age of Empire* covers the era of
western imperialism and examines the forces that swept
the world to the outbreak of World War I – and shaped
modern society.

Abacus
0 349 10598 7

Now you can order superb titles directly from Abacus

☐	The Age of Revolution	Eric Hobsbawm	£12.99
☐	The Age of Empire	Eric Hobsbawm	£12.99
☐	Age of Extremes	Eric Hobsbawm	£12.99
☐	Bandits	Eric Hobsbawm	£9.99
☐	On History	Eric Hobsbawm	£9.99
☐	Revolutionaries	Eric Hobsbawm	£8.99

Please allow for postage and packing: **Free UK delivery.**
Europe; add 25% of retail price; Rest of World; 45% of retail price.

To order any of the above or any other Abacus titles, please call our credit card orderline or fill in this coupon and send/fax it to:

Abacus, P.O. Box 121, Kettering, Northants NN14 4ZQ
Tel: 01832 737527   Fax: 01832 733076
Email: aspenhouse@FSBDial.co.uk

☐ I enclose a UK bank cheque made payable to Abacus for £ ....
☐ Please charge £.............. to my Access, Visa, Delta, Switch Card No.

☐☐☐☐☐☐☐☐☐☐☐☐☐☐☐☐☐☐

Expiry Date ☐☐☐☐   Switch Issue No. ☐☐

NAME (Block letters please) ....

ADDRESS ....

....

....

Postcode ....Telephone ....

Signature ....

Please allow 28 days for delivery within the UK. Offer subject to price and availability.

Please do not send any further mailings from companies carefully selected by Abacus ☐